*Other Books by Edith Sitwell*

# THE QUEENS AND THE HIVE

THE ERMINE PORTRAIT OF QUEEN ELIZABETH I

# THE QUEENS
# AND THE HIVE

BY

EDITH SITWELL

WITH ILLUSTRATIONS

*An Atlantic Monthly Press Book*

LITTLE, BROWN AND COMPANY
Boston                    Toronto

LIBRARY OF CONGRESS CATALOG CARD NO. 62-17059

*Second Printing*

ATLANTIC—LITTLE, BROWN BOOKS
ARE PUBLISHED BY
LITTLE, BROWN AND COMPANY
IN ASSOCIATION WITH
THE ATLANTIC MONTHLY PRESS

PRINTED IN THE UNITED STATES OF AMERICA

TO
GEORGE CUKOR

# ACKNOWLEDGMENTS

THE small numbers in the text of this book are intended to refer the reader to the end of each chapter for Notes on the sources from which quotations and other material have been taken. These sources are often books or documents belonging to the period of which I have written, or fairly close to that period; but others are much more recent works, and I have to acknowledge my indebtedness to all concerned for excerpts or information I have drawn from these.

I have to mention with particular gratitude the following: Mr. Michael Stapleton, for his great help in the preparation of the book; Miss Elizabeth Salter; Dodd, Mead & Company Inc., for the use in Chapter Fifty-five of some information from Frederick Chamberlin's *Elizabeth and Leycester*; and The Hutchinson Publishing Group, for the use of some quotations from A. E. Waite's translation of Eliphas Lévi's *History of Magic*.

# CONTENTS

# ILLUSTRATIONS

THE QUEENS AND THE HIVE

# Prologue

THE clangour of mailed footsteps, sounding like a storm of hail in the passages of the Tower of London, died away ; and now a black frost of silence sealed the world from all life.

The outer world seemed dead. The memorials of King Henry's vengeance, the eternal smiles, the unheard laughter fixed to the turrets of the Tower, did not relax their soundless merriment at the thought — visiting, perhaps, the heads from which the brain had long since disappeared — that the daughter of the woman for whose sake they had reached this show of gaiety might soon be going to join her.

Round that laughter, black rags (of cloud ? of some remnants left of their humanity ? of the wings of birds of prey ?) flapped lazily.

The young girl with the lion-coloured hair and the great golden haunting eyes who had just entered the Tower by the Traitor's Gate sat, quite quietly, looking at the door of her prison, as if she waited for someone.

And still there was no sound, save that of distant weeping.

The tears of Mrs. Ashley, the governess of this twenty-year-old girl waiting for death, if this could be encompassed by the Council and her sister's lawyers, fell from a heart that knew the nobility, the Christian love and forgiveness of that elder sister's soul and heart, before these were poisoned, when she became Queen, against the forlorn being she had befriended. Black bitterness, a slow, sure poison had been skilfully instilled into that noble heart, assured at last of Elizabeth's treachery towards her — indeed that she had connived at the plot of the traitor Sir Thomas Wyatt, son of the poet, to seize the Crown on her behalf, and end not only Mary's reign, but her life. Had not Wyatt denounced her, when he was taken, in the hope of saving himself?

Mary, now thirty-eight, had forgiven, had not visited upon her half-sister the endless and intolerable insults, injuries, and dangers that had fallen upon her since Elizabeth's birth — had forgiven her own bastardisation brought about in order that the baby Elizabeth should take her place as heiress to the throne, had forgiven being sent to the baby's household, not as a Princess, but as a dependent, with the order from her step-mother, the usurper-Queen, Anne Boleyn, that if she persisted in retaining her state as Princess, and refused to eat at the common table, she was to be deprived of food, and 'beaten and buffeted like the cursed bastard that she was'.

But soon the baby who had been proclaimed heiress to the throne of England in Mary's place was, following her mother's execution, pronounced, in Parliament, a bastard.

It was then that Mary's true nobility showed itself. In answer to the dying prayer for forgiveness from the woman who was the author of the tragedy, she protected and loved the little creature, aged three and a half years, who now had 'neither gown nor kirtall [slip], nor petticoat, nor no manner of linnen, nor foresmocks [pinafores], nor kerchief, nor rails [nightgowns], nor mofelers [mob-caps], nor biggens [night-caps]', and who now shared the nursery palace with her.* Her tenderness, her care for that forlorn child were endless.

And this was the being who all the while (so she was told) had laughed at her, mocked her, and who had now plotted her death.

Before Elizabeth was sent to the Tower, she wrote Mary a letter, imploring her to admit her to her presence, saying 'I pray to God I may die the shamefullest death that any one ever died, if I may mean any such thing' (as to try to encompass Mary's destruction) '. . . practised, counselled, nor consented to anything that might be prejudicial to your person in any way, or dangerous to the state by any means . . .

* See *Fanfare for Elizabeth*, p. 96.

'I pray God . . . evil persuasions persuade not one sister against the other, and all for that they have heard false report, and the truth not known. . . .'

But the Queen did not answer.

.    .    .    .    .

To come to any understanding of the being in whose reign the greatness of England began, and to understand her relations with her sister Mary, we must consider the circumstances of her birth.

To Anne Boleyn, Elizabeth's mother, and to many others, that birth in 1533 had been like the birth of Fate.

It was preceded by the Sophoclean drama of King Henry's escape from a real or imagined incest (that of his marriage with his brother's widow, Mary's mother) — cursed by Heaven with the decree that no male child born of that marriage should live.

That drama of passions, faiths, lusts, and ambitions that had the fever of lust, was brought about in part by a spiritual upheaval in the history of mankind, in part by the absolute necessity, if the country were to be preserved from civil war, that King Henry should provide a male heir to the kingdom.

King Henry, that lonely being, a giant in scale, a creature of powerful intellect and insane pride, of cruelty, vengeance, and appalling rages, of regal generosity and breadth of understanding, helped to bring about a tragedy through two factors — his kingly sense of duty to his people, and his curious power of self-deception, which enabled him to see his long infatuation for Queen Catherine's maid of honour, Anne Boleyn, as a part of his duty.

He put aside his Queen, and married the object of his infatuation, who, was young, and would surely bear him a son.

The King, the Princess of Aragon who was his Queen — a dark and sombre Niobe, weeping for the death of her sons — and Anne, the light summer existence that supplanted her,

these played out their tragedy lit by the fires in which the
martyrs perished, kindled in vindication of Henry's regency
under God in place of the Pope — who had refused to allow
the King's divorce from Queen Catherine, and whose power,
therefore, the King defied — and in homage to the son who
was soon to be born to the witch-Queen Anne and to Henry,
that almost supreme being.

But 'to the shame and confusion of the physicians, astrologers, witches and wizards', who had assured the King that
the coming child would be a son, 'the Lady', as the Ambassador
to the Emperor Charles the Fifth persisted in calling her, was
delivered of a daughter.

The King's fury, raging for three days, breaking from the
fires and darkness of his nature, had been terrifying to see.
. . . The child a *girl* ? Was it for *this* that he had defied
the Pope, denied his supremacy, overthrown the established
church in England ? Was it for *this* that he had risked war
with the Emperor, Queen Catherine's nephew, so that he
might marry Anne Boleyn, with the great slanting black eyes
and a long throat on which was a mole like a strawberry —
this being kept hidden by a collar of big pearls which, from
time to time, she would pull aside with her left hand, on which
was a rudimentary sixth finger, the sure sign of a witch. It had
been whispered — and now the King was sure of it — that
not Sir Thomas Boleyn, but the Prince of the Powers of the
Air, was the new Queen's father.

Listening to her, as in her rages she revealed her vanities,
her self-seeking greed, the King began to notice things to
which he had blinded himself. He still watched her every
movement, as he had done in the long years of his infatuation
for her before their marriage — those seven years in which he
had longed for her, and she had resisted him. But he did not
watch her, now, from love. He was seeing, for the first time,
her empty pretensions, her unfitness to be Queen.

She saw that he looked at her strangely — she knew that
something was happening in his mind, a change that she did
not understand.

But she had never understood anything in his nature, excepting the elementary fact that if something was withheld from him, his desire for it grew. She did not understand his gigantic vanity, nor his sense of kingship. Above all, she did not understand that with all the deformities, the monstrous pride of his nature, he was yet a great King.

She had raged at him. And she had tried to rule him.

What, he asked himself, had he got from this marriage for which he had risked the threat of excommunication, involving not only earthly ruin (the sentence that no son of the Church must speak with him or give him food, and that his body must lie without burial) but the appalling sentence of everlasting damnation — that his soul, blasted by anathema, should be cast into Hell for ever ?

This he had risked. And what had he obtained from that marriage ? Gusts of rage. An endless emptiness. A useless daughter.

The King was *bored*. To this she had brought him, after all those years of infatuation.

But still he must show his omnipotence. And to do this, he must prove that he still lay under the spell of his new Queen. Any person who denied that she was the rightful Queen was executed as a traitor. And three months after the birth of Elizabeth, the Imperial Ambassador told his master: 'The King, at the solicitations of the Lady, whom he dare not contradict, had determined to place the Queen [Catherine] in a house surrounded by deep water and marshes. . . . And, failing all other pretexts, to accuse her of being insane' (like her sister, Queen Juana of Castille, the Emperor's mother, who lived for forty-nine years in raging madness).

She was not taken to that house, but lived in one equally gloomy, rising in the depth of each night to pray, as if she were a nun, wearing under her dress the rough habit of St. Francis of the Third Order, and fearing, each hour of the day or night, to die by poison, or to be struck down by assassins hidden in her room.

The Imperial Ambassador was warned that the King said

he had grave doubts if Catherine, who was his Queen, would live long. She had a dropsy, he said.

The Ambassador replied sternly that the Queen had no dropsy. But he knew, or thought that he knew, the meaning that lay behind the King's words. This illness was to be induced by artificial means, or she would die by some subtle poison which would produce the symptoms of dropsy.

Anne, the supplanter Queen, had, it was thought, laid her plans. And she had become openly threatening, both to the life of the true Queen and that of Mary. In the summer of 1534, she was overheard telling her brother Lord Rochford that when the King went to France and she was left as Regent, she intended to have Mary executed for disobedience. Rochford warned her of the King's rage (for, in spite of his threats, he still loved his elder daughter) but she replied, violently, that she would do it, even if she were skinned or burned alive as a punishment.

In November 1535 the King uttered a threat against the life of his first Queen and their daughter Mary. Four weeks later, Catherine was seized with a mysterious illness, that came and went for a little, leaving the waxen figure a little more shrunken and twisted.

Her death took place on the 7th of January 1536. And, although it was a cold winter day, the Keeper of the house decided that she must be embalmed that same night, and enclosed in lead, far from the eyes of men. The work was done quickly, as if the fires of the sun that flare over the dead woman's native Granada were at their height.

In the early morning following the night they had spent with the dead Queen's body, the embalmers told her devoted Spanish servants that her heart, when it lay exposed to their eyes, was entirely black, and hideous to the sight. . . . They washed the heart, strongly, in water that they changed three times. But that frightful blackness did not alter. Then one of the embalmers clove the heart in two, and they found a black thing clinging to the core, with such force that it could not be dislodged. That black heart, and the body it had consumed as a fire melts wax, were shut away in a covering of lead before the light of day could witness the fate that had befallen them.

Next day, which was a Sunday, the Court rang with the noise of balls and feasts.

The King exclaimed, 'God be praised that we are free from the danger of war' — with the Emperor. And the father and brother of Anne, openly exulting, declared that the only thing they regretted was that the Lady Mary was not keeping her mother company.

The King and his new Queen wore yellow — for mourning, it was said.

At the Court Ball in the afternoon, the King sent for the baby Elizabeth and, wrote the Emperor's Ambassador, carrying 'his little bastard' in his arms, he 'showed her first to one, then to another'.

Watching the little child, leaping up and down in her father's arms, where the great fires lit the winter dusk, who could imagine this being as she would be in sixty-five years' time ? — the old sandalwood body smelling of death, the beautiful hands, that were like long leaves, grown a little dry from age, so that the lines on the palms were like those on a map. Then, too, she would leap into the air like a thin flame — like the flames she saw as she was about to die. ('I saw one night', she told one of her ladies, 'my body thin and fearful in a light of fire.')

In the last days of her life she danced to the sound of a pipe and a drum, alone in a small room, excepting for the musicians and her faithful friend and lady-in-waiting, Lady Warwick. She danced, as she did everything, to fight the shadow of Death. When she could no longer dance, she would sit and watch the maids of honour dancing — to the sound of the Dargason or Sedany, Flaunting Two (a country dance), Mopsy's Tune, Turkerloney, Frisks, the Bishop of Chester's Jig, Dusty, my Dear — and perhaps the wonderful Lachrimae Pavanes of Dowland, published three years after her death, with a number of other Pavanes, Galliards, and Almands, in a book with the title *Lachrimae, or Seaven Teares, figured in Seaven Passionate Pavanes*, the last words being :

Happy, happy they that in Hell feel not the world's despite.

But, a little child, she knew nothing of that despite, and sang in imitation of the music.

Yet even then she was the heroine of a triumph brought about by Death — that of her mother's rival — Death, that was to follow her everywhere. But the triumph was to be that of Death, not of her mother.

Three weeks after the funeral of Catherine, whom she had once served, after some hours of a slow-dragging agony, the new Queen gave birth to a dead child. And that child was a son.

Entering her room, merciless, without pity for her pain or her humiliation, the King, fixing her with his formidable stare, told her that he knew, now, that God would not grant him male children. 'I will speak to you', he said, 'when you are well.'

For the rest of the time that remained to her — she was led to her death less than five months after the death of the Queen she had supplanted — Anne was alone with her splendour. But she continued in her pride.

This being whose extraordinary will to live and conquer was such that it seemed as if it must stain the air through which she passed, leaving upon it some colour of summer and its wilfulness, impressing upon the air for ever some memory of her being — how could she dream that one day she would be enveloped by the waiting darkness, and that all her thoughts and hopes, and all her summer existence would soon be forgotten !

Like her daughter, she 'danced high'. But she did not, like that daughter, 'dance disposedly'.

The year before, an old and great man, Sir Thomas More, waiting for death in the Tower because he refused to renounce the power of the Pope, or to acknowledge the usurper Queen, had asked his daughter one day how the Queen fared. 'Never better,' she answered. 'There is nothing in the Court but dancing and sporting.'

'Alas,' he sighed, 'it pitieth me to think into what misery she will shortly come. Those dances of hers will spurn off our heads like footballs, but it will not be long ere she will dance headless.'

She had borne a useless daughter and a dead son. The violence of her pride, her interference with public affairs, the fact that her continued existence prevented friendship with the Emperor — these were a menace to England. So she must go.

A few indiscreet words, spoken to a Court musician, and to certain of the King's gentlemen, and blown away by the spring wind — a little foolish vanity, beginning in nothing and ending in nothing. This was all that was needed.

A little careful planning on the part of the King's chief minister Cromwell, and all was arranged. (The present writer assumes she was innocent of the charges against her, although it is *possible* that she was guilty, and fell into a trap. That there *was* a trap is certain.)

The men who were chosen to die with her were carefully chosen, so that, they having been always close to the King's person, the Queen's sin, supposed or real, would become almost a physical presence to the King — would follow him, wherever he went.

At first her husband — bored by her temper and bold manners and already attracted by a young woman whose face had a strange and rather beautiful greenish pallor, like that of the flower of the hellebore, a young woman whose speech was all of virtue and duty, Jane Seymour — was amused by the stories against Anne, which, at first, were discreet. Then, after a while, he began to understand that his supremacy as man and as King was in question. Slowly his anger grew.

Anne had resisted the King of England during seven years, and now, as Queen, she had given herself to a groom of the chamber (a man of the people), and to various of the King's courtiers.

Nothing, excepting the diatribe in which King Lear pours scorn upon the race of women, can give the likeness of a being such as that into which this light native of the summer was transformed :

> But to the girdle doe the gods inherit,
> Beneath is all the Fiends,
> There's hell, there's darkness, there is the sulphurous pit,
> Burning, scalding, stench, consumption, Fye, fye, fye.

The following charges were made :

'That whereas Queen Anne has been the wife of Henry the Eighth for three years and more, she, despising her marriage and entertaining malice against the King, and following daily her frail and carnal lust, did falsely and treacherously procure by means of base conversations, touchings, gifts, and other infamous incitations, divers of the King's daily and familiar servants to be her adulterers and concubines, so that several of the King's servants yielded to her vile provocations. . . . Furthermore, that the Queen and other of the said traitors, jointly and severally, compassed and imagined the King's death ; and that the Queen had frequently promised to marry some one of the traitors, whenever the King should depart this life, affirming she would never love the King in her heart.'

In addition, she was accused of being a poisoner. It was said that she had given Norreys, one of the men accused with her, a locket — presumably a receptacle of poison to bring about the death of Queen Catherine.

Before the day of the trial she knew, not only that she must die, but that nothing in all her life, no pure happiness, no natural impulse, remained unfouled by her enemies. Even her natural love for her brother was transformed by those enemies into a love 'against the commands of God Almighty and all laws human and divine'. There was no reason now why she should wish to preserve her broken life.

Anne Queen of England was sentenced to be beheaded or burned at the King's pleasure.

Saying only that she was innocent, and that the men

charged with her had been falsely accused, she told her judges she held herself 'saluée de la mort'.

That poor ghost, with her gay light dancing movements, went to her nameless grave in the Tower. And her daughter would never, in all her long life, speak her name. The fact that it had once been part of a living reality must be kept in silence for ever, like some appalling obscene secret. Yet through all the life of that child, until she was an old woman, the unnamed ghost, the phantom of her mother's supposed sin, would rise from the grave and come, in the warmth of the sun and the fire of the full moon, bringing the chill of its death and the real or imagined fever of lust that not even death could assuage, to stand between Elizabeth and happiness, or to add its own horror to a later horror, its blood to blood that was still wet. . . .

After the execution of Mary Queen of Scots, those floods of tears, that refusal to eat and inability to sleep. . . . What did Elizabeth see, as she stared before her ? Two heads, not one, lying in the dust — a head with greying hair, and a young head with long black hair and great slanting eyes ?

The child of the collision between these two beings, Henry and Anne, who like disastrous comets had rushed to meet their fiery doom in each other, sat now in the shadow of Death, staring at the door of her room in the Tower. Whom was she awaiting ? Who did she think, when night fell, would come to her through that door ?

# Chapter One

IN the late autumn of the year 1558, the night, lying over England, was a pall of darkness that shuddered like the ash left over from remembered fires.

The land seemed as if poisoned, like the land of the Atridae, which, we read, was 'a land of Fire, of thirst, and of delirium', as if it must still give forth the exhalations of monstrous deeds.

All day long, in the murky, marshy air, strange apparitions had been seen, tall pale flames suspended high up in the air, above the heads of the passing people. They had been seen in Finsbury Fields, in Moorfield, and by a certain Dame Annie Cleres, 'above the Dog-house'. Passers-by, terrified by these apparitions, had the furtive air and livid faces of ghosts, or seemed like phantoms of the sun that 'on foggy days hid his head, or appeared with a discoloured face, pale, or dusky, or bloody, as if all Nature were to suffer some agony'.

The people passed silently ; and on the brows of some the reflections of those ghosts of flames suspended high above their heads cast a scarlet mark like the brand of Cain. For were not those apparitions of fires the ghosts of the martyrdoms ?

The sun hung in the firmament like a lump of blood.

Lit by those flares high up in air, and by that phantom sun, the false saints and prophets went, seeking their own destruction.

No longer did the cries of 'There are no fires in Hell', 'The Millennium is here', sound in the streets. The falsely illuminated prophets from whose mouths those cries had sounded were gone. The fires of Hell were here. The Millennium was come. But still you could not tell against whom your sleeve brushed in the street. For other madmen walked those streets, lit by the sheet lightnings of the martyrdoms — fleeing from, as they thought, but actually approaching ever nearer to, the flames.

Some denied the Godhead of the Holy Ghost. They would not say 'God have mercy upon us, miserable sinners', for the reason that they were not miserable, nor would they have it said that they were. Some would not use the Lord's Prayer, for they could not pray 'Thy Kingdom come', since God's Kingdom was already come upon earth. Nor could they pray 'Forgive us our trespasses', since they were sinless.

These went to join the martyrs in the flames.

But in the night through the streets of London sounded strange wandering cries. Not like the shrieks that arose from the Maryan martyrdoms, that arose from the martyrdoms under King Henry; but as if ghosts cried out in warning.

It was not always possible to discern what was said. But now and again, coming nearer to the Palace of St. James, in which the sleepless Mary waited for one who would never come again, those cries, sounding close, then wandering away again, bore this meaning: 'Bloody Bonner is Bishop of London'.

And the Bishop shook in his Palace. . . . There were six martyrs awaiting their death by fire; but he did not dare to burn them in the sight of day, because the people of London had uttered threats against him. So they must be tried in secret in his Palace at Fulham, and burned by night at Brentford — consumed to ash like the heart and hopes of the Queen.

'So good and virtuous a lady!' This was said of her by de Noailles, the French Ambassador. But where had that good lady gone? At this time, when her life would soon be over, the warmth of her heart, her pity for the poor, her loving charity, her loyalty to her friends, were forgotten.

Even her appearance was so changed by illness and despair that it lent colour to the belief in her wickedness. The eyes that had been 'dark and lustrous, and vehemently touching when she fixed them upon anyone', now started from her wasted face, and had a peculiar, fixed, and menacing glare :

The Nightmare Life-in-Death was she,
Who thicks man's blood with cold.

Kneeling in the silent Palace, where the wandering cries awakened no sleepers, this unhappy being bent her head, that had been fox-coloured, red as a winter sun, but was now dank from her approaching death, in supplication. Lower and lower it sank, as, with lips wet from her tears, she murmured the prayer written for her by her cousin Cardinal Pole, who was her only earthly consolation now that the being she loved was gone, and her life was going :

'Domine Jesu Christe,

'— Lord Jesus Christ, Who art the true husband of my soul, my true King and my master. . . . Thou didst choose me for spouse and consort a man who, more than all others in his acts and his guidance of mine, reproduced Thy image — Thy image Whom Thou didst send into the world in holiness and justice ; I beseech Thee by Thy most precious Blood, assuage my grief.'

But there was no answer. No one came to lift the darkness. Her grief remained with her, seeming a part of time, that would only leave her when time was no more.

In the days before her husband had gone (in those days in which she believed that the death she carried within her was a living child), in every room of the Palace there was some record of her hope and of her agony. Her prayer-book, for instance, dropped by her hand at a moment when faintness overcame her, with the page open at the prayers for women in childbirth, wet with her desperate tears.

It was long ago — aeons ago — the time of those prayers that had been said in vain. Now the forlorn creature that was Queen of England rose from her knees and wandered through the Palace. Every night, had anyone been wakeful, they could have heard that sound of a ghost drifting through the rooms. Loitering sometimes, at a remembered scene, to impress it upon the eyes that would soon see no more — or walking quickly, as if hunted, or as if searching for something. For

what ?   For some word from her mother's tomb, bringing
her forgiveness for a terrible, though unwilling betrayal —
the document signed, in order to save her and her faithful
servants from the axe :  ('Item :  I do freely, frankly, and for
the discharge of my duty towards God, the King's highness,
and his laws, without any other respect, recognise and acknowledge that the marriage hitherto had between his majesty and
my mother, the late princess dowager, was by God's law and
man's law incestuous and unlawful').   For some belated words
from Philip, telling her that he loved her (those words that had
never been borne in his heart) — Philip, who had left her, and
whom she would never see again ?

From time to time she would pause in one of the rooms,
and hurriedly turn over the contents of a drawer, only to find
an unwanted, long-forgotten letter — one, perhaps, from a
little boy, Lord Darnley, the son of her cousin Margaret
Douglas, Countess of Lennox, thanking her for a gold chain
she had sent him as a reward for an exercise he had written,
and telling her he wished his 'tender years' had not prevented
him from fighting against her rebels.

No, that was not what she was looking for.   Nor for these
old records of past small happinesses, or of a time when she still
believed that happiness might be hers, in a velvet-covered book
containing her accounts, which she always superintended per-
sonally :  'Item :  5s. for the woodbearer, bringing the white
larke from Hampton', 'To my lady of Troy's woman for
bringing two swans and eight turkey hens for my lady grace's
larder'.  'For straunge minstrels.'  'To a poore woman bringing her a bird in a cage.'  (Long years ago.  And dust had long
stopped the bird's sweet voice.)  'One penny, for needles for
Jane the Fole' (who had been ill and had amused herself with
needlework till she should be well again).  Money for presents
to her godchildren, when she, still a girl, had walked in the
green forest lanes with her ladies, visiting the cottages.

Small and pathetic reminders of the time that lay between
her mother's tragedy, and the tragedy of her own love for
Philip.

Or was she looking for some memorial of the first Christmas she had spent with the King her father after their estrangement had ended ? Then, everything seemed made of gold. The King had given her a bordering of goldsmith's work for a dress. She had lost six gold angels at cards. That Christmas time there had been much music ; the Court danced to the sound of Mrs. Winter's Jumpp, and King Henry's Galliards. But the music had faded.

Now, as she sat at a table reading these records of past happiness, the gold light from the fire fell on her haggard cheek, turning it to gold as it had done on a Christmas Eve at Greenwich when she was a little child of four. Then, too, everything had seemed of gold — the gold cup given her by Cardinal Wolsey, the two small gold flagons from Princess Katherine Plantagenet, the gold pomander from her aunt, Queen Mary of France. . . . There was even a rosemary bush hung with spangles of gold, brought by a poor woman of Greenwich for the King's little daughter. And the King had swung her round and round the rosemary bush till he seemed, with his beard of gold, like the sun, and she a little planet in her course round that sun.

Long ago. Now all the gold had gone.

Looking round, she told herself that there was someone she had come to meet. Not Philip — for he would never come again. Not Renard, the Emperor's Ambassador, for he, too, had gone — though still the Palace seemed to echo with his whisper, bringing death to those of whom that whisper spoke.

No. It must be her lost self whom she had come to meet.

But would she know her now ? What mirror would restore to her that lost and laughing woman of the few short months of her illusory happiness ?

How cold it had become ! She had thought it was spring, but it was winter. Why, of course — a few weeks more, and it would be the time of the coming of the Christ Child.

But before that, she must be gone.

# Chapter Two

AFTER the Atridaean tragedy of King Henry, the imagined incest and curse from Heaven, the coming and death of the witch-Queen, there was a pause, during which Edward, son of Anne Boleyn's supplanter, Jane Seymour, reigned — the phantom of Henry's huge passions. But the little ghost-King dwindled, like a sorcerer's wax image before the flame.

For days before the King's death, it was rumoured that he had gone. . . . Then a white despairing face was seen looking through a window of the Palace — a face with no hair.

After his death, the rumour spread everywhere that he had been poisoned. A contemporary letter [1] said : 'That wretch, the Duke of Northumberland' (who had wrested the Protectorship from the Duke of Somerset, and had plotted that his daughter-in-law, Lady Jane Grey, daughter of the Duke of Suffolk, should reign instead of her cousin Mary after the King's death), 'has committed an enormous crime. Our excellent King was taken off by poison ; his hair and nails fell out.'

It was thought that the Duke, having induced the dying boy-King to disinherit his sisters Mary and Elizabeth in favour of their cousin Lady Jane (married to Lord Guildford Dudley, the Duke's fourth son), had considered it dangerous to wait, and so assisted the King to his death with poison.

The Emperor's Ambassador, Simon Renard, told his master that when, on Mary's accession, she had the King's body examined, it was found that 'les artoix des pieds et des doigts lui estoient tumbez et qu'il a esté empoisonné'.

At one moment, it was suggested that the Duke should be

charged with his King's murder. But opinion varied as to who actually administered the poison. John Hayward, in his life of the young King, wrote that another of the Duke's sons, Lord Robert Dudley (afterwards Earl of Leycester), had been sworn one of the King's Gentlemen of the Bedchamber, and that 'after his entertainment into a place of near service, the King enjoyed his health not long'.

At that time Lord Robert was but nineteen. And it is probable that the King died from the effects of minerals mixed, with the best intentions, with his medicines ; and from some form of tuberculosis.

July 1553 was a month of flame. But on the afternoon of the 6th an appalling blackness enveloped the city, the houses shook beneath the rolling thunder as if in an earthquake. The tempest increased in terror, and after the young King's death (at six that evening) it was said that the rolling, earthquaking noise was not that of thunder, but of King Henry the Eighth bursting open his tomb in his rage at this defiance of his will, the death of his son.[2]

The young King dwindled away to nothingness on that evening when hail the colour of fire fell in the city, through the burning heat, melting in the yet more fiery hearts of the roses and carnations in the city gardens. And all night long a horseman galloped in wild haste to Hunsdon to warn Mary, the rightful Queen, that she must fly immediately. The Duke of Northumberland's fellow conspirators and followers had risen and were in arms. She was to be inveigled to the Tower to receive the crown, the gates would be locked behind her, and she would be at their mercy, and her cousin crowned in her stead.

Not an instant must be lost. She must fly to Norfolk, where the Howards awaited her, and, as she went, must issue proclamations that she was the true Queen, and that all loyal Englishmen must rise to defend her.

Early next morning, when Lord Robert Dudley arrived to take her to the Tower, she had gone.

.     .     .     .     .

The Northumberland rebellion rose like a wind, died like a wind.

The boy and girl who Northumberland had hoped would be King and Queen of England were prisoners in the Tower, where they had spent Jane's nine days of Queenship.

Then the rightful Queen made a triumphal entry into the city, and beside her rode Elizabeth. On all state occasions, Elizabeth took her place as Princess of England and the Queen's successor. The Queen embraced her warmly. They walked hand in hand.

But not for long.

.        .        .        .        .

The red-haired Queen reigned, and, walking behind her in the rooms of the Palace, came Renard the Fox, the Emperor's Ambassador (successor to Queen Catherine's friend and adviser). A marriage between Philip, the son of the Emperor Charles the Fifth, and the Queen of England would mean almost world-domination for the Emperor. For what could the ambitions of France united with Scotland achieve against such a force? It would mean, also, the restoration in England of the Catholic Church.

Therefore, under the insinuating whisper of Renard, the real Philip was replaced, gradually, by a being who was the evocation of Mary's sick and disordered fancy.

It has been said of Philip that he sealed the doom of Mary. But that doom sprang from her own heart, and from the tragedy of her early youth. By the very circumstances of that youth she had been taught to distrust all thoughts of love. Had she not lived under the shadow of an evil enchantment masquerading under that name?

She had known, in the thirty-eight years of her life, little affection, and no love. But for all that original distrust, she had always longed to give and to receive it. Surely, somewhere in the world, she told herself, there was a being who would value her heart at its true worth.

This forlorn and unloved creature had once bestowed a

timid kiss on a Prince to whom her father had, at the moment, determined to marry her. But then the King changed his mind, and the Prince went away, never to return. And though the King her father, and, later, her brother, had engaged her, in all, seven times, any talk of her marriage had never been for long.

In her youth, knowing that happiness could not exist for her in the actual world, she had spun for herself, web by web, a world of fancy which, she told herself, would suddenly be made real (she did not know how, or when) by some romantic and unexpected happening. Spain and Flanders formed the landscape of that world. Spain had been the home of her mother, that beloved and betrayed being. And was not the Emperor, when Mary was a girl, her only hope of safety? Would she not have been sent to her death, had it not been for fear of his vengeance? Surely, then, the only chance of happiness must lie with those trusted beings, the Emperor and his son.

The task of Renard was easy.

Under the spell of the Ambassador's insinuating speeches, the Queen was already half in love with the cousin she had never seen; but she succeeded in persuading herself that she was contemplating entering this marriage only for the good of her people.

Her mind was still not wholly made up, when a rumour reached her. It was hinted that Don Carlos, born of Philip's first marriage, was by no means his only child. He had numerous other children, born out of wedlock. (The Prince of Orange, in his Apologia, wrote that even before Philip's first marriage he had conferred the title of wife on Doña Isabel de Osario, the sister of the Marqués d'Astoya. This is incorrect, but he had lived with her since his wife's death, and she had borne him several children.)

On hearing this rumour, the Queen summoned Renard, and begged him to tell her truthfully if the Prince was the paragon of virtue he had described to her. 'Madam', said the Ambassador, 'he is the very paragon of the world.'

The Queen took his hand. 'Oh!' she cried. 'Do you speak as a subject whose duty it is to praise his sovereign — or do you speak as a man?' 'Your Majesty may take my life', was the reply, 'if you find him other than I have told you.'

'Oh, that I could but see him!' she murmured.

A few days later the Ambassador was summoned again to a room in the Palace in which he found, besides the Queen, only Lady Clarencieux. On an altar was the Holy Wafer.

She had spent her days and nights in tears and in prayers to God to guide her, she told him. And, falling on her knees with her two companions, they sang the *Veni Creator*. Then, rising to her feet, she told him of the Divine message. The Prince of Spain had been chosen by Heaven as husband to the virgin Queen. No malice of the world should cause her to disobey God's word. No one should keep the Chosen from her. To him alone would she give her love, her utter devotion, and not even by a wayward thought would she give him cause for jealousy!

The Ambassador noticed, with cynical amusement, that since she had begun to think of Philip, all dark colours had been banished from the Court, which was now as bright as a flower-garden with the Queen's preferred colours — ruby, crane, drake, 'flybert' (filbert?), 'goselinge', horseflesh, Isabella (a pale yellow), and willow. The Queen's hoarse laughter was heard more frequently than formerly.

She was seen, more than once, examining her face in a mirror, as if it were the face of someone she had once known but had long lost sight of. But she never scrutinised that face when the sun was likely to shine upon it.

. . . . .

A second rebellion, that of Wyatt — its purpose, Wyatt said, when captured, being to dethrone the Queen and give Elizabeth the crown — rose like a wind, died like a wind.

And, walking behind the red-haired Queen in the rooms of the Palace, came Renard the Fox. Wherever the Queen went, that figure stepped from the shadows, and, after bowing profoundly, moved, darker than those shadows, behind her, whispering in her ear, fanning the latent sparks of madness in her.

Old King Henry's body lay in earth, his spirit was in Heaven or in Hell. (The child of his rightful wife had masses said for his soul. But the people said of her that she had instigated an ecclesiastical Council to exhume her father's bones that they might be burnt for heresy.)

Anne Boleyn, the light laughing woman, 'la grande putain', she, too, was gone, and the son who was to save England. Only the child of the woman for whose sake so much blood had been shed, and for whom Henry's soul, many believed, had been plunged into eternal damnation — only Elizabeth, and Mary, the child of the rightful wife, only these remained.

The tragedy of the real or imagined incest was forgotten by the busy world, but there was a dark place in Mary's heart in which that terrible memory remained — a spark to be fanned into flame by the whisper. The Atridaean tragedy was not dead, but sleeping.

'Traitors', said the whisper, 'require to be taught that for the principals in treason there is but one punishment.'

(The wind that came and was gone !)

'Your Majesty', the whisper had said, even before the Wyatt rebellion, 'would do well to discover if Madam Elizabeth does not see her reign as near.'

(Madam Elizabeth, whom she had loved and befriended when her sister was a little disinherited child, Madam Elizabeth whom the Court was bound to treat as a Princess and the Queen's sister, Madam Elizabeth who had plotted, so she was told and believed, to take both her crown and her life.)

Ah, she was the true daughter of 'la Manceba', 'la grande putain', the witch-queen who had said of Mary, 'She will be my death, or I shall be hers — so I will take good care she does not laugh at me after my death.'

The head of La Manceba had rolled in the dust, and Mary was Queen.

But still there was no laughter.

And now what was the whisper saying ?

'While such dangerous traitors live as the lady Elizabeth, the precious person of Prince Philip could not be entrusted to her.'

This was said on the 8th of March 1554. Elizabeth must be condemned to death. This was the Emperor's price for the marriage. And in an agony of fear for her happiness, the Queen cried that this should be arranged. Yes, she must die !

'The Queen's blood is up at last' — the exultant Ambassador told the Emperor.

Elizabeth, who was seriously ill and in the country, received an urgent command to come immediately to London.

At first she was unable to travel, then was carried in a litter to London, by slow degrees, the journey taking several days.

On the day when she reached the city ('crowded with gibbets, and the public buildings crowded with the heads of the bravest men in the kingdom' — so the French Ambassador wrote) the Princess Elizabeth was thus described by Renard : 'the lady Elizabeth arrived here yesterday [the 23rd of February 1554] dressed all in white surrounded with a great company of the Queen's people, besides her own attendants. She made them uncover the litter in which she rode, that she might be seen by the people. Her countenance was pale and stern, her mien proud, lofty and disdainful, by which she endeavoured to conceal her trouble.'

She passed through the silent crowds, staring at her as they had stared at her mother on that afternoon when a barge took her to the Tower, and she disappeared through the Traitor's Gate, to be seen no more. . . .

The cortège passed Smithfield, where the fires of the martyrdoms were soon to be lit, passed down Fleet Street, and on to Whitehall, entering through the garden to the Palace.

Arrived at Court, the Queen refused to see her.

Death was now very near. . . .

The letter written to her by Wyatt, which she denied receiving, had been found, and Renard decided to use Lady

Wyatt as a tool. He swore to her that if her husband would implicate the Princess still more fully, his life would be spared.

This he did. But unfortunately, wrote Renard, there were not enough proofs to bring about, by English law, the Princess's death on the block. She was, however, sent to the Tower on Palm Sunday, the 18th of March 1554.

As she was being led through the garden of the Palace to the barge, she, looking up at the windows of the Palace, cried, 'I marvel what the nobles mean by suffering me, a Prince, to be led into captivity ; the Lord knoweth wherefore, for myself I do not'.

She declared she would not be landed at the Traitor's Gate, 'neither could she, unless she should step into the water over her shoe'. And when one of the lords in attendance told her she could not choose but do so, and then, as the rain was pouring down upon her, handed her his cloak, 'She dashed it from her, with a good dash', wrote Speed, and, mounting the stairs, said, 'Here lands as true a subject, being prisoner, as ever landed at these stairs. Before Thee, O God, I speak it, having no other friend but Thee alone.'

After Wyatt exonerated the Princess, at his execution, of any implication in the plot, it was rather difficult to know what to do with her. She might, perhaps, be sent to Pomfret Castle. After all, the cries of King Richard the Second within those walls had not been heard. But then might there not be the danger of vengeance from Lord William Howard, her great-uncle, who was Lord High Admiral, with the whole of the Navy under his command ? What if he should join the French and the exiled rebels ? It might be better to take her to Wood-stock, where she could be kept in semi-imprisonment until they dared take her to Pomfret. . . .

She was released from the Tower on the 19th of May 1554, and taken down the Thames — as she believed, to her death.

The Queen, listening at a window of the Palace, heard the firing of guns from the Steelyard — the sign of the people's joy that their Princess was freed from the Tower.

The Queen's misery, already great, was increased by that

sound, and it grew from day to day. Already she foresaw, perhaps, the terrible passion that was to devour her like fire, and which would set alight the fires of the martyrdoms, knew that she was to love one who would never love her in return — one whose bride, whose love (so her people believed) was the flame that, burning men's bodies on earth, would cast their souls into the flames of Hell.

Her days were given up to waiting for news of Philip. He did not write. Or, if he wrote, his words were lost.

But worst of all was the sadness of awakening before dawn, from dreams in which she was young and beloved, to the truth that she was growing old. Of those nights when she saw the truth and was filled with despair. Then her agony was such that de Noailles, the French Ambassador, reported it to his King, who, though not her friend, pitied her.

'Quelques heures de la nuict', wrote the Ambassador, 'elle entre en telles rêveries de ses amours et passions que bien souvent elle se met hors de soy, et croy que la plus grande occasion de ses douleurs vient du déplaisir qu'elle a de voir sa personne si diminuée et ses ans multiplier en tel nombre. . . .'

'The unhappy Queen', wrote his master, before these revelations of her ladies to his Ambassador had reached him, 'will learn the truth when it is too late. She will wake, too late, in misery and remorse. . . .'

### NOTES TO CHAPTER TWO

[1] Burcher to Bullinger.
[2] Elizabeth Jenkins, *Elizabeth the Great*.

# Chapter Three

ON Monday the 23rd of July 1554, a procession made its way from the sea towards Winchester. And, at the head of the cortège, riding through the rain that shone with such brilliance, fell with such violence, that it seemed forked lightning, rode a figure in a black velvet suit with a felt cloak of 'damned-colour' (flame or black) thrown over it — a figure with a face as pale as that of the White Horseman of the Apocalypse — Prince Philip, only lawful son of the Emperor, Charles V.

From his earliest childhood, indeed from his birth, duty flowed in his veins instead of blood. Grandeur was his relentless fate. There could be no yielding to impulse, no softening, no natural expression of pain or of distaste.

His mother the Empress, in her birth-pangs, being implored by one of her Portuguese ladies to allow herself to yield to her agony, was so conscious that she was giving birth to one who would rule over half the world, that afraid to detract, by relapsing into ordinary humanity, even for a moment, from the greatness of that supreme hour, she replied, 'Die I may, but wail I will not'. And she ordered the ladies in attendance upon her that her form and face should be shrouded in darkness, so that the light could not shine upon that human failing, pain.

This seemed a portent of her only surviving son's whole life — (other sons she had, but these soon died of epilepsy). It gave him, perhaps, the 'marble serenity' of which Martin Hume spoke — a serenity as of the tomb — and his supreme dignity of demeanour.

Looking at his portraits, it is difficult to understand what there was in his appearance, in that cane-coloured hair and beard, and the tepid blue moleskin-soft eyes that not even cruelty could fan into flame — (for cruelty was not, with Philip, a main characteristic, was indeed, when brought into being, purely the result of intellectual processes and a sense of duty) — to arouse a desperate passion.

Mary's heart was invaded, and killed, by a chimera, a vampire masquerading as a dream, and born of her own nature.

Philip was a cold, not a bad man, and his character was just. He would not tolerate the enslaving of the Indians in his American colonies, nor the importation of negro slaves, and this at a time when the English made a prosperous trade out of this barbarity. (Horrible cruelties were, however, perpetrated in his dominions, induced by the hideous greed of the colonists.)

He has been vastly misjudged. He was blamed by the English for the fires lit by Mary, but he was in no way guilty of them. When the sparks from Mary's madness lit the countryside with a wild-beast glare as of blood, the King's principal confessor denounced the burnings in a sermon, probably instigated by the King, and certainly approved by him.

Francesco Soranzo, the Venetian Ambassador to Spain, wrote, after the King's death, that 'he was profoundly religious and loved peace. He had vast schemes, of which he never counted the cost, but in small matters he was rather parsimonious. He feigned not to feel small injuries, but never lost an opportunity of avenging them.' It was said of him that 'his dagger followed close upon his smile'. But again, according to the Venetian Ambassador, he was 'patient, flegmatic, temperate, melancholy, hated vanity, was never in a rage, had his desires under absolute control, and an immutable temper'.

When he was sixteen and a half years old, the Emperor's son was given in marriage by his father to Maria, daughter of King John the Third of Portugal and the Emperor's sister Catherine. For King John ruled over the infinite riches of the Portuguese East Indies. But the marriage ended, eleven months later, with her death — brought about, it was said, by her being left alone while the ladies in attendance on her after the birth of Don Carlos ran to witness the processions and judgment of the Auto da Fé. While they were gone, she imprudently (so soon after the birth of her son) ate a lemon, which caused her death.

For three weeks the Prince, mourning for his young wife, remained unseen by the people. From duty? From grief?

When, nine years later, he was told that it was his father's will that he should marry his cousin Mary — shrunken, ageing, and ill — and must go to live in a cold and sunless land, he answered that the Emperor's commands must be obeyed.

This, he knew, was to be the end of his personal happiness. But what did personal happiness matter when religion and the needs of the Empire bade him put it aside ! To the wife of an officer in his train who enquired if they should sell all their possessions, that they should not be an encumbrance, he replied, 'I do not order you either to sell or not to sell your property, for know ye that I am not going to a marriage feast, but to a fight'.

On the 14th of May 1554, the Prince, with the Dukes of Alva and Medina Celi, the Count of Egmont, the Count de Feria, Ruy Gómez, and twenty other of the highest grandees of Spain, followed by nearly a thousand horsemen, the Prince's Spanish and Teuton Guards, and three hundred servants in the red and yellow livery of the King of Aragon, rode through the flaunting yellow dust, yellow as the sanbenitos of the prisoners of the Inquisition, yellow as the flames in which they were consumed, from Valladolid to Tordesillas, where the Prince would say farewell to his grandmother, the mad Queen Juana of Castille.

The old Queen, who at seventeen had been married to Philip of Burgundy, whom she loved passionately, and who was unfaithful to her, began to go insane at the age of twenty-three; then, when she was twenty-six, flamed into raging madness brought on by the mysterious death of that beloved traitor. (Some said her father, King Ferdinand, had caused him to be poisoned.)

The mad Queen rushed, like a comet, in the darkness of each night, across Spain to Granada, in her flight from those who would take her husband from her ; but from time to time she would stop, and force her attendants to open the coffin, that she might see the dead body of her husband had not escaped from her ; for one of these days he would surely rise from his coffin, as she had often seen him rise from his bed after a long sleep. And this time he would not look at her coldly, but with a smile. But now no woman must approach him, lest she should steal him from Juana ! . . . And when, one night, she halted in the dark countryside with her train, only to find that she had taken the dead man, unwittingly, into a convent of nuns, she fled again, and, in that night of storm, insisted on the coffin being opened, that she might see, by the wind-blown light of torches, that the dead man was still there.

She lived, in raging madness, for forty-nine years.

The old madwoman and her grandson said farewell in the darkness of the Castle. Then he made his way once more into the flaunting sunshine, the fluttering banners of the yellow dust. The procession wound down the great roads to the ship *The Holy Ghost.*

Scarlet silk streamers and banners of many colours floated from end to end of the ship. Huge standards of crimson damask thirty yards long, on which were painted the Imperial arms and gold flames, and other standards bearing the royal devices, floated from every mast, bulwark, castle. The Prince's cabin was of scented woods and gold ; and the ship was manned by three hundred sailors in scarlet liveries.

But the Prince was going to a land where his food must be prepared by his own servants, for fear he should be poisoned. He was twenty-seven, and was going to a bride who, at thirty-eight, had been withered and aged by misery, by illness, by fear, beyond her years.

It was after he had been received in Winchester Cathedral by Bishop Gardiner in full pontificals, with many priests singing the Te Deum, it was after many prayers, that, at ten o'clock at night, the bridegroom was led across a dark garden to a moated house to meet his bride. . . . (The yellow, shrunken face that seemed a part of the dust, or like faded yellowing flowers thrown away from some ancient bridal bouquet . . . the dwindling form that was soon to be distorted by the dropsy from which she died . . . the relentless greed for possession with which she received him, as the grave receives the dead. . . .)

The wedding, which took place on the 25th of July, was of the utmost magnificence — the Queen (whose train was borne by her cousin Lady Margaret Douglas) and the bridegroom wore garments that glittered like starlight.

There was great pomp and splendour. There was courtesy ; there was consideration. And yet, something was missing. What could that something be ?

.    .    .    .

In Spain, in a dark palace whose rooms never knew the arid, many-coloured fires of that country's sun, Juana, the nineteen-year-old widowed Princess of Portugal, whom her brother Philip had left as Regent, presided over the upbringing of his little nine-year-old half-mad son, Don Carlos. He was not as yet subject to the ferine rages that filled the whole Court with terror.* But he was even then becoming increasingly strange. And the quality of strangeness in him was equalled by that in his aunt.

The Princess of Portugal seems to have inherited some of the madness of her grandmother. Her religion was of the deepest gloom — a blackness not even shot through with the lightnings of that madness. All was darkness, all was silence.

She was in the habit of dropping a long black veil over her face before she gave audience to a foreign Ambassador. But, in order that he should not think he was being received by a ghost, or a spy, she would, at his entrance, raise her veil, stare at the Ambassador with eyes like phantom suns in her ghostly

* See Appendix D.

pale face, then drop her veil again.  The rest of the audience would be conducted with the Ambassador speaking to a veil behind which there was no sign of life.

At one moment the Princess formed the 'unusual determination'[1] to become the bride of the nine-year-old Carlos. And this she only relinquished because he did not grow quickly enough.

This was the strangeness, the accustomed gloom, that Prince Philip was forced, by duty, to exchange for a gloom to which he was unaccustomed.

### NOTE TO CHAPTER THREE

[1] Hume, M. A. S., *Two English Queens, Mary and Elizabeth, and Philip.*

# Chapter Four

A TALL figure robed in scarlet, with the long, ascetic, beautiful face of the Plantagenets, mounted the stairs of the Palace at Whitehall, and was greeted with tears of joy by a woman who was about to bear a child. The Queen's cousin, the long-exiled Cardinal Pole, now Papal Legate to England, greeted her with the words of the Angel to the Holy Virgin : 'Ave Maria gratia plena, Dominus tecum, benedicta tu in mulieribus'.

Supreme hour of happiness and of hope ! 'It was the will of God', said the Cardinal, 'that I should have been so long in coming. God waited till the time was ripe.'

It was indeed, as he might have foreseen, the hour of a miracle. For hardly had he reached his private rooms in Lambeth Palace, before a message was rushed to him from the Queen. In answer to the angelic salutation, 'the babe had leapt in her womb'.

The cannon thundered. The Te Deum was sung in every church. The proof of Heaven's mercy to England was the theme of every pulpit next day, which was a Sunday.

.     .     .     .     .

In the months since she had felt the stir within her of the child, the miraculous being who was to save England, other and humbler lives — each green life guarded by its particular star — stirred in the gardens of Hampton Court, sheltered by the walls to which rosemary was nailed. The roots of the violets, the primroses, the bears'-ears that were 'of a fine light browne-yellow colour, which wee doe usually call Haire-colour', with their 'large leaves which are meally withall' felt their lives stir under the manure of strawberry rot. Soon

33

in the Palace, that is of the colour of strawberries or of a bull-finch's rosy feathers, the life that was to be the flower of the kingdom would come into being.

On the 20th of April 1555, the Queen went into seclusion at Hampton Court, to await the birth of the child. The cradle-rockers, the physicians, the nurses, had long been ready. In the still-rooms of the Palace, remedies, restoratives, sweet waters, were being prepared. 'Rose shredde small and sodde in clarified hony, maketh that hony medicinable with gode smell and this comforteth . . . and defyeth glemy [gloomy] humours.' 'Some do put rose water in a glasse and they put roses with their dew thereto and they make it to boile in water then they sette it in the sun till it be redde.' 'Also drye roses put to the nose to smell do comfort the braine and the hart and quencheth spirits.'

But how can the heart that is dying, or is already dead, be comforted ?

Processions of bishops and priests walked through the London streets chanting litanies. Another procession of bishops, in vestments of cloth of gold, bright as the fires that were so soon to be lit, walked round and round Hampton Court, with King Philip at their head, praying for the most serene auspicious delivery of the Queen, while she watched them from a window.

On the 30th of April, the supposed birth-pangs began. The bells rang, the Te Deum was sung in St. Paul's, bonfires were made ready for lighting and tables for feasting in the streets. But where was the child ?

The blasting curse from Heaven upon the Atridaean sins had descended upon Mary. She convinced herself that she was unable to bear her child because Heaven was offended by two frightful and unexpiated sins — her leniency towards the heretics, and that document denying the supremacy of the Pope, denying her mother's legal marriage to her father, signed at a moment when she had succumbed to King Henry's will because she and her servants were in danger of death by the axe.

The signing of that paper brought the hereditary madness that had flamed in Juana of Castille, her mother's sister, nearer. It lit the first sparks of the martyrdoms. Mary knew, now, that she must give a sign to Heaven of her repentance for those mortal sins.

Therefore the heretics must be proceeded against. Sheets of fire ran along the ground like lightning, or like water.

The crowds saw Rogers, Canon of St. Paul's, who, with Coverdale and Tyndall, had translated the Bible, 'bathing his hands in the flame as if it were cold water'. They heard Bishop Hooper, who had fed the poor, crying, in his agony, 'For God's sake, good people, let me have more fire ! [that his torture might end the sooner]. Lord Jesu, have mercy upon me ! Lord Jesu, receive my spirit !' But still his hands were seen to beat upon his breast, after those cries had ceased. It was three-quarters of an hour before his spirit left his crumbling body, and that body fell to ashes. The crowds saw Thomas Hawkes (who had told his friends that 'if the rage of the pain was tolerable and might be suffered he should lift up his hands towards heaven before he gave up the ghost') after he 'had continued long in the fire . . . reach up his hands, burning in a light fire ; which was marvellous to behold, over his head to the living God, and with great rejoicing, as it seemed, strike and clap them together and so, straight way sinking down into the fire, he gave up his spirit.'

And from the crowds a hoarse murmur arose.

They saw the burning of the aged Archbishop Cranmer. To him Cardinal Pole had written : 'Compared with you, all others who have been concerned in these deeds of evil, are but objects of pity. You exhorted your King with faire words to put away his wife. . . . You parted him from the Church, the common mother of the faithful ; and thenceforth, throughout the land, law has been trampled under foot, the people bound with tyranny, the churches pillaged, the nobles murdered, one by another . . . [an old grey head, honoured and loved, the head of the Cardinal's mother, the Countess of Salisbury, hacked from her shoulders by many strokes, and lying in the dust . . .] I say, were I to make my own cries heard in heaven, I would pray God to demand at your hands the blood of his servants.' . . .

Terrified by this denunciation, in unspeakable fear of an agonising death, the Archbishop, hoping for mercy, signed a paper acknowledging that he was a blasphemer, had persecuted the truth, and deserved eternal damnation. But when all hope was gone, he went to his death bravely, 'renouncing and refusing those papers' and holding the hand that signed them in the flames, to 'suffer just punishment'.

In the midst of his own agony, did Bishop Latimer remember the words he had written, *in jest*, to Cromwell, when, in King Henry's reign, another man was to perish in even greater torments, purposely prolonged, because he was steadfast in his faith ? 'If you wish me to *play the fool* [my italics] in my customary fashion when Forest shall suffer' — (the saintly Father Forest, who was suspended in an iron cage above the flames) — 'I wish my stage to stand near Forest, so that he may hear what I say, and perhaps be converted.' He added, however, 'If he [Forest] would yet with heart return to his abjuration, I would wish his pardon, such is my foolishness'.

Did the Bishop remember, also, the horrible letter he had written to Cromwell about Cardinal Pole, at a time when he knew the execution of the Cardinal's mother had been planned ? 'Blessed be the God of England whose instrument you be ! I heard you say, once, after you had seen that furious invective of Cardinal Pole, that you would make him eat his own heart, which you have now, I know, brought to pass, for he must needs now eat his own heart and be as heartless as he is graceless.'

The man who had eaten his own heart had now arisen to confront the Bishop, and there was no heart to which any supplication could be offered — no heart to hear those anguished cries.

The horrors of the Maryan reign in no wise excelled those of King Henry's. The crowds might well have remembered the cry of a Catholic saint in that earlier reign, as his heart was torn from his living body : 'What wilt thou do with mine heart, O Christ?' But they could not remember, because they had not seen, how three out of the eighteen gentle, guilt-less monks of the Charterhouse had been chained, standing upright, to the wall of their prison for thirteen days and nights, before being dragged on hurdles through the city to suffer unspeakable and most obscene mutilations, while still alive and conscious — in the full view of crowds, which included many of the King's courtiers.

In thinking of the frightful cruelties enacted in the Maryan Age, we are apt to forget two things. The first is that (mon-strous and unpardonable as is the cruelty) it is no more cruel to burn a living being in the name of a travesty of Almighty God, made in our own image, endowed with our own cruelty and foolish vanity, than it is to commit the unspeakable obscenity of disembowelling, emasculating, and tearing the heart from a living being in the name of another travesty.

This last, Henry sanctioned, Elizabeth sanctioned.

We must remember, too, thinking of the crimes com-mitted by both sides, that to the men who perpetrated the Maryan martyrdoms, the blasphemy of those who denied the Transubstantiation was as frightful as to mock at the living Body of Christ upon the Cross. . . . If He were not present in the Consecrated Bread and Wine, would it not mean that He had deserted us ? Those martyred under Mary had — in the minds of those who burned them — cast away from us, horribly, unforgivably, the Body of Christ.

There is no excuse for the cruelties of either side, but, again, the Protestants may have remembered the garish horror of that unspoken, appalling blasphemy the Blood of Hales (bird-lime coloured with ochre, compounded by priests and held at the Monastery of Hales) to which the people flocked in thousands, like the birds caught in that lime, believing, in the words of Archbishop Cranmer, 'that it is the very Blood of Christ, and that it puts all men in a state of salvation'.

The cruelty on each side was responsible for that on the other. 'The villainy you teach me I will execute,' said a creation of the greatest man ever born in England, 'and it shall go hard, but I will better the instruction.'

.        .        .        .        .

Standing naked in an ocean of fire, these men of the Maryan reign perished.  Yet Heaven was not appeased.

On the 27th of June, the agitated Renard wrote to the Emperor : 'Our doctors and ladies were two months out in their reckoning. . . . If, by God's mercy, she does well, matters will have a better turn, but if not, I foresee trouble, and a great disturbance, so great, indeed, that the pen cannot express it.  For it is certain that they have managed so ill with the succession, that if anything untoward happens, Lady Elizabeth will have the preference.  [Lady Elizabeth, who had been imprisoned in the Tower, and in danger of death by the axe or by poison.]  I am not at all sure that the King and the Court will be safe. . . . Some say the Queen is not pregnant at all, and if a fitting child had been found, there would not have been so much delay.'

Even before the conflagrations had begun, hatred of the Queen had risen like a pestilence from kennels and slums.  A placard had been found nailed to the door of St. James's Palace the day after the announcement that the Queen was to bear a child : 'Are we such fools, oh noble English, that we can believe our Queen is enceinte of anything but an ape or a dog ?'

One day a dead dog was thrown through the window of her Presence Chamber, tonsured, and with cropped ears, and a placard hung round its neck saying that all the priests in England should be hanged.  Papers, strewn by an unseen hand, were found on the floors of her private apartments, even of her bedroom, telling her she was hated by the whole nation.  Terrified, her ladies would burst into tears in her presence.

There was no charge against her that was not believed.  As we have seen, it was said that she was about to have the body of the King her father disinterred that it might be burned as that of a heretic, deserving everlasting damnation — (she who had masses said for the soul of that beloved heretic). This was believed because she had, as Sir Thomas Smith declared, 'showed cruelty, or rather a raging madness, on the bodies of God's servants long before buried — drawing them forth of their graves to burn them as heretics'. And the long-dead body of an ex-nun, the wife of Peter Martyr, had been dragged from its grave and thrown upon a cesspool.

There was now no low mockery, no indignity, which was not heaped — the mockers being safe in their anonymity — on this agonised creature whose child could not be born.

A passer-by in the galleries of Hampton Court would see, slumped on the floor, her knees gathered up to her head, a figure that he took to be that of a dead woman. As he came nearer, that heap upon the floor would seem to be that of a beggar woman fallen there in her hunger and despair.

Then a physician and ladies-in-waiting would rush in, and as they lifted the fainting figure to its feet, the passer-by would see it was that of no dead woman, no beggar fallen from hunger, but that of a woman seemingly about to bear a child — the Queen of England.

But, as they carried her away, and the glamours of the summer light fell upon her haggard cheek, her distorted body in its ermine-trimmed dress, the nature of the burden she carried within her could be seen.

The child she was about to bear was Death. This was the child that Philip had given to her and to England.

# Chapter Five

To these agonies was now added that of jealousy.

If the strange and significant moments of Elizabeth's life, after her release from the Tower, could have remained, as the fires of the martyrdoms had left their ghosts in the air, what should we see ? What should we hear ?

Two sisters meeting for the first time after nearly two years — the younger going to meet the elder through the dark and glittering leaves of the garden, lit only by a torch — then ascending a secret staircase, up and up, until a gallery was reached : the sisters brought face to face — the older ape-like and wizened by pain, the younger with a pride like that of summer, so that it seemed the air through which she passed must retain some colour of summer. . . . The Queen's denunciation ; her sister's tears of denial. The Queen, after these denials, muttering to herself, in Spanish, 'Sabe Dios', 'God knows'. The husband of one sister hiding behind the arras to see the younger sister for the first time.

At first, this had not seemed strange to the Queen. . . . And yet . . . what interest had he in her whom he had never seen, that impelled him to hide behind the tapestry during that interview, in order to watch her, himself unseen ? And why, having seen her, did he not speak of her, keeping silent as if the whole episode had been a dream ?

The Queen thought of her sister's magnificent youthfulness, the high nostrils that looked as if they were breathing fire, the strange animal force that seemed to emanate from her, the strong aura of a grand physical life. She thought of her own ageing and withered face, her distorted form. And her hatred rose. . . .

. . . . .

Now there was silence in the Palace. One by one, the nobles that had crowded to Court to await the birth of the heir, the midwives, the nurses, the cradle-rockers, had gone, and soon the moment for Philip's release from that joyless marriage would come, and Mary would be alone.

Before it was known that the child she would bear was Death, the birth of a living child had been awaited by none more eagerly than the King, for that birth would mean his instant release from captivity. The Venetian Ambassador told the Doge, on the 1st of June, 'he [the King] will then cross the Channel instantly. . . . One single hour's delay seems to him a thousand.'

Such was the King's impatience to be free of this ageing, half-dead woman that when the marriage had lasted only six months, Renard had been obliged to remonstrate with him. The King must bear in mind, he said, the purpose for which he had come. No doubt he wished that the Queen was 'more agreeable. But he must remember that she was infinitely virtuous.' And with this cold comfort he had had to be content.

But now the Emperor was about to abdicate and retire to a monastery ; the raging madness of Philip's grandmother, Queen Juana of Castille, was over, for she was dead, and Philip could make it his excuse that the business of the Empire called him away. Soon he would be gone. And Renard, the Queen's adviser. And only her cousin, the Papal Legate, the fires of the martyrdoms, and her grief, would be left.

At first the King had tried to hide from her the truth. But, one by one, the Spanish grandees were missing from the Court. The Queen, noting their absence, dared not ask the reason. But, looking at Philip with anguish, she knew what it meant. He would not stay with her. He was going, and she would be alone.

It was only for a few weeks, he explained. If she liked, she could accompany him to the place of his embarkation, and wait for his return. But she was not deceived. She had seen on his face the marks of his eagerness to be gone.

The rumour spread that the Queen had died. So the night before the King's departure, a procession must go through the streets of London to show the people that she still lived.

The night of the 26th of August 1555 seemed laden with fire. So burning was the heat that the airs that came and went seemed plumed with flames, the river made of black fire. And in the streets the fevered dust seemed as if it might contain all the tropical diseases from Philip's dominions — the *tabardillo*, or yellow fever, the *calentura*, or heat-stroke, the *Cámaras de sangre*, or tropical dysentery.

The procession made its way through the silent streets of midnight, lit by a hundred torches. (Did not Nero find his way by night, by the light of human torches that were being consumed to dust in his honour ?) From a litter, the face of this new Nero, this Nightmare Life-in-Death, looked out through the heat.

The procession was on its way to Greenwich Palace, where the Queen was to bid her husband good-bye.

.     .     .     .     .

As she saw him step on to the barge that was to take him far away, out of her life, to where her love could never reach him, she hid her face. But not before her desperate, heart-stricken tears had been seen — tears that she must hide, for was she not the Queen ?

Had she known it, he would come again, as it were in mockery, in order to complete her ruin by involving England in his war with France, so bringing about the loss of Calais. And once again she would believe she was to bear a child.

Then, some instinct of pity, some stirrings of the feelings of a gentleman in his cold heart, moved him to foster this belief in her. But then he went again. And when she lay dying he would not come. Her usefulness had gone. It was time, now, for him to look to Elizabeth.

He was far away, yet, lying on her death-bed, looking at the door, she still expected him to enter. And still the Queen, to whom Death, that awaited child, was so long in coming, heard the whisper that had fanned her madness into flame.

But now only the darkness in the Palace echoed with the name that whisper had so often uttered . . . 'Elizabeth' . . . 'Elizabeth' . . .

# Chapter Six

FOR days, the hard black winter roads echoed with the sound of the flying hoofs of horses — a sound like that of black armour clashing on black armour. The courtiers were leaving the Palace in London where the Queen lay dying, for another Court, deep in the country, where a twenty-five-year-old Princess sat waiting for news.

But still she is alone, save for her ladies; sitting, in spite of the winter weather, under an oak tree in the park, looking at the snowflakes flying like bees, she does not see us, and is not trying to deceive us, and so for a moment we may see her, perhaps, as she really is.

Though her face and form are reflected in the mirror of History — her pulses, the tempestuous tides of blood, the depth of that lion-great but fearful heart — a heart that never yielded to its fear — are not seen. Only the outer covering, the swaddling of the sun and darkness of her spirit, these are given us.

We see a thin-waisted gold body, like that of the Bee-Priestesses, with a high ruff and sleeves like the thin wings of these : we see a gown that seems descended from the Minoan or Cretan civilisations.

Her appearance was that of the Plantagenet race. Her ugly face, so full of fire, so full of intellectual power, wisdom, vanity, and a strange fascination, was the face of the Plantagenets. She had the great, hauntingly beautiful eyes of Anne Boleyn, but the high, thin, and arched nose, whose nostrils seemed as if breathing fire, the long carved eyelids, the long and flawlessly beautiful hands, were the Plantagenet nose, eyelids, and hands.

For all this subtlety in the shape of her face and hands, there was a strange animal breath about her, so that we think of the Dauphin's horse that was 'all air and fire, chez les narines de feu'. 'Let me be your Prometheus', she wrote to Sir Henry Sidney. And she, nailed to the rock of her greatness, under the shadow of the eagle's wing, brought fire to her countrymen. Those wild sparks fell in the hearts of the adventurers, lit a torch in the blood of the greatest man ever born in England, William Shakespeare.

She was born at the time of the martyrs' fires under King Henry. At all moments of greatness, her Promethean fires burned in her speech, which was of a transcendental grandeur.

'I know that my kingdom is small', she told the French Ambassador ; 'it is therefore all the easier to defend.' 'Although I am a woman', she said, on another occasion, 'nevertheless I am the daughter of predecessors who knew how to deserve their kingdom.' To Fénelon she said, 'Although I may not be a lion, I am a lion's cub, and I have a lion's heart'.

One amongst the many contradictions in her was the difference between her speech at times of peril, or at any time when the sun of her greatness was at the height of its heaven, and her speech when an Ambassador was to be drawn into a web. She had learned during the terrible years of her childhood and early youth not to speak unwisely. Hasty speech led to death. She would therefore, in conversation with Ambassadors and certain others, enwrap their senses with a web of words, no thread of which seemed to lead anywhere. Then, having lulled and bemused them into a sense of security so that they were unprepared for shock or danger, she would, without the slightest warning, shoot with a terrifying force and directness straight to the heart of the matter.

A sense of fun would, from time to time, cause her to utter the most bewildering statements, especially to the Spanish envoys, whose grave stateliness, she thought, made them particularly desirable as victims. 'I yearn', she told the Spanish Ambassador, when she was twenty-six years of age, 'to be a nun and pass my days in prayer in a cell.' Bishop de

Quadra, reporting this to his King, remarked : 'It is a pretty business to deal with this woman who, I think, must have a hundred thousand devils in her body, in spite of her forever telling me the above.'

The impulses, the springs of life in this strange nature, have never been understood. Nor has the greatness of her indomitable spirit.

She inherited, in her blood, a dark strain of animality from her mother, and from the Minotaur, her father. But in spite of all the impulses that sprang from this inheritance, in spite of the frequent pretences at flirtation, those *fêtes galantes* that were a mask for her misery, she loved but one man in all that long life. That man was Robert Dudley, Earl of Leycester.

The scandals told of her had no foundation in fact. The contradictions in her nature gave her, together with those impulses, a fastidiousness equally strong.

Only one thing did she love more than Leycester and that was England.

'Have a care to my people', said this young woman of twenty-five to her judges on their assumption of office. 'You have my people — do you that which I ought to do. Every man oppresseth and spoileth them without mercy. They cannot avenge themselves, nor help themselves. See unto them — see unto them, for they are my charge. I care not for myself; my life is not dear to me. My care is for my people. I pray God whosoever succeedeth me, be as careful to them as I am.'

So she spoke when young. Many years later, she said to the crowds in the Strand, as she returned by torchlight from a Council meeting held after the defeat of the Armada : 'Ye may have a greater prince, but ye shall never have a more loving prince.'

For England's sake, she renounced all personal happiness.

Sometimes, in the rage of her misery, she would pretend to herself as well as to others that she would marry and have an heir. She would deceive her suitors into believing that she intended to marry them. She would accept their compliments and protestations of devotion with all the appearance of belief in their reality. Then the tragic and bitter humour in her heart would break from her like a flash of lightning ; and in that brief flash it could be seen that she had known all the truth from its deepest roots — that she was undeceivable. To the Duc d'Alençon, in answer to his telling her that, rather than give her up, he would see them both perish, the forty-eight-year-old Queen said : 'You must not threaten a poor old woman in her own kingdom !'

She would pretend to enjoy, perhaps even did enjoy, fulsome compliments on her beauty. This being who was lonely as the sun in his heaven longed to believe that she could be loved for herself.

When the slow wrinkles, soft as the first flakes of snow, fell upon her cheeks, thicker and thicker, until at last winter came to her heart, she could not bear to pass a mirror, so that all these were banished from her presence. This has been regarded, not as the outer sign of her tragedy, of her unspeakable anguish — all chance of happiness gone, no child to inherit her kingdom and save it from civil war — but as the displeasing and laughable vanity of a foolish old woman.

'Dead but not buried' — 'dead but not buried' — this was her cry, during the last two years of her life. 'Affection is false', she said. . . . (Leycester, whom she loved, and who had married, secretly, her evil and hated cousin Lettice — for whose sake it was supposed by some that he had murdered her first husband. . . . Essex, that cousin's son, who she had pretended to herself was *her* son . . . and who must soon die.

Dead and gone and false to the core.)

This strange contradiction of a woman, whose life, seen from one angle, was so barren, but, seen from another, was infinitely fertile, was constant only in her greatness and in her affections. That high courage of the lion, and the lion's heart, and the lion's rages, contrasted with the subtle mind. Sir Christopher Hatton, who knew her character, said, 'The Queen did fish for men's souls, and had so sweet a bait that no-one could escape from her network'.

Sir John Harington, 'the boy Jack', her godson, declared :

'When she smiled, it had a pure sunshine that every one did choose to bask in if they could ; but anon came a sudden gathering of clouds, and the thunder fell in a wondrous manner on all.'

Though the most feminine of women — (the ridiculous female-impersonator's appearance, the fishwifely back-slapping jollity and familiarity imputed to her by certain writers in later times, are singularly remote from this being of air and fire) — she yet had a masculine sense of justice, evinced, sometimes, in terrible words.  She told the French Ambassador, Fénelon, when he begged her not to visit upon the Queen of Scots the guilt for the massacre of St. Bartholomew's Eve : 'The Queen of Scots has enough sins of her own to answer for, without ascribing to her those of other people'.

What black and unresolved hatred, resulting, perhaps, from unplumbed depths of suffering, made this otherwise great woman capable of unreasoning, sensual cruelty ?  Made her capable of permitting the vile horrors, the unspeakable cruelties that were perpetrated by her troops in Ireland — the monstrous cruelties inflicted on the Catholic martyrs ?

'The rack was in constant use during the latter part of her reign', wrote one Catholic authority, Father Herbert Thurston, S.J.  'The total number of Catholics who suffered under her were 189 — 128 being priests, 58 laymen, and three women.  To these should be added, as Law remarks in his *Calendar of English Martyrs*, 32 Franciscans who were starved to death in the prisons.' [1]

What caused that hideous cruelty ?  The fear that was ever present with her, but that never caused her to flee from danger ?  The fear brought upon her by her terrible childhood, by the horror of her mother's and her stepmother's executions (so mysterious in their implications to a child of three, a child of nine) — by the danger in which she lived during Mary's reign, the daily, nightly danger of death by a dagger, a poisoned cup ?

What were those unexplained illnesses that fell upon her, going as suddenly as they came, but fear ?  'Queen Elizabeth, going of late to her church, was on the way suddenly stricken with some great Fear, that she returned to her Chamber to the admiration [amazement] of all present', wrote Thomas Morgan from Paris to Mary Stuart. And there were times when Leycester must sit by her side and, with her ladies, watch over her through the night.

The fires and the rivers of blood of the Henryan martyrdoms heralded her coming. And now, Death's shadow followed her everywhere, as it had done when she was a little child, seeming, then, only a shadow in the heat of the day. She would be playing, perhaps, and there would be Death, waiting quietly, or playing with her. She would think she spoke with her familiar servants, but through their lips the voice of Death would speak. 'Has the Queen my mother gone away?' 'Gone away.' 'Where is she? At Hampton Court?' Silence.

Then Death would come again. Her stepmother, the lewd, sly, pitiable little ghost Katherine Howard, who came back to haunt the King from the tomb of her cousin, Elizabeth's mother, vanished. 'Where is she gone?' 'The King's Grace was angered with her. So she is dead.' 'Dead?' 'Yes. The King's Grace had had her put to death because she was wicked.'

Thus the word 'Death' echoed through the Palace, throughout that lonely childhood.

In the time of her sister's reign the shadow was ever there, waiting for her. It followed her to her imprisonment in the Tower, where she must have seen, in imagination, a young head with long black hair, great slanting black eyes, severed from the body of that summer existence that had laughed so lightly. That sight confronted her through all the long days and nights in the Tower when she awaited her own end.

The shadow of Death was not to leave her until that of Mary went to join it, and, together, the two shadows disappeared. For a while only. Then the shadow of Death returned, and this time for ever.

She defied Death in every action of her life. When she

danced 'high and disposedly' on the threshold of the grave :
when she saved, not once, but over and over again, the life of
her cousin and enemy for whose sake, and with whose connivance (so she believed), her own death had been plotted,
not once, but many times.

But the presence of that shadow cannot possibly excuse
the martyrdoms of men who died for their faith, and for no
political activities.

And what of the personal cruelties, the delight in bear-
baiting, the cruelty to the deer at Kenilworth whose life, after
a hunt, the Queen spared, but whose ears were shorn off as
ransom ?

Thinking of that soft and helpless creature, sobbing in its
pain, I see the earless deer rising, upon the Judgment Day, to
confront her — one of the flames, perhaps, in which, as she
lay dying, she saw her 'lean and fearful body' wrapped.

But that death would not be for forty-seven long years.
Meanwhile, youth, and love, and glory were hers.

.        .        .        .        .

So we see her as she sits under the oak tree, looking at the
snowflakes and waiting for news.

At seven o'clock the next morning, the vast swell and
tolling of the great bells and the roar of the cannon sounded
like the rushing of the winter seas upon the shores of England.

The waxen form of the Queen whose child was Death lay
silent now, her red hair spread on either side of her like spent
flames.   At the same hour that night, the life of the Papal
Legate ceased.

### NOTE TO CHAPTER SIX

[1] *Catholic Encyclopaedia.*

# Chapter Seven

OF the four men who were to be the chief Councillors to the new Queen, it was said that Lord Robert Dudley (afterwards Earl of Leycester) 'seemed wiser than he was ; but Sir Nicholas Bacon was wiser than he seemed to be ; Lord Hunsdon (Anne Boleyn's nephew) neither was wise, nor seemed to be'. As for Sir Nicholas Bacon's brother-in-law, Sir William Cecil — afterwards Lord Burleigh — he was 'the youngest, the oldest, the gravest and greatest councillor in Christendom'.

'There was, before his death,' said a writer of the time, 'never a counsellor left alive in Europe, that was counsellor when he was first made one. He was made a counsellor at twenty-five years of age. And so continued foure yeares, in King Edward's time — and was the first counsellor Queen Elizabeth had.

'And so continued to the fortieth yeare of her reign. A long, happie tyme, to live in such a place, in so great account and reputation ! And, in the end, having lived so honourablie, virtuouslie, peaceablie, to die so goodlie, is an example of God's wonderful and rare blessinge, seldome found in men of his estate and employment.'

Now, unobtrusively, in his country house, he was waiting for the news that would summon him to Hatfield.

One candle threw a thick gold thread over the snow that was dark green as strawberry leaves under the shadow of the winter trees. Then even that thread of light was extinguished, and the cares and hopes of the day were forgotten by him who, when old, used to say 'when he put off his gown : "Lie there, lord treasurer", and, bidding adieu to all state affairs, he would dispose himself to his quiet rest.' [1]

His escapes from danger, his variations from truth-telling

boldness to subterfuge, had, during the last years, been of a startling character. He had, with some difficulty, avoided being involved in the disgrace of the Protector, the Duke of Somerset, to whom he was secretary. At the time of that disgrace, he crossed over to the enemy, and became secretary to the Duke of Northumberland, who superseded the disgraced man.

At the time of the Northumberland rebellion, he had thought it best to absent himself from Court, giving an imaginary illness as his excuse. But this illness, owing to fright, soon became a reality. So much so, indeed, that his kinsman, Lord Audley, wrote to him, advising him : 'Good Mr. Cecil, be of good comfort and plucke up a lustie merrie heart, and thus shall you overcome all diseases'. He recommended him to take, as remedy, 'A Porpin, otherwise called an Englishe Hedgehog, and quarter hym in peeces, and put the said Beeste in a styll with these Ingredients : item : a quart of Red Wine, a pinte of Rose-water, a quart of Sugar, Cinnamone and great Raisines'.

Whether or not this was, as Lord Audley claimed, 'a proved Remedie', the sufferer's health improved. But this may, perhaps, be ascribed to the fact that Lady Bacon, his sister-in-law, one of Queen Mary's ladies, had succeeded in averting from him the Queen's wrath.

When we think of him, we see him (perhaps because of his great wisdom and experience) as an old man, one full of cares and honours — see him as when, like another old counsellor,

> His beard was white as snow,
> All flaxen was his poll.

But at the time of Queen Elizabeth's accession, he was aged thirty-eight, and his hair was brown — it had not yet faded to flaxen like the dying snow ; and he walked with a lively step, not yet having been afflicted by that 'unhappie griefe in the foote', the gout. 'He was rather meanely statured', wrote the author of *Desiderata Curiosa*, 'and more well-proportioned than tall. . . . He was verie well-favoured, and of an excellent Complexion. Inasmuch as even in his later dayes, when he was well and warme, or had newe dined or supped, he had as good a colour in his face as most faire Women.' (Of 'an orient colour', perhaps, like his prized gilliflowers who 'stayed till hotter beams are prepared to infuse a spicy redness into (their) odours, and tincture (their) complexion with the deepest crimson'.)

'I think', continued the same writer, 'there were few who knew him but will say he was one of the sweetest and most well-mannered olde Men that hath beene seene. . . . He liked not an indirect or frivolous answere. Nor a tedious tale. Yet would he heare all though sometimes telle their faults.

'Most parte of the tyme, he was noted to be most patient in hearing (and so milde and readie answering as no Man went away discontented or without a reasonable Answere and quicke Despatch). Until three or foure yeares before his Deathe, when surprised with Age's Imperfections, he was a little sharpe in wordes, sometymes ; but it would vanishe like the Winde.

'In his old Age, if he could gett his table sette round with young, littel children, he was then in his Kingdome. And it was an exceeding pleasure, to heare what sporte he would make with them, with such prettie Questions, and wittie Allurements, as much delighted himselfe, the Children, and their hearers. . . . Or if he could get anie of his old Acquaintance, who could discourse of their youthe, or of thinges past in olde tyme, it was notable to heare what merrie tales he would tell.

'He had a great Household, and manie Gentlemen's sonnes among them.

'Bookes he loved, but after bookes, his Garden was his chiefe pleasure.'

This garden was ruled over by John Gerard, the herbalist —John Gerard with eyes as dark and clear and flashing as thieving blackbirds, and a ruff as clear and fresh as one of his own pinks. The Lord Treasurer's garden was full of gilliflowers discovered and fostered by Master Ralph Tuggie,

Gerard's friend, whose garden in Westminster was famous :
'The Princesse, the fairest of all these variable tawnies, of a
stammell* colour, striped and marbled with white stripes and
veines'. 'Master Tuggie's Rose Gilliflower, onely possessed
by him that is the most industrious preserver of all nature's
beauties, being of a fine stammell colour, very like unto a
small rose, much like unto the red Rose Campion, both for
forme, colour, and roundnesse, but larger for size.' 'A Gillo-
floure with yellow flowers, the which a worshipful Merchant
of London, Mr. Nicholas Leete, procured from Poland. . . .'

These were the delight of the leisure of that 'industrious
perceiver of all nature's beauties', Queen Elizabeth's chief
statesman.

> .          .          .          .          .

The wise old man was in the habit of saying, 'That nothing
was truly for a prince's profit, that was not for his honour'.
'That war is soon kindled, but peace very hardly procured.'
'He would often say that he thought "there was never so wise
a woman born, for all respects, as Queen Elizabeth. For she
spake and understood all languages. Knew all estates and
dispositions of all princes. And (particularly was) so expert
in the knowledge of her own realm and estate as no counsellor
she had, could tell her what she knew not before.

'She had also so rare gifts, as when her Counsellors had
said all they could say, she would then frame out a wise
counsel beyond all theirs.'"

> .          .          .          .          .

On Sunday the 20th of November, the new Queen gave
her first audience to her Ministers.

After the oaths of allegiance had been taken, the Queen
addressed the assembly :

'My Lords,

'The laws of Nature move me to sorrow for my sister ;
the burden that has fallen upon me maketh me amazed : and

* Scarlet.

yet considering I am God's creature ordained to obey His appointment I will thereto yield ; desiring from the bottom of my heart that I may have assistance of His Grace, to be the minister of His heavenly will in the office now committed to me. And as I am but one body naturally considered, though by His permission a body politic to govern, so shall I desire you all, my Lords, chiefly you of the nobility, every one in his degree and power to be assistant to me ; that I with my ruling and you with your service may make a good account to Almighty God, and leave some comfort to our posterity on earth. . . .'

As Sir William Cecil knelt before the Queen, and took his oath of allegiance as Secretary, she said to him, 'I give you this charge that you shall be of my Privy Council, and content yourself to take pains for me and my realm. This judgment I have of you, that you will not be corrupted by any manner of gifts, and that you will be faithful to the State ; and that without respect of my private will you will give me that Counsel which you think best ; and if you shall know any-thing necessary to be declared unto me of secrecy, you shall show it to myself only ; and assure yourself, I will not fail to keep taciturnity thereto.' [2]

To these charges he was faithful to his death.

So he was seen by most observers. But the light could change the shadows cast by him to strange shapes. Those shadows could be dark and deep.

At this same audience, Sir Nicholas Bacon was made Lord Keeper, and Cecil's kinsman and friend, the fat and fussy Thomas Parry, was knighted and made Controller of the Queen's household.

This Polonius of a man, this old courtier whose ear, one imagines, was always at the keyhole, whose tongue was never silent, whose speeches were like a swirl of dry dust in a little air, had been in her life since her early childhood.

He had been forgiven for his gross indiscretion, years ago, when Admiral Seymour, the Protector's brother (a

strong-voiced, gallant, swashbuckling, thirty-eight-year-old
man — 'fierce in courage, courtly in fashion, in personage
stately, in voice magnificent, but somewhat empty of matter' [3]),
having succeeded in marrying King Henry's widow Catherine
Parr — secretly, for his brother would not have allowed the
marriage — turned his attention, immediately after his wife's
death, to the fifteen-year-old Elizabeth.[4]

Before the Queen's death, when the Princess was living
in her stepmother's house, Mrs. Ashley, the girl's governess,
had strongly disapproved of the Admiral's conduct.  However, as soon as he became a widower, she and Parry, the
Princess's cofferer, did their utmost to further his new ambition,
with the result that they brought, not only their lives, but that
of the Princess, into danger.  When the news reached the
Princess's house that the Admiral had been sent to the Tower
on the charge of high treason (an attempt to get possession
of the person of his nephew the boy-King), and that 'my lord
Great Master and Master Denny' had arrived to arrest both
governess and cofferer for advancing the Admiral's ambition
to marry the Princess, 'the Cofferer turned horribly pale, went
hastily to his chamber, and said to my lady his wife "I would
I had never been born for I am undone" — and wrung his
hands, and cast away his chain from his neck and his rings
from his fingers'.

Thomas Parry and Mrs. Ashley were sent to the Tower.
There, in fear of his life, he repeated all Mrs. Ashley's indiscreet
remarks.

That lady had many virtues, but discretion was not among
them.  Her tongue was a babbling brook, and she could not
conceive of a heaven in which there was neither marrying
nor giving in marriage.

That babbling tongue had helped to bring them to the
Tower.  After Queen Catherine's death, on Twelfth Night,
she told the cofferer that the Queen's ladies had said evil things
. . . that 'the Admiral had loved the Princess but too well,
and had so done for a long while' ; and that 'the Queen,
suspecting too often access of the Admiral to the lady Eliza-

beth's Grace, came suddenly upon them, when they were all alone (he having her in his arms). Whereupon the Queen fell out both with the Lord Admiral and with her Grace also. . . . And this was not long before they parted asunder their families [households]. I do not know whether . . . she went herself, or was sent away. . . .' 5

This was the gist of Thomas Parry's revelations in the Tower. . . .

One false step on the part of this fifteen-year-old girl, left alone, with no one to advise her . . . then the Tower — the headsman's block for herself, and for others.

The questioners were unable to bring Elizabeth to say one thing which could inculpate Mrs. Ashley or Parry. They, and in particular Parry, had told everything which could reflect discredit upon the young girl in their charge. But, with the true Elizabethan greatness, that young girl asserted their entire innocence. They had never, she declared, tried to further the Admiral's plans.

On their release, the Princess received them back into her household, and Thomas Parry had, though a Protestant, been allowed by Queen Mary to attend the Princess at Hatfield, though not to live actually in the house. Incurably addicted to the promotion of matrimony, and not in the least discouraged by his sojourn in the Tower for that offence, he was soon to become one of the chief instigators of the plan that the Queen should marry Lord Robert Dudley.*

He was not to serve his mistress for long. He died on the 15th of December 1560 of 'mere ill humour'.

* So it is said. But the present writer does not see, considering the date of his death, how this was possible.

### NOTES TO CHAPTER SEVEN

1 F. Peck, *Desiderata Curiosa.*
2 Froude, *Domestic MS. Elizabeth*, vol. i.
3 Heylin, *History of the Reformation.*
4 See the author's *Fanfare for Elizabeth*, p. 163 *et seq.*
5 Confessions of Katherine Ashley, *Domestic Papers Edward VI*, vol. vi, *Fanfare for Elizabeth.*

# Chapter Eight

OVER the wide roads, a winter firmament of black glass, from which the hooves of a thousand horses splintered great stars, moons, planets, and meteors, the procession made its way towards the capital, and, at the head of the cortège, a blazing comet in the melancholy day, rode the Queen, and next her, a magnificent figure whose face, as yet, could not be seen clearly — Lord Robert Dudley, her Master of the Horse. As he was born on the same day of the same year as his Queen, their lives were ruled by the same planet, and according to Camden this was the reason for their life-long infatuation with each other.

It was along this road that she had been carried in a litter, to enter the Tower by the Traitor's Gate, and to die by the axe if her sister's counsellors and lawyers could encompass that death.[1]

At Cripplegate she was received by the Lord Mayor and civic authorities. Riding along London Wall (then a fortification), which was hung with tapestries, she was greeted by exultant crowds. Then, as she reached the entrance to the Corn Market, the guns from the Tower began their thunder.

As she entered the Tower, the Queen said to the company : 'Some have fallen from being princes of this land, to be prisoners in this place. I am raised from being prisoner in this place to be prince of this land. That dejection was a work of God's justice ; as they were to yield patience for the axe, so I must bear myself to God thankful and to man merciful for the other.'

She remained in the state apartments of the Tower until the 5th of December 1558, holding each day Councils of state ; the main purpose of which was to decide who among the dead Queen's Catholic advisers could remain in harmony with the new members of the Council — Cecil, Bacon, Parr, Russell, Sadler, Lord Robert Dudley — many of whom had served under King Edward. The other purpose was to formulate the religious policy.

The clergy and the lawyers alike were consulted about the latter. In a paper named 'Distresses of the Commonwealth', the writer (possibly Armagil Wade, Clerk of the Council at the time of King Henry's death) advised 'wary handling'. 'The Catholics were in the majority in every county except Middlesex and Kent.' 'The Pope was a dangerous enemy.' 'Theological intolerance was not found by experience to produce healthy convictions.' Goodrich, a lawyer, advised that in the coming Parliament, it would be better to do nothing but repeal the Lollard Statutes of Henry the Fourth, and Henry the Fifth, revived by Queen Mary. 'Her Majesty', he continued, 'might by licence of law use the English Litany and suffrages used in King Henry's time', and 'Her Majesty . . . might use the Mass, without lifting up of the Host, according to the ancient canons ; and might also have at every Mass some communicants with the Minister in both kinds'.[2]

This, the Protestants felt, was good as far as it went. And yet, they could not but feel disappointed. They had looked forward to persecuting the Catholics to their hearts' content. But now they were forbidden even to *irritate* them — and as for invectives and persecutions, they were told these must be kept for Arians and Anabaptists !

.    .    .    .    .

On the 5th of December, the Queen left the Tower, going by water to Somerset House 'with trumpets playing, and melody and joy and comfort to all true English men and women'.[3]

For the Queen, in her daily progresses through the streets of London, had already fired the imagination and hearts of her people . . . 'in coupling mildness with majesty as she did', wrote a contemporary, 'and in stately stooping to the meanest sort. . . . Her eye was set upon one, her ear listened to another, her judgement ran upon a third, to a fourth she addressed her speech ; her spirit seemed to be every where. . . . Some she pitied, some she commended, some she thanked, at others she pleasantly and wittily jested, contemning no person.'

She was gracious equally to the poor and to the richer citizens ; she reined in her horse to speak, long and sweetly, to the ill Marquis of Northampton, the brother of her step-mother Queen Catherine Parr, whom she had espied at a window.

But King Philip's Ambassador, the Count (afterwards Duke) de Feria, told his master that the reason for that gracious-ness was that Lord Northampton had been a great traitor to her sister ; and as for the shouting in the streets, he was not at all sure that these were entirely due to the new Queen's popularity. Could they not be the echoes of the shrieks that still haunted the heaps of ash in Smithfield ?

The happy days flew by, but there was still a dark memory that must be buried and forgotten.

On the 13th of December 1558, the late Queen was borne to her grave.

The procession started early in the day from St. James's Palace, where she had died. A herald who was an eye-witness wrote : 'So up the highway went the foremost standard, the falcon and the hart. Then came a great company of mourners. Then another goodly standard of the lion and the falcon, fol-lowed by King Philip's servants, riding two and two. Then the third standard with the white greyhound and falcon. The Marquis of Winchester bore the banner of England on horse-back ; Chester herald, the helm, the crest, and the mantle ; Norroy, the target, with the crown of England and the order of the Garter ; Clarencieux, the sword, and Mr. Garter King-at-Arms her coat armour — all on horseback. The Somerset, Lancaster, Windsor, and York heralds carried four white banners of saints embossed in fine gold. Then came the corpse, in a chariot, with an exact image representing Queen Mary dressed in crimson velvet, with many gold rings on her hands. The pall over the coffin was black cloth of gold, intersected by a cross of cloth of silver. The body was followed by the chief mourners ; the Queen's ladies came after on horseback, but their black trains were long enough to sweep after them on the ground.

'Before the corpse and following after it, came processions of monks, mourning their own fate as well as the death of Mary. Such was the procession that passed by Charing Cross, and arrived at the great door of Westminster Abbey, where everyone alighted from their horses. There, waited gentlemen, ready to take the Queen out of her chariot. The Earls and Lords went before her. . . . The effigy above mentioned was carried between men of worship. At the great door of the Abbey, four Bishops and Abbot Feckenham *in pontificalibus* met this procession and censed the corpse. The royal corpse was then placed on the hearse, and watched the live-long night of December the 13th. A hundred poor men in good black gowns and hoods, bearing long torches, with the Queen's guard in black coats, bearing staff torches, stood round the hearse that night, and wax-chandlers were in attendance to supply any torch that burnt out.

'The next morning, December the 14th, was the Queen's Mass, and all the people offered ; the Queen's body armour, her target, her banner of arms, and three standards, were all offered, her heralds standing round the coffin. The Bishop of Winchester preached. . . .

'Then Her Grace was carried up to that chapel King Henry VII builded, attended by mitred Bishops. When the heralds brake their staffs and flung them into the grave, all the people plucked down the hangings, and the armorial bearings round the Abbey, and everyone tore him a piece as large as he could catch it.'

Long years afterwards, the sister from whom she was so deeply divided in life was carried to a grave beside her. And, a life-time after that second burial, when, in 1670, the royal vault was opened, a mischievous little boy dipped his hand into the sisters' urns, and, for a moment, held in that small hand the heart of fire and the lesser heart — 'now but a kind of glutinous red substance, somewhat resembling mortar'.[4]

.          .          .          .          .

The new Queen listened with some interest to Dr. White's funeral sermon. It was in Latin, which the Queen understood as she understood English, and it could not be said to be fortunate. Sir John Harington, the Queen's godson (always addressed by her as 'Boy Jack'), called it 'a black sermon'.

After sobbing so violently, as he described the late Queen's sufferings, that for some moments he was unable to continue his sermon, the Bishop (when at last his speech returned to him) added, perhaps as an afterthought, 'that Queen Mary had left a sister, a lady of great worth, also, whom they were bound to obey' : for, he reminded the congregation, '*melior est canis vivus leone mortuo* . . . better a living dog than a dead lion'.

It is scarcely surprising that as the Bishop left the pulpit, the Queen ordered him to be arrested. He defied her, and threatened her with excommunication. The order was not withdrawn. It is said that the Bishop desired martyrdom. But the Queen had not, as yet, descended to persecution.

On the 23rd of December, the Court removed to Whitehall for the first Christmas of the reign.

It had been thought by all that Christmas would have been celebrated in the Palace according to the rites of the Catholic Church. On Christmas morning, the Queen appeared, in great state, in her closet in the Chapel, accompanied by her ladies and the officers of state. Oglethorpe, the Bishop of Carlisle, was at the High Altar, preparing to celebrate the Mass. But at the end of the Gospel, when all present expected that the Queen would make the usual offering, she rose to her feet and, followed by her whole train, withdrew from her closet to her apartments — greatly to the astonishment of the spectators.

Was the Queen ill ? So it might be supposed. But shortly afterwards, a proclamation was issued that from the first day of the New Year, the Litany, Epistle, and Gospel should be read in English in the Queen's Chapel and in all churches.

It had, however, been determined that the Queen should be crowned according to the rites of the Catholic Church, and the time having now come when the date of the Coronation must be fixed, the Master of the Horse, Lord Robert Dudley, and Lord Pembroke, rode through the bear-furred winter woods to the house of the mathematician, scientist, and (it was supposed) necromancer, Dr. John Dee, to enquire the most auspicious day foretold by the stars for the holding of the ceremony.

John Dee, the inventor of the Paradoxicall Compass, was the future friend and adviser of twenty-six-year-old Mr. Hakluyt, of the Middle Temple — whom he told about the conquest by King Arthur of Gelindis, 'recently called Frise-land' — the future friend and adviser of young Mr. Gilbert, John Davis, and young Mr. Hawkins 'who had been with Mr. Drake' (and who, long years after Dr. Dee had been con-sulted about the time for the Coronation, 'had been to my house in Mortlake'. Indeed, Dr. Dee was the friend of all mariners and adventurers. Did he not, in 1580, draw a chart and write instructions for Captains Charles Jackson's and Arthur Pett's North-East voyage to Cathay ?

He was a cousin of the elderly Blanche Parry, who had held the little Elizabeth, as a child, in her arms. He had a firm friend in Secretary Cecil, having been introduced to him and presented to King Edward by the King's tutor and Cecil's brother-in-law, Sir John Cheke. Queen Elizabeth was in the habit of consulting him, and he was tutor in alchemy and astronomy to her confidential maid-of-honour, Blanche Parry.

But his future had not always seemed so clear. In the reign of Queen Mary he had been in considerable danger. During the early spring of 1555, certain members of Princess Elizabeth's household at Woodstock were accused of witch-craft, 'for that they did calculate the King's, the Queen's, and my lady Elizabeth's nativity, whereof one Dee, and Cary, and Butler, and one other of my lady Elizabeth's (household) are accused that they should have a familiar spirit, which is the more suspected, for that Ferys, one of their accusers, had, immediately on the accusation, both of his children stricken, the one with death, the other with blindness'.[5]

But nothing could be proved against the accused, and Dr. Dee, with the others, was acquitted.

The day blessed by the stars for the Queen's Coronation, he told the two emissaries, was Sunday the 15th of January 1559.*

* For more information about Dr. Dee see Appendix A.

NOTES TO CHAPTER EIGHT

[1] Froude, *History of England, Reign of Queen Elizabeth I.*
[2] Froude, *op. cit.*
[3] Neale, *Queen Elizabeth.*
[4] Manuscript Diary of William Taswell, D.D., Rector of Newington and St. Mary, Bermondsey.
[5] Thomas Martin, Letter to Earl of Courtenay.

# Chapter Nine

KING PHILIP had not yet returned to his Palace in Spain, darkened against the coruscations of the many-coloured fires of the sun, and haunted by his ghost-like, black-veiled sister and her constant companion, his little half-mad son. But in Brussels, a martyr to matrimony, he was facing anew the fact that once more he must offer himself as a sacrifice on the altar of his religion and his country.

The news from England had been anything but satisfactory.

From a benevolent wish to guide his sister-in-law, 'a young untried lass', as his Ambassador, Count de Feria, described her, he had sent that gentleman, a few days before Queen Mary's death, to assure the Princess of the King's continued friendship.

Count de Feria was received, he told his royal master, 'well, though not so cordially as on former occasions'. He supped with the Princess, Lady Clinton, and three of the Princess's ladies-in-waiting, Lady Troy, Lady Gard, and Mary Norn.

The Princess declared her pleasure at the Count de Feria's visit, and spoke of the King with cordiality. But when the Count gave her to understand that she owed the reversion of the Crown to His Majesty's will, she evinced some surprise.

Shortly before this, two members of the Council had visited her, to inform her that it was 'the Queen's intention to bequeath to her the royal crown'. To which she replied: 'I am very sorry to hear of the Queen's illness, but there is no reason why I should thank her for her intention of giving me the crown of the realm, for she has neither the power of bestowing it, nor can I lawfully be deprived of it, since it is my peculiar and hereditary right'.

Something of the same kind she conveyed to the Ambassador. The uncomfortable impression made on him by this interview was intensified by his treatment when the new Queen went into residence in London.

You would have thought, would you not, that he would have been given a room in the Palace, and would have received all the Queen's most secret confidences. Not at all ! 'They run away from me as if I were the devil !' he told the King. And as for being given a room in the Palace, when he suggested this, the Queen sent a message by the Lord Chamberlain that 'she was astonished at his wishing such a thing, which had never been granted to the Minister of any Prince. It was done for me during the late Queen's life because she was the wife of Your Majesty, while she [Queen Elizabeth] was still unmarried'.

The Ambassador, determined not to forgo the wished-for room without a struggle, told Bishop de Quadra, his assistant, to ask Cecil to explain the matter to the Queen. It was for the sake of *convenience* that he asked to be given a room in the Palace. He was there to serve the Queen in all things, and should be given every facility to do so. (But actually his reason was that the Councillors were lacking in tact. They had formed the trying habit of following the Ambassador whenever he wished to have a private conversation with the Queen. By living in the Palace, he hoped to circumvent them.)

At last, to the utter amazement of the Ambassador and the Bishop, it was explained that his request could not be granted as the Queen was a young unmarried woman and the Ambassador a bachelor !

Astonishing ! The Ambassador exclaimed that, though still a bachelor, he was about to be married (to Jane Dormer, one of Queen Mary's maids-of-honour). The Ambassador, whose high shoulders looked always as if they had just been shrugged, and were about to be shrugged again, seemed even more cynical than ever.

Things went from bad to worse. He himself was, as he

complained to the King, 'nothing but a cypher'. As for the
King — 'his voice had no more weight with the Council than
if he had never married into the realm. In all likelihood', he
continued, 'there would be an insurrection, of which the
French would take advantage to invade the realm'. Indeed,
'the realm is in such a state that we could best negotiate sword
in hand'.

Spain was determined that England should not come under
the influence of France (with whom the war still continued) —
still less under French rule. . . . And there was grave danger
of the former happening, without any need for an invasion.
The Queen had instructed her Ambassador to tell the King of
Spain that France had made advances to her, had proffered a
separate peace.

The King of France, that 'diamond dolphinical dry lecher',
had written congratulating her on her accession, assuring her
that he had been and would be her truest friend, and adding
that with the death of the late Queen, he trusted the only
reason for differences between England and France had gone.
The English Ambassador added that he was instructed to say
that the Queen would do nothing to injure her alliance with
Spain, without a previous warning to the King. But that
England had been dragged into war with France against the
wishes of her people, and that she would not think it right to
refuse an offer made to the advantage of her country.

The King of France had instructed Guido Cavalcanti to
say that 'although Calais was of the ancient patrimony of
France and the French would give all their substance to keep
it', yet, 'where there was a will on both sides, no difficulties
were insuperable'. . . . 'So long as it was uncertain where
the Queen might marry, he might, if he restored it, be opening
a door to give his enemies an entrance into his kingdom.'
(To which the Queen replied that, as to Calais falling to
Spain, she was of English descent, not Spanish like her sister,
and she and her people might be trusted to take care of it.
She was good friends with the King of Spain, but not otherwise
than was for the good of her people.)

If, the French King told her, the Queen would marry in a quarter from which France had nothing to fear . . . an expedient would be found for Calais to the honour of both princes and the satisfaction of their subjects . . . while an alliance might be formed between himself, the Dauphin, the Dauphine Mary (who claimed to be Queen of England as of Scotland) and Elizabeth, for a perpetual union of England, France, and Scotland, with a final determination of all quarrels, rights, and pretensions whatever.

This must be prevented at all costs !

The King of Spain instructed his Ambassador to *spare no expense* in the Palace or outside it, in order to find out the truth of the Queen's relations with France, the possibilities of a separate peace, etc.

At first, all went splendidly. The new Lord Treasurer, and the new Lord Chamberlain, Lord William Howard, accepted with delight the offer of pensions to be paid them by Spain. What made these acceptances particularly fortunate was that Lord William was to succeed the Earl of Arundel (held by the Ambassador in peculiar detestation) as delegate to the Peace Conference to end the war between Spain and France . . . and Lord William would be in the pay of Spain !

The Ambassador suggested that they should have a quiet talk, an invitation that Lord William accepted with alacrity. In the course of the talk, the Ambassador assured him that not only would he receive the pension yearly, but that the King would add to this, each year, a valuable sable coat, the perquisite of the Lord Chamberlain's office. It gave the King particular pleasure to think of the coat having so worthy a wearer ! There was no need — the Ambassador was particularly emphatic on this point — that anybody should know about the transaction : the payment and presents would arrive under cover, through Luis de Paz, a Spanish agent in London.

Lord William was profuse in his thanks, the farewell was cordial in the extreme, and the Ambassador relaxed, and waited for news.

News came — but not of the order the Ambassador had expected. Instead of going straight to the Conference at Château-Cambrécis, Lord William and his train were to stay in Brussels, where the King of Spain was at that time, in order to see him. . . . Why? The Ambassador was completely in the dark. His spies seemed even more stupid and inept than usual, and could tell him nothing.

The Ambassador, therefore, sent Luis de Paz to Lord William to express his delight at the news. But travelling in state, and entertaining in a suitable manner, were a heavy expense. If Lord William needed ready money, there was Luis de Paz only waiting to give it to him. (Surely this added proof of generosity and thoughtfulness must entangle Lord William even more inextricably in the web of Spain !)

To the Ambassador's amazement, Howard replied that 'he was provided with money for the present', and that 'hitherto he had done no more than other councillors, and did not require the money'!

It was evident, either that the Lord Chamberlain had taken leave of his senses, or that he had been so indiscreet as to consult somebody, and had received bad advice.

But worse was to come.

The Ambassador was still suffering from shock when he received another and even worse one. The Lord Chamberlain sent a servant to say that he had thought the matter over and had changed his mind. 'He could not accept what I had offered him previously until he found the Queen's pleasure in the matter ; but now that she had given her consent, he would be glad if I would give him the money.' So the Ambassador told his King. It was obvious that you could not trust this perfidious race an inch. 'This is to let your Majesty know', the Ambassador exclaimed, 'what sort of people these are !'

Lord William made a sensational attendance at the Peace Conference, where he shouted so loudly that he caused the Constable Montmorency to swear in church.

Disgusted and disillusioned, the Ambassador did not look

forward to his next interview with the Queen. The conduct
of that 'young untried lass' was, however, as usual, unpredictable. With great sweetness of manner she told him there
was no objection, as far as she was concerned, to his spending
his master's money in that way if he liked. It would be an
economy for her to employ people whose wages were paid
by somebody else. She even said, 'She hoped Your Majesty
would not be offended if she, on her side, employed some of
the servants you have here'.

De Feria replied that he was sure His Majesty would be
delighted. He told the King that he thought the surplus of
the money which might, alas, have been so usefully expended,
had better be distributed among the loyal Bishops in the Tower,
rather than 'on these renegades who have sold their God and
the honour of their country !'

And yet, in spite of this, in spite of the fact that she had
refused him a room in the Palace, it was obvious to the Ambassador that the Queen had changed from her former cold
attitude to him. She told him gossip, invited him to plays.
She undoubtedly, he thought, enjoyed her conversations with
him. (There, he was right !) She now consulted him about
everything, listened to his advice with a countenance of the
most flattering attention, agreed to follow it — and it was, of
course, only due to accident that she never by any chance did
so. The look she turned upon him was of the utmost innocence. She enjoyed, particularly, their theological discussions,
and, sighing, said that she wished that religion had played a
larger part in her upbringing. He sent her books on the subject, which, she assured him, were of the greatest profit to her.

But strangely enough, they did not influence her behaviour. The truth of the matter was, as he realised, that the
'young untried lass's' *stupidity* was the cause of these strange
discrepancies between her conversation and her conduct!

But the lightning changes from day to day — each day
bringing some scheme more impossible than the last — were
beginning to tell on the Ambassador's nerves. It was impossible to foresee what she would say or do next. He feared that

she would 'marry for caprice'. This would be fatal. He must 'get in a few words about it'. He did, and often. Each time that he did so, the Queen listened with a pretty air of deference. She had, she said, been about to consult him. She had practically made up her mind to marry So-and-so — in every case someone who was obviously out of the question. What did the Ambassador think ? The Ambassador gave full rein to his eloquence. From time to time, leaning back in her chair of state with its shining cover of peacocks' feathers sewn together, she would shield her face with her hand, as if dazzled by so much brilliance. Once, from behind the hand, came a slight sound, gone almost as soon as heard. The Queen, perhaps, had caught her breath ? Perhaps. The next moment, the hand was withdrawn, and the young, serious face, the candid eyes, regarded him. Sighing, she declared he had convinced her. But next day she consulted him about marrying somebody even more impossible.

The Ambassador was in despair. The Queen seemed determined on her own ruin. And as for her obstinacy ! And yet . . . 'She seems to me', he wrote, 'incomparably more feared than her sister, and gives her orders and has her way as absolutely as her father did.'

This was true. 'Che grandezza !' an Italian onlooker observed, as she — then an old woman — walked by. That *grandezza* had been with her from the beginning. And the Houses of Parliament, to their astonishment, were soon to know what lay in that heart of fire, that temper of the finest steel, that man's brain in a woman's body. She ruled Parliament as her father had done, spoke to them as a King, not as a woman. When, years afterwards, the Commons thought to force her to marry by including her promise to do so in their subsidy book, she said to them : 'I know no reason why my private answers to the realm should serve for prologue to a subsidy book ; neither yet do I understand why such audacity should be used to make, without my licence, an act of my words'. Then in the same session of Parliament she said : 'Let this my discipline stand you in stead of sorer strokes, never to tempt too far a prince's patience, and let my comfort pluck up your dismayed spirits, and cause you think that . . . you return with your prince's grace, whose care for you, doubt you not to be such as she shall not need a remembrancer for your weal'.    And, turning to Bacon, she said, 'My Lord Keeper, you will do as I bid you'.    Bacon said, 'The Queen's Majesty dissolves this parliament.    Let every man depart at his pleasure.'

They feared and loved her.

As for her people : she who, many years after, wrote a Latin prayer in her prayer-book, the last words of which, translated by Frederick Chamberlin, are 'Give to me, the Queen, Thy commands, that I may judge Thy people in justice, and Thy poor in understanding', was already, at the beginning of her reign, beloved by them.    She could say of their love then, as she said to the French Ambassador when she was an old woman, 'It seems incredible, and I love them no less, and I can say that I would rather die than see any diminution of it on one side or the other'.

The unfortunate Spanish Ambassador was soon to find, as Parliament found, that she had inherited King Henry's temper.    'I have', she said, 'the heart of a man, not a woman, and I am not afraid of anything.'    And, years later, 'I am more afraid of making a fault in my Latin than of the Kings of Spain, France, Scotland, the House of Guise, and all their confederates'.

It was useless for the King of Spain to urge him to terrify the young untried lass with the Dauphine Mary's claim to the throne, or with the Pope.

What was to be done ? . . . Perhaps even better than that Spain should 'negotiate sword in hand', would be the Queen's immediate marriage to a prince who could be ruled by Philip — his cousin, the landless Philibert of Savoy, perhaps ? . . . But he had already been suggested and refused, before her accession.

'If she marry out of her own realm', the Ambassador wrote, 'may she place her eyes upon Your Majesty.'

# Chapter Ten

FRANCE and the heretics — the heretics and France ! . . . Something must be done, and that quickly — for the Queen's suitors were increasing in number. Soon it might be too late.

In addition, the King of Spain had been considerably alarmed by the suggestion that Elizabeth might marry 'in a quarter whence France had nothing to fear'.

This could not be risked.

But was there to be no end *ever* to the sacrifices the King was required to make ?

The Ambassador urged him to come to an immediate decision. But the time was not an auspicious one. The King was at that moment plagued with the million points that had to be made at the Peace Conference, with the details of his own delegates' interviews, with preparing arguments for his allies the English, and with making arrangements to bribe the French. If the Conference broke down, there would be another immediate war, and that would mean finding all the money available. The Pope insisted that heresy must be suppressed among the King's subjects in the Low Countries, and that immediately. His generals harassed him ceaselessly with demands to know how they were to proceed with the fortifications of Metz.

But letter after letter reached him from England, adding to the burdens on his mind.

On the 9th of January 1559, he was still undetermined. On the 10th, he was resolved. The sacrifice should be made.

He did not doubt this would be accepted. For how was

it possible that any woman could be so foolish as to refuse him as a husband ? Was he not, by the grace of God, King of Spain, Naples, and Jerusalem, Duke of Milan, Burgundy, and Brabant, Prince of Sicily ; Archduke of Austria, Count of Hapsburg, Flanders, and the Tyrol ? Had he not, also, roused in Mary's heart a desperate and undying passion ?

.        .        .        .        .

The man who had been the deeply disinclined husband of Mary, and who now resolved, once more, to sacrifice himself on the altar of his duty, wrote to his Ambassador : 'Touching the Queen's marriage, I directed you in one of my last letters to throw all possible obstacles in the way of her marriage with a subject. For myself, were the question asked, I bade you say nothing positively to commit me, yet so to answer as not to leave her altogether without hope. In a matter of so great importance I had to consider carefully ; and I wished before coming to a resolution to have the advice both of yourself and others. At length, after weighing it on all sides, I have concluded thus :

'There are many and serious reasons why I should not think of her. I could spend but little time with her ; my other dominions require my constant presence. The Queen has not been what she ought to be in religion ; and to marry with any but a Catholic will reflect upon my reputation. I shall be committing myself, perhaps, to an endless war with France, in consequence of the pretensions of the Queen of Scots to the English crown ; my subjects in Spain require my return to them with indescribable anxiety ; while so long as I remain in this country [Flanders] the hospitalities expected of me are, as you well know, a serious expense ; and my affairs, as you know also, are in such disorder that I can scarce provide for my current necessities, far less encounter any fresh demands upon me.

'There are other objections besides these, equally considerable, which I need not specify. You can yourself imagine them.

'Nevertheless, considering how essential it is in the interests of Christendom to maintain that religion which by God's help has been restored to it — considering the inconveniences, the perils, the calamities which may arise, not only there but in these states also, if England relapse into error — I have decided to encounter the difficulty, to sacrifice my private inclination in the service of our Lord, and to marry the Queen of England.

'Provided only and always that these conditions be observed : First and chiefly, that you will exact an assurance from her that she will profess the same religion which I profess, that she will persevere in it and maintain it, and keep her subjects true to it ; and that she will do everything which in my opinion shall be necessary for its augmentation and support.

'Secondly, she must apply to the Pope for the absolution of her past sins, and for the dispensation which will be required for the marriage ; and she must engage to accept both these in such a manner that when I make her my wife she will be a true Catholic, which hitherto she has not been.

'You will understand from this the service which I render to our Lord. Through my means her allegiance will be re-covered to the Church. I should mention that the condition that gave the Low Countries to the issue — should any such be born — of my marriage with the late Queen cannot be again acceded to. It is too injurious to the rights of my son Don Carlos.'

He was particularly insistent that he could spend but little time with the Queen, but must come and go. But it would be better if the Ambassador did not mention this, or any of the other conditions which would have to be made, until he had found out if the Queen was inclined to accept his proposal and see his self-sacrifice in its true light. On no account must the King be exposed to 'a refusal which would make his con-descension appear ridiculous'. The Count must use tact.

He did. The first thing for him to do, he realised clearly, was to consult with the Queen's ladies and inform them of the gist of the letter — including, one imagines, the reference to the sacrifice of the King's personal inclinations, and his condescension.

The ladies, enchanted, rushed to Her Majesty with the news.

# Chapter Eleven

On the Saturday before the Coronation, the Queen went by water to her state apartments in the Tower — this being the custom with sovereigns about to be crowned.

Her progress was accompanied by 'such a gathering of ships, galleys, brigantines', wrote a Venetian eye-witness, Il Schifanoya, in a letter to the Castellan of Mantua, 'of such splendour that he was reminded of Ascension Day at Venice, when the Signory go to espouse the sea'.

Drums beat. Cannon thundered. Bells played. Music sounded. And almost louder than these were the roars of the crowd watching from the banks.

The Queen's barge was covered with tapestries, both externally and internally, and was towed by a long galley rowed by forty men, with a band of music. Her Majesty having passed the Bridge, the guns from the Tower roared in welcome. She entered by her private stair seen, said Il Schifanoya, 'by but few persons'.

On Saturday the 14th of January 1559, the Procession of Recognition began in the morning and continued throughout the afternoon. This being over, she went in state to Westminster.

As she passed to her litter through the gates of the Tower, the Queen stood still for a moment, and, looking up to heaven, said: 'O Lord, Almighty and everlasting God, I give Thee most humble thanks that Thou hast been so merciful unto me as to spare me to behold this joyful day; and I acknowledge that Thou hast dealt mercifully and wonderfully with me, as Thou didst with Thy servant Daniel, whom Thou deliveredst out of the den, from the cruelty of the raging lions; even so

77

I was overwhelmed, and only by Thee delivered. To Thee only, therefore, be thanks, honour, and praise for ever. Amen.'

Her Majesty entered her litter.

'The Court so sparkled with jewels and gold collars', wrote Il Schifanoya, 'that they cleared the air, though it snowed a little.'

Amidst the shouts of acclamation from the crowds, the Queen passed from street to street in the city beneath houses hung with carpets, rich stuffs, and cloth of gold, windows from which banners floated.

On both sides of the streets were 'wooden barricades on which the merchants and artisans of every trade leant in long black gowns with hoods of red and black cloth, such as are usually worn by the doctors of universities in Italy, with all their ensigns, banners, and standards . . .'. 'The number of horses was in all 1000, and last of all came Her Majesty in an open litter, trimmed down to the ground with gold brocade with a raised pile, and carried by two very handsome mules covered with the same material, and surrounded by a multitude of porters in crimson velvet jerkins studded with massive gilt silver, with the arms of a red and white rose on their breasts and backs, and the letters E.R., for Elizabeth Regina. . . . The Gentlemen Pensioners of the Axe walked at her side, with hammers in their hands, and clad in crimson damask, given them by the Queen for livery.

'Behind her litter came Lord Robert Dudley, Master of the Horse, mounted on a very fine charger, and leading a white hackney, covered with cloth of gold. Then came the Lord Chamberlain and other Lords of Her Majesty's Privy Chamber, who were followed by nine pages dressed in crimson satin on very handsome chargers richly caparisoned, with their Governor and Lieutenant.'

The noise was like that of the sea.

The Queen passed through a triumphal arch 'which', said Il Schifanoya, 'was very lofty, divided into three floors. In the first were King Henry the Seventh, of the House of Lancaster, with a large red rose in front of him, and his wife the Queen Elizabeth of the House of York, with another large white rose in front of her, both in royal robes.

'On the second floor above these were seated King Henry the Eighth with a white and red rose in front of him, with the pomegranate between them, and Queen Anne Boleyn, mother of the present Queen, with a white eagle and a gold crown on the head and a gilt sceptre in its right talon, the other resting on a hillock ; and . . . in front of her, small branches of little roses, the coat of arms and device of the same Queen.

'On the third floor above, a Queen was seen in majesty, to represent the present one, who is descended from the aforesaid.

'Externally and above, as façade, there were the royal arms of England, trophies, festoons, etc.

'Further on, she came to the Conduit, which is a small tower having eight points called the Standard, and on it were painted to the life all the Kings and Queens chronologically in their royal robes down to the present day.

'At a short distance hence she found the great Cross, like a pyramid, completely gilt and somewhat renovated, with all the saints, in relief, they being neither altered nor diminished. . . .'

'The crowds lining the streets', says Miss Elizabeth Jenkins, in the best description of the scene that I have read, 'broke into exclamations at the sight of her, with prayers, welcoming cries and tender words.' [1]  Those within ear-shot heard her reply to them 'in most tender language', those who could see her saw her gesture with her hands towards them.  As she was borne along, some sixth sense told her when to halt. 'How often stayed she her chariot when she saw some simple body approach to speak to her.'  What they saw when they pressed up to the chariot was a straight and narrow figure in a cloth-of-gold dress, under a cloth-of-gold mantle with an ermine cape.  From a gold circlet, limp strands of red-gold hair fell down, framing the delicacy and strangeness of an oval, pale face, a face with faint brows spanned like Norman arches, and heavy-lidded golden eyes, smiling at them.

Sometimes the procession would halt, that the Queen might receive a little bunch of grey winter rosemary from a poor woman. 'How many nosegays', wrote George Ferrers, an officer in the procession, 'did Her Grace receive at poor women's hands ! . . . That bunch of rosemary given to Her Majesty with a supplication about [near] Fleet Street Bridge, was seen in her chariot when Her Grace came to Westminster not without the wondering of such as knew the presenter, and noticed the Queen's reception of the same.'

Or she would pause to receive a purse of crimson satin containing a thousand marks in gold from the Recorder of the City on behalf of the Lord Mayor. Thanking 'My Lord Mayor, his brethren and all', she said, 'and whereas, Master Recorder, your request is that I may continue your good lady and Queen, be ye assured, that I will be as good a lady unto you as ever Queen was to a people'.

In Cheapside she was seen to smile, and being asked the reason, replied, 'Because I have just heard one say in the crowd, "I remember old King Harry the Eighth".'

### NOTE TO CHAPTER ELEVEN
[1] Elizabeth Jenkins, *op. cit.*

QUEEN ELIZABETH IN CORONATION ROBES

# Chapter Twelve

MASS was served for the Coronation at Westminster Abbey, 'which was decorated', wrote Il Schifanoya, 'with the handsomest and most precious tapestries that were ever seen, they having been purchased by King Henry the Eighth, representing at one side the whole of Genesis, on the other side the Acts of the Apostles, from a design by Raphael d'Urbino ; and the other chambers were hung with the history of Caesar and Pompey. At one of the sides the buffet was prepared with raised steps, on which were 140 gold and silver drinking cups, besides others which were below for the service.

'The Queen was received by the Archbishop and another Bishop, they having previously perfumed her with incense, giving her the holy water and the pax, the choristers singing ; then the Earl of Rutland followed her Majesty with a plain naked sword without any point, signifying Ireland, which has never been conquered ; then came the Earl of Exeter with the second sword ; the third was borne by Viscount Montague ; the Earl of Arundel having been made Lord Steward and High Constable for that day, carried the fourth (sword) of royal justice with its scabbard loaded with pearls. The Orb was carried by the Duke of Norfolk, Lord Marshal, and in advance were knights clad in the ducal fashion, carrying the three crowns, they being three Kings-at-Arms ; they bore the three sceptres, with their three crowns of iron, silver, and of gold on their heads, and in their hands three naked iron swords, signifying the three titles of England, France, and Ireland.

'In this way they proceeded to the Church, the Queen's long train being carried by the Duchess of Norfolk, after whom followed the Lord Chamberlain, upon purple cloth spread on the ground ; and, as Her Majesty passed, the cloth was cut away by those who could get it.

'Then followed the duchesses, marchionesses, and coun- tesses, dragging their trains after them.'

Who then remembered that other glittering train at the ceremony of the 10th of September 1533 — that company 'like shadows haunting faerily the brain' — the beings that seemed planets with their long gold trains like the heat of the sun, and that would so soon be gone ?

For even then, at the christening of this child of a great fate, the shadow of a triumph brought about by Death was present. Some of those glittering beings would die by the axe, some by a strange and unexplainable accident.

But now the shadow of Death seemed far away.

'On Her Majesty's arrival', continued Il Schifanoya, 'all the bells in London ringing, she ascended her lofty tribune erected behind the high altar and the choir, and being thus exhibited to the people, it was asked if they wished her to be crowned Queen. Whereupon they all shouted "Yes" and all the organs, pipes, trumpets and drums playing, the bells also ringing, it seemed as if the world would come to an end.

'Descending from her throne, the Queen placed herself under the royal canopy ; and then the choristers began the Mass, which was sung by the Dean of the Chapel and her Chaplains.

'The Mass concluded, Her Majesty then retired behind the High Altar, and having offered up her crown, robes, and regalia in St. Edward's Chapel, she appeared again, robed in violet velvet, ermine, and a crown of state, and the great train returned to Westminster Hall.

'Meanwhile, the Lord Marshal, the Duke of Norfolk, and the Lord Steward, the Earl of Arundel, in accordance with their offices, proceeded to arrange the banquet. . . .' They were attired in 'short capes according to the Spanish fashion — the Earl of Arundel in cloth of gold, and the Duke of Norfolk in silver tissue, both their capes being lined with sables.

'They then mounted two fine chargers, each of which had housings of the same material as their rider's apparel, the Duke's horse being covered with white lions rampant. The Duke was bare-headed, and had a silver truncheon in his hand, indicating the office of Lord Marshal. Arundel bore a silver staff in his hand, indicating the office of Lord Constable, who for that day commanded the Duke and everybody. Each of them went about the victuals ; and after 3 P.M. when the Queen commenced washing her hands, the water and the napkins were given her by the noblemen who had waited on Her Majesty as server and as carver : Lord Howard of Effingham, Lord High Admiral, and the Earl of Sussex, the former carving, and the latter placing and removing the dishes, both of them serving on their knees.

'Beside Her Majesty stood the two Earls who had supported her to the Abbey by the arms : Shrewsbury and Pembroke, with the sceptre and orb in their hands ; the others likewise being in the Queen's presence with the aforesaid iron swords. They all remained covered with their Coronets on their heads, and although Her Majesty spoke occasionally to some of them, they never uncovered, except when she drank all their healths, thanking them for the trouble they had taken. . . .'

     .      .      .      .      .

According to Holinshed, 'Sir Edward Dimmocke, Knight, her Champion-in-Office, came riding into the hall in faire complet armour, mounted upon a beautiful courser richly trapped in cloth of gold and . . . cast down his gauntlet, with offer to fight with him in her quarrell that should denie her to be the righteous and lawful Queene of this Realme. The Queene, taking a cup of gold full of wine, drank to him thereof, and sent it to him for his fee, together with the cover. Now after this, at the serving of the wafers, the Lord Mayor of London went to the cupboard, and filling a cup of gold with ipocrasse, bare it to the Queene and kneeling before her, tooke it, gave it her, and she receiving it of him and drinking of it, gave the cup with the cover to the said Lord Mayor for his fee, which cup and cover weighed sixteen ounces Troy weight.

'The Banquet lasted till the ninth hour of the night' (1 hour, 18 minutes, A.M.) and 'shortly afterwards, Her Majesty rose, and by a covered way returned to the Palace of Westminster by water.'

.          .          .          .          .

So great was her exhaustion, owing to this, and a severe cold, that the Queen remained in bed for a week. Then, on the 28th of January, she was carried to the first Parliament of the reign.

She listened, in the House of Lords, to a speech by the Lord Chancellor on the change in religion, the alteration in the penal laws, and the necessity for heavy taxation in order to carry on the war with France.

Then, in the House of Commons, the Queen having taken her place on the throne, Sir Nicholas Bacon rose and spoke :

The Parliament, he said, must eschew all private interests. They must avoid frivolous arguments and quiddities, and, moreover, they were required by the Queen to 'eschew contumelious and opprobrious words, as "heretic", "schismatic", and "Papist", as causes of displeasure and malice, enemies to concord and unity, the very marks which they were now to shoot at'.

He told Parliament that the Crown had fallen to 'a princess that never for private affection would advance the quarrel of a foreign prince and impoverish her realm' ; a princess to whom 'nothing — no worldly thing under the sun was so dear to her as the love and goodwill of her subjects'.

.          .          .          .          .

The young woman whose childhood had been spent in dependence on her father's whims, and who was now Queen of England, lived surrounded by magnificence.

Her bedroom at Windsor Castle was that in which King

Henry the Sixth had been born. The Queen's bed, wrote her contemporary Hentzner, 'is covered with curious hangings of embroidery work. The tapestry represented Clovis, King of France, with an angel presenting to him the fleur-de-lis. . . .' This tapestry was a prize taken from France by Henry V.

In the room was a table of red marble with white streaks, and a cushion 'most curiously wrought by Her Majesty's own hands.'

At Hampton Court, 'in one chamber were the rich tapestries, which are hung up when the Queen gives audience to foreign ambassadors ; there were numbers of cushions ornamented with gold and silver, many counterpanes and coverlids of beds, lined with ermine . . .' and from the windows, the Queen could look down on the great flower gardens.

At Whitehall, the queen's bed was 'ingeniously composed of woods of different colours, with quilts of silk velvet, gold, silver, and embroidery'. And the room contained two little silver cabinets, 'in which', said Hentzner, 'the Queen keeps her paper, and which she uses for writing-boxes. Also a little chest, ornamented with pearls, in which she keeps her bracelets and rings.'

Here the young woman born to be Queen spent her days.

'Her Highness', her godson Sir John Harington wrote, years afterwards, 'was wont to soothe her ruffled temper with reading every morning, when she had been stirred to passion at the Council, or other matters had overthrown her gracious disposition. She did much admire Seneca's wholesome advisings when the soul's quiet is fled away, and I saw much of her translating thereof.

'Her wisest men and best Councillors were oft so troubled to know her will in matters of state, so covertly did she pass her judgment, as seemed to leave all to their discreet management ; but when the business did turn to better advantage, she did most cunningly commit the good issue to her own honour and understanding ; but when aught fell out contrary to her will and intent, the Council were in great strait to defend their own acting and not blemish the Queen's good judgment. Herein, her wise men did often lack more wisdom, and the Lord Treasurer [William Cecil, later Lord Burleigh] would oft shed a plenty of tears on any miscarriage, well knowing the difficult part was not so much to mend the matter itself, as his mistress's humour, and yet did he most share her favour and good-will, and to his opinion she would oft-time submit her own pleasure in great matters. She did keep him till late at night in discoursing alone, and then call out another at his departure, and try the depth of all around her sometime.

'Walsingham * had his turn, and each displayed his wit in private. On the morrow, everyone did come forth in her presence, and discourse at large ; and if they dissembled with her, or stood not well to her advisings before, she did not let it go unheeded, and sometimes not unpunished. Sir Christopher Hatton † was wont to say, "the Queen did fish for men's souls, and had so sweet a bait that no-one could escape from her net-work".

'In truth, I am sure her speech was such as none could refuse to take delight in, when frowardness did not stand in the way. I have seen her smile, in sooth with great liking to all around, and cause every one to open his most inward thought to her, when on a sudden she would ponder in private on what had passed, write down all their opinions, and draw them out as occasion required, and sometime disprove to their faces what had been delivered before. Hence, she knew every one's part, and by thus "fishing", as Hatton said, "she caught many poor fish who little knew what snare was set for them".'

* Sir Francis Walsingham: Secretary of State, jointly with Sir Thomas Smith, and head of the Secret Service.

† Sir Christopher Hatton : one of the Queen's favourites ; subsequently Lord Chancellor.

# Chapter Thirteen

AT one moment, during the long discussions about Calais at the Peace Conference, the French had enquired to whom, in truth, did Calais belong? Not, surely, to Elizabeth, since not she, but Queen Mary of Scotland, the Dauphine, was Queen of England, since, they said, she was the legitimate granddaughter of King Henry the Eighth's sister, the Queen of Scotland, whereas Elizabeth was Henry's daughter by his second wife, married while his first Queen was yet alive, and was therefore illegitimate.

The English Commissioners, according to themselves, did not know how to answer this — which seems strange — and without showing any sign of indignation, wrote home for instructions.

The Queen, in a fury, asked how they had dared to discuss their sovereign's right to the throne of her ancestors — how they could permit such a statement to be made in their presence, no matter by whom, whether by Frenchman or Spaniard — how they had dared to ask her pleasure in such a matter !

The grief of the Commissioners on receiving this letter was not to be borne. Sir John Mason assured the Council that rather than their sovereign mistress should have such an opinion of them, they would infinitely prefer to be out of this world. They implored him to assure her that it was all due to a misunderstanding — they had not expressed themselves properly, had, perhaps, not been precise enough. They were appalled by the letters from the Council, but that from Her Majesty had placed them beyond comfort. They were clean amazed. Indeed, two of them had been so stricken that they would carry the matter to their graves. Poor Doctor

Wotton 'had fallen half into an ague, marry, rather an ague of the mind than of the body, and was sore broken'. As for the Bishop of Ely, he had been rendered senseless. 'For the love of God', Sir John implored Cecil, 'help to salve this sore and move the Queen to heal the wounds she hath given by some comfortable letter . . . for the senses of her ministers are clean taken away by sorrow.'

Then it became known to Sir William Cecil that, under the influence of the King of France, his fifteen-year-old daughter-in-law, the Queen of Scotland, had assumed the royal arms of England. 'On the 16th of January 1559', he noted in his diary, 'the Dauphin of France and the Queen of Scotland, his wife, did, by the style and title of King and Queen of England and Ireland grant the Lord Fleming certain things.'

A brief entry, but one that seemed like a long shadow — red as if the being that cast it had been too long in the light of the sun. (When Mary was a child, the Queen of France, watching her playing, asked Nostradamus, her astrologer : 'Do you perceive any calamity threatening that fair head ?' 'Madam,' he replied, 'I see blood.')

It was now obvious to the Council that only one life lay between England and its annexation by France.[1] The question of the Queen's marriage and the birth of an heir eclipsed, therefore, all others in importance. So, on the 6th of February, the Privy Council, the Speaker, and thirty members of the House of Commons asked for an audience of the Queen, and, without naming either the man or his nationality, begged her, in the name of the nation, to take a husband.

On the morning of the 10th, they were summoned to the Palace to receive the Queen's answer.

'Concerning marriage, which ye so earnestly move me to,' she said, 'I have long been persuaded that I was sent into this world by God to think and do those things chiefly which may tend to His Glory. Hereupon have I chosen that kind of life which is most free from the troublesome cares of this world, that I might attend to the service of God alone. From which if either the tendered marriages of most potent Princes, or the danger of Death intended against me, could have removed me, I had long agone enjoyed the honour of an Husband.

'And these things have I thought upon when I was a private person. But now that the public care of governing the Kingdom is laid upon me, to draw upon me also the cares of marriage, may seem a point of inconsiderate Folly. Yes, to satisfy you, I have already joined myself in Marriage to an Husband, namely, the Kingdom of England. And behold', said she, 'which I marvel you have forgotten, the pledge of this my Wedlock and Marriage with my Kingdom.' And therewith she drew the ring from her finger and showed it, wherewith at the Coronation she had in a set form of words solemnly given herself in Marriage to her Kingdom. Here having made a pause, 'And do not', saith she, 'upbraid me with miserable lack of Children : for every one of you, and as many as are Englishmen, are Children and Kinsmen to me ; of whom, if God deprive me not (which God forbid) I cannot without injury be accounted Barren. But I commend you that ye have not appointed me an Husband, for that were most unworthy the majesty of an absolute Princess, and unbecoming your wisdom, which are subjects born.

'Nevertheless, if I enter into another course of life, I promise you I will do nothing which may be prejudicial to the Commonwealth, but will take such an Husband, as near as may be, as will have as great a care of the Commonwealth as myself. But if I continue in this kind of life I have begun, I doubt not that God will so direct mine own and your Counsels, that ye shall not need to doubt of a Successor which may be more beneficial to the Commonwealth than he which may be born of me, considering that the issue of the best Princes many times degenerateth. And to me it shall be a full satisfaction, both for the Memorial of my Name, and for my Glory also, if, when I shall let my last breath, it be engraven upon my Marble Tomb : Here lieth Elizabeth, which Reigned a Virgin, and died a Virgin.'

In spite of this statement, wooers and their ambassadors

flocked to the Palace. Distant potentates offered themselves, their sons, their brothers. And the Queen's subjects were among her suitors : nor did she seem by any means disinclined to consider them.

It seemed, indeed, likely at one moment that she might marry a subject, the Earl of Arundel — or else Sir William Pickering, once Queen Mary's Ambassador in France.

The former, a widower aged forty-seven, was, at the time of her accession, head of the English delegation to the Peace Conference, but he returned to England immediately to offer himself as the Queen's husband. Another passenger on the same ship was de Quadra, Bishop of Aquila, the Spanish Ambassador's aide. The sea was extremely rough, and seemed determined that the ship should not reach England. The Bishop suffered greatly at sea, as the Ambassador told his King : 'but I believe the tears of the Earl of Arundel floated them into port, for he (the Bishop) says the Earl cried like a child'.

A few days afterwards, however, the Ambassador was sorry to see Lord Arundel at the Palace, 'very smart and clean ; and they say he carries his thoughts very high'. And a fortnight after that, the Ambassador was obliged to tell his King 'the Earl of Arundel has been going about in high glee for some time ; and is very smart. He has given jewels worth 2000 pounds to the women who surround the Queen, and his son-in-law Lord Lumley has been very confidential with her. I was rather disturbed at this for a time, as an Italian merchant from whom he has borrowed large sums of money (lent, no doubt, on his expectations) told others that he was to marry the Queen ; but I did not lose hope, as the Earl is a flighty man of small ability.'

The anxieties of King Philip rose. Was it *possible* that she could refuse so magnificent a marriage as that which he offered her ? It was obviously impossible ! But then again, might he not be obliged to withdraw the offer, if she persisted in her heresy ? It was doubtful how much longer he would be able to induce the Pope to refrain from excommunicating her.

But the Duke of Alva, on being consulted, reassured him. It was out of the question that the Queen should refuse him. And once he became King of England, he could impose his will on her and on the whole nation. They would be forced to obey him.

But the King, still anxious, impressed upon de Feria that he must warn Elizabeth of the dangers she was running. He must try to frighten her, once more, with the name of the Queen of Scots. He must even, if she persisted in her folly, threaten her with the danger of losing him !

When, after his voluminous correspondence with his King, the Ambassador at last informed the 'young untried lass' of the honour awaiting her, she seemed neither surprised nor overwhelmed. The Ambassador had kept the matter an absolute secret — confiding it only to the Queen's ladies — and yet, he could almost have sworn that the proposal had been awaited. The Queen's speech in answer to him might have been prepared beforehand : it showed no sign whatever of the astonishment, pride, and joy that he had expected.

She spoke of her profound respect for the King, both as man and monarch ; but said that she must be given time to consider the matter, and to consult Parliament. She asked the Ambassador to assure the King (and such was her tone that he felt certain she would have liked to express herself even more warmly) that if she should marry, he would be preferred before all.

But as time went on, there occurred, in the Queen's conversations with the Ambassador on this subject, phrases that awoke a strange echo in his mind. It was extraordinary ! They might almost have been phrases taken verbatim from His Majesty's own letters. She feared, she said, that the King would spend but little time with her. He would marry her but to leave her. He would come and he would go.

It was evident to the harassed Ambassador that 'the devil had taken possession of her'. She would not listen to entreaties. Menaces could not frighten her. The Pope would not allow her to marry her brother-in-law, she said. (What of that long-past divorce between the King her father and Queen Catherine ?) And as for the fear of France, 'her realm was not too poor, nor her people too faint-hearted to defend their liberties at home and to protect their rights abroad. She would not marry, and she would agree to no peace without the return of Calais — that was her answer.' [2]

On the 19th of March, after another confidential talk with Her Majesty, the Ambassador told his King, 'After we had talked a short time, she said she could not have married Your Majesty because she was a heretic'. (Those letters again !) 'I said I was astonished to hear her use such words. I asked her why her language was now so different from what it had been ! But she would give me no explanation ; the heretics, with their friend the devil, are working full speed ; they must have told her that Your Majesty's object in proposing for her was only to save religion.

'She spoke carelessly, indifferently, altogether unlike herself, and she said positively she meant to do as her father had done.

'I told her I could not believe she was a heretic — I could not think she would sanction the new laws — if she changed her religion, she would ruin herself. Your Majesty, I said, would not separate yourself from the Church for all the thrones in the world.

'"So much the less", she replied, "should Your Majesty do it for a woman."

'I did not wish to be too harsh with her, so I said men sometimes did for a woman what they would do for nothing else.'

Then, just as Her Majesty had called the English Bishops 'a set of lazy scamps', in came 'Knolles to tell her that supper was ready — a story made for the occasion, I fancy. They dislike nothing so much as her conversations with me. I took my leave for that time, saying merely that she was no longer the Queen Elizabeth whom I had known hitherto, that I was ill-satisfied with her words to me, and that if she went on thus she was a lost woman.'

In a later conversation, the Ambassador told her he knew what her resources were ; 'I knew also', he wrote to his King, 'what Your Majesty's resources were, and what those of France were, and her only chance was to remain on good terms with Your Highness.

'She said she did not mean to quarrel with France ; she intended only to maintain herself in her own realm as her father had done.

'I told her she could not do it. She talked of imitating her father ; and yet she kept about her a parcel of Lutheran and Zwinglian rogues that King Henry would have sent to the stake. May God and Your Majesty provide a remedy for those misdoings.'

But the hour was late ; and the King of Spain knew now that he must sacrifice himself elsewhere.

One of the conditions of peace proposed at the Conference in the previous autumn, was a marriage between Don Carlos and Elizabeth, daughter of the French King and Catherine de' Medici. Now the King of Spain proposed that he, instead, should be her husband.

On the 2nd of April, the suggestion was put forward openly by Montmorency (who had been in correspondence with the Duke of Alva on the subject). It was accepted immediately, and the marriage was arranged so quickly that the treaty was completed and signed next day.

The Queen of England, when she was told the news of the marriage, 'affected one or two little sighs, and then observed, with a smile, that her name was a fortunate one. I told her', the Ambassador wrote, 'I was very sorry but the fault was more with her than with Your Majesty ; she knew how unwilling I had been to accept her refusal.

'She admitted the truth of my words ; but she said Your Majesty could not have been so very much in love with her, or you would have waited three or four months. She did not seem to like it, though two or three of the Council, she told me, were delighted.'

He added : 'Both she and they are alarmed at your alliance

with France, and fear that it bodes no good for them. That pestilential scoundrel Cecil tried to persuade me that they would have liked nothing better than to go on with the war. I bade them go say that to someone less well acquainted with the state of the country than I was.'

But 'the country is lost to us now — body and soul', for 'it has fallen into the hands of a woman who is the daughter of the Devil'.

Or the granddaughter, perhaps. For had it not been said that Anne Boleyn was the daughter, not of Lord Wiltshire, but of the Prince of the Powers of the Air ?


NOTES TO CHAPTER THIRTEEN

1 Froude, *op. cit.*
2 de Feria to King Philip.  29 February, 1559.

# Chapter Fourteen

WHETHER the Queen was the granddaughter of Lord Wiltshire or of the Prince of the Powers of the Air, the suitors of
their Ambassadors thronged the Court, and were

> . . . brighter than stars in the sky,
> (The stars thick as roses in hot July) —
> As bright as the raindrops and roses in June,
> And many and merry as notes in a tune.

But still the Queen could not make up her mind which to
choose.

In August, Paolo Tiepolo and his Colleague Extraordinary,
Marc Antonius da Mula, Venetian Ambassador to King Philip,
informed the Doge and Senate that 'the Ambassador of the
King of Denmark in England, to demonstrate his King's love
of Queen Elizabeth, wore upon his gown a crimson velvet
heart pierced by an arrow'.

At one moment it seemed as if she favoured the Archduke Charles. . . . Lady Mary Sidney, sister to Lord Robert
Dudley, had come with a secret message to the new Spanish
Ambassador, Bishop de Quadra. No word of what she was
about to say, she told him, must be even whispered. There
were spies everywhere. But the Queen had been in appalling
danger. A plot had been discovered to poison the Queen
and stab Lord Robert Dudley at a supper party given by his
eldest brother, Lord Warwick. (There had been strange dark
rumours about Lord Robert. It was said he was casting a
shadow over the name of the Queen, and there were men who
thirsted for his blood. And were there not those who wished
her dead also ?) The Queen knew now, Lady Mary told the

95

Ambassador, that only in marriage with the Archduke could she find safety.

But when questioned, the Queen said she could not marry a man she had never seen. Nor could she invite a man to come to London to marry her. Also might he not, would he not, almost certainly hear rumours against her reputation ? And, if so, might he not refuse to marry her ?

The Bishop reassured her. The Archduke was a gentleman. He reminded her also (we do not know in what spirit) that he — the Bishop — *knew everything that happened at Court.* Nothing was hidden from him, and that if there had been any truth in the whispered scandal, he would have known it.

But before the Archduke's visit could be arranged, the Queen's fancy — or so it seemed — veered again. Now she was considering the suit of Eric, the eldest son of the King of Sweden, who sent his younger son, the Duke of Finland, to lay the proposal before the Queen.

'There are ten or twelve Ambassadors of us here', de Quadra told de Feria (the 29th October 1559), 'all competing for Her Majesty's hand, and they say the Duke of Holstein is coming next, as a suitor for the King of Denmark. The Duke of Finland, who is here for his brother the King of Sweden, threatens to kill the Emperor's man ; and the Queen fears they may cut each other's throats in her presence.'

The Duke of Finland was uncouth, and made a bad impression on Sir William Knollys, who was sent to meet him when he landed. When Sir William was shown into his presence, the Duke, remaining seated, held out his hand to be kissed by Sir William. But Sir William, reporting the matter to Cecil, said : 'The writer has been brought up otherwise than to kiss the hand of any subject other than of the parentage of his own Prince. Therefore, having with reverence kissed his own hand, the writer joined his hand with that of the Duke after the manner of his own native country.'

But for all the Duke's uncouthness, he scattered silver like a shower of falling stars in the London streets, and told the crowds that whereas he scattered silver, his brother would scatter gold.

The King of Sweden died, and the Queen's suitor succeeded him. And nothing could deter him from his wooing — he received refusal after refusal, but would not accept them. Neither seas, enemies, nor any imaginable dangers should keep him from her. He would fly to her side.

Indeed, in August 1560, he started to do so, and though the winds were dead against him, and he was forced to return, he started again. This time his fleet was scattered by the winds. 'Fortune', he declared, 'had been harder than steel and crueller than Mars — but, as he had dared storms and raging seas to come to her side, so would he brave armies of foes to come to her.'

The Queen had retained Roger Ascham, her old tutor, as Latin secretary, and she would sometimes ask his advice about important matters. He told his friend Sturmius, who was corresponding with him, advocating the Queen's marriage with the Swedish King, 'I have nothing certain to write to you, nor does anyone truly know what to judge. I told you rightly in one of my former letters, that in the whole ordinance of her life, she resembled not Phaedra but Hippolyta, for by nature, and not by the nature of others, she is thus averse, and abstinent from marriage.'

Was it the ghost of Anne Boleyn, with her gay light laughing movements, bringing down doom upon herself and so many others — and the ghost of Katherine Howard, the later phantom of Anne's imagined sins, rising from their graves in the warmth of the sun and the fire of the full moon, to bring the chill of their deaths and the real or imagined fever of lust that not even death could assuage — was it these ever-young ghosts that stood between Elizabeth and happiness?

As the months went by, the wooers were anything but 'merry as notes in a tune'. Discord was everywhere. 'Here is great resort of wooers and controversy among lovers', wrote the harassed Sir William Cecil. 'Would to God the Queen had one, and the rest were honourably satisfied.'

But there seemed little chance of that. For a dark and magnificent tall shadow had been cast upon the realm and the name of the Queen — a shadow dark and glittering as moonlit water, and water-deep — a mysterious being, a

High, hollow, fateful rider,

who seemed always as if attired in dark armour (but under that armour was a human heart, and this was often bruised by a hard and undeserved treatment) : Lord Robert Dudley, the only love of his Queen's long life — Lord Robert Dudley, the son and grandson of beheaded traitors, the husband of a wife, perhaps deserted, certainly hidden from the world.* Lord Robert Dudley, the suspected poisoner, the companion of witches. For was it not believed that he employed Dr. Dee and Dr. Allen as 'conjurors' of the dead, and to cast horoscopes and, no doubt, spells ? And witchcraft was one of the deadliest perils to the realm.†

* See Chapter Twenty.            † See Appendix B.

# Chapter Fifteen

LORD ROBERT DUDLEY (later Earl of Leycester) had several earthly siblings, but he had also, in the fires of Hell, according to many people, one far nearer to him in spirit :

> . . . that first archetype
> Of pride, and paragon of all creation,
> Who, of the light impatient, fell unripe.

('of the light impatient' : intolerant, unable to endure the light.)

But Leycester did not fall unripe. He lived until his usefulness was finished, and then died, a few weeks after the victory over the Armada.

There is practically no evil, physical or spiritual, that has not been ascribed to him : (for was he not, in the eyes of the world, most highly favoured by fortune, and must he not therefore, if possible, be pulled down into the mud, made equal with those who envied him ?) But not one crime or other evil has ever been *proved* against him, or could, I think, be believed in by any serious reader.

His sin in the eyes of the world was that he had that fallen angel's glittering beauty, look of fiery pride, and dark magnificence ; that he was tall, of great physical strength, was not one to 'sit among the cinders', and that he was loved by a Queen.

The accusations against him are so multitudinous, the sins ascribed to him of such a magnitude as to be most impressive.

'What a monster of a man was Leycester, who first brought the art of poysoning into England.' [1]

'If any of his enemies', wrote Edmund Bohun, in 1693,[2]

'had at any time a little too freely expressed their resentment against his Dishonesty, Wickedness, Injuries, Power, or Perfidy . . . he seldom failed to have them treacherously murdered. Many fell in his time (saith a great man of that age) ³ who saw not the hand that pulled them down ; and as many died that knew not their own disease. He would not trust his Familiars above one year, but either transported them to Foreign Services, or wafted them to another World. And then it is said that some noble families he utterly extinguished.' Mr. Frederick Chamberlin, quoting this, says that 'no man of that age . . . said anything of the sort', as far as he could learn.

It was said that he murdered his first wife. The jury found that she died through an accident. He was supposed to have 'procured by an artificial catarrh that stopped his breath' the death of Lord Sheffield, in order that he might marry his widow, Douglas.

The only thing against that story is that Lord Sheffield died two years after Leycester was supposed to have killed him, and that the teller of the tale was an old lady over a hundred years of age, who had lost her memory.

He is said to have married the widow secretly, and then deserted her. There is no proof of the marriage, and her suit to have it acknowledged after Leycester's death was dismissed by the Courts. She did, however, bear him a son, and to that story we shall come later.

He was supposed to have murdered Lord Essex (father of Queen Elizabeth's young favourite) and yet, according to an eye-witness of Essex's death (the Master of the Rolls, writing from near Dublin, in September 1576, to his 'Dear Good Lord Burleigh'), 'I was much in the later ende of his sicknes. . . . He doubted that he had bene poysoned . . . and of that suspicion acquitted this land.' And Sir Henry Sidney told Walsingham, 'When he was opened, it could not appeare that one Intrall within his Body, at any Tyme, had bene enfected with any Poyson'.

But that, no doubt, was because (according to *Leycester's*

*Commonwealth*) he had in his employ, besides Dr. Dee and Dr. Lopez, and Julio the Italian, Doctors Bayly and Culpeper, 'once Papists, now Galenists, poysoners so subtle that they can make a man die of any sickness as long after as they like'.

Leycester married Lady Essex, not immediately, but two years all but a day after her husband's death, and, according to *The Dictionary of National Biography*, 'there is no proof that the Countess intrigued with Leycester in her husband's lifetime'.

Amongst other accusations, he was supposed to have poisoned Cardinal Châtillon, Sir Nicholas Throckmorton, and the Countess of Lennox, and attempted the murder of the French Envoy, Simier. But indeed his assassinations were so numerous that it would be tedious to mention them all.

As for his morals ! According to Edmund Bohun [3] 'he gave himself up entirely to the exercise of a most wicked and universal Luxury . . . and brought into England from Foreign Countries many new and unheard of Pleasures. . . . He would drink dissolved Pearls and Amber to excite his Lust.'

And 'as his lust and lyking shal varie' (said the anonymous author of *Leycester's Commonwealth*) 'wherein by the judgment of all men he surpasseth, not onlie Sardanapalus and Nero, but even Heliogabalus himself ; so his Lordship also chaungeth wives and minions, by killing the one, denying the other, using the third for a time, and then fawning upon the fourth'.

He was accused, also, of incest — with 'the keeping of the mother wyth two or three of her daughters at once or successively . . .' this being 'no more with him, then the eating of a hen and her chicken together'.

One of the shocked protagonists of *Leycester's Commonwealth*, on hearing that at one time Leycester was living simultaneously with Lady Sheffield and Lady Essex — (he did nothing of the kind) — declared, 'I never heard or red the like to this . . . yet have I red especialie of the Emperor Heliogabalus who passed all other, and was called Varius, of the varitie of filth that he used in this kind of carnalitye, or carnall beastliness. Whose death was, that being . . . slaine by his own souldiers [he] was drawen through the Citie upon the Ground like a dogge, & caste into the common privie, with this Epitaphe. . . . "Here is thrown in a Whelp of unrewlie and raging luste" : which epitaphe, may also one day chance to serve my L of Leycester.'

It is strange that, as far as the present writer knows, the only women in Leycester's life, apart from the Queen (with whom his relationship was platonic), were his first and second wives, and Douglas Sheffield, to whom he does not seem to have behaved dishonourably.*

According to his detractors, his frauds, his sales of benefits, his treacheries, were as numerous and shone as brightly as the stars. In addition, he was a fool. And yet the Queen, who was not supposed to be one, placed him in supreme command of the army at the time of the Armada !

The *Commonwealth* is supposed to have consisted of a conversation between three persons, the anonymous author, (under the pseudonym of 'Scholar'), 'a verye worshypfull and grave Gentleman', and 'an Auncient man that professed the law'. It is pleasant to know that the Gentleman, as befitted his status, ended the conversation with 'Craving pardon of my Lord of Leycester for my boldness, yf I have bene to plaine wyth him. And so I pray you let us go to supper.'

But although this delightful person was, according to himself, a gentleman, Lord Leycester, according to the same authority, was not.

To this, his nephew, Sir Philip Sidney, in his *Defence of Leycester*, answered, 'Now to the Dudleys . . . When he [the author of the *Commonwealth*] saith they are no gentlemen, affirming that the Duke of Northumberland was not born so . . . I am a Dudley in blood, that Duke's daughter's son, and do . . . say, that my chiefest honour is to be a Dudley. . . .

'In one place of his book he greatly extolleth the great nobility of the house of Talbot. . . . And yet this Duke's [Leycester's father's] own grandmother, whose blood he makes so base, was a Talbot, and sole heir to the Viscount of Lisle . . .

* See Appendix G.

'The house of Grey is well known ; to no house in England inferior in great continuance of honour, and for number of great houses sprung from it, to be matched by none ; but by the noble house of Nevill, his mother was a right Grey, and a sole inheritrix of that Grey of the house of Warwick which ever strove with the great house of Arundel, which should be the first Earl of England ; he was likewise so descended . . . being the only heir to the oldest daughter, and one of the heirs of that famous Beauchamp, Earl of Warwick, that was Regent of France . . . and of the house of Berkeley, which is affirmed to be descended lineally from a King of Denmark . . . this Duke was the only heir general. . . . So that I think it would seem as great news as if they came from the Indies, that he, who by right of blood, and so accepted, was the ancientest Viscount in England, heir in blood and arms to the first or second Earl of England, in blood of inheritance a Grey, a Talbot, a Beauchamp, a Berkeley, a Lisle, should be doubted to be a gentleman. . . .'

He had inherited danger and tragedy.

His grandfather had been beheaded in 1510, 'as a sacrifice to the importunate clamours of the people'. His father, the Duke of Northumberland, was restored in blood by King Henry VIII ; but after the rebellion, he, too, was condemned to die by the axe.

All five of his sons, including the twenty-year-old Robert, were condemned (the latter was reprieved). These youths, waiting for death, occupied themselves with carving their devices in their cells — Warwick's name appearing with two bears and ragged staves surrounded by acorns, roses, honeysuckles, and gilliflowers, representing the initials of his four brothers — with Robert Dudley's device, a sprig of oak.

On the 22nd of August (1553) the father was beheaded on Tower Hill — his death witnessed by his five sons from the windows of their cells.

On the 13th of November, Guildford, the husband of the little usurper Queen Jane, was condemned to be beheaded, and his sixteen-year-old wife to be burnt to death or beheaded at the Queen's pleasure. She went to her release from her most unhappy life without flinching.

Five days before her death, she, who with her husband and their brothers had been brought into the rebellion through the ambition of their fathers, wrote to hers : 'Father, although it hath pleased God to hasten my death by you, by whom my life should rather have been lengthened, yet can I patiently take it, that I yield God more hearty thanks for shortening my woeful days, than if all the world had been given into my possession, with life lengthened at my own will. . . . My dear father, if I may, without offence, rejoice in my own mishap, herein I may account myself blessed, that washing my hands with the innocence of the fact, my guiltless blood may cry before the Lord "Mercy to the innocent". . . . The Lord . . . so continue to keep you, that at last we may meet in heaven with the Father, Son, and Holy Ghost. Amen. I am, your obedient Daughter till Death, Jane Dudley.'

She saw, from her window, the body and the head of her young husband carried away. Then, an hour afterwards, went to her own death. Four hours after that death, her body and her head, lying on the straw in such a sea of blood that de Noailles, the French Ambassador, wondered so much could come from so little a body, could still be seen by her four brothers-in-law from their cells.

Next would come the turn of Robert Dudley. On the 22nd of January 1554, brought up before the Lord Mayor of London and the Earl of Sussex, he did not deny the treason (that of loyalty to his father, brother, and sister-in-law) and was condemned to death. But for some reason that death was delayed.

.        .        .        .        .

After the execution of Guildford, only six of the Duke's children were left — the four brothers, and their sisters,

Mary (Lady Mary Sidney), and Catherine (the Countess of Huntingdon).

Their unhappy mother, like some forlorn little bodiless air, haunted the Court. . . . If only someone would listen to her, she felt sure that her remaining sons would be spared — would be set free. But her voice could not make itself heard in the noise of the preparations for Queen Mary's marriage.

Then came the dark foreign faces ; and some of these were kind. Besides, the ladies had not overmuch to do. They did not care to venture often into the city, for their lords were hated. So they listened, and received, from time to time, small presents of little value from this old woman, reduced now to extreme poverty, whose husband, and one of whose sons, had been executed, and whose other sons were in the Tower.

On the very day of her death, the 22nd of January 1555, the kindness of the Spanish lords and ladies to her bore fruit. 'We, the aforesaid King and Queen, moved to pity of our own special grace and certain knowledge . . . have pardoned, remitted and released . . . in as much as is in us . . . Robert Dudley.'

Three days after he and his brothers were set free, the eldest, Warwick, worn out by his long imprisonment and by the horror of those deaths he had witnessed, died.

About two years after that pardon, the property of Robert Dudley was restored to him, by the King's and Queen's goodness.

Then, on the 17th of March 1557, 'cam rydyng from King Phelype from beyond the sea unto the Court at Grenwyche, to our Quen, with letters in post, my lord Robert Dudley . . . [saying] that the Kyng would com to Cales the xvii day of March' — on his way to Greenwich, to complete her ruin.

The Duchess of Northumberland, on her death-bed, did not forget her benefactors. She had not much to bequeath them ; but to one among 'those that did my sonnes good' — 'a Spanish lord that is beyond the seas', the Lord Dondagoe Damondesay, she left her 'book clock that hath the sun and the moone on it', to the Duchess of Alva her green parrot, 'having nothing worthy of her else', with a prayer to 'continue a good ladye to my children, as she has begun'. To Robert's wife Amye, whom he had married when he was nineteen, she left 'a gown of wrought velvet'.


### NOTES TO CHAPTER FIFTEEN

[1] Howell's Letters.
[2] *Character of Queen Elizabeth.*
Waldman, *Elizabeth and Leycester.*

# Chapter Sixteen

IN July 1559, the new Spanish Ambassador, Alvarez de Quadra, Bishop of Aquila, told his King, 'Thomas Randolph has come in haste from France to say that the Dauphin, after having publicly assumed the royal arms of Scotland, is about to be proclaimed King of Scotland, England, and Ireland.'

The Queen of England, when she heard of it, said she would take such a husband as would make the King of France's head ache ; and that he little knew what a buffet she would give him !

It was with some difficulty that the Earl of Arran, next in succession to the Scottish throne, who was to be the means of administering the buffet, was smuggled into England from France, where he had been Captain of the Scottish Guard ; but it was done, and the Queen of Scots burst into tears of rage when she heard of it — knowing well what that visit to England might portend.

The omniscient Bishop de Quadra told his King : 'We shall soon hear more. . . . She would not have received him here with the certainty of giving mortal offence to France, if it were not a settled thing that the Earl was to be more than a guest. I have my spies about the Queen's person ; and I know every word that she says.' It is not impossible that the Queen was aware of this, and made full use of it.

The new suitor was received by the Queen, in what was supposed to be secrecy, in the gardens of Hampton Court. 'Divers conceits' had not, as yet, troubled his mind ; he had not, as yet, shown open signs of the madness that was soon to engulf him. But there must have been, even then, a certain strangeness about him. In any case, the Queen decided not to take him as a husband ; and at the beginning of September 1559, he made his way, under an assumed name, to Scotland, where it was hoped he would cause the maximum of trouble.

. . . . .

Though the peace treaty between France and England had been signed, an unquenchable fire of hatred separated the two countries, since, by adding the title of Queen of England to that of Queen of Scotland and Dauphine of France, Mary Stuart had not only insulted the national pride of England, but had proclaimed her cousin Elizabeth a bastard.

Her hand, as she signed documents with these titles, was guided by that of her father-in-law, King Henri the Second. . . . But greater influences than his were brought to bear upon her.

Throughout her childhood, and that part of her early youth that was spent in France, their lengthening shadows ever falling before her, as if cast by her, the sinister dark figures of her uncles the Duc de Guise and the Cardinal of Lorraine, moved beside her. All the actions and thoughts of this seeming somnambulist, this beautiful, doomed being, were guided by them.

If the events that followed are to be understood in the slightest degree, the scene must now be shifted to Scotland — a land of high romance, chivalry, bravery, and of such fiery imagination as that which caused the heart of Bruce to be sent to fight in the battle against the Saracens, and to visit the Holy Land, — that sent, also, the heart of the murdered James the First, that King of a giant's strength and savagery, on a pilgrimage to the Holy Land, — that heart being brought back to its home in Scotland, from Rhodes, by a Knight of St. John.

Al was this land fulfild of fayerye.

It was in this strange and beautiful country of legends (such as that of an incestuous Princess of great beauty, the sister of James the Third, seduced by a lord out of revenge against the King, who had corrupted his wife) — in this land soaked by the blood spilt in the feuds between the great nobles, that Mary was born. And Shadow was her companion from the moment of her birth. So had Tragedy been her young father's twin-brother, inseparable from him, his bed-fellow.

John Knox, the Reformer, a great writer (capable of a grandeur of utterance, and, at other times, of a mean squalor) who was afterwards to be the scourge of that monarch's daughter, wrote thus of the time preceding Mary's birth and the death of her father, James the Fifth.

'So far had that blinded and most vicious man, the Prince (most vicious, we shall call him, for he neither spared man's wife, nor maiden, no more after his marriage than he did before) — so far . . . had he given himself to obey the tyranny of those bloody beasts [the Bishops] that he had made a solemn vow, That none should be spared that was suspect of heresy, yea, although it were his own son. . . . And yet did not God cease to give to that blinded Prince documents [signs] that some sudden plague was to fall upon him, in case he did not repent his wicked life ; and that his own mouth did confess. For after that Sir James Hamilton [for long a favourite of the King, then accused of treason in 1546] justly or unjustly, we dispute not, was beheaded . . . this vision came unto him, as to his familiars himself did declare : The said Sir James appeared unto him having in his hands a drawn sword, by the which from the King he struck both his arms, saying to him these words, "Take that while [until] thou receive a final payment for all thy impiety". This vision, with sorrowful countenance, he showed on the morrow, and shortly afterwards died his two sons, both within the space of twenty-four hours ; yea, some say, within the space of six hours. . . .'

(James the Fifth's only legitimate sons, James and Arthur, died in 1541, Arthur eight days after his birth, James, who was about a year old, four weeks after his brother.)

'How terrible a vision that said Prince saw lying in Lin-lithgow that night that Thomas Scott, Justice-Clerk, died in Edinburgh — [he had proceeded against men charged with heresy. . . .] For, afraid that midnight or after, he cried for torches, and roused all that lay beside him in the Palace, and told them that Thomas Scott was dead ; for he had been at him with a company of devils, and had said to him these words "O woe to the day that ever I knew thee or thy service, for, serving of thee against God, against his servants, and against justice, I am adjudged to everlasting torment".

'How terrible the voices the said Thomas Scott pronounced before his death, men of all estates heard ; and some that yet live can witness : his voice was ever "Justo Dei judicio condemnatus sum" : that is, "I am condemned by God's just judgment". None of these forewarnings could either change or mollify the heart of the indurate, lecherous, and avaricious tyrant ; but still does he proceed from impiety to impiety.'

But that heart, that pride, were to be overthrown.

It was decided to invade England. At Solway Moss, 'fires were kindled and almost slaked on every side ; Oliver, the great minion [Oliver Sinclair], thought time to show his glory, and so, incontinent, was displayed the King's banner ; Oliver upon spears was lifted up upon men's shoulders, and there with sound of trumpet, was he proclaimed general lieutenant, and all men commanded to obey him as the King's own person under all highest pains. . . .

'Great was the noise and confusion. . . . The day was near spent, and that was the cause of the greatest fear. . . . The soldiers cast from them their pikes, culverins, and other weapons fencible, the horsemen left their spears, and so, without judgment, all men fled.

'The sea was filling, and the water made great stop ; but the fear was such that happy was he that might get a taker. . . . Such as passed the water, not well acquainted with the ground, fell into the Solway Moss. . . . Stout Oliver was without stroke taken, fleeing full manfully. . . .

'The certain knowledge . . . coming to the King's ears . . . he was stricken with a sudden fear and astonishment, so that scarcely could he speak. . . . The night constrained him to remain where he was, and so yead [went] to bed ; but rose without rest or quiet sleep. His continual complaint was "Oh, fled Oliver ! Is Oliver tane ? Oh, fled Oliver !" And these words in his melancholy, and as it were carried away in a trance, repeated he from time to time, to the very hour of his death. Upon the morn . . . returned he to Edinburgh, and so did the Cardinal [James Beaton, Archbishop of St. Andrews] from Haddington. But the one being ashamed of the other, the bruit of their communication came not to public audience. The King made inventory of his poise [treasure], of all his jewels. . . . And thereafter, as ashamed to look any man in the face, secretly departed to Fife. . . .'

And to his servants he said '"Or [ere] Yule day ye shall be masterless, and the realm without a King . . . ". And albeit there appeared unto him no signs of death, yet he constantly affirmed, "before such a day, I shall be dead".

'In the meantime was the Queen upon the point of her delivery in Linlithgow, who was delivered the eighth day of December, in the year of God 1542, of Marie, that then was born, and now does ring [reign] for a plague to this realm.'

Knox declares that when the King was told of the birth of his daughter, he cried '"Adieu, fare well, it came with a lass, it will pass with a lass",* and turned his back to his lords and his face to the wall'.

But, though 'after that he spake not many more words that were sensible . . . ever he harped upon his old song "Fye, fled Oliver : Is Oliver tane ? All is lost."'

Then the Cardinal came to him and said '"Take order, Sir, with your realm : who shall rule during the minority of your daughter ? Ye have known my service : what will ye have done ? Shall there not be four Regents chosen ? And shall not I be principal of them ?" Whatsoever the King answered, documents were taken that so should be as my Lord Cardinal thought expedient. As many affirm, a dead man's hand was made to subscribe a blank, that they might write above it what pleased them best.'

* The lass with whom it came was Marjorie Bruce.

So, on the 14th of December 1542, six days after the birth of his daughter, died James the Fifth.

It was from the darkness of such a night that the dream-bright Mary was born.

.     .     .     .     .

According to Knox, when the Cardinal went straight from the King's death-bed to the Queen, she said to him, 'Welcome, my Lord. Is not the King dead?'

From which Knox deduced that the Cardinal was the Queen's lover, and that between them they had poisoned the King.

.     .     .     .     .

The hatred between Scotland and England persisted.

On the 3rd of May 1544, a great fleet of ships was seen approaching towards the north. . . . 'Upon the Saturday, before noon. Question was: What should they mean? Some said, "It is no doubt but that they are Englishmen, and we fear that they shall land."'

They did.

The Cardinal was present at the first fight, dressed in a 'casacque de vellour jaulne fort découppé pleine de taffetas blanc avec listes d'or que floquent par les descoupeures'; but he was said to be 'the first man that fled . . . a valiant champion. . . .'[1]

He was not to remain long in his power. After the burning of George Wishart, the Protestant, he was told that he was in danger; but 'in Babylon, that is in his new block-house [the Castle of St. Andrews] he remained without all fear of death [saying], "Is not my Lord Governor [a member of the house of Hamilton, who, according to Knox, had the wicked ever blowing in his ears] mine? . . . Have I not the Queen at my own devotion? . . . Is not France my friend, and I friend to France? What danger should I fear?"'

But that danger was real. At five in the morning, on the 29th of May 1546, murderers, breaking open the outer doors of that Babylon, and the doors of his bedchamber, put him to death with many wounds, and, after mutilating him, hung him by a pair of sheets over the wall by the arm and foot, 'and bade the people see there their God'. He died unshriven of his sins, having spent the night before with his mistress.

His murderers, pious men, were much commended by Knox, — who wrote, also, 'The death of this foresaid tyrant was dolorous to the priests, most dolorous to the Queen Dowager ; for in him perished faithfulness to France, and the comfort to all gentlewomen, and especially to wanton widows'. One wanton widow, according to Knox, being the Queen Dowager.

Two years after this time, the baby Queen of Scotland, who was affianced to the Dauphin of France, sailed for her future husband's country, arriving there on the 13th of August 1548. She was then aged five and a half years ; but Knox wrote : 'And so the Cardinal of Lorraine [her uncle] got her in his keeping, a morsel, [I] assure you, meet for his own mouth'.

.        .        .        .        .

Eleven years after the little Queen's departure from Scotland, John Knox returned to his native country in 1559, after a chequered career.

This extraordinary mixture of greatness, pettiness, appalling spiritual arrogance, spiritual bravery, and spiritual courage (this, however, deserted him entirely when 'mischievous Mary' — as he called Queen Mary Tudor — came to the throne of England), honesty and self-deception (black could be transformed to white at a moment's notice when this was convenient) regarded himself, and was regarded by others, as a Man of God. He was certainly not one who would say, with Oliver Cromwell, 'I beseech ye, brethren, in the bowels of Christ, think it possible ye may be mistaken'.

John Knox could never be mistaken. And this gave him the right, indeed the duty, to speak and write to whom he chose, as he chose.

In his portraits we see a sturdy, rather short person with bear-brown hair framing a non-committal face that shows nothing of the fires, the ardours, the coldness, the hatred, within his soul. Physically he resembled, to some degree, a brown bear. One would imagine the hug would hold.

Any hug born of affection in him enclosed very young girls — both his wives (he married the second when he was fifty-nine years of age) were barely sixteen at the time of their marriage. His reproofs to those succumbing to the lusts of the flesh were particularly severe.

His career knew as many contrasts as his character. Formerly a priest of the Church of Rome, he became an apostate, and, after rebelling against Mary of Guise, Queen Regent of Scotland, he was sentenced to a year and a half as a slave in a French galley. On his release, he took refuge in England, where he remained until the accession of 'mischievous Mary', when, deeming it his duty not to accept martyrdom (although he reproved in no measured terms others who had felt the same dictates of conscience), he repaired, in some haste, to Geneva and Zurich, for conversations with Calvin and others, on certain especially delicate spiritual problems.

From these far cities, the Reformer lectured his fellow Protestants who, left in England, were faced with the probability of being burned alive, on the subject of their behaviour and outlook.

They must not, he insisted, 'hate with any carnal hatred these blind, cruel and malicious tyrants'. Any hatred they felt must be purely spiritual. No doubt, in his own mind, his references to the 'loathsome legs' of Mary of Guise, dying of dropsy, and his delighted record of the murder and subsequent treatment of the body of Cardinal Beaton ('these things we write merrily'), were inspired purely by spiritual, not carnal, hatred. But hatred, actually, had replaced love in his heart, and was regarded by him as a virtue.

From the safety of Dieppe, the Reformer sent also a tract to the 'Professors of God's truth in England'. After indulging in a good many comparisons of Queen Mary Tudor with certain undesirable persons described in the Old Testament, he prayed that 'God, for his great mercy's sake, stir up some Phineas, Elias, or Jehu, that the blood of abominable idolaters · may pacify God's wrath, that it consume not the whole multitude'.

'In casting such a pamphlet into England at the time he did', wrote his biographer Hume Brown, 'he indulged his indignation, in itself so natural under the circumstances, at no personal risk, while he seriously compromised those who had the strongest claims on his most generous consideration.'

This was the man who, great in his way, small in his way, now returned to his native country and proceeded to exhort the godly and to defy the Queen Regent. It must be said that he found some of his natural enemies, the Catholic Prelates, behaving in a manner calculated to inspire him to eloquence.

The Prelates had not, of recent years, been popular in Scotland. It was only a matter of time before they would be seen to 'cast no shadows' and to have cloven hooves. But at the moment they contented themselves, according to their detractors, with producing 'a flock of bastard birds', amongst the most active in this respect being (according to a letter from Randolph, the English Ambassador, to Cecil), the Bishop of Dunblane. Of him 'it were shameful to speak ; he spareth not his own daughter'.

Of this conduct, Knox, who seems to have had a peculiar gift for inducing acute hysteria in his hearers, made full use in his oratory, for which he can scarcely be blamed ; and the resultant excitement spread like wildfire.

NOTE TO CHAPTER SIXTEEN

1 Hume Brown, *John Knox : a Biography*.

# Chapter Seventeen

In the French Court, the Queen of Scotland was exposed to a more unwholesome atmosphere, more dangerous morally, than any to be found in her native country. In this she spent her childhood and early youth.

Her father-in-law, King Henri the Second, had been married at the age of fourteen to a child-bride, Catherine de' Medici, the daughter of a marriage in which there was a second bridegroom, 'Mounseer Dry-Bone, the Frenchman', * who took to himself the bride fifteen days after the birth of her child, and his rival bridegroom six days after that, and who was to be the shadow of all the children born to the child of that marriage — following them in the light of the sun, changing their aspect to his own.

For years, that shadow would allow her no children ; yet at length, by some supreme effort of will, they were born. But they were his for all their short life-time.

Catherine's husband — as hard of heart as he was weak of will — was so backward mentally that he seemed to be of the vegetable nature. 'Monsieur d'Orléans, a large round face [but not like the large round face of the sun], who does nothing but give blows, and whom no man can master.' So said a contemporary.

In after years, the face which had been round lengthened ; from that malignant face, which showed both the hardness of his heart and the weakness of his will, two cunning eyes were constantly at watch. The moustache round his mean, thin mouth, and his beard, were equally thin and weak.

* Mounseer Dry-Bone, or syphilis, the appalling disease which, since the capture of Naples by the French in 1495, had ravaged Europe, rivalling and eclipsing leprosy in its horror.

He and his deceased elder brother had been hostages in Spain, and the thought of this captivity remained ever with him. He was never seen to smile.

It must be said of him that he had great physical courage.

He became an all-too-willing prisoner, at the age of nineteen, in the toils of Diane de Poictiers (widow of the Grand Sénéchale of Normandy, and afterwards Duchesse de Valentinois), who was, at the time when she took possession of him, and of the kingdom, aged thirty-eight. It is said that she was beautiful, but her portrait gives no indication of this — showing a reddish nose with a fat tip, thin expressionless lips, and pale meaningless eyes, like holes in a canvas shrouding nothingness. The only thing to be gathered from that face is that she was cautious. During the life-time of her elderly husband, she had lived virtuously, and on this she prided herself. The greed for possessions was, perhaps, her only passion, if we exclude that for outward respectability.

Unfortunately the King, while furthering the first passion, disregarded the second. Having fallen under this enchantment, he was tireless in insulting his wife — his otherwise inactive brain showing an extraordinary fertility in inventing new ways of doing so.

When the Queen was ill, this woman remained at her bedside ; when the royal children permitted her by the Grande Sénéchale were born, this fleshly shadow of the King was present. The mistress chose the persons who were to educate the King's legitimate children. They were, in all but the fact of birth, her children, not the Queen's.

On the Progresses made by the King and Queen, every possible affront was offered to the long-suffering woman who was, in name only, Queen of France. The hangings of the canopies bore the interlaced letters H and D (Henri and Diane). The nobles of the cities visited, paraded first before the King, then before the mistress, then (as an afterthought, presumably) before the Queen. At galas, the Sénéchale sat beside the Queen, cloaked with ermine as if she were Queen of France, and wearing the Crown jewels, given her by the King.

The unremarkable face (more French in character than Italian) of that most remarkable woman who bore the title of Queen, and whose protruding myopic eyes saw everything, betrayed nothing. It is doubtful if that inexpressive face was given as much as a glance by the mistress, who was occupied with her own beauty and her triumph.

With this *faisandée* old lady, the little Dauphine was allowed to hold daily, familiar intercourse ; the child's instruction in manners was placed in her hands. And as part of this instruction, she was trained to speak insolently of the Queen, and of her descent from Florentine merchants.

The Queen of France, perhaps influenced by her daughter-in-law's friendship with Madame de Valentinois, never held her in affection. Catherine was, it may be supposed, frozen at heart by the treatment she had received, and, withdrawing from ordinary humanity, was surrounded (finding in them, perhaps, some relaxation from the public façade of indifference, of nullity she was forced to assume) by mental and physical deformities, misshapen from birth, as she had been misshapen by the years, — by dwarfs, by fools (one, named La Jardinière, was a particular favourite, and had, as companion, a parrot and an ape 'dont la main velue porte bonheur' [1]), and by necromancers and astrologers, chief of whom was Nostradamus.

. . . . . .

In July 1559, preparations were being made for the marriage, by proxy, of the King of Spain with the French King's daughter ; and the canopy of the thrones, the hangings of the galleries, the sleeves of the heralds, were embroidered with the arms of England.

Among the other celebrations, a great tournament was to be held, in which King Henri, insulting, as usual, his Queen, carried on his lance the colours of Madame de Valentinois.

The tournament began at nine in the morning, to the sound of trumpets. The Queen, sitting with Madame de Valentinois in her near neighbourhood, was, naturally, ignored. But if anyone had had the time to cast her a casual glance, it would have been seen that her normally ruddy face was white.

At the time of her marriage she had been told by the astrologer and mathematician Luc Gauric that a duel would end her husband's reign and life. Even the manner of wound from which he would die was foretold, and she was warned that, especially between his fortieth and forty-first year, he must avoid taking the field in single combat, for a wound in his head would lead to death.

Nostradamus had prophesied :

> Le lion jeune, le vieux surmontera,
> En champ bellique, par singulier duelle,
> Dans cage d'or les yeux lui crevera. . . .

The forty-year-old King entered the lists.

The third passage of arms, against the tall, powerful young Comte Gabriel de Montgomery, Seigneur de Lorges, should have been the last in which the King would take part. The combat ended, the Queen, whose face had grown even whiter, sponged her forehead, and the colour returned to her face. The prophecies had been false.

Then, to the astonishment of the Court, when Monsieur de Vieilleville, who was to take the King's place in the lists, advanced, fully armed, the King told him that he wished to break a further lance with the Comte de Montgomery, nor would he listen to any remonstrances. To the Queen's message, imploring him, for love of her, to desist, he answered — ironically — 'Tell the Queen that it is precisely for love of her that I am breaking the lance'.

Monsieur de Vieilleville, in grave tones, said, 'Sire, I swear before the living God that for more than three nights I have dreamt that some misfortune would befall you, and that this last day is fatal'.

At this, the Comte de Montgomery felt fear rise in his heart. 'I implore Your Majesty', he said, 'not to persist.' To which the King replied, in irritation, 'Make ready to enter the lists against me'.

The combat began. . . . The Comte de Montgomery galloped towards the King, almost obscured by a cloud of dust. His lance clashed against the King's vizor with an extraordinary violence, broke, and pierced the King's right eye, issuing through his ear.

The King reeled, then slumped over the pommel of his saddle.

The Queen gave a piercing shriek, then she, her son, and daughter-in-law, fainted. The Cardinal, the Duc de Guise, and their enemy the Constable, bearing the weight of the King's sagging body, still upright on his feet, helped him to his bed. As he reached it, he felt for it as if he were already blind, pitched on to his back, and with an effort placing his hands together, began to pray.

During the eleven days of torment he was to know before his death, the Queen, the Duc de Savoie, the Duc de Guise, the Cardinal of Lorraine watched, in turns, by the bedside.

But one person was absent — the omnipotent figurehead of vice and hypocrisy who had reigned over the kingdom for so many years. Her daring, her insolence, had deserted her, and she was alone. 'Is the King dead?' she asked again and again of her servants. For while he lived, nobody would risk touching her. But she was soon to know what lay behind the inexpressive face at which she had never troubled to spare a glance. Just before the King's death, the Queen sent a message addressed to 'la mère Poictiers', ordering her to leave the Palace and retire to her house, to relinquish the Crown jewels and all other properties given her by the King, with the exception of one house.

Her reign was over; and so, the glories of this world having been snatched from her greedy hands, she made an attempt to seize those of the next, and, until her death seven years later, the priest in charge of 'les filles repenties' would exhort his flock, at every Mass, to 'pray to God for Diane de Poictiers'.

The King's last words as, blinded, he groped for his son's hand, were : 'My son, you are about to lose your father, but not his blessing. I pray God that he make you happier than I have been.'

Strange and affecting farewell ! Perhaps, in the midst of all the pain he had inflicted, he, too, had suffered.

---

## NOTE TO CHAPTER SEVENTEEN

[1] Castelnau, Michel de, *Mémoires*.

# Chapter Eighteen

THE Queen of Scotland's young husband, Francis — that little pale phantom, so like, in his coming and going, to her cousin Edward the Sixth of England — was now King of France.

And once again Catherine de' Medici was to be eclipsed. She had expected to rule France. Now she found that the title of Queen Mother, bestowed on her by her son out of courtesy, meant nothing. The boy-King was entirely ruled by his wife, and on him, as on her, were cast the dark glittering shadows of her uncles, the Duc and Cardinal de Guise.

One of the young Queen's first actions was to urge her husband to send troops to aid her mother against the Scottish rebels, and this, she said, 'he has promised to do, and I will not allow him to forget it'.

The rebellion, taking the form of a religious war, was now spreading, and was increased by the miseries of the poor and the eloquence of Knox.

On the 1st of January 1559, the beggars fastened a paper called 'the Beggars' Warning' to the gates of the monasteries. The priests and monks, they said, had taken what was rightfully theirs, with the consequence that they were destitute. On Whit Sunday, they warned the occupants of the monasteries, they would seize what was theirs and would turn their oppressors into the streets.

Of course the beggars got nothing. The nobles of the 'Congregation' — the name by which the Protestant rebels were known — saw to that. But the Abbey of Scone was 'committed', wrote Knox, 'to the merciment of fire', and as for 'the Black and Grey Thieves [or friars] their monuments of idolatry . . . were so destroyed that only the walls remained'. When this was reported to the Queen Regent, she

YOUNG FRANCIS

was 'so enraged that she did avow "utterly to destroy Saint Johnston, man, woman, and child, and to consume the same by fire, and afterwards to salt it, in sign of a perpetual desolation"'.

Had the Queen Regent dismissed the French troops, as the Congregation demanded, she would have been condemning the priests of her creed to instant death at the hands of the Congregation. The French troops remained, and, on the 8th of July 1559, it was known to Cecil that fresh French troops were massing at Havre en route for Scotland. 'And when Scotland is quieted', de Quadra, the new Spanish Ambassador to England, wrote to the Emperor, 'it will be England's turn.' Indeed, the Bishop of Arras told Sir Thomas Chaloner, the English Envoy to Philip in Brussels, that the whole reason for the French preparations was that the young Queen of France intended to seize England.

Cecil was convinced that the English, for their own safety, must send an army to turn the French out of Scotland and come to the aid of the Scottish rebels. But the Queen realised that it would be difficult to explain sending arms and men to aid rebels against their monarch. It might set a bad example. Therefore, Sir William wrote to her, 'with a sorrowful heart and watery eyes, I, your poor servant and most lowly subject and unworthy Secretary, beseech Your Majesty to pardon this my lowly suit. That considering the proceeding in this matter for removing the French out of Scotland doth not content Your Majesty, and that I cannot with my conscience give any contrary advice, I may with Your Majesty's favour and clemency, be spared to intermingle with it.' He would willingly, he said, serve her as her gardener, or in some such humble capacity. But her Minister he could not be.

It was then decided, for the moment, that England would confine herself to sending money secretly to the rebel Lords.

Unfortunately, the Queen Regent discovered that Cecil had been corresponding with her rebels, and she sent a protest, through the French Ambassador, to the Queen of England, presumably without mentioning Cecil by name. In answer

to 'The Right High and most Excellent Princess, our dear
Sister', the Queen expressed her astonishment that any of her
subjects should, 'regardless of her displeasure, have sought to
meddle with any such people'. Who could the culprit be ?
She begged her dear sister to tell her exactly what she complained of, in order that she might go into the matter, and, if
it were proved, chastise such as had offended.

For it would be convenient to find out just how much her
dear sister knew.

The Congregation was, by this time, in desperation, and
begged for the armed aid of England. Their hope that this
might be forthcoming had not been advanced by the candour
of Knox. Elizabeth had been deeply displeased by his *First
Blast of the Trumpet against the Monstrous Regiment of Women*,
nor had she been soothed by Calvin's apology to Cecil on the
subject. 'Two years ago', he wrote, 'John Knox asked of
me, in a private conversation, what I thought about the government of women. I candidly replied that, as it was a deviation
from the original and proper order of nature, it was to be
ranked no less than slavery among the punishments consequent
on the Fall of Man.' There were, however, 'occasionally
women so endowed, that the singular good qualities which
shone forth in them, made it evident that they were raised
up by divine authority ; either that God designed by such
examples to condemn the inactivity of men, or for the better
setting forth of His Glory'.

The moment of his country's appeal to England was now
judged propitious, by the Reformer, for delivering a homily
to the English Queen. He had received no answer to a
message sent her through Cecil, and wrote to her, therefore,
as follows :

His book, he assured her, only concerned her if she deserved
it to do so. If she continued to defend God's truth God would
defend her, and he and God's friends would pray for her.

'But consider deeply', he continued, 'how for fear of
your life ye did decline from God and bow to idolatry [on
an occasion in Queen Mary's reign when Elizabeth went to

Mass and *he* was having those interesting conversations with Calvin, far from England]. Let it not be a small fault in your eyes that ye have declined from Christ Jesu in the day of His battle. . . . God hath preserved you when ye were most unthankful, and hath raised you from the ports of death to rule above His people, for the comfort of His Kirk. . . . But, if you begin to brag of your birth, and to build your authority upon your own law, flatter you whoso list, your felicity shall be short.

'Interpret my rude words as written by him who is no enemy of Your Grace. By divers letters I have required licence to visit your realm — not to seek for myself, neither yet my own ease or commodity — which if you now refuse or deny, I must remit myself unto God, adding this for conclusion : that such as refuse the Counsel of the faithful, appear it never so sharp, are compelled to follow the deceit of flatterers to their own perdition.' (20th July 1559.)

It cannot be said that the letter was well received, nor that it made the present task of Cecil — that of inducing the Queen to make open war on Scotland — any easier.

Cecil had himself been allowed a taste of the Reformer's eloquence, having been bombarded from Dieppe by letters, unanswered by him, and followed by duplicates. In these, Cecil was lectured on his duties, was reminded that he had, 'by silence, consented and subscribed . . . to the shedding of the blood of God's most dear children', and that although, in spite of this 'most horrible defection', God had spared him, yet, 'Very true love compelleth me to say [love took the strangest forms in the Reformer] except the Spirit of God purge your heart from that venom, which your eyes have seen to be destruction unto others . . . ye shall not long escape the reward of dissemblers.'

All this added up to the fact that what the Reformer wanted was to come to England, and that the Queen was determined that he should not. But he was forgiving. He was even able to make allowances for her, seeing 'the miraculous work of God, comforting his afflicted by an infirm

vessel' (the Queen, unfortunately born a female). He reminded the recipient of this letter that 'this is the third time I
have begged licence to visit the hungry and thirsty among
you'.

To his surprise, he received no answer to this letter, and,
finding that the subsequent bombardment by duplicates produced no effect, he set sail for Scotland, landing there on
the 3rd of May 1559, and sending Cecil, on the 20th of July,
the letter of surpassing length, already referred to, which he
asked should be given to the Queen.

The Congregation, meanwhile, was putting up a feeble
fight against the Queen Regent's partisans, and Knox told
Cecil, on the 18th of November, 'Friends do fail and fall back
from the enterprise. The whole multitude — a few excepted
— stand in such doubt they cannot tell to which part they
shall incline.'

Then, suddenly, the Congregation entered into open
rebellion against their ruler. They renounced Mary Stuart,
they renounced France, they renounced their ancient hatred
against England, and made a formal offer to the Queen of
England of the Crown of Scotland, so that the two realms
should be united in one, to be known by the ancient name of
Great Britain.

No longer was her marriage with the mad Lord Arran,
next in succession to the Scottish throne (a marriage which
had been considered), made a condition, although it must have
been understood as a possibility.

This was not the first time that such an offer had been
made to England by Scottish rebels. On the 27th of December 1531, the Lord Bothwell of that time, with Angus,
described as 'ever in harte as trew and loyal as any of his house
hath ben afore time', had suggested crowning King Henry
the Eighth in Edinburgh, as King of Scotland.[1]

For Elizabeth to have accepted the Scottish offer would
have meant immediate war with France. And she would
have been forced to ask the aid of Spain. But could she rely
on this ? The Spanish enmity towards England was growing,

although it was mixed with fear of the outcome should England be defeated ; for if, as the Duchess of Parma wrote to King Philip, 'the French once established themselves in Scotland, England is theirs ; and with England they will have the Low Countries. . . . And when we are overrun, you must judge for yourself how it will fare with Spain and the Indies.'

It was thought that the time had come for the King of Spain to consider the interests of his own country, for the Queen of England had done everything that he had advised her most strongly not to do, and now he must 'provide for his own safety as best he might'. In short, Spain did not intend to fight France in defence of England. Questioned on this point by Sir Thomas Chaloner, the British Ambassador, the Bishop of Arras replied that it was strange that England thought the world did not know her weakness. 'I demand what present store of expert captains or good men of war ye have ?'

But the Bishop of Arras was wrong in thinking there were no 'expert captains or good men of war' !

On the 29th of December 1559, young Admiral Winter set out with his Fleet for the Forth, with orders to cause as much trouble as possible. He was to prevent any more French from entering Scotland, and to destroy their vessels if they attacked him. If they refused a quarrel, he was to persist until he drove them to it. He must challenge the right of the French commanders to carry the English royal arms, and was to declare that, as an Englishman, he would not endure it. But on no account must he say that those were the Queen's orders.

This denial that he was under orders would make him liable, if he were caught, to be hanged as a pirate. But he did not care.

A few days before the sailing of Admiral Winter's fleet, the French reinforcements, under the Queen Regent's brother, d'Elbœuf, left Dieppe. They should have reached Scotland before Winter, but a gigantic storm arose, splintering half the French ships, the mountains of waves carrying on their peaks soldiers, sailors, horses. Though the English fleet was caught, also, no ships were damaged.

When Winter arrived, he seized barques full of ammunition and of provisions waiting to be sent to the French army now marching on St. Andrews. Those that he did not seize, he drove on shore to be taken by the rebels. Luckily, also, the French, believing his fleet to be the awaited fleet of d'Elbœuf, fired a friendly salute, thus giving him the chance to say that the French had fired on him, so that he had the right to fire back.

When the Queen Regent sent a herald and trumpeter to ask the meaning of the Admiral's peculiar behaviour, he replied that it had just been an idea of his. No, he did not know what had put it into his head. Certainly not his Queen! She knew nothing about it. He had simply been sent to act as escort to ships carrying ammunition to the English garrison at Berwick. But there was nowhere for him to sink anchor at Berwick. Therefore, not having the slightest suspicion that the Scots were at war with his Queen, or that anyone whatsoever had any quarrel with her, he had gone with his Fleet to the Forth. The French had fired on him. Naturally he was not going to put up with that without making some rejoinder, so he had fired back. And then, remembering the cruelties of the French towards the Congregation, he had grown angrier still, and that was why he had decided to help the latter by seizing the barques full of ammunition and provisions destined for the former.

The Queen of England, when she was told of her Admiral's conduct, was astonished. She told the Queen Regent that she could not condemn the Admiral unheard, but that she had given orders to the Duke of Norfolk, in command of the English garrison at Berwick, to arrest him immediately.

The Duke seems to have been singularly dilatory in carrying out his orders, for the Admiral was not arrested, but was left to carry out his train of thought unhampered in any way by his compatriots.

The English troops lay idle at Berwick. The French in

the fortress of Leith showed increasing determination, and the Congregation grew ever more helpless and tepid in spirit. On the 25th of February 1560, the most energetic member of the Congregation, Mary Stuart's bastard half-brother, Lord James Stuart (afterwards Earl of Moray), came to Berwick to arrange the terms on which Elizabeth would allow her army to join the rebels. She must know, he was told, how, if she expelled the French from Leith, the Scots were prepared to prevent them from returning. France would probably declare war on England, and if England was invaded, could she depend on Scotland? Finally, were the Congregation prepared to form a lasting alliance with England, which would render the keeping of troops on the Scottish border unnecessary?

The reason given for the English invasion of Scotland was the alleged French attempt to annex Scotland; for this reason, England would fight to preserve Scottish liberty. A solemn declaration was made that this, and this only, was the reason for the appearance in Scotland of the English army. No attempt was to be made against the authority of the Queen of Scotland.

On hearing this, King Philip sent an envoy, the Seigneur de Glasion, to the Queen of England to tell her that he was astonished and pained at her proceedings. If she sent an army into Scotland, she must recall it immediately, and, instead, *he* would send an army there to restore order. If she did not follow his instructions, not only would he leave her to the destruction that would fall on her, but, should the French declare war on her, he might even feel it his duty to make that destruction doubly sure by coming to the aid of the Queen of Scotland.[2]

Elizabeth was roused to fury by these threats.

The understandably nervous French Ambassador, de Sèvre, forced in the course of his duties to protest to the Queen (he had not orders to declare war), tried to induce the Spanish Ambassador and the King of Spain's envoy to accompany him to the audience. Equally understandably, they declined.

He found the Queen in a violent passion.

'You complain', she said, 'of the fleet and army which we have sent to Scotland. What were we to do? You challenge our Crown; you deny our right to be Queen. You snatch the pretext of a rebellion to collect your armies on our Borders, and you expect us to sit still like children. . . .

'We know what was intended for ourselves — some of your own statesmen have given us warning of it. Your Queen claims our Crown; and you think that we shall be satisfied by words. You say you recalled d'Elbœuf. The winds and the waves recalled him; and our Fleet in the Forth frightened him from a second attempt. You have given us promises upon promises; yet our style is still filched from us, and your garrisons are still at Leith. We have forborne long enough.' (15th April 1560.) [3]

The English army, by now, was a mile from Leith. The time preceding the siege is best seen through the magnificent description by Froude.

'. . . Day and night the English batteries flashed and roared. On the evening of the 30th of April the town was observed to be on fire. Fanned by a fresh breeze, the blaze rose into the sky, lighting up the masts and spars of Winter's fleet, and throwing its red glare on the walls and chimneys of Edinburgh. The English skirmishers, to assist the confusion, attacked the enemy's lines; and amidst the shouts of action and the roar of the artillery, Grey, the General, sat in his tent writing an exulting despatch to Norfolk. A third part of Leith was in ashes ere he closed his letter. The flames shot up again as he was writing the last words, and an eager postscript added — "Yet it burns — yet it burns."'

Leith was on fire, yet 'On May the 1st', wrote Andrew Lang (*History of Scotland*), 'the gay defenders crowned the walls [of the fortress] with May-poles and May-garlands'.

On the 7th of May, between two and three in the morning, 'the whole English line advanced'. With them were a thousand Scots.[4] But they came to a wide, deep moat, and beyond that, a huge stone wall with great towers. That wall was impossible to scale ; the ladders were too short by six feet.

The invaders clung despairingly to those huge walls, but soon found even this impossible, and, as they fell to the ground, they were bombarded by shots from cannon, by vast blocks of stone, and by blazing pitch. 'The Frenchmen's harlots' — so Froude described these Scottish viragoes — rushed to join the men on the battlements, carrying great 'chimneys of fire', loading the cannon, rolling the barrels of tar, carrying seething cauldrons with which to set on fire and flay the invaders.

Sir James Crofts was the general responsible for the assault. He did not arrive in time, and his division was absent.

The invaders kept up their despairing attempt for two hours. But they could not even reach the enemy. When half their officers had been killed, and eight hundred of the common soldiers were either dead or wounded, on the ground outside those impregnable walls, the bugles sounded the retreat. The slaughter was over.

Now panic reigned, and the Edinburgh townspeople refused even to take the wounded, for whose aid they had asked, into their houses. They left them to die under the hot skies.

'The Queen Regent', wrote Knox, 'sat all the time of the assault (which was both terrible and long) upon the fore-wall of the Castle of Edinburgh ; and when she perceived the overthrow of us, and that the ensigns of the French were again displayed upon the walls, she gave a gawfe of laughter, and said "Now will I go to the Mass, and praise God for that which my eyes have seen !" And so was Friar Black ready for that purpose, whom she herself a little before had deprehended [apprehended] with his harlot in the chapel.' (16th May 1566.) . . .

'The French, proud of the victory, stripped naked all the slain, and laid their dead carcasses before the hot sun along the wall, where they suffered them to lie more days nor one ; unto the which, when the Queen Regent looked, for mirth she happit [skipped] and said "Yonder are the fairest tapestry

that ever I saw : I would that the whole fields that is (*sic*) betwix this place and yon were strewn with the same stuff". *
. . . Against the which, John Knox spake openly in pulpit, and boldly affirmed "That God should revenge that contumely done to his image, not only in the furious and godless soldiers, but even in such as rejoiced thereat".' His 'sound northern courtesy', — so much admired by Froude, caused him to add : 'And the very experience declared that he was not deceived ; for within few days thereafter (yea, some say that same day) began her belly and loathsome legs to swell, and so continued, till that God did execute his judgment upon her'.

Her fate, — that 'judgment' which was to fill Knox with triumph, was swift. On the 8th of June, this indomitable woman, once the greatest beauty of the Court of France, now swollen with dropsy, old, and almost friendless in this alien country, sent for her husband's bastard son Lord James Stuart, and for the Duke of Châtellerault.

She was dying, and she knew it. In her failing voice she told them that she grieved for Scotland's sufferings, and for any part that she might have had in them. She asked them not to leave her. They were with her when, at midnight between the 10th and 11th of June, she died.

When the news of the defeat at Leith reached Elizabeth, she 'renewed the opinions of Cassandra', Killigrew told Throckmorton on the 13th of May. And he was informed by Cecil, on the same day, that 'God trieth us with many difficulties. The Queen's Majesty never liketh this business in Scotland.' He added, in cipher, 'I have had such a torment herein with the Queen's Majesty as an ague hath not in five fits so much abated me'.

* The editor of *The Reformation in Scotland*, Dr. William Croft Dickinson, says, 'It may be questioned whether it was physically possible for the Queen Regent to see, from the walls of Edinburgh Castle, the dead on the walls of Leith'.

### NOTES TO CHAPTER EIGHTEEN

1 State Papers.  　　　　　　　　　2 Froude, *op. cit.*
3 Teulet. vol. ii, p. 21, abridged by Froude.
4 Froude, *op. cit.*

# Chapter Nineteen

ON the 7th of September 1560, Sir William Cecil held with the Spanish Ambassador, Bishop de Quadra (whom he might have been supposed to regard with the highest distrust), a conversation of great strangeness.

Before considering that strangeness, it may be useful to turn over a few pages of the Chief Secretary's past life.

'The old fox', said his nephew Nicholas Bacon, long after this time, 'crouches and whines.' That crouching, whining habit was to be seen in all his dealings with 'great men' — whilst their greatness was in the ascendancy.

'Be sure', he wrote in his Precepts for his son Robert, 'to keep some great man thy friend ; but trouble him not for trifles. Present him with many yet small gifts and of little charge. And if thou hast cause to bestow any great gratuity, let it be some such thing as may daily be in his sight. Otherwise in this ambitious age thou shalt remain as a hop without a pole living in obscurity, and be made a football for every insulting companion.

'Towards thy superiors be humble yet generous ; with thy equals familiar, yet respective ; towards thy inferiors show much humility with some familiarity, — as to bow thy body, stretch forth thy hand and uncover thy head, and such like compliments. The first prepares the way for thy advancement ; the second makes thee known as a man well bred ; the third gains a good report which once gotten is easily kept.'

Of comparatively modest birth (his grandfather was a yeoman of the King's chamber under Henry the Eighth, his father a royal page who had risen to be groom of the chambers), he had risen by his own efforts, built on the scaffolding

133

(in more senses than one) of two great patrons, to be Chief Secretary to the Queen of England. His talent for pliancy, when, in his youth, this could be of use to him, had gained for him gifts of lands.

He had married wisely and well, having, while at Cambridge, met and courted the daughter of a beadle whose widow kept a small wine shop. A humble beginning ; but John Cheke, tutor to King Edward the Sixth, was his bride's brother. A useful connection !

That he set much store in the choice of a wife is evident from the precepts to his son already referred to.

'When it shall please God to bring thee to man's estate, use great providence and circumspection in choosing thy wife. For from thence will spring all thy future good or evil. And it is an action of life, like unto a stratagem of warre ; wherein a man can erre but once. If thy estate be good, match neere home and at leisure ; if weak, far off and quickly. Enquire diligently of her disposition, and how her parents have been inclined in their youth. Let her not be poore, how generous soever. For a man can buy nothing in the market with gentility. Nor choose a base and uncomely creature altogether for wealth ; for it will cause contempt in others and loathing in thee. Neither make choice of a dwarf or a fool ; for, by the one thou shalt beget a race of pygmies ; the other will be thy continual disgrace ; and it will irk thee to hear her talk. For thou shalt find to thy great grief, that there is nothing more fulsome than a she-fool.'

His son Robert was to prove a complete satisfaction to him.

We have seen in an earlier chapter the roseate portrait of William Cecil as an old man. And indeed, I believe his character was so changed, in the reign of the great Queen, by the quality of his labours, that could we forget some terrible charges of cruelty brought against him, we should see that portrait was the accurate representation of his old age.

But in his earlier life there was a darkness in him — a second self, hidden under that discreet, middle-class respectability, but afterwards to be banished as the great character of his labours purified him. For, from a cocoon woven about him from outside by circumstance, from inside, as the silk-worm spins silk, from the central fault in his own nature that was the cause of his worldly success, greatness, eventually, would emerge.

He had a prodigious memory — always brought into play when it would be useful — and, one supposes, an equally prodigious gift for putting it aside when it might disturb his complacency. When, as an old man, he 'disposed himself to his quiet rest', it may be doubted whether that virtuous sleep was ever disturbed by the blood-stained ghosts of the two men to whom he owed his fortune and his lands, and whom he had helped to betray to their death.

He had been, at the age of twenty-eight, a member of the Duke of Somerset's household. He became Master of Requests, which post, highly confidential, entailed dealing with all applications to the Protector, of every kind. From this post, he advanced to that of the Protector's chief secretary, being in possession of all his patron's secrets.

No need, now, to keep this 'great man' his friend by giving him small gifts or great. He had the great man where he wanted him, having all his secrets. The great man's fate was in the watchful, respectful, and respectable Cecil's hands.

The Protector had been useful to him in many ways — as to advancement, as to the acquisition of property. Cecil was not rich, and he wished for a grant of Wimbledon ; when it was found that he could not be given this, he was granted instead, at Somerset's request, the park and lodge of Mortlake. Tyrwhit, the owner, in a letter to Cecil dated the 12th of April 1550, said 'I have received my Lord Grace's letter o'er yours for the lodge and park at Mortlake for your commodity to have it, because his Grace would have you near him'.[1] For Somerset trusted him completely.

When John Dudley, Earl of Warwick (afterwards Duke of Northumberland), returned from his victory at Dussindale, his first act was the overthrow of Somerset. But months before that time, Cecil had been receiving from his patron's deadly and implacable enemy letters addressed to 'My very loving friend, Mr. Cecill'. For it was now time for Cecil to serve a great man other than his first patron (of whose greatness, soon, nothing would be left).

So, under the spell of this new devotion, Somerset's secretary set himself, as was his duty, to bring about the Protector's attainder and death on the charge of treason.

Businesslike and cool as ever, he began to make a list of witnesses (he who knew all his patron's secrets), to interview them, and to frame questions to be asked at the trial, of a 'subtlety that would not let the accused man see the concealed trap until it was sprung'.

The preparations were made with great secrecy, but the Protector seems to have become suspicious. 'The Duke', said King Edward in his Journal, 'sent for the Secretary Cecil to tell him he suspected some ill. Mr. Cecil answered, that if he were not guilty, he might be of good courage ; if he were, he had nothing to say but to lament him.'

It is said that Somerset 'defied him'. But there was nothing to be done. He was condemned to death.

For the sake of decency, one supposes, Lord Warwick's 'very loving friend' was sent to the Tower at the same time as the man who had founded his fortunes. But he was in no danger. . . . In three months' time he emerged, as bright, and as brisk, and as businesslike as ever, and soon afterwards devoted himself openly to the service of his former patron's destroyer.

He was warmly congratulated, — by the Duchess of Suffolk, mother of Lady Jane Grey, among others (2nd October 1550), — on 'the good exchanges you have made, and on having come to a good market'. As one of his correspondents said, with great acumen, 'It were a way to make an end to amity, if, when men fall, their friends should be troubled'.

Cecil was not. One must, of course, look after one's own interests, and he had really done very well.

The new great man, now Duke of Northumberland, was soon to find the nature of his 'loving friend's' devotion.

When the Northumberland rebellion in favour of Lady Jane Grey began, the night before the Duke and his army started for the north, he called all the Council together at supper, and made them swear not to betray him nor the cause of the sixteen-year-old girl whom they had been so eager to acclaim as Queen. Among the company was his 'loving friend', as useful, as watchful, as discreet as ever.

The Duke left his friend with certain definite orders. He was to send his horses and retainers to join Northumberland at Newmarket. He did nothing.

He was to rouse the chief noblemen of Lincolnshire, Northamptonshire, and the West Country, and urge them to join Northumberland's army with all their retainers with the greatest speed. He told them to join the army of Queen Mary at Framlingham.

He was to seize Windsor Castle for Queen Jane. He ensured that it was held for Queen Mary.

He was ordered to make certain that Mary's tenants at Wimbledon joined Northumberland's army. He advised them to stay at home.

All his own retainers were to be sent to join his patron ; he sent eight, and told his tenants to stay where they were.

The armed men and horses that were to have reached the Duke from Northamptonshire were 'ambushed and detained by other servants of his' (Cecil's).

For the astute man had realised, by now, who, in all probability, would win the day. And it was his duty to himself to be on the winning side.

He went, says Chamberlin, to the Market Cross in Cambridge, threw his hat full of gold coins to the gaping crowd, and called for cheers for Queen Mary. He went from that Cross to King's College, a prisoner.

In case he found himself on the losing side, after all, he had had all his movable belongings sent abroad, and his horses were saddled and ready in case he must flee to the coast.

For *still* he could not be quite certain of the outcome.

Even on the morning of the 19th of July, he was uncertain. The Council was shilly-shallying again. One moment they were for Queen Mary, the next, in a fright, for Queen Jane. However, he succeeded, at last, in bringing them to reason, and — it is impossible to guess by what means — they succeeded in inducing the Duke of Suffolk, the little Pretender Queen's father, to let them leave the Tower. Dashing to Baynard's Castle (near St. Paul's) they summoned the Lord Mayor, the Recorder, and the Chief Aldermen, and all signed the proclamation that Mary was Queen.

It was all over, excepting the taking of prisoners and the execution of the rebels.

But the situation, for Sir William, was exceedingly delicate, and must be handled with extreme care. He travelled to Essex, and placed in the hands of the rightful Queen a most humble submission, assuring her that any ostensible disloyalty was in appearance only.

Mary's character was devoid of vindictiveness, excepting towards heretics, and, owing to the prayers of one of her ladies, Lady Bacon, sister of his second wife, Sir William was pardoned. Five years of darkness — then the light of the new rising sun, Elizabeth.

But that new day had not brought him the fortune he expected. Quite the contrary. The Queen was lavishing favour and fortune on Lord Robert, son of that betrayed patron. (What did she see in him ? 'A Vertue of his, whereof he gave some shadowed tokens' [2] — to her, if to no others ?) And each gift, each honour, compromised her more deeply in the eyes of the world. And here was he, William Cecil, working without a salary, even allowed to pay his own expenses on that most important journey to Scotland, to attempt to arrange a treaty, the terms of which were that the English and French troops should alike withdraw from Scotland, that Calais should be restored to England (but on this he did not insist), that the Queen of Scotland would cease the use of the royal arms of England and her pretensions to the

Crown, and that the King and Queen of France would promise liberty of conscience to their subjects.

But, as he said, 'What was to be expected, when the Duke of Norfolk, a rare nobleman and a kinsman of the Queen, was merely thanked for his services and sent home without allowance or promise ? He himself (Sir William) would feel the pinch of his expenditure for seven years ; yet he had saved the Queen £15,000 in one day by his prompt discharge of her forces.'

Yet here was Lord Robert Dudley, who, Sir William thought, had done nothing to deserve it — (he had, in the time of Queen Mary, sold land in order to come to the aid of Elizabeth) — made Master of the Horse, with a payment of a thousand marks a year, with his own table at Court, such as was 'furnished for the Lords', at no cost to himself, and with all the men in the royal stables under his command, — made Constable of Windsor Castle and forest, and keeper of the great park — made a Knight of the Order of the Garter — whilst *he* . . .

Why did this man who, to say the least of it, had a businesslike attitude towards life, work thus, for no pay ?

From a true love of England ? From a recognition of greatness when he saw it ?

The following conversation with de Quadra is the only recorded instance of his having shown Elizabeth even the slightest disloyalty. He was faithful to his country and to her, to the end.

But at this time, tired and dispirited, he was thinking of leaving her service.* And here he was, on the 7th of September 1560 (and it is the *date* we must note), meeting the Ambassador and, simple man that he was, confiding in him.

'I met the Secretary Cecil', the Ambassador told the Duchess of Parma, 'whom I knew to be in disgrace. Lord Robert, I was aware, was endeavouring to deprive him of his place.

'With little difficulty I led him to the subject, and after

* See Appendix C.

many protestations and entreaties that I would keep secret what he was about to tell me [Cecil knew, naturally, that the Bishop would do nothing of the kind], he said that the Queen was going on so strangely that he was about to withdraw from her service. It was a bad sailor, he said, who did not make for port when he saw a storm coming, and for himself he perceived the most manifest ruin impending over the Queen through her intimacy with Lord Robert. The Lord Robert had made himself master of the business of the State and the person of the Queen, to the extreme injury of the realm, with the intention of marrying her [he had been a married man for eight years], and she was shutting herself up in the palace to the peril of her health and life. That the realm would tolerate the marriage he said that he did not believe ; he was therefore determined to retire into the country, although he supposed they would send him to the Tower before they would let him go.

'He implored me for the love of God to remonstrate with the Queen, to persuade her not utterly to throw herself away as she was doing, and to remember what she owed to herself and to her subjects.' (What game was this ? Both the speaker and the hearer knew perfectly well that the latter had no influence whatsoever over the Queen.) 'Of Lord Robert', the Ambassador continued, 'he twice said he would be better in Paradise than here.

'I could only reply that I was most deeply grieved ; I said he must be well aware how anxious I had always been for the Queen's well-doing. I had laboured, as the King my master had directed me, to persuade her to live quietly and to marry (with how little effect he himself could tell). I would try again however as soon as I had an opportunity.

'He told me the Queen cared nothing for foreign princes ; she did not believe that she stood in any need of their support. She was deeply in debt, taking no thought how to clear herself, and she had ruined her credit in the City.

'Last of all he said that they were thinking of destroying Lord Robert's wife. They had given out that she was ill ;

but she was not ill at all ; she was very well, and was taking care not to be poisoned ; God, he trusted, would never permit such a crime to be accomplished or allow so wicked a conspiracy to succeed.'

The last suggestion — that 'they were thinking of destroying Lord Robert's wife' — was common gossip. But it seems strange that this most wily, most experienced servant of the state, 'the old fox', made this communication at *this moment* to the Spaniard, a man who, he knew, was the employer of spies, and who would be certain to repeat the conversation.

Lord Robert may have desired his wife's death. But as his subsequent letters show, he knew that if that death were accompanied by the least suspicion of murder, any hope he might have of becoming the Queen's husband would be at an end. Others knew this also.

He had many enemies.

## NOTES TO CHAPTER NINETEEN

[1] P. F. Tytler. *England under the Reign of Edward VI and Mary.*
[2] Camden, Book 1.

# Chapter Twenty

THE days had seemed too short for the Queen's happiness.

In the afternoons on the long river (dark green as the waters of Lethe), in this happiness, floating onward, sometimes playing the lute or talking a little, and then falling silent, might not the Queen, with Lord Robert sitting beside her or lying at her feet, and sometimes with the grave dark presence of the Spanish Ambassador, shadowing nothing, and seemingly threatening nothing, forget the morrow?

Robert was the husband of another woman. Still, she must have told herself, often, 'It will always be like this. . . . We shall always be young, happy. . . . Tomorrow may never come.'

Tomorrow . . .

. . . . .

On Sunday the 8th of September 1560, the day after Sir William Cecil had held with the Spanish Ambassador a strange conversation, a young woman was walking downstairs, in a house that was otherwise deserted — or so she thought. For she had sent all her servants that morning to a fair at Abingdon, and they would not return till night.

Was that the sound of a heavy door behind her — a door at the head of the stairs, that she had thought closed, being opened? — slowly and stealthily at first, then more and more quickly . . .

Only the wind. And that other sound — it could not be that of approaching footsteps? . . . Only the rustling of leaves coming to her through a window.

That morning (so it is said, but it is obvious that the next morning is meant, since the servants did not return till night) one of Lord Robert's gentlemen, a distant cousin named Thomas Blount, left Windsor, where the Queen was in residence, with Lord Robert in her train, for Cumnor Hall, where he had business to transact in Lord Robert's household. When he had ridden for some hours, he was met by a horseman galloping in the direction of Windsor — Bowes, one of Amye Dudley's servants. Seeing Blount, he stopped and gasped out the news. . . . His lady was dead. He did not know how. There had been a fall down a pair of stairs — that was all he knew. . . . No, he could not tell at what time it had happened, for there was nobody in the house. The lady had insisted that all the servants should go, that morning, to Abingdon Fair, and not return till night. He did not know who had found the body, or when. . . .

Continuing the letter to the Duchess of Parma referred to in the last chapter, the Spanish Ambassador wrote, on the day following, 'The Queen told me, on her return from hunting, that Lord Robert's wife was dead — or nearly so, and begged me to say nothing about it'.

He added, 'Since this was written, the death of Lord Robert's wife has been given out publicly. The Queen said in Italian "che si ha rotto il collo"' — she had broken her neck. She had been found dead at the foot of a staircase.

This did not seem to the Ambassador, in spite of his 'anxiety' for the Queen's well-being, to be an unmitigated misfortune. The fury of the populace would undoubtedly be aroused. 'They [the people] say that she and her lover are likely to go to sleep in the Palace and wake in the Tower.'

'Si ha rotto il collo.' Immediately the evil rumours arose. According to *Leycester's Commonwealth* 'she had the chaunce to fal from a paire of staires, and so to breake her necke, but yet wythout hurting of her hoode that stoode upon her head. . . . Sir Richard Varney, who by commaundment remayned with her that day alone, with one man onelie . . . can tel how she died, which man being taken afterward & offering to publish the maner of the said murder, was made awaye privilie in the prison. . . . Sir Richard . . . dying about the same time in London . . . cried pitiouslie, and blasphemed God . . . & said that the divels in hell did teare him in peeces.'

A century later, it was stated in *The Life and Times of Anthony Wood* that 'They [Varney, Forster, the master of the house, and one man only] whether first stiffling her or else strangling her, afterwards flung her doune a paire of staires and broke her necke, using much violence upon her. . . .' However, 'her father Sir John Robertset' [*sic*], with commendable energy (he had, at the time of her death, been in his grave for six years), at once 'came with all speed thither', and insisted on an inquest.

There were other versions concerning her death. According to the same, I am afraid not very able, writer, 'In this house [Cumnor Place] Leycester layed a plott with ye aforesaid Forster, his Tenant, to make away his Wife . . . ye Plot being laid, and ye night appointed, they made advantage to convey her to another chamber, where her bed's head should stand just against a doore which she did not know of ; in ye middle of ye night came a man with a spitt in his hand, open the privy doore, run ye spitt into her head, and tumbled her downe staires. To make ye people believe she had killed herself, they bury her immediately, but her father caused her to be taken up again, enquires into ye business, and prosecutes it. . . .'

An Italian, Baptista di Trento, had another account. It was not a spit, but 'five nails six fingers long driven into her head'.

Nobody foresaw more clearly than the dead woman's husband what would be said.

'Cousin Blount,' he wrote to his gentleman, already at Cumnor, 'Immediatelie upon yr. departing from me, there came to me Bowes, by whom I do understande that my wife is dead, and, as he saithe, by a falle from a paire of stayres ; little other understandinge can I have of him. The greatnes and the suddennes of the mysfortune doth so perplex me untill

I do heare from you how the matter standethe, or howe this evill shuld light upon me ; considering what the malicious world will bruyte, I can take no rest. And, because I have no waie to purge my-selfe of the malicious talke that I knowe the wicked worlde will use, but one, which is the verie plaine trothe to be knowen, I DO praie you, as you have loved me and do tender me and my quietnes, and as nowe my special trust is in you, That you will use all the devices and meanes you can possible for the learnyng of the trothe, wherein have no respect to any living p-son ; And, as by your owne travell and diligence, so likewise by order of lawe, I meane by calling of the coroner, and charginge him to the uttermost from me to have good regarde to make choyse of no light or slight p-sons, But the discretest and substancial men, suche as . . . maye be able to serche thorowlie . . . the bottome of the matter. . . . And that the bodie be vewed and searched accordinglie by them, and in everie respecte to procede by order and lawe. . . . Prayinge you even, as my truste is in you, and as I ever loved you, do not dissemble . . . neither let anythinge be hidd from me. But send me yr. trewe con-ceyte and opinion of the matter ; whether it happened by evill chaunce, or by Villainye . . . in moch haste from Windsore, this IX of September, in the eveninge (Monday)

yr. lovinge frende and kynsman<br>moch perplexed<br>R.D.

I have sent for my brother Appleyarde [Amye's half-brother] and other of her frendes also, to be theare, that they may be previe, and se how all things do proceade.'

Here was no pretence at grief. His wife had long been dead to him — not even a ghost, rising up at the Court banquets to confront him, sighing to him from among the weeds on that river green as the waters of Lethe. . . .

But had *he* been a ghost to *her*, haunting her day and night, coming to share her utter loneliness, speaking to her with the voice of her dead love ? Or again, not speaking, with a silence more terrible than sound ? And was it to end that ghosting that she died ?

His cousin's reply to this letter was dated two days later. On his way to Cumnor he had spent the night at Abingdon. There the landlord told him the news (which he had heard already) and said, 'Some were disposed to saie well and some evill. . . .' But 'the great honestie' of Mr. Forster (Dudley's tenant, in charge of the house) 'dothe moche cutt the evill thoughts of the people'.

Immediately on reaching Cumnor, Blount had inter-viewed the distracted servants. Their lady had, apparently, been particularly insistent that they should go, that day, to the Fair. She had even quarrelled with Mrs. Odingsells, a guest of Forster, because she wished to remain at home, — had, indeed, shown great anger : 'The same tale doth Pirto', Amye's maid, 'who doth dearlie love her, confirm. . . .

'In askinge of Pirto what she might thinke of this matter, either chaunce or villany, she saide, "By her faithe she doth judge it verie chaunce, and neither done by man nor by her-selfe". "For her-selfe," she saide, "she was a good virtuous gentlewoman and daielie would praie upon her knees ; and divers times . . . she hath harde [heard] her praie to God to deliver her from Disperaconne." Then said I, "she myght have an evell eye in her mynde". "No, good Mr. Blount", said poor Pirto, afraid that the beloved dead woman might be suspected of the mortal sin of suicide, "do not judge so of my words".'

Again and again, the husband of the dead woman insisted that the truth must be known. The Coroner's court gave the verdict that the death was from a 'mischaunce'. Lord Robert asked that a second jury should be called. The verdict was the same.

The death was a mysterious one. Why did this young woman who, it seems, could never bear to be alone, insist that the whole household, on that day, should go to the Fair ?

What was the 'desperation' from which she prayed God to deliver her ? She had been in 'a strange mind'. Had she heard the hideous rumours — unfounded — that her husband was planning her death ? Did she feel herself to be a hunted creature, fearing death from every cup, every dish ? Was this the 'desperation' — or was it her knowledge that she had long since been deserted ? Did she — it is possible — kill herself for revenge ? Was she murdered by an enemy of her husband's ? Or by someone employed to discredit the Queen, and make the path of the Queen of Scots to the English throne more safe ?

We know nothing of her.

Had tears like rivers of fire burned their way through her eyes from some hidden volcano in the heart, in the darkness when not even Echo, drifting to her on the night wind as it came to her through her window, would speak her name in the voice she would hear no more — (a name that voice had almost forgotten) ? That name had once meant something to her. Did she, in the days, in the lonely woods, speak that name to impress it on her own memory — only to hear Echo, the mocking Echo that would not come to her in the nights, repeat it to her loneliness ?

Was it for hatred that she died — so that a Fury might dip a torch in her blood and write that name on the conscience of every subject of the woman who had taken her husband from her ?

We shall never know.

All that we know is that if she brought about her own death, the Fury must have come to her suddenly. For only two weeks before, the small occupations of life were still with her. She was preparing for a winter other than that to which she must go. 'My very frinde Willgam edney the tayler . . . at tower rill' received a letter from her 'to deseir ye to make this gowne of vellet whiche I sende you with such A collare as you made . . . my rosset taffyta gowne you sente me last. . . .'

Seven years after she died, John Appleyard, who had, possibly, tried a little blackmail which had been unsuccessful, 'let fall words of anger, and said that for Dudley's sake he had covered up the murder of his sister'. Cecil examined him on this, and he then said that the enquiry had not been pushed to its furthest point. He had often begged Lord Robert to give him leave and to countenance him in the prosecution of the murder of his sister — adding that he did take Lord Robert to be innocent thereof : but yet he thought it an easy matter to find out the offenders . . . showing certain circumstances which moved him to think she was murdered. . . . But Lord Robert always assured him that he thought it was not fit to deal any further in the matter, considering by order of law it was found otherwise.[1]

Sir Henry Neville, writing of this to Sir John Thynne, said 'On Fryday in the Star-Chamber was Appleyard brought forth [from gaol, where he had spent the last seven years] who showed himself a malytyous beast, for he did confesse he accused my Lord Leycester only of malys : & that he hath byn about yt thes 3 years, & now bycause he cold not go thoroghe with his business to promot [promotion] he fell in this rage ageynt my lord. . . . I thinke his end wyl be the pillyry.'

.    .    .    .    .

The sensation caused by the mysterious death of the wife of the Queen's favourite was, naturally, immeasurable. So was the horror of Her Majesty's Ambassadors.

Randolph wrote from Scotland : 'The news so passioneth my heart, that no grief I ever felt was like unto it'.

As for the Ambassador to France, Sir Nicholas Throckmorton, described, most justly, by Strype, as 'a busy intriguing person', he told the Marquis of Northampton, in a letter dated the 10th of October, that he wished 'he were either dead or hence that he might not hear the dishonourable reports that are made here of the Queen, and the great joy of the Princes here for the success they take it they are likely to have in England [i.e. winning the throne for the Queen of Scotland] not letting [omitting] to speak of the Queen and some others that which every hair on my head stareth at, and my ears

glow to hear'. He added that he was 'almost at his wit's end,
and knoweth not what to say. One laugheth at us, another
threateneth, another revileth the Queen. Some fail not to say
"What religion is this that a subject should kill his wife, and
the Prince not only bear withal, but marry with him?"
rehearsing the father and the grandfather [beheaded as traitors].
All the estimation the English had got is clean gone, and the
infamy passes the same so far, as his heart bleeds to think upon
the slanderous bruits that he hears. Which if they be not
slaked, or if they prove true, their reputation is gone for ever,
war follows and the utter subversion of the Queen and
country.'

Sir Nicholas implored Lord Northampton to help to slake
these rumours, and only prayed that God would not suffer
the Queen to be 'opprobrium et abjectio plebis'. Finally, 'with
weeping eyes' he took his leave.

But on the very same day we find Sir Nicholas writing
to Lord Robert, saying he has 'learnt of the death of my Lady,
your Lordship's late bedfellow', and condoling with him,
thanking him for his present of a nag, and adding that he
'would thank him even more if he (Lord Robert) would find
means for him to come home in post to hunt and hawk in
England, which it would be more meet for him to do than
to be Ambassador here, as things have fallen out!'

A man of the world!

A few months later, he told Cecil that though he liked
Lord Robert well enough, yet the love he bore the Queen and
her realm took more place in him than friendship. If the
marriage between the Queen and Lord Robert took place, he
did not know to what purpose any advice or counsel could
be given. 'I conjure you', he wrote, 'to do all in heaven to
hinder that marriage. For if it takes place, they will be
opprobrium et abjectio plebis. God and religion will be out of
estimation, contemned and neglected, and the country ruined
and made prey.

'Wherefore, with tears and sighs as one being already
almost confounded, I beseech you again set your wits and all

your help, to support the commonwealth, which lieth now in great hazard. . . .

'For your letters, they be as safe in my hands as in your own, and more safe than in any messengers'. Think it assuredly I am as jealous of your safety and well-doing as yourself, and so conceive of me.'

He added that if Cecil was minded to send him letters, his (Sir Nicholas') cousin, 'a faithful young man, can bear the letters, and he prayed Sir William to deal with his letters as Sir Nicholas did with those of Sir William, for "all is not gold that glitters"'.

At last, Sir Nicholas' lamentations and prognostications of disaster became of so dangerous a character — (there were spies everywhere) that the distracted Sir William found it necessary to tell him (on the 15th of January 1561) that he, Sir William, had always professed earnest friendship for Sir Nicholas, and therefore advised him not to meddle with the affairs of the Court otherwise than he may be well advised from hence (from London). 'What the Queen will determine God alone knows. But writings remain ; and coming on the other hand, servants or messengers may be reporting to whom they list,' and therefore it was impossible for Sir William to give the Ambassador a plain counsel as he would like to do. But in one word, he bade Sir Nicholas 'not to contend where victory cannot be had'.

Cecil seems not to have believed in Dudley's guilt, and to have visited him in a friendly manner (which makes his conversation with the Spanish Ambassador all the more mysterious). For, in the month in which his wife died, Lord Robert wrote him the following letter :

'Sir, I thank you for your being here, and the great friendship which you have shown towards me, I shall not forget. I am very loath to wish you here again, but I would be very glad to be with you there. I pray you let me hear from you what you think best for me to do. If you doubt, I pray you ask the question, for the sooner you can advise me thither the more I shall thank you. I am sorry so sudden a chance should breed in me so sudden a change ; for methinks I am here all this while as it were in a dream, and too far — too far from the place where I am bound to be ; when methinks also this long idle time cannot excuse me from the duty I have to discharge elsewhere. I pray you help him that seems to be at liberty of so great bondage. Forget me not though you see me not, and I will remember you and fail ye not ; and so wish you well to do. In haste this morning.

R. Dudley.

I beseech you, sir, forget not to offer up the humble sacrifice you promised me.'

What is the meaning of this ?

When the news of Amye's death reached the Queen, she sent for Lord Robert. No one was present at that meeting but the two principals, and nothing is known of what was said but that she ordered him to retire to his house till the Coroner's verdict was known. The Court went into mourning.

Was 'the great friendship which you have shown me' due to the very real kindness in Cecil's nature and that was given play whenever it did not interfere with his interests ? Or did it mean that the wise, the subtle, the wily Cecil knew that Lord Robert had been rendered safe. His marriage with the Queen could now easily be prevented. And the son of the beheaded Northumberland could no longer hold any thought of revenge. Northumberland was dead and best forgotten, and Cecil, by interceding with the Queen on that son's behalf, would hold him, for the future, in his hands.

Not only Amye Robsart lay dead, that September day, at the foot of a staircase in Cumnor Hall.

Six years after this time, when it was again hoped that the Queen might marry the Archduke Charles of Austria, the cautious Chief Secretary made out a paper weighing the qualifications of the Archduke as against those of Lord Robert, by then Earl of Leycester, to be husband to the Queen.

## TO BE CONSIDERED IN THE MARRIAGE

| Convenient person | Carolus | Earl of Leycester |
|---|---|---|
| In birth. | Nephew and brother of an Emperor. | Born son of a knight, his grandfather but a squire. |
| In degree. | An Archduke born. | An earl made. |
| In age. | Of — and never married. | Meet. |
| In beauty and constitution. | To be judged of. | Meet. |
| In wealth. | By report 3000 ducats by the year. | All of the Queen, and in debt. |
| In friendship. | The Emperor, the King of Spain, the Dukes of Saxony, Bavaria, Cleves, Florence, Ferrara and Mantua. | None but such as shall have of the Queen. |
| In education. | Amongst princes always. | In England. |
| In knowledge. | All qualities belonging to a prince — languages, wars, hunting, and riding. | Meet for a courtier. |
| In likelihood to have children. | His father, Ferdinando, hath therein been blessed with multitudes of children. His brother, Maximilian, hath plenty. His sisters of Bavaria, Cleves, Mantua, and Poland, have already many children. | 'Nuptiae steriles.' No brother had children, and yet their wives have — Duchess of Norfolk. Himself married, and no children. |
| In likelihood to love his wife. | His father, Ferdinando, ut supra. | Nuptiae carnales a laetitia incipiunt et in luctu terminantur. |
| In reputation. | Honoured of all men. | Hated of many. His wife's death.[2] |

As for Sir Nicholas Throckmorton, he died in Lord Leycester's house. Writing to Walsingham, two days after that death (on the 14th of February 1570) his host said : 'We have lost, on Monday, our good friend Sir Nicholas Throckmorton, who died at my house being there taken suddenly in great extremity on the Tuesday before. His lungs were perished. But a sudden cold he had taken was the cause of his speedy death. God hath his soul : and we his friends [have] great loss of his body.'

Years afterwards, a contemporary, Pennant, wrote of the great reluctance of persons who had offended Lord Leycester to accept his invitation to dinner — 'remembering Sir Nicholas Throckmorton who was said to be poisoned by a fig eaten at his table'.

### NOTES TO CHAPTER TWENTY

[1] Note of the Examination of John Appleyard in Cecil's hand. Hatfield.
[2] MSS. Notes in Cecil's hand. Hatfield.

# Chapter Twenty-one

BISHOP DE QUADRA, even for an Ambassador, was an unusually busy man. His visitors were innumerable, and of an exceedingly varied kind, having little in common excepting their desire to be unnoticed.

This being so, it was fortunate that Durham Place, where he lived, had a water-gate leading to the Thames, through which Irish chiefs, Catholics anxious to replace the government by one of their own religion, disaffected nobles, and even Ministers of State, were able to come and go unseen.

The Ambassador had, for instance, interesting talks with the great Irish chieftain, Shan O'Neil, who, after defeating the Queen's troops in Ireland, visited her Court, and whilst there, called, in an unobtrusive way, on the Spanish Ambassador.

'The Irish chiefs', he told his King, in July 1559, 'have communicated with me. They request you to receive them as your subjects. You have but to say the word, and the country is yours.'

That Durham Place was the centre of every conspiracy had long been known to Cecil. Every plot Cecil formed, a counterplot arose to circumvent it, and he knew that De Quadra was the counterplotter. But, although he realised that the Queen had, of late, become on much more confidential terms with the Bishop, the Chief Secretary did not know as yet to what degree. He was meditating what course to take, when the Bishop, one day, sent to him his confidential secretary, Borghese Venturino — a person who seems to have had in him a strong admixture of Machiavelli and Iago — with some message.

Once in Cecil's presence, actuated by — according to Cecil

— 'some unkindness' between the Bishop and himself, by — according to less innocent minds — Cecil's bribes, or, as de Quadra firmly believed, by the Devil — Borghese declared his willingness, indeed eagerness, to disclose to Cecil all he knew of the Bishop's proceedings ; of his incessant plots and non-stop mischief-making.

And what he knew was *everything* !

Nothing had remained unnoticed or unrecorded. He had ciphered all the Bishop's letters and had, unknown to that gentleman, kept accurate copies of every letter.

Borghese had lately accompanied a priest, Dr. Turner, to Flanders to try to get support for Lady Lennox's proposed attempts on the throne. . . . Dr. Turner had taken with him a list of the disaffected nobles and other Catholics, with details of what they proposed to do, should the King of Spain lend them his support.

Turner died in Flanders, leaving all his papers in the possession of Borghese — and the prudent man took copies of these before returning them to his employer. Amongst them was a letter in which the Ambassador strongly recommended the King of Spain to lend his aid to Lady Lennox and her son, for, if he did so, eight or ten of the nobles, he declared, would rise in their favour and the Queen would be overthrown.

The Ambassador had always advised a marriage between the Queen of Scots and Don Carlos, who could then expel Elizabeth from her kingdom, and become King of England as well as of Scotland.

Amongst the Bishop's more ordinary mischief-making was his reiterated statement that the Queen had always favoured the heretical party in Scotland (in other words the rebels), and had tried to induce the Queen of Scots to marry Lord Arran in order to 'facilitate her own marriage with Lord Robert'.

According to him, 'the ships departed to Guinea, though pretending to be trading vessels, are in reality intended to prey upon the Spanish fleet returning from the Indies'. The Queen, too, was very hostile to the King of Spain, and had expressed herself openly to that effect when speaking at Richmond Palace of the departure of the Spanish troops from Flanders. 'Let the negroes', she had said (referring, it was supposed, to the Spaniards' dark complexions), 'go and roast in the torrid zone, and when they are gone I shall have as many friends in Flanders as the King has.'

More was to come. The revelations were not yet complete. Cecil directed Borghese to return to Durham Place and continue his activities as a spy.

But unhappily Cecil was not the only person who employed spies. The Bishop did, also, and in Cecil's household, and these were quick in telling him of his secretary's treachery.

A few days later, one of the Ambassador's couriers, going with his despatches to Flanders, was seized by two highwaymen, who opened his portmanteau on the pretence that they were looking for gold he was smuggling out of England against the law. After searching the portmanteau thoroughly, the highwaymen *appeared* to put everything back in its place. But, unfortunately, in appearance only. The highwaymen in question were two high-spirited young gentlemen named Cobham, who had held up the courier in order to abstract all his despatches.

Cecil pretended to believe the story was 'a device' of the Ambassador's, when he complained. But he told the Ambassador to Spain, Sir Thomas Chaloner, that he thought it best to warn him ; for the episode, real or imaginary, might have put ideas into the Bishop's head, who on his part might try some such device on Chaloner's courier, coming to or from England.

But the story was true. The papers had been taken ; and the next that the Ambassador knew was that two of his friends were in the Tower.

Borghese would have to be murdered. That was evident to the Bishop. But on reflection he realised that the instigation of this act on the part of a Prince of the Church might be misunderstood in England. A fatal accident could be more easily — more tactfully — arranged abroad. He therefore ordered Borghese to go to Brussels. . . . Once there . . .

But Borghese, while the Bishop was thinking out his next move, fled from Durham Place and took refuge in Cecil's house, where he proceeded to tell everything he knew. And from that house he refused, with unaccountable obstinacy, to move. Nothing the Bishop could say or do had the slightest effect.

'I have done my best', the afflicted man told Cardinal Granvelle (the 8th of June 1562), 'to repair this disaster, but I have failed. The devil that has entered into my servant will not be exorcised. I have tried to induce him to leave the realm, I have entreated, bribed, threatened, promised, all to no purpose ; and to put him to death as he deserved would have been awkward. I would have consented to it myself, and for the nonce would have broken the rule of my habit ; but I should only have irritated them the more, and increased their suspicions.'

The situation was desperate.

He went to the Queen. After all, she was a woman of the world. She could understand, he said, that he had only refrained from having the man murdered in England because that would make a disturbance. Would Her Majesty be good enough to have him expelled from the country ?

Her Majesty seemed not to understand. Instead of having Borghese expelled, she had him arrested, to the Bishop's horror, and sent the latter a message saying that if he had any complaint to make, she was ready to hear it.

Arrested ! He was at large in Cecil's house, where the Bishop could not get at him, but Cecil could ; and his depositions were being taken down.

The Bishop asked for another audience with the Queen and was refused. But he was, according to the injured Borghese, 'still a persecutor'. For inspired, one supposes, by the example of the two young Cobhams, the Bishop succeeded in getting some of his own, extremely compromising letters stolen.

'The Ambassador', complained his secretary, 'has just played me a shrewd trick. Having left a trunk in Brussels which contained certain of my effects, I arranged with a Flemish carrier for its conveyance hither. The Bishop caused it to be intercepted, and has possessed himself of the writings it contained.' These were of great importance, 'consisting of autograph letters from the Bishop to the writer, then in Flanders, which might be considered as summaries of his correspondence from London with Flanders and Spain. There were also some concerning the concubines and children which the Bishop had in England, instructions about affairs which the writer managed for him, and vouchers for money expended for the Bishop in Flanders, which he fears he cannot now recover. The knavish carrier is said to have returned to Flanders, but it is probable that he is secreted at Durham Place. The writer craves Cecil's protection and assistance.'

The English nobles who were most incriminated by Borghese's revelations were the Earls of Northumberland and Westmorland, and Lord Montague. Lord Derby might also be implicated, but this was not certain, so a letter supposed to be written by the King of Spain and full of promises, was left, mysteriously, at his house. Lord Derby, believing it to be genuine, asked the Bishop for an explanation, and being warned, was able to save himself.

But Cecil's worries, in spite of his triumphs over the Ambassador, were acute. . . . There had been those advances, of which he now heard for the first time in their entirety, made to the King of Spain by the Queen and Lord Robert . . . those secret communications with the Ambassador : for instance, the visit from Sir Henry Sidney, Lord Robert's brother-in-law, in which he said that should the King of Spain further the project of the Queen's marriage with Lord Robert, the King would find Lord Robert 'as ready to obey him and do him service as one of his own vassals . . . especially he would be ready in restoring the religion, seeing clearly that it ought to be done, and that it was this which had separated England from His Majesty and forfeited his protection'.

The Queen would therefore be forced to act with caution. It was lucky that the extreme insolence with which the Bishop had invariably referred to her could be used against him.

When Borghese had finished his revelations, the Queen sent for the Bishop, and told him, coldly, that she had to complain of the language he had used about her to the King of Spain. . . .

'It is a pretty business to deal with this woman, who, I think, must have a hundred thousand devils in her body, in spite of her forever telling me. . . . "I yearn to be a nun and pass my days in prayer in a cell." . . . The spirit of this woman is such that I can believe anything of her. She is possessed by the devil, who is dragging her to his own place.' (30th May 1559.) . . . 'As for this woman, you must expect nothing from her. . . . If Your Majesty were to save her life a second time, she would be no more faithful to you than she is now. If she can spread the poison, and set Your Majesty's Low Countries on fire she will do it without remorse. . . .' (July 1559.)

Awkward ! . . . Then he remembered, with satisfaction, those secret communications. . . . No, there was not much that she could do.

The Ambassador, in answer to the Queen's reproof, told her that she had been pleased to listen to the tales of a treacherous secretary, and had therefore heard things that it was quite unnecessary for her to know. He considered it a bad precedent.

Lord William Howard and Dr. Wotton produced the Articles against the Bishop, and amongst the minor complaints were these : 'That you, the Ambassador, did send to the King of Spain a book by the heretic Doctor Ball in which the King of Spain and the Spanish nation were evil spoken of ; and that you did say that His Majesty might judge from it what was the disposition of the Queen of England towards him'.

*Answer :* 'It is true that I did send such a book. I had remonstrated with her till I was weary, of the perpetual books, plays, and songs which were written in the King's dishonour.

The Queen had promised me many times to stop them, and had not done so.'

.    .    .    .    .

'That you, the Ambassador, told the King of Spain that the Queen had privately married Lord Robert in the Earl of Pembroke's house.'

*Answer :* 'I wrote what I said to the Queen herself, that it was reported all over London that the marriage had taken place.  She betrayed neither surprise nor displeasure at my words.  She told me merely that not only the world outside the palace believed it, but that the same evening the ladies of her own bedchamber, when they saw her enter with Lord Robert, asked whether they were to kiss his hand as well as hers.  She told them that they were not to do so, and that they should not credit such stories.  Two or three days after, Lord Robert informed me that the Queen had promised to marry him, but that it could not be this present year.  She said herself to me, with an oath, that if she married an Englishman, it should be him.  Had I so pleased, I might have written all this to His Majesty ;  nor do I think I should have done wrong had I told him the world's belief she was married already.  I did not write it however, and sorry I am that I cannot write it with truth.' [1]

Cecil did not wish the Bishop to know the full extent of his secretary's betrayals, for fear that he might warn the nobles implicated.  And these it would be unwise to arrest.

So the matter was dropped.  But the Queen's confidential messages to the Bishop ceased.

.    .    .    .

Then, at the very beginning of January 1563, an Italian Calvinist in the train of the Vidame de Chartres happened to be passing Durham Place when an apparently unoccupied stranger, lolling against the door, suddenly drew a pistol and fired at him, missing him but wounding an Englishman behind.

EARL OF LEYCESTER

Chased by an infuriated crowd, the assailant dashed into the Bishop's house. The Bishop (to whom he was a stranger) realised that the man aimed at was a heretic, and ordered his servants to open the water-gate. The would-be murderer rushed down the steps and into a boat, but was caught at Gravesend, and, being tortured, confessed that the would-be murder was at the instigation of the Provost of Paris, who had bribed him to commit it.

The Bishop, this time, had gone too far. Having made himself an accessory after the fact, he was told he must give up the keys of his house. When his steward refused to do so, the Lord Mayor sent workmen to change the locks.

The Bishop sought an audience of the Queen. This was refused ; and he was told that he could not be allowed to remain at Durham Place, and Cecil added that all the trouble in the realm originated from there, and that if it had not been for the Queen's incessant watchfulness, he would have been murdered, long since, by the mob.

'I am not to remain in the house', the Ambassador told his King, 'because it has secret doors and entrances which we may use for mischief. They are afraid, and they have cause to be afraid. . . . A few days ago, the Lord Keeper [Bacon] said that neither the Crown nor religion were safe so long as I was in the realm. It is true enough, as Cecil says, that I may some day be torn to pieces by the populace. . . . Did they but dare, they would not leave a Catholic alive in the land. . . .

'London indeed is bad enough ; it is the worst place in the realm ; and it is likely — I do not say it in any fear — that if I reside within the walls of the city something may happen to me. The Council themselves tell me that if I am detected in any conspiracy my privilege as Ambassador shall not save me. They wish to goad me on to violence that they may have matter to lay before the Queen against me.' (10th January 1563.)

Two days afterwards, on the day of the Opening of Parliament, two sermons were preached — (it was the first

Convocation of the Church of England). One, at St. Paul's, was preached by Day, Provost of Eton, the other, at Westminster, by Dr. Nowell. 'The subject of both', says Froude, 'was the same : the propriety of killing the caged wolves [the Catholic Bishops in the Tower] with the least delay.'

But this Christian aspiration came to nothing.

As for Bishop de Quadra, all that happened was that the Queen wrote to his King [2] that 'she has occasion to doubt whether his Ambassador rightly reports her mind to him. Although she will not deny his zeal, he meddles with affairs that do not pertain to his office, and he has implicated himself with affairs tending to disturb the tranquillity of the realm. She has therefore ordered her Ambassador to request that he may be commanded to desist from these proceedings, or that he may be recalled home, and another sent in his place.'

His King was highly indignant at the treatment of him. He remained at his post, and although the house was watched night and day, all comers and goers were questioned, the water-gate shut, and sentinels posted at the lodge, the Bishop was allowed to live at Durham Place.

For a short while only. He was not much longer for the light of the sun.

NOTES TO CHAPTER TWENTY-ONE

[1] MS. Simancas. Froude, VII.
[2] 9th January. *Calendar of State Papers.*

# Chapter Twenty-two

PORTENTS of danger to France appeared in October 1559 in an anonymous pamphlet threatening the government ruled over by the Guise family.

There was a lull. Then, at the beginning of February 1560, the French Court received a more ominous warning of a conspiracy. But time passed, and still nothing happened.

The Court was at Amboise. Then, on the 2nd of March, as everything still seemed normal, the young Queen of France and Scotland and the Queen Mother decided to go to Tours.

On the following day, two messengers arrived : one from the Duke of Savoy, the other from Granvelle in Brussels, saying the plot was ripe. The royal family had three more days to live. On the 6th of March, the King of France, the two Queens, the royal children, the Duc de Guise, and the Cardinal de Lorraine were to be murdered. The leader of the plot was 'a great Prince'.

But the days passed, and they still lived. The King resumed the wild, mad hunting-parties in which he spent his days.

On the 15th the Prince de Condé arrived at Court, and was coldly received.

The Court was in a panic. 'I have never', wrote Throckmorton, the English Ambassador, 'seen people more terrified and more abandoned to their fears. They do not know their friends from their enemies, they give orders and counterorders, and suspect everyone they employ.'

It was at dawn on the 17th, when the Court was still sleeping, that a company of horsemen was seen approaching Amboise on the road from Blois. By the time the alarm had been given, these had already attacked the city gate. Eventually, however, they were routed, and made their escape. But a few prisoners remained, and these revealed that their orders came from the Prince de Condé, the leader of the Protestants. The cautious Duc de Guise ordered that this must be kept secret, for the Prince de Condé was of royal blood.

When it was known that another much larger army was massing, the Prince embarrassed the Duc de Guise considerably by insisting on taking part in the preparations for the siege.

By this time increasing numbers of prisoners were being brought in, and the rebels were tied together in sacks, and drowned in the Loire, were hanged, or were beheaded, their bodies being hung from the ramparts. Only thirty-one died on the first day, but the pace soon increased. On the 18th, the young Duc de Lorraine, who had been invited to join the King in his hunting-parties, galloped to Amboise with new prisoners, and as there was no room for them in the prisons, these had to be emptied by death.

On a single day, fifty-six died, one by one, by the axe, watched by spectators from the outlying countryside, in tiers of seats as in a Roman theatre, and by the King, his wife, his mother, his two little brothers and his sister, seated in a window, with the Cardinal of Lorraine towering above them and bending, sometimes, to whisper in their ears. The Duc de Guise, mounted on horseback, presided over the executions.

These continued. At the end of ten days, the reek of blood from the soaked earth seemed to have taken possession of all the air; the smell, the glare of blood was everywhere, and the young King's health was endangered by this. For Francis the Second was already ill; and the illness from which he suffered came from some unknown cause.

The year sank in a mist of blood. Through that mist, the shaping of the things to come could not be seen.

Then came a temporary quietness. The Furies were sleeping. But not for long.

On the 1st of March 1562, at Vassy, in France, the followers of the Queen of Scots' uncle, the Duc de Guise, set on and murdered a congregation of Huguenots. As a result, the following month saw the beginning of a new war — or the resumption of the old — between the French Catholics and Protestants. The English Ambassador to France, Throckmorton, seeing that the foreign Catholic powers would intervene on the side of their co-religionists, urged the Queen to come to the aid of the Prince de Condé, the leader of the Protestants. For, as the high-minded followers of both sects would be getting whatever they could as a reward for their services, why should not the Queen of England ? Condé might even restore to her Calais, give her Dieppe or Havre.

There was again a temporary lull, a tentative effort to make peace. Then, on the 12th of July, France broke into flames, every kind of atrocity was practised, and Elizabeth saw that there was nothing for England to do but to support the Prince de Condé. In early October, in accordance with her treaty with Condé, the English army, under the generalship of the Earl of Warwick, Lord Robert's brother, occupied Havre.

But on the 25th of March 1563, following the capture of Condé and the murder of the Duc de Guise, the civil war ended, and the whole of the French nation, with a really remarkable unanimity, considering how lately they were at war, turned on England.

The Prince de Condé, who had declared that he took up arms for the sake of freedom of conscience, and had chosen to assume that Elizabeth did so for the same reason (for of course Calais did not come into the question), wrote on the 8th of May that neither Admiral Coligny, his fellow leader, nor he had given Havre to the English. But that he, the Queen Regent, and the whole of the nobility of France would swear to renew in all formality the clause in the Treaty of Cambray promising to restore Calais to the English in 1567. That he would repay the money lent by the Queen and would admit the English to free trade and intercourse with the whole of France. England was, it seems, to receive little or no reward for her intervention (for Elizabeth regarded Calais as English property).

The Queen and her people were furious. . . . The garrison at Havre, who, when peace was signed, were about to leave the city, were enthusiastic at the thought of reopening the war ; and when, a few days later, they knew that they were about to be besieged, they swore that 'Lord Warwick and all his people would spend the last drops of their blood before the French should fasten a foot in the town'.

Then came the discovery of a paper hidden in the clothes of a peasant carrying chickens into the town. . . . Held to the fire, the paper revealed a conspiracy to murder Lord Warwick and admit the French army. The whole of the French population was promptly turned out of the town, and the garrison prepared for a siege by the army their Queen's money had helped to raise.

'The false Prince de Condé', said the Queen, was 'a treacherous inconstant perjured villain.'[1]

She sent for his envoy, de Briquemaut. 'Her rights to Calais', she said, 'being so notorious, she required neither hostages nor satisfaction ; she would have Calais delivered to her ; she would have her money repaid ; and she would not relinquish Havre until both Calais and money were in her hands.'

In that case, de Briquemaut said as he left her presence, the Queen must prepare for war.

Recruits for the garrison were raised among the gentlemen of England and the prisoners in Newgate waiting for execution. England commanded the sea, and it was thought that the whole of the force of France could be defied.

But on the 7th of June 1563, an enemy more terrible than France made its first appearance — an enemy moving slowly at first, secretly, and almost in disguise. Nine men in the garrison, Warwick wrote to Cecil, had died of a strange disease.

.     .     .     .     .

In England the year 1560 had been one of strange portents. There was such incessant rain that it might have been asked : 'How many Oceans of Water would be necessary to compose this great Ocean, rowling in the air without bounds or

banks ?' and answered : 'Some great violence has been
offered to Nature, such as we suppose to have been in the
General Deluge when the frame of the Earth was broken'.[2]

A child was born, with a ' great collar of flesh and skin
growing like to a ruff of a shirt and neckerchief, coming up
above the ears, plaiting and folding. . .'.[3]

The rain had faded with the fading of the last year, and
now it seemed as if the weather had been set on fire.

In the blood-red heat of Havre, bounded by a sea that
seemed of the element of fire, not water, in the filthy narrow
streets that seemed cut by a knife between the tall, black,
rocking houses, — here, where seven thousand men existed
with no water (owing to the drought), with nothing to drink
in the dark stinking rooms but tepid wine and cider, with
neither fresh meat nor vegetables, the progress of the enemy
soon quickened. . . . By the 27th of June, sixty men a day
fell to it, by the 29th, the deaths had been five hundred. By
the end of the month only three thousand out of the five
thousand men of the garrison were living. Those other two
thousand lay on the shore of the sea of fire — for there was
none to bury them.

The name of that strange disease was now known. It
was the Plague. . . .

On the 26th of June, the Prince de Condé had written to
the Queen : 'To prevent war, the King and Queen, the
Princes of the Blood, the Lords of the Council, the whole
Parliament of Paris would renew the obligation to restore
Calais at the eight years' end. It was an offer which the Queen
of England could accept without stain upon her honour, and
by agreeing to it she would prove that she had engaged in
her quarrel with a chief eye to the glory of God and the
maintenance of truth.'[4]

But the Queen would have none of it. She would send
another army to replace the army of the dead.

The reinforcements came. . . . In a few days or even
hours they too were gone. Fifteen hundred men were left
by the 11th of July. Another ten days, Warwick wrote, and

three hundred men would be left. . . . Anything, anyone available was sent, to add to the horror. Then came storms to isolate the city : and soon would come famine.

Sir Francis Knollys, in command at Portsmouth, told the Council they must empower Warwick, immediately, to make what terms he could. . . .

The French general assault had been planned for the morning of the 27th of July. And the night before, those who remained of the garrison knew they, too, would be dead before another night. Then came the Queen's letter . . . the surrender of the city . . . the return of those few that lived to England.

A few only. . . . But they cast a long shadow. . . .

The Queen had wished to risk infection from the Plague by going to thank her returned soldiers for their incomparable bravery, but this could not be allowed : her life was too precious to England. In a proclamation signed by her own hand she told the country that these men were England's sacred charge. Their every want must be alleviated. . . . Each person in authority, civil or religious, must come to the aid of any of these who were in need 'lest God punish them for their unmercifulness'. Nor must any blame them for their surrender of the city ; 'they would have withstood the French to the utmost of their lives ; but it was thought the part of Christian wisdom not to tempt the Almighty, to contend with the inevitable mortal enemy of the Plague'.

But the shadow cast by those who had returned, lengthened.

'Art thou all spotted over ! They are God's rich Ermines, to Inroabe thee like a King, and to set a Crowne of Glory on thy head.'

Those rich ermines were to clothe many.

In London, the deaths from the Plague began by being two hundred a week . . . then in August, seven hundred . . . a thousand . . . in the last week of that month, two thousand . . .

The doctors were powerless. . . . 'Galen', wrote Dekker

of a later Plague (that of 1603),[5] 'could do no more good than Sir Giles Goosecap . . . [they] were at their wits' end, or rather, I think, at the world's end, for not one of them durst peepe abroad ; or if any of them did take it upon him to play the venturous Knight, the Plague put him on his nonplus ; in such strange and such changeable shapes did this chameleon-like sickness appear.'

The Queen and the Court retired to Windsor.

At first, a few swashbucklers remained, — such as 'Signor Ginglespur . . . the first gallent I met in Powles * . . . (there) deceast about three hundred that daye. . . . What dare you venture, Sig [Signor] at the latter end of a Fraye now ? I meane not at a Fraye with swordes and Bucklers, but with sores and carbunckles : I protest you are a strong Mettalde Gentleman, because do you not feare the dangerous Feather-beds of London, nor to be tost in a perilous Blancket, or to lie in the fellowes of those sheetes that two dead Bodies were wrapt in some three months before.'

Then the streets became full of the echoing sound of flying hooves, as all those who could, fled from the city. The lodging-houses outside London were crowded. 'Six houres sleepe could not be bought under five shillings' [then a large sum] ; 'And (having learned the tricks of London Sextons), there they laid foure or five in a bed, as here these other Knaves of Spades thrust nine and ten into one grave. . . .'

Soon the city was almost deserted. 'There was never a Gilt Spur to be seene all the Strand over, never a Feather wagging in all Fleet Street. . . .' And no sound, excepting that of the bells 'ringing all about London as if the Coronation day had beene halfe a yeare long'.

And sometimes a long black shadow would be thrown across the otherwise empty street ; but who could tell if it was a shadow or a man, until one saw that it was a being 'miching and muffled up and downe with Rue and Worme-wood stuft into [his] eares and nosthrils, like (a) Boreshead stufft with branches of Rosemary. . .'? For the smell of

---

* St. Paul's was the meeting-place of beggars and the homeless.

rosemary was believed to be a defence against the Plague. And some profited by Death. . . . 'Hearbe-wives and Gardeners, that never prayed before, unlesse it were for raine or faire weather, were now day and nighte uppon their maribones, that God would blesse the labours of these molecatchers [diggers of graves]' because 'the price of flowers, hearbes and garlands, rose wonderfully, in so much that Rosemary which had wont to be solde for 12 pence an Armefull, went now for sixe shillings a handfull.'

Not only men, but dogs were stricken, and 'fell thicker than acorns'.

Once and again would come the hollow sound of hooves, in the empty city, and by would come 'a fearefull pitiful Coach . . . all hung with Rue from the toe to the Boote, to keep the leather and the nayles from infection ; the very Nosthrilles of the Coach-horses were stopt with herb-grace, that I pittied the poore Beasts being almost windless, and having then more Grace in their Noses than their Maister had in all his bosome, and thus they ran . . . just in the middle of the street, with such a violent trample as if the Divell had been Coachman'.

Otherwise silence . . . excepting for those bells that rang . . . the bells of Death, or the bells that told the hour in Bedlam.  But who rang them, since the city was deserted ?

On the 26th of August, in the silence of the city, a brave man, Luis de Paz, went to a man who lay dying of the Plague in Durham Place.  'He knew me', wrote his fellow Spaniard, 'and answered bravely when I spoke to him.  He was grieved to end his services at a moment when he hoped to be of use. "No puedo más", he said.  "I can do no more." '

Those were the last words of Alvarez de Quadra, Bishop of Aquila, who for all his faults had, as Froude said, 'the courage of an Ignatius and a Cortez' . . . who was 'free from selfish and ignoble desires, and loyal with an absolute fealty to his creed and his King. . .'.

His pay as Ambassador had been pitifully small.  When he died, his debts were so great to tradesmen and to his household (some of whom had received no money for years) that for more than eighteen months the body of this man who had died of the Plague was not taken to his own country for burial, as the executors feared that, in the passage from England, it would be seized, terrible as it was, by his creditors.

---

### NOTES TO CHAPTER TWENTY-TWO

1 Burnet, *The History of the Earth.*
2 Neale., *op. cit.*
3 De Quadra to Philip, 9th May 1563.
4 Forbes II. Froude, *op. cit.*, VII, 513.
5 The other quotations in this chapter are from Dekker's Plague Pamphlets.

# Chapter Twenty-three

FOR some time before the events described in the previous chapter, that unhappy child Francis the Second, King of France (he was only sixteen at the time of his death in 1560), had been in a strange condition. He had long suffered great pain from an abscess in the ear. His face was discoloured by vermilion patches that seemed attempting some ghastly, despairing, mimicry of health. Rumours flew over the countryside. Was it possible, the whispers asked, that he had leprosy — due to his mysterious conception by a sterile mother, brought about by some violence offered to nature? Women gathered up their children and fled at his approach as he galloped past, spurring on his horse.

He had worn out his body by ceaseless hunting, — as if, by this endless pursuit of living creatures, he could, at the same time, escape from something. From what? From his heredity? From the memory of that scene in the Tournament in which his father was struck down — (that scene that had been prophesied so long before) — from his father's last whispered words?

He became stranger every day. Now, in his wild pursuit of living creatures, as if, by their deaths, the lives that he had taken from them might ensure his — he would suddenly turn in his tracks, and fly with an equal frenzy of speed in the opposite direction.

For what purpose? Did he know that all pursuit and all flight were in vain, and that he must now return to meet his fate? Or was there no longer any purpose in his haunted mind?

At eleven o'clock at night, on the 5th of December 1560,

'lo ! The potent hand of God', wrote Knox, 'sent unto us a most wonderful and most joyful deliverance ! : For unhappy Francis, husband to our Sovereign, suddenly perisheth of a rotten ear . . . the death of that child was not only the cause of joy to us in Scotland, but also were the faithful in France delivered, as it were, from the present death. . . .

'As the said King sat at Mass, he was suddenly stricken with an apposthume in that deaf ear that would never hear the truth of God.' And thus would 'those cruel and conjured enemies of God and all godliness', the Guise family, be deprived of putting their 'bloody counsel in execution' against the Protestants.

For a new persecution was being planned.

After the King's death, the young Duc de Lorraine remembered that a court lady had told him of a strange dream she had had on the night before King Henri's death in the lists. In that dream she had seen him fall before the lance, and she had seen a splinter from the lance of Montgomery strike the Dauphin in the ear.

Not only the virtuous rejoiced at his death. According to Sir James Melville, the Scottish Ambassador, 'The Queen Mother was blithe of the death of King Francis her son, because she had no guiding of him, but only the Duke of Guise and the Cardinal his brother. . . . And for their sake she had a great misliking of our Queen.' Étienne Pasquier, one of Catherine de' Medici's most malevolent haters, declared that the King's mother had bribed his barber to put some poison in his ear — this report being fostered by her almost undisguised joy at his death.

It was now time for Mary to make her first departure from the light of the sun. In her white dress of mourning, she, veiled with tears, looked like a white-flowering thorn tree full of light and of dew. One could not see the thorns for the flowers.

Before the preparations for her journey to Scotland, she had sent the French Ambassador to ask the Queen of England for a safe-conduct, either by sea, or, should she be in danger or ill, to land in England and so travel to her own country.

Remembering her assumption of the royal arms and title of Queen of England, and the fact that Mary had not signed a treaty, Elizabeth, in the presence of the whole Court, answered, in a loud voice, and with a look of great anger, 'The Queen of Scotland should ask no favours till she had ratified the treaty of Edinburgh'.

When this answer was repeated to the eighteen-year-old Queen of Scotland, she sent for the English Ambassador, Sir Nicholas Throckmorton. Anxious to show the superiority of her queenly manners over those of her cousin, she signalled to the courtiers to withdraw, and said : 'My lord Ambassador, as I know not how far I may be transported by passion, I like not to have so many witnesses of mine infirmity, as the Queen your mistress had, when she talked, not long since, with Monsieur d'Oysell. There is nothing that doth more grieve me than that I did so forget myself, as to have asked her a favour, which I could well have done without. I came here in defiance of the attempts made by her brother Edward to prevent me [ships had been sent by England to try to intercept her, on her journey to France — since it had been intended by Henry the Eighth that England and Scotland should be united by the marriage of Mary with his son], and by the grace of God, I will return without her leave. It is well known that I have friends and allies who have power to assist me, but I chose rather to be indebted to her friendship. If she choose, she may have me for a loving kinswoman and useful neighbour, for I am not going to practise against her with her subjects as she has done with mine ; yet I know there be in her realm those that like not of the present state of things. The Queen says I am young, and lack experience : I confess I am younger than she is, yet I know how to carry myself lovingly and justly with my friends, and not to cast any word against her, which may be unworthy of a Queen and a kinswoman ; and, by her permission, I am as much a Queen as herself, and carry my courage as high as she knows how to do. She hath heretofore assisted my subjects against me ; and now that I

am a widow, it may be thought strange that she would hinder
me in returning to my own country.'

She added that her husband had not wished her to sign
the Treaty of Edinburgh, and that during his lifetime she must
follow his wishes ; now, her uncles said that, being peers of
France, they could not advise her in the matter : she must
consult her Council.

Throckmorton reminded her that she and her husband
had assumed the title of King and Queen of England.  She
looked surprised.  'My late lord and father, King Henri, and
the King, my late lord and husband, would have it so.  I was
then under their commandment, as you know, and since their
death I have neither borne the arms, nor used the style of
England.' [1]

On that long, tedious, and infinitely dangerous journey,
beginning at St. Germain-en-Laye on the 25th of July 1561,
Mary was accompanied by two of her uncles, six score French
nobles (among them, Brantôme), a doctor of theology, two
doctors of medicine, a young man named Chastelard, her four
Maries (her maids of honour), and the other women of her
Court.

Ronsard wrote of this beautiful, doomed creature's departure from France : '. . . As a lovely mead despoiled of its
flowers . . . thus will France grieve, bereft of her ornament,
losing that royalty which was her flower, her colour, her
beauty. . . . Ha !  Scotland !  I would that thou mightest
wander like Delos on the face of the sea, or sink to the pro-
foundest depths, so that the sails of the bright Queen, vainly
stirring to seek her realm, might turn and bear her back to her
fair Duchy of Lorraine.'

Leaving that lovely mead and the warmth of the sun,
'unlike Dido', said one writer, 'who looked evermore towards the sea — her eyes were fixed upon the land that was
receding from her sight for ever.  Before she retired, she
requested the pilot that in the event of France being still
visible, as soon as it should be light, to direct her ladies to
awaken her, no matter how early it might be.'

One of her first thoughts was for the wretched galley slaves, and she gave orders to the overseers that they were not to be lashed while she was on her journey. 'For', said Brantôme, 'she had an extreme compassion for those unfortunates, an innate horror of cruelty, and a heart that felt for all suffering.'

The English Fleet were in readiness to intercept her. 'Off Flamborough Head [according to Rupert Gore-Brown in *Lord Bothwell*] two great galleys [the Queen of Scotland's galley and its escort] loomed out of the mist, within a furlong of the pier. The larger was all white, the second was flying a blue pennant with the arms of France and a white flag that glistened like silver at the stem. Both vessels cast anchor, and put out two men stripped to swim, and boats to take soundings. The mist lifted and revealed thirty-two "tall ships" farther out to sea and on the horizon twenty more.

'Mist descended to prevent an engagement. . . . The galleys that bore the Queen and her train anchored at Leith at nine in the morning of the 19th of August.'

The mist which had saved the Queen of Scotland changed to a thick fog, and this, according to John Knox, was sent as a warning to Scotland of the wrath to come should the Scots put up with their Queen's conduct.

'The very face of heaven at the time of her arrival', wrote the Reformer, 'did mournfully speak what comfort was brought into the country with her — to wit, sorrow, dolour, darkness, and all impiety ; for, in the memory of man, that day of the year was never seen a more dolorous face of the heaven than was at her arrival, which two days after did so continue; for, beside the surface wet, and corruption of the air, the mist was so thick and dark that scarce might any man espy another the length of two pair of buttes ; — the sun was not seen to shine two days before, nor two days after. That forewarning God gave unto us, but alas, the most part were blind.'

What evil had been brought into their midst in the shape of a laughing, gay, beautiful creature not yet nineteen years old !

MARY QUEEN OF SCOTS AGED SIXTEEN

In the last two years the Reformer had been by no means inactive. Publicly, in a sermon delivered at St. Giles, he had thanked God that the Queen's mother, Mary of Guise, was dead. He had prayed that his Queen might die before she returned to her kingdom. But here she was, and he must do his utmost to thwart her in every way, backed up in his opinion of her by the behaviour of the weather.

## NOTE TO CHAPTER TWENTY-THREE

[1] Throckmorton's letter to Elizabeth in cipher.

# Chapter Twenty-four

BOTH heaven and earth seemed resolved to remind the recently returned Queen of Scotland of her bereavement. Enormous black mourning wreaths and trains of weeping cloud descended to join the black mists, the impenetrable fogs in which, according to John Knox, her coming had involved the realm.

Every morning, in her room shrouded from these, and lit by candles, she, sitting up in her great bed of 'fresit [frosted] cloth of gold, with draughts of red silk in figures of gennets and personages and branches of holine [holly] — the hangings fringed with thread-of-gold and cramosy silk'[1] — eating a boiled egg (as she was to do in a room hung with black the morning after her second husband's murder), was told of the continued impenetrable mourning of the heavens.

Sitting patiently at Council, sewing — (a wedding-dress or a shroud?) for a little work-table of sandalwood with her work-basket upon it was always placed near her chair of state, says Agnes Strickland — or listening to the chatter of her four Maries and of her fool La Jardinière (who was rigorously chaperoned by her governess as was Mary by Madame de Briante or de Brêne), each day seemed to her full of new troubles, new bewilderments.

There was little movement in Edinburgh Castle, excepting when the Court gathered for dinner, and then there would be a chattering as of starlings. The Queen's governess dined at a table with the four Maries, and two other ladies — each of whom had a manservant (who dined with an officer of the household called 'The Usher of the Ladies', and with an embroiderer). The ladies' maids dined with La Jardinière the fool, her governess, the wife of William de Vienne (one of the Queen's butlers), and Annibal, one of her pages.

The Queen's musicians dined with the valets de chambre and René the perfumer.

It was some time after the landing in Scotland that the French musicians were joined at table by a Piedmontese named David Riccio — black-visaged, and twisted of body.

.        .        .        .        .

The Queen was subjected to the constant reproofs of John Knox, in whose eyes the nineteen-year-old girl who had returned to be the bane of Scotland could do nothing right. She insisted on practising her religion, was at the same time incurably addicted to 'joyosity', enjoyed 'fiddling and fling-ing' (in other words music and dancing) and could not be prevented from 'skipping' — 'an occupation not very comely for honest women'.

'I would be glad to be deceived,' he told Cecil, 'but I fear I shall not ; in communication with her, I espied such craft as I have not found in any age.'

In short, as the English Ambassador, Randolph, told Cecil, the Reformer was 'as full of mistrust of her as if he were of God's privy council and knew how He had determined of her from the beginning, or that he knew the secrets of her heart so well, that neither she did or could have for ever one good thought of God or of the true religion'.

He was tireless in denouncing her from the pulpit and to her face. Usually she endured the tirades with extraordinary patience. (Undoubtedly a very great man, he had, unfortu-nately, little or no tolerance for any point of view but his own.)

On one occasion (in 1563), when he had preached a sermon publicly denouncing the possibility of the Queen contracting a foreign marriage, she sent for the Reformer and was reduced by him to 'owling'. Crying out that 'never was Prince so handled as she was', she declared, 'I have borne with you in all your rigorous manner of speaking, both against myself and against my uncles ; yea, I have sought your favour by all possible means. I offered unto you presence and audience whensoever it pleased you to admonish me, and yet I cannot be quit of you. I vow to God, I shall be revenged.'

'And with these words,' wrote Knox, 'scarcely could Marnock, her secret chamber boy, get napkins to hold her eyes dry for the tears', and 'with tears and the owling she could say no more'.

The patient man endured the 'owling' for some time. Then, when he was able to make himself heard, he declared to her that his 'vocation and conscience demand plainness of speech' — and warned her against taking an 'unfaithful husband' — (one who was not of Knox's faith), adding that should the nobility allow this, 'they renounce Christ and betray the realm'.

The Queen was seized again with a violent fit of 'owling'. The Reformer again bore this in silence, then said : 'Madam, in God's presence I speak ; I never delighted in the weeping of any of God's creatures ; yea, I can scarcely abide the tears of my own boys whom my own hand corrects ; but seeing I have but spoken the truth as my vocation craves of me, I must sustain your Majesty's tears rather than hurt my conscience'.

Soon after her arrival in Scotland, after she had been subjected to a long harangue, the Queen was silent for an age, standing, the Reformer declared, 'as if amazed'. When, at last, she was able to speak, she said, 'Well then, I perceive that my subjects shall obey you, and shall do what they will, and not what I command ; and so must I be subject to them, and not they to me'. 'Nay,' he said, 'let Prince and subject both obey God. Kings should be foster fathers of the Kirk and Queens its nursing mothers.' 'You are not the Kirk that I will nurse', she said. 'I will defend the Kirk of Rome, for that I think is the Kirk of God.' 'Your will, Madam,' he returned, with the 'sound northern courtesy' so much admired by Froude, 'is no reason, neither does your thought make the Roman harlot the spouse of Jesus Christ.'

She tried to please him in small ways.

The morning after one of his exhortations, 'Whether it was the night's sleep or a deep dissimulation locked in her breast, that made her to forget her former anger, wise men may doubt.

'In any case, she did not speak of it, but said merely that she had been offered a ring' (a little ring with a pointed diamond in it, which the sinister giver declared would keep the Queen from poison) by Lord Ruthven, 'whom I cannot love,' she said, 'for I know him to use enchantment, and yet is he made one of my Privy Council.' She spoke then of her half-sister Lady Argyll 'who was not as circumspect in all things as she would wish her to be. Nor did her husband always treat her godly.' It was worse, she said, than the Reformer knew, and she begged him to 'put them at unity'. (He wrote Lord Argyll a letter of remonstrance that was both wise and kindly.) But still the Queen could do nothing right, and according to the Reformer it was her fault that a grievous famine arose.

The gloom by which the Queen was surrounded continued. The priests of her religion were in constant danger of death from the lords of the Congregation. For the virtuous Scottish Protestants were determined to 'renounce the congregation of Satan'. In pursuance of this high ideal, Erskine of Dun had murdered the priest in the bell-tower of Montrose. His father paid his blood price.

After a private Mass had been celebrated in the Queen's chapel, several 'Men of God' as Knox called them, the Master of Lindsay among them, gathered outside the chapel door, yelling that 'the idolatrous priest should die the death'. But this Christian aspiration was foiled by the Queen's half-brother, Lord James Stuart — afterwards Earl of Moray — a staunch Protestant. He held the door of the chapel — he was a man of extreme bravery — while Lord Robert and Lord John Stuart guarded the priest on his way to his chamber. 'And so the godly departed with great grief of heart', deprived of their prey.

Although Mary was Queen, it was that most remarkable man, James Stuart, her elder half-brother, who was in all but name ruler of Scotland.

At first, until her duplicity, the constant rumours (untrue, at first) that she was involved in plots to bring about his death, changed him towards her, he seems to have loved her. In any case he did his utmost to protect her — *at first*. But soon he was to believe that heart of diamond held a black light, dark and fathomless depths, within it. And soon, not only was he to change towards her, but her affection for him was to change to a murderous hatred.

It was his misfortune and Scotland's that he was not King.

He was the illegitimate son of James the Fifth by Margaret Erskine, sister of John, sixth Lord Erskine. His mother had been taken by the King from her husband, to whom she had been married against her will. James's petition to the Church that she should be divorced, in order that he might marry her, was refused. She bore him several children.

In James (a strange character not given to much outward expression), great strength of will, great courage, were allied to an equally great acquisitiveness.

Lang said of him, 'History sees him, as, in Lethington's phrase, "looking through his fingers" — looking at Riccio's and at Darnley's murders'. Those fingers hide the face.

'At the hypocrisies and falsehoods of his party, deeds of treachery and blood, Moray looked through his fingers.'

He was sixteen when he fought at the Battle of Pinkey Cleugh. Three years later, although his royal father had made him Prior of St. Andrews, he entered into a contract of marriage with Christian Stuart, the young girl who was heiress to the Master of Buchan, killed in that battle, and consequently to the Earl of Buchan, her grandfather, whose lands were mortgaged.

Lord James bought the rights of redemption from the Queen Regent. The old Earl died. The long engagement to Christian languished, then died. . . . But the lady's property remained with Lord James, and when his brother Lord

John (seemingly without consulting him) married the deserted lady, Lord James complained passionately to his mother about this marriage to 'that innocent', and swore that whoever tried to wrest from him the lady's property would have to pass over his dead body.

.          .          .          .          .

On the 22nd of July 1562, Sir Henry Sidney told the Queen of Scotland that the meeting with his Queen that had been arranged could not take place for a year. She therefore planned that 'terrible journey to the North' (as Randolph called it in a letter to Cecil), and started on this about the 10th of August.

The reasons for the journey are mysterious, but it is certain that among those reasons was the fact that, as Randolph told Cecil, on the 18th of September, 'She has just cause for misliking the Earl of Huntly, of long time [he was a northern noble of the highest power] whose extortions have been so great, and other manifest tokens of disobedience such, that it was no longer to be borne.

'The first occasion was this : the Laird of Findlatter [Sir John Gordon, Lord Huntly's son, who had committed murder] being commanded to ward in Edinburgh, broke prison ; and being afterwards summoned to the assize at Aberdeen, disobeyed also a new command from the Queen to enter himself prisoner in Stirling Castle. The Queen, thinking this to be done by the advice of his father, refused to come to his house, she being looked for and provided for. He, inadvisedly, conceiving the worst, took the worst way, and supported his sons to manifest rebellion. At her arrival at Inverness on the 9th, she proposed to lodge in the Castle, which belongs to her, and the keeping only to the Earl of Huntly . . . but was refused entrance and forced to lodge in the town. That night the castle being summoned, answer was given that without Lord Gordon's command it should not be delivered.'

The Queen was 'of the blood of the Lion', and this conduct was not to be borne.

'Next day the country assembled to the assistance of the Queen. The Gordons . . . finding themselves not so well served by their friends [who had above 500 men] as they looked for, rendered up the Castle, not being twelve or fourteen able persons . . . the Captain was hanged, and his head set over the Castle.'

'The Earl of Huntly keeping his house', Randolph told Cecil ten days after his previous letter, 'would have it thought that his disobedience came through the evil behaviour of his sons.' And Lady Huntly (reputed by the Protestants to be a witch) was fervent in expressing her and her husband's loyalty to the Queen.

But 'when he [Huntly] understood that the Queen had caused the captain of the Castle of Inverness to be hanged, and committed the others to prison, he thought there was no other way with him but to execute his former determination, or to be utterly undone'. (Randolph to Cecil : 24th September.)

On the 28th of October (Randolph to Cecil, 2nd November), 'he, marching on Aberdeen, was surrounded by the Earls of Moray [Lord James Stuart] Athol, Morton, and 2000 others, so that after some defence he yielded himself up, as did John Gordon and another son, Adam, seventeen years of age. . . . The Earl, after he was taken, without either blow or strike, being set on horseback before him that was his taker, suddenly falleth from his horse stark dead, without word that he ever spake, after that he was upon horseback.'

. . . . .

The dead body of the Earl of Huntly was brought to Aberdeen, where it was to be decided what should be done with it — whether it should immediately suffer a second death — that of a traitor — and be beheaded, disembowelled, mutilated . . . or whether it should be kept for trial before Parliament. The latter was decided on.

The dead body was tried, with its living co-traitor, Sutherland, in Parliament. The Queen, in royal robes, sat in state.

The description of the trial is given in the Rutland MSS. of May the 28th.

The coffin was set upright, as if the dead man, in his grey, steel-cold Knight's armour of Death, stood upon his feet, to face his judgment — 'with his arms fast pinned'.

'His accusation being read, his proctor answering for him as if he, himself, had been alive, the inquest was impannelled. The verdict was given that he was found guilty; and judgment given thereupon as by the law accustomed.

'Immediately hereupon the good black cloth that hung over the coffin was taken away, and in the place a worse hanged on, the [coat of] arms torn in pieces in sight of the people, and likewise struck out of the herald's book.'

His son, John Gordon, was to suffer death. He had become Laird of Findlatter owing to the somewhat unfilial behaviour of the original heir to the Lairdship.

'Touching the Laird of Findlatter', Randolph told Cecil, 'there is a strange story. If your honour call it to remembrance, there was one Findlatter, Master of the Household to the Queen's mother, that had commission many times to confer with your honour and the rest of the commissioners on your being at Edinburgh. This Findlatter was disinherited by his father, and his land given to John Gordon, second son to the Earl of Huntly. Two principal causes there were that moved Findlatter's father thus to do : the one that he solicited his father's wife, being his mother-in-law, to dishonesty [adultery] not only with himself but with another man ; the other, which is marvellous strange, that he took purpose with certain as well-conditioned as himself to take his father and put him into a dark house, and there to keep him waking until such time as he became stark mad. And that being done, he thought to enter himself in possession of the house and lands.

'This being done, and sure token given unto his father that this was true, he, having no other issue, by persuasion of his wife (who was a Gordon) gave the whole land unto John Gordon, who after the death of the said Findlatter married her, and so had right unto the whole living. To see how God

hath plagued the iniquity of this same woman — in one month
after his marriage, John Gordon casteth his fantasy unto another, and because he would not depart from the land which
was hers for her lifetime, he locked her up in a close chamber
where she remaineth.'  (30th September 1562.)

The Queen was forced by her brother to witness John
Gordon's execution from her window. . . . As he was about
to place his head upon the block, Gordon raised it, and looked
up at the Queen.  The headsman, nervous, made false stroke
after stroke ;  rivers of blood streamed from the neck of the
wretched man.  The Queen, always merciful, hated cruelty,
gave a piercing shriek and fainted.  After she had been carried
away, the headsman recovered his nerve, and severed the head
from the shoulders.

Why had James Stuart forced his sister to witness that
appalling spectacle ?  To answer this question, we must
examine the various theories about the reason for which the
Queen's journey to the North was arranged.

The journey may have been planned — according to a
tentative suggestion by David Hay Fleming [2] — 'by Lord
James for his own aggrandisement'.  'According to Chalmers,
Lord James — anxious to secure the Earldom of Moray —
saw that a handle might be made of Sir John Gordon's escape
from prison ;  and therefore persuaded Mary to go to the
North, where, "being egregiously imposed upon by a thousand of his fictions and falsehoods", the Queen was made at
once the victim of his ambition and the instrument of his
murders.' [3]  Hosack holds Lord James was in no way responsible for the rebellion of the Gordons'.[4]  Or else the journey
was 'intended by Mary for (his) Lord James's destruction [for
the iron hand of her brother already weighed heavily upon
her, however affectionately laid upon her shoulder] as Knox
suspected ;  or undertaken for her deliverance from his power
and for her marriage to Sir John Gordon'.

Sir John had already, as we know, a wife, although she
was hidden in 'a close chamber'.  It is *possible* that, wife or no
wife, a fresh marriage was planned for him ;  but I think it

unlikely.   Yet the Queen told Randolph 'how detestable a part Huntly thought to have used against her ;  as to have married her where he would'.[5]   In any case, that journey had resulted, says Hay Fleming, 'in the disgrace, defeat, and death, of the virtual ruler of the north and the entire ruin, for the time being, of his house'.

.         .         .         .         .

The young girl, with her 'fiddling and flinging', continued, like the Princess in Grimm's fairy tale, to dance her slippers away every night until they vanished like the starlight.

NOTES TO CHAPTER TWENTY-FOUR

[1] *Royal Wardrobe Book*, ed. T. Thomas.
[2] *Mary Queen of Scots.*
[3] *Life of Mary.*   1818.
[4] *Mary and her Accusers.*
[5] *Foreign Calendar.* Elizabeth, V, 421.

# Chapter Twenty-five

'UPON the 20th day of January 1563,[1] there fell [in Scotland] wet in great abundance, which in the falling freezed so vehemently that the earth was but a sheet of ice. The fowls both great and small freezed and might not fly : many died, and some were taken and laid beside the fire, that their feathers might resolve. And in that same month the sea stood still ; as was clearly observed, and neither ebbed nor flowed the space of twenty-four hours. In the month of February, the 15th and 18th days thereof, was seen in the firmament battles arrayed, spears and other weapons, and, as it had been the joining of two armies.' (Presumably, said the editor, the Northern Lights.) 'But the Queen and Court made merry. There was banquetting upon banquetting.'

.　　　　.　　　　.　　　　.　　　　.

> The courts with feather litter of the cold are filled
> And the dead woods hear no hunting horn.[2]

In the new year festivities, the Court, as usual, amused itself with 'the ordinary recreations, which we have in Winter, and in most solitarie times busie our minds with, as Cards, Tables, and Dice, Shovel-board, Chesse-play . . . shuttle-cocks, billiards, musicke, masks, singing, dancing, Yule-games, frolicks, jests, riddles, catches, purposes, questions, and com-mands, merry tales of Errant Knights, Queens, Lovers, Lords, Ladies, Giants, Dwarfs, Thieves, Cheaters, Witches, Faynes, Goblins . . . etc. . . . and the rest, which some delight to heare, some to tell, all are well pleased with'.[3]

But above all, the Court amused itself with dancing, and

amongst those who danced with the Queen was a French youth named Chastelard.

This intolerable person was a collateral descendant, on his mother's side, of the Chevalier Bayard ; he wrote verse, and was an accomplished musician. As part of the suite of Domville, son of the Constable of France, he sailed in the ship that bore the Queen to Scotland, and 'drawn perhaps', said Hay Fleming, 'by that inchantment whereby men are bewitched', he returned to Scotland in the following year. According to the Spanish Calendar [4] he said, on his way through London, that he was 'going to Scotland to see his lady love'.

According to Knox's version of the events that followed — all versions of the story differ — 'Chastelard was so familiar in the Queen's cabinet that scarcely could any of the Nobility have access to her. The Queen would lie upon Chastelard's shoulder, and sometimes privily she would steal a kiss of his neck. And this was honest enough ; for it was the gentle entreatment of a stranger.'

His head seems to have been completely turned.

On the 12th of February, the Queen having been kept long in Council — until well after midnight — her ladies had fallen asleep, and so this youth was able to steal into her bedroom and conceal himself under her bed. Here he was found by two grooms of the chamber, whose duty it was, each night, to look behind the tapestry and under the bed.

The Queen herself only heard of this monstrous behaviour next day, — whereupon he was commanded to leave Scotland. But within twenty-four hours, as she opened the door of her bedroom in the house where she spent the night en route for St. Andrews, Chastelard rushed from a closet in which he had hidden himself, and implored her forgiveness. Her ladies screamed for help, Lord Moray (Lord James Stuart) rushed in, and the Queen cried, 'Thrust your dagger into the villain'. But her brother, taking him prisoner, told her, quietly, that 'it would not be for her honour if he were punished by a summary act of vengeance, but that he must be dealt with according to the laws of the realm'.[5]

According to Knox's version, Moray, falling upon his knees before the Queen, said : 'Madam, I beseech your Grace, cause me not to take the blood of this man upon me. Your Grace has entreated him so familiarly before that ye have offended all your Nobility, and now, if he shall be secretly slain at your commandment, what shall the world judge of it ? I shall bring him to the presence of Justice, and let him suffer by law according to his deserving.' 'Oh,' said the Queen, 'you will never let him speak.' 'I shall do,' said he, 'Madam, what in me lieth to save your honour.'

Brought to trial at St. Andrews, he was condemned to death, and the Queen, merciful as she was by nature, refused, resolutely, to pardon him, in spite of all efforts to induce her to do so.

On the 22nd of February, he was executed, boasting on the scaffold, showing off, and refusing spiritual aid. 'If I am not without reproach like my uncle the Chevalier Bayard,' he cried, 'I am, at least, as free from fear.' Instead of praying, he, according to Brantôme, recited Ronsard's 'Ode to Death', and his last words were 'Adieu, the most beautiful and the most cruel Princess of the world'.

The Knox version declares that this gallant gentleman 'begged licence to write to France the cause of his death, which, said he, in his own tongue, was "Pour estre trouvé dans un lieu trop suspect"'.

'And so', added the chivalrous Reformer, 'received Chastelard the reward of his dancing, for he lacked his head, that his tongue should not utter the secrets of our Queen.'

Mary's behaviour seems, if we regard the Reformer's imputations as having any foundation, a little inconsistent. Why did she have him turned out of her bedroom if she wanted him to be there ?

A month after the execution, one of the Lords, Lethington, told Bishop de Quadra that Chastelard had 'said that he had been sent from France by persons of distinguished position' to 'try to make himself so familiar with the Queen and her ladies, that he could seize an opportunity of obtaining some appearance of proof sufficient to sully the honour of the Queen' ; that his intention, therefore, had been 'to remain that night underneath the bed, and go out in the morning, so that he could escape *after being seen*'. (The italics are mine.)

It was, he said, 'Madame de Curosot' who had given him his principal instructions ; but in a letter to Lethington, Mary said 'the other names could not be intrusted to letters'.[6]

To what names can this refer ? And what was the reason for this secrecy ?

The Venetian Ambassador was told by Madame de Guise that Chastelard had 'confessed to having been sent by Madame de Cursolles', a lady in great favour at the French court, 'and supposed to be of this new religion, so that by this means she might defame that Queen, in order to thwart any marriage that might be treated for her' (*i.e.* for which a treaty might be signed).[7]

Lang says that 'Curosot is the Spanish cipher name for Châtillon, and the wife of the Admiral Coligny is intended ; or the real name is de Cursol or Crusolles, later Duchesse d'Uzès. Chastelard was, perhaps, a Huguenot.'

## NOTES TO CHAPTER TWENTY-FIVE

[1] Knox, vol. ii.
[2] Sacheverell Sitwell, 'Dr Donne and Gargantua'.
[3] Burton, *The Anatomie of Melancholie.*
[4] Elizabeth I, 314.
[5] Strickland, *The Life of the Queen Elizabeth.*
[6] *Spanish Calendar*, I, 314.
[7] *Venetian Calendar*, VII, 365. Hay Fleming.

# Chapter Twenty-six

ON the 15th of October 1562, nine days after three thousand English troops occupied Havre, the Queen of England had sent to her sister of Scotland a letter of the true Elizabethan greatness :

'My Own Dear Sister, — Were it not a thing impossible for us to forget our own hearts, I should fear you might think that I had drunk the waters of Lethe ; but there is, I assure you, no such river in England ; and of the fault, if fault there be, you are yourself the chief cause ; for if your messenger who you told me long ago was coming had not delayed so long, I should have written to you as usual ; but when I heard that you were going so long a pilgrimage and so far from the English border, I thought this had perhaps hindered you ; while on my part I was kept silent by another motive — I feared to distress you with the tale of the tragedies with which each week my own ears were grieved. Would to God they had been as unknown to others as they were passed over in silence by me ; and I promise you on my honour that till the ravens cried out upon me, I would have stopped my ears with oblivion. But when I saw that all my advisers and my subjects considered me too blind — too dull — too improvident — I roused myself from that slumber. . . .

'Far sooner would I pass over those murders on land ; far rather would I leave unwritten those noyades in the rivers — those men and women hacked in pieces ; but the shrieks of the strangled wives, great with child — the cries of the infants at their mothers' breasts — pierce me through. What drug of rhubarb can purge the bile which these tyrannies engender ? My own subjects in many places have lost goods,

QUEEN ELIZABETH I, 1563

ships, and life, and have been baptised with another name than their sponsors gave them in their baptism — the name of Huguenots. The blame of this treatment has been cast upon the poor soldiers, but the fault rests with the wicked leaders of the quarrel, who, when complaint is made to them, instead of correcting one ill deed commit twenty.

'I received letters from the King and Queen — letters which they cannot deny — from which I learn clearly that the King is but King in name, and that others have the power. And seeing this I have set myself to prevent the evils which might follow if the quarry of this realm was in their talons. But I shall so rule my actions that the King shall hold me a good neighbour, who rather protects than destroys. Your Kinsmen shall have no cause to deem me vindictive. I shall do them no hurt unless they commence with me. . . . I send my fleet, and I send my army, but with no thought except to do good to the King, and to all, unless they will first injure me ; and that the world may know the desire I have for peace, and remove all suspicions which may be engendered of me, I make this declaration without any reserve whatever. I trust therefore you will think as honourably of me as my good-will towards you deserves ; and though I am not ignorant what arts will be or have been used with you in this respect to induce you to withdraw from the affection which I am assured you bear me ; I nevertheless have such trust in this heart which I hold so precious [a heart set with diamonds had been sent to Elizabeth by the Queen of Scots] that I think the rivers will sooner run upwards to the mountains than it shall change towards me. The fever under which I am suffering forbids me to write further.' [1]

'The fever under which I am suffering . . .'

On the day when that letter was written, the Queen, who was at Hampton Court, had felt an increasing malaise. Hoping that fresh air would revive her, she left the Palace for the chilly gardens. In a few hours she was in a raging fever. A famous foreign doctor, Burcot, was summoned. Immediately he saw her, he exclaimed, 'My liege, thou shalt have the pox !'

She shrieked with horror, and said, 'Have the knave out of my sight'.

But smallpox it was; the cold air had driven the eruption inwards, and Cecil, sent for in the middle of the night, was told by the doctors that unless a miracle took place, the Queen was dying.

Next morning her state was unchanged, and the Council was summoned. That evening she became unconscious, 'without speech', and in the antechamber of the Queen, who lay within a few hours, it was believed, of her death, the Council sat in the night to discuss the question of the succession.[2] Some of them put forward the claims of Lady Catherine Grey, some (including Lord Robert Dudley) were in favour of Lord Huntingdon. The Queen of Scots was hardly considered.

In despair, the Queen's attendants sent for Burcot once again; but he had been deeply offended, and refused to come. Eventually he was taken to the Queen's side, almost by force. Saying to her, 'Almost too late, my liege', he ordered a mattress to be put by the fire, and wrapping her in a great length of scarlet cloth, he held a drink to her lips.

At midnight the miracle occurred. The Queen returned to this life.

Yet she believed she was dying, and, to the Council who now filled her room, she spoke her first words since the danger began. Those first words, those first thoughts, were of Lord Robert. She entreated the Council that he should be made Protector of England. Then, as her mind grew stronger, she said that 'she loved him dearly, and had long loved him; but she called God to witness that nothing unseemly had ever passed between them'.

She then spoke of members of her household who must be given pensions. After which the Council retired.

Next morning the danger was over. The eruption had appeared.

The Queen remained in her private apartments till the last traces of the illness had vanished. She was unmarked.

But Lady Mary Sidney, who had nursed her, caught the disease and was so terribly disfigured she would never again appear at Court without a mask.

The Queen gave Dr. Burcot land, and gold spurs inherited from Henry the Seventh.

This illness had shown the Council the magnitude of the danger to England, if she should die before naming a successor.

When Maitland, the Scottish envoy, urged the Queen of England to name his mistress as her successor, she said that while she lived she would be Queen of England. 'When I am dead, they shall succeed that have most right. If the Queen your sovereign be that person, I shall never hurt her ; if another have a better right, it were not reasonable to require me to do a manifest injury.

'Think you', she asked, 'that I could love my winding-sheet, when the examples show, princes cannot even love their children who are to succeed them ?

'I have good experience of myself in my sister's time, how desirous men were that I should be in place, and earnest to set me up, and if I would have consented, I knew that enterprises would have been attempted to bring it to pass. Now,' she added, 'the affections of some people were perhaps altered. As children dream in their sleep of apples, and weep when they awake in the morning and do not find them, so every man who bore me goodwill when I was Lady Elizabeth, imagined that immediately she came to the throne he would be rewarded according to his own fancy ; and finding now that the event had not answered his expectation, could perhaps be content with a new change on the chance of faring better. No prince's revenues be so great that they are able to satisfy the insatiable cupidity of men.'

At last she instructed Randolph, her Ambassador to Scotland, to make the following formal declaration to the Queen of Scots : that she was anxious to settle the question of the succession, and, if possible, to name Mary as the heiress to the throne. Parliament had wished to erase her claim to the succession, but this wish had been combated by the Queen, who was anxious for the union of the two countries, and whose private opinion it was that Mary had the first claim to succeed her. But, should she be acknowledged heiress to the crown, it was necessary that she should accept the Reformation as the law of England.

With her own hand, the Queen wrote that she 'did not believe that the Queen of Scots meant anything against her'; but that there were dangerous elements in England, against which she must warn the Queen of Scots, begging her not to be misled by these, and so fall into a course of conduct that might 'become a perpetual reproof to both of them throughout all posterity'.

She warned the Queen of Scots that should the latter marry the Archduke Charles of Austria (the name of Don Carlos, also, must have been in Elizabeth's mind) this would be regarded as an act of war against England.

What would be most satisfactory to England would be her marriage with an English nobleman. . . . Then, inspired by who knows what despair, what self-abnegation, she declared that 'she could be content to give her one whom perchance it could be hardly thought she [Elizabeth] could consent to'.

Randolph, writing to Cecil on the 4th of September 1563, said the Queen of Scots had received him graciously, and had declared her gratitude to Elizabeth for her sisterly interest.

Exactly a month later, Knox discovered and disclosed to Cecil what had been planned secretly. Mary had no intention of marrying the Archduke. The King of Spain had suggested her marriage with Don Carlos. Catherine de' Medici had proposed she should marry Catherine's second son, Charles the Ninth. If Philip could be held to his offer, it was this she would accept. If not, she would marry the King of France.

In February 1564, Mary, explaining to the Chancellor Granvelle that she was unable to marry the Archduke, tried, at the same time, to learn if she could be sure of marriage with Don Carlos, saying that if that marriage fell through, her party in England wished her to marry Lord Darnley. . . . She set herself to try to manœuvre Elizabeth into a position where she would suggest this.    Once she was acknowledged the heiress to the throne, and was the wife of the head of the Catholic faction, her way would be easy.

At first she would act with caution, moving, day by day, a little nearer to her goal, increasing her claims, almost imperceptibly, until the moment came — as it surely would — when she could satisfy her hatred of her cousin, the bastard who, as she thought, had usurped her throne, — could seize the Crown, and bring about her utter ruin.

But Darnley was the last person whom Elizabeth would wish to see married to Mary.   She understood clearly what the outcome of that marriage would be.

It was whilst this plan was still maturing in Mary's mind that she found that the English nobleman who Elizabeth had suggested should be her husband, was not Lord Darnley, but Lord Robert Dudley.

Disguising from Randolph her fury, seeing herself about to be thwarted, and offered as husband her cousin's favourite, she told him that Lord Robert's inferiority in rank, should she marry him, would be a blot on her honour.[3]

To this Randolph replied that 'It was honour enough to inherit such a kingdom as England'.   Mary answered that she did not expect to inherit England, for her sister might marry, and was likely to live longer than herself ; she was therefore obliged to consider her own and her friends' expectations, and she did not think they would agree that she should abase her state so far.   She asked him to tell his Queen that she had no personal objection to Lord Robert ;  but that he was beneath her in rank, and so unsuitable.

'Ah !' said the Queen of England to the Scottish Ambassador, Melville, whom she saw each day, discussing with him, ceaselessly, the question of his mistress's marriage.  'You make little of Lord Robert."

Had it been possible, she said, she would have married Lord Robert.   This she could not do, so wished him married to her sister of Scotland, for 'that done', she would have no fear of any usurpation before her death, 'being assured that Dudley was so loving and trusty that he would never permit anything to be attempted during her time'.[4]

For what other reasons did she wish — if indeed she *did* wish — that he should become the husband of Mary? Did she wish to ensure that he should become what she had hoped to make him — a King, even though it meant that she must relinquish the love of her life? Was she inspired by some obscure hatred of Mary, some wish to humiliate her? It is impossible to tell. What is known is that he himself feared that marriage, dreaded the consequences to himself of that marriage having been suggested.

On Michaelmas Day, 1564, Lord Robert Dudley was created Earl of Leycester in the presence of the Scottish Ambassador, in order that he should appear to be more suitable as a husband for the Queen of Scotland.

Robert Dudley's life at Court had been anything but easy, and the Queen's passion for him, and her knowledge that she could never marry him, made that life more difficult.

His pride almost equalled hers, and was, perhaps, one of the reasons for that passion. But she would fall into rages with him and deliberately humiliate and insult him. At one moment, about nine months after the death of Amye Robsart, she had told Robert that she intended to invite the King of Sweden to England, with a view to marriage. He told her the King was an idiot — which was true — whereupon she flew into a rage. What business was it of his? she enquired. Who was he to speak disrespectfully of a Prince? He replied that her marriage was very much his business. Did he imagine, she exclaimed, that she would dishonour herself by a marriage with such as he?

If that was her feeling, he replied, he would ask her permission to leave the realm and go to sea.

But she changed her mind again. The King of Sweden did not come and Dudley did not go to sea.

One could give many instances of such insults, with

their origin, one supposes, in some fit of anger or despair. She repeated to him the Queen of Scots' gibe about her intended marriage to her 'Horsemaster'. She reminded him that more than one of his ancestors had been attainted for treason.

She spoke of him to others, sometimes, in a manner most cruelly humiliating. In 1565, when the French Ambassador suggested Leycester should be sent on a mission to the King of France, she said, 'It will not greatly honour me to send a groom to so great a prince, and I could not be without him once a day ; he is like my little dog, so much so that when they see him enter anywhere they say at once that I am coming'.

But still he continued to behave as if he were her favoured suitor.

At this time, when she was pretending to arrange his marriage with the Queen of Scots, the Scottish Ambassador Randolph had been scandalised by the report in the Scottish Court that while Leycester and the Duke of Norfolk were playing tennis in the presence of the Queen, 'Lord Robert being very hot and sweating, he took the Queen's napkin out of her hand and wiped his face', and that the outraged Norfolk had threatened to break the racket over his head.

The Duke of Norfolk and Lord Arundel spoke angrily to him on the subject of his conduct. He had gone, they had heard, into the royal bedchamber before the Queen was out of bed (some of the Lords, among them Leycester, as Master of the Horse, had the right of entry at certain times). Nor was that his only indiscretion. He had the habit of kissing the Queen's Majesty uninvited. To their astonishment, he answered peacefully, thanking them for their advice.

All this was, naturally, repeated at the Court of the lady to whom the Queen of England seemed intent on giving Leycester as husband.

'She appeared', wrote Melville, 'to be so affectionate to Queen Mary, her good sister, that she had a great desire to see her, and because that could not be she delighted oft to look

on her picture.  She took me to her bed-chamber, and opened
a little lettroun [desk ?] where there were divers little pictures
wrapped up in paper, their names written with her own hand.
Upon the first she took up was written "My lord's picture".
This was Leicester's portrait.  I held the candle, and pressed
to see my lord's picture.  Albeit she was loth to let me see it,
but I became importunate for it, to carry home to my Queen ;
she refused, saying she had but one of his.  I replied, "She
had the original !"  She was then at the further end of her
bed-chamber, talking with Cecil.  Elizabeth then took out
my Queen's miniature, and kissed it.  Whereupon the Scottish
Ambassador kissed her hand.

'She shewed me', he wrote, 'a fair ruby, great like a racket
ball.  I desired she would either send it to my Queen, or the
Earl of Leicester's picture.  She replied : "If Queen Mary
would follow her counsel, she would get them both in time,
and all she had. . .".'

And England's Prometheus felt the eagle-beak in her heart
— the coldness of the rock to which she was nailed.

.        .        .        .        .

In the possibility of this marriage Elizabeth still pretended
to believe, and Melville, the Scottish Ambassador, still pretended to believe.  But the Queen was not deceived : 'You
like better yon long lad', she said to the Ambassador, pointing
at her cousin, the eighteen-year-old Lord Darnley.

The Ambassador assured her that this was not so —
'although', he wrote, 'I had a secret charge to deal with Lady
Lennox to procure liberty for him to go to Scotland'.

For the 'long lad's' mother had long since begun her
plots.  A marriage between her son and the Queen of Scotland
would mean not only the fulfilment of her and her husband's
insatiable ambition, but it would enable her to defy and insult
Elizabeth, whom she hated passionately.

In the time of King Henry, the Earl of Lennox had claimed
that he, and not the Duke of Châtellerault, was heir to the
kingdom of Scotland, in default of the royal line.  King Henry

had found him a useful tool ; but he was a fool, and an intriguing fool, driven from Scotland and forced to remain in England as a grumbling and greedy pensioner. He married the King's niece (the daughter, by her second marriage, of Margaret Tudor, Queen of Scotland) and she, it is evident, was the leader in all their ambitious schemes.

At the time of her marriage, Lady Lennox was over thirty-two years of age. She was, therefore, in late middle age at the time when she began her plots for 'the long lad'. Though dangerous in conversation to a most reckless degree, you would have said, looking at her, that not only slyness (which was a principal constituent in her character), but also caution (which most certainly was not), had seeped into her blood.

In the only portrait I know of her, painted when she was an old woman, all that could be concealed (excepting her inexpressive hands, that might have been the hands of anyone) is hidden. Her circumspect bell-shaped black velvet gown (with two hanging bell-ropes of some gold material ending in tassels), reaching from her shoulders to the ground, shrouds her feet, which must have moved, always, with a mouse-like caution, but in the most unexpected directions. The neck that was more than once in peril from the axe has a high ruff that reaches to the chin — (that, of course, was the fashion of the time). Her face, with the exception of her anxiously-peering cunning dark eyes, tells us nothing. It bears no trace of the Plantagenet fire and arrogance.

Perhaps this physical habit of concealment made her believe her scheming was equally hidden. It was not.

This singularly detestable woman, who seems to have been incapable of loyalty to anyone, excepting her husband, had, at the time when Elizabeth was arrested on suspicion of being involved in the Wyatt rebellion, insulted her publicly (safe in Elizabeth's defencelessness), had repeated everything that would be likely to injure her with Mary, and had done all in her power to induce Mary to execute her.

Such was her pettiness, that when the Princess was ill, Lady Lennox had her hangings taken down, and caused a kitchen to be installed over her head, with the usual bangings and bumpings, shouts, comings and goings.

She was as impudent as she was troublesome, and it was probably at her instigation that Lord Lennox wrote to Cecil (30th November 1562) a grumbling whining letter complaining about the Earls of Morton and Glencairn, 'the first being chief keeper of his wife's inheritance unjustly (taken) from her, the other having ungratefully deceived King Henry VIII and the writer. . .'. He added that he hoped 'he and his wife (would) prosper, for it would redound more to the Queen's commodity [credit ? advantage ?] than anything they go about'.

The letter was a mistake as a move. It was written to the wrong person.

Sir William wrote that 'if Lord Lennox alleges strait handling, or brag, upon the covenants of Henry VIII, he shall be answered as follows : That all covenants are fulfilled, and 100,000 crowns more are distributed without fruit, for the Earl's advancement'.

He reminded Lord Lennox (for he was perfectly aware of Lady Lennox's intrigues about their son) that he was 'sworn a perpetual subject, promising that he should never enter into any private bond or practice with any state, without the Queen's license'. 'It would seem that where he countenances [pretends] to labour for his living in Scotland, it is not so, but a colour for a higher feather . . .' (a coloured feather, gilded like a crown, for that popinjay Lord Darnley ?)

The Secretary added that 'the Queen is good lady to Lord Lennox in suffering them to enjoy these great livings without disturbance, considering what faint hearts they bear her, and against their own commodities seek to be her enemy. Lord Lennox enjoys more of the Queen's liberality than he thinks she knows of, which is meet to be restored.'

I do not know what answer was returned to that appalling snub.

Now that the woman whose death she had tried to encompass had come to the throne, Lady Lennox was tireless in inventing gibes, and listening to, and spreading, evil stories about her ; and a mischief-making busybody called Yaxlee, a gentleman of the Queen's bedchamber, was encouraged to spy, and to report all the gossip that became known to him. Unfortunately for Lady Lennox, the Queen heard of this. Yaxlee was arrested, Lord Lennox sent to the Tower, and Lady Lennox ordered to appear at Court immediately, to answer for her behaviour.

William Forbes, one of her servants, testified against her. 'I have heard her say', he declared, 'that either Queen Mary or the Queen's Majesty, Elizabeth, behoved to be a bastard. As for Queen Mary, all the world knew that she was lawful ; and for herself, she desired nothing but her right, which she knew God would send her one day.' She had allowed the household Fool to rail against the Queen and Lord Robert, calling his blood 'traitor birds' and 'saying that he caused kill his wife . . . with most odious words that I will not rehearse'. 'And said to Hew Allen [I suppose he means that Lady Lennox said] that he [Lord Robert] was lying ill of the pokkes.' He swore that 'I know she sat herself down, held up her hands, and gave God thanks for preserving the Scottish Queen from the Queen's Majesty's ships when she passed to Scotland, saying "How God preserves that Princess at all times"'. The preservation in question being, it was thought by some, the result of Lady Lennox's witchcraft. According to Forbes, not only were 'the curtains of her bed and those of Lord Darnley pinned round with idols', but she frequented witches, and, indeed, had one living in the house.

Lady Lennox had intended to brazen this out, but was given no chance. She was arrested on the charges of treason and witchcraft, and was sent to imprisonment in the house of Lord and Lady Sackville. Lord Lennox was sent to the Tower — *alone*. And solitude was his terror.

He lived in such deadly fear of the young ghosts that might come to companion him when he was in solitude and in silence, that Lady Lennox feared for his life. Had not the Queen herself advised that he should never be left alone ? —

knowing that he 'was guilty of a deed of blood which whispered despair to his soul whensoever it communed with itself — a deed that had drawn down upon him the execration of all humanity'.[5]

In the terrible invasion of Scotland of 1547, a body of Scottish horsemen had been forced into his ranks by the fact that he held their children as hostages. They deserted. . . . So eleven of the boys were hanged by his orders.[6] One, Lord Herries . . . 'had the rope round his neck'. But he was so young, so pitiful, that the English soldier who was to be his executioner turned sick with horror, and could not bring himself to pull the rope. So the boy survived. From that time, Matthew, Earl of Lennox, dared not be alone.

His wife bombarded Cecil with letters. Her husband, if she was not allowed to join him, could not, because of this terror, 'continue long of his life, which to Her Majesty should be small pleasure'. In the same month, she reminded Cecil that her husband 'had a disease which solitariness is most against, as heretofore, to my comfort, her Majesty willed me to cause him always to be in company. . . . I assure you, Master Sekretary, it is a great grief to me, and the greatest that I ever had, to perceive the little love and affection that her Majesty bears me.'

And, later, '. . . If my lord and I might find the Queen's Majesty so good and gracious to us, as to hear our accusers and us, face to face, I would be out of doubt to find shortly some part of Her Highness's favour again'.

For, like her future daughter-in-law, she was so optimistic as to think that, if she were brought into the presence of the most astute woman in Europe, any lie she chose to tell would be believed.

No doubt she told herself that if the Queen of England would not see her, the Queen of Scotland would come to her rescue. Mary's ambition at that time, however, was still centred on marrying Don Carlos — sane or mad * — and in this way possessing herself, through King Philip's help, of

* See Appendix D.

England.    And the fate of Lord and Lady Lennox and their son mattered little to her.[7]

Lady Lennox was eventually restored to Court, and resumed her intrigues.   And Lord Lennox was allowed to cross the Border — this being less troublesome than to imprison him once more.

As for the new Earl of Leycester, that gallant gentleman to whom the Queen of England had given her love, who thought himself worthy to be the husband of the Queen of England, made the most abject apologies to the Queen of Scotland's Ambassador that he should ever have appeared to dare be her suitor.

The day after he was created Earl of Leycester, he 'desired', wrote Melville, 'to know what the Queen my mistress thought of him, and the marriage that Mr. Randolph had proposed. . . . Then he began to purge himself of so proud a pretence, as to marry so great a Queen, declaring that he did not esteem himself worthy to wipe her shoes ; declaring that the invention of that proposition of marriage proceeded from Mr. Cecil, his secret enemy.   For if I, says he, should have appeared desirous of that marriage, I should have offended both the Queens and lost their favour.   He entreated me to excuse himself at her Majesty's hands, and to beg, in his name, that she would not impute that matter to him, but to the malice of his enemies.'

This is the most unworthy thing that, in the present writer's opinion, can be proved against him.


NOTES TO CHAPTER TWENTY-SIX

[1] Translated by Froude from the French.
[2] Froude, *op. cit.*
[3] Froude, *op. cit.*
[4] Froude, *Melville's Memoirs.*
[5] Strickland, *op. cit.*
[6] Holinshed, *Chronicles.*
[7] Neale, *op. cit.*

# Chapter Twenty-seven

THE long and boneless Waxworks King, Lord Darnley, with his white, flaccid, meaningless face, like the taffeta mask he was so soon to be obliged to wear, with his curling marigold-coloured hair, and his long hands like satin gloves filled with damp sand, arrived at Edinburgh on the 12th of February 1565. He was presented to the Queen a week afterwards, dancing with her, and whispering in her ear.

On that night, the clash of weapons wielded by ghostly warriors was heard in the streets — a terrifying omen that occurred for three nights in succession. But the Queen continued her Herodian dancing. The omens were outside the Palace. . . . How could they threaten her ?

Preceding his son by three months, came the hated Earl of Lennox (with those ghost children unseen by all but him, but never absent from his company — waiting for the moment when he should be alone).

On the 2nd of December 1564, Randolph had written to Cecil, 'I am evil willing that my Lord of Darlie [sic] should come hither'. On the 14th of that month he said he feared his own Queen would be blamed for 'sending home so great a plague into this country'.

Mary was — or pretended to be — deeply impressed by the newcomer. Soon she allowed it to be understood that she had fallen in love with him. She loaded him with presents — violet velvet for a dressing-gown, cloth of gold for the caparison of his horse, bonnets with feathers for his fools. . . .

Amongst Darnley's principal favourites at the Court was a small, mis-shapen, evil-favoured, black-visaged, but merry, man of mean birth — David Riccio, who had been retained by the Queen when his Savoyard master, with whom he had come to Scotland, left the country, because of his skill as a musician, since she needed a singer for the fourth part to be sung by 'the varlets of the chamber'. On the evening of the day he entered her employment (the 8th of January 1562) the clerk's entry for the expenses of the day included, 'To Anthony Geddes, for keeping of her Grace's dogs, twelve pounds. item. to David Riccio, varlet in the Queen's Grace's chamber, one pound.' As we have seen, the varlet dined, at first, at the same table as the three other singing varlets, René the perfumer, and a tailor. But that was long ago. He was now high in the Queen's favour, was her French secretary, and accepted everywhere.

He and Darnley became inseparable. He became Darnley's confidant, his adviser in everything. Such was their friendship that they would sometimes 'lie in one bed together'. Nobody was more eager in his advocacy of the Queen's marriage with the Waxworks King.

Then, suddenly, there was a new arrival at Court — the man who was to be Mary's enchanter, conjuring up the evil spirit soon to be engendered in her — the Earl of Bothwell. This 'rash, glorious, dangerous young man' had been 'put to the horn' (i.e. had been declared, by three blasts on the horn, an outlaw). Yet here he was, coming boldly into the Queen's presence, — and not a man dared lay a hand upon him.

Soon it became certain that the Queen was determined on the marriage with Darnley. . . . For love ? Is it possible that this, in many ways, very great woman could have loved this meaningless, flaccid, arrogant boy ? . . . From hatred ? More probably. For by now the ruling passions of her life were her hatred of her cousin Elizabeth, her hatred of her half-brother Moray (who understood her only too well, and so could not be forgiven), and her ambition to seize the crown of England ; and marriage with Darnley, the grandson of Margaret Tudor, sister of Henry the Eighth, would be a step towards this. To satisfy any of these three passions she would almost sacrifice her life.

Maitland, the envoy to England, had said of her : 'The Queen my mistress is descended of the blood of England, and is of the race of the Lion on both sides. I fear she would rather be content to hazard all than to forgo her rights.' The same could be said of those ruling passions. Maitland was not deceived : he declared 'the foundation of the matter might have been anger or despite'.

Mary was strangely altered. 'Her Majesty is laid aside', said Randolph the English Ambassador ; 'her wits not such as they were ; her beauty other than it was ; her cheer and countenance changed into I wot not what — a woman more to be pitied than ever I saw.'

She had, perhaps, understood to what a fate devouring ambition, intolerable hatred, had led her — a bottomless emptiness, lit only by the little flares of Darnley's vices.

As for the Waxworks King, he seemed to be worked by some alien spirit, guiding his movements, ever nearer, to the mouth of the abyss.

Later, the English Ambassador wrote that 'David Riccio is he that now worketh [arranges] all, chief secretary to the Queen and only Governor to her good man. . . . The hatred towards Lord Darnley and his house (is) marvellously great, his pride intolerable, his words not to be borne : but where no man dare speak again [i.e. answer] he spareth not also in token of his manhood to let blows fly where he knows they will be taken. Where men have said all and thought what they can, they find nothing but that God must send him a short end or themselves a miserable life. . . .'

Even so early was that self-wooed death foreseen.

Half the English Council, aware of the danger to Elizabeth's crown if the marriage took place, advised her to demand the instant extradition of her subjects, Darnley and his intriguing father, and, if this was refused, to declare war.

The French Ambassador was sent to the English Queen to endeavour to induce in her a change of mind. He found her sitting at a table whose top was of red coral, playing a game of chess. De Foix spoke with some nervousness. 'This game',

MARY QUEEN OF SCOTS
Deuil Blanc

he said, 'is an image of the words and deeds of men. If, for example, we lose a pawn, it seems but a small matter ; nevertheless the loss often draws after it that of the whole game.' The Queen looked up, for a moment only, and answered : 'I understand you : Darnley is but a pawn ; but he may well checkmate me if he be promoted'.

And she moved another silver chessman on the board.

On the 14th of June 1565, the Queen of Scotland sent a letter declaring that her only reason for contemplating this marriage was to 'meet her dearest sister's wishes'. Her dearest sister replied by ordering her subjects to return to England immediately.

When Randolph presented the letter, Mary burst into tears, Lennox was struck speechless ; but the young fool his son said, boastfully, that he had no intention of returning. When Mary recovered herself, she said that she hoped her good sister did not mean what she said, to which Randolph replied that she most certainly did mean it, and if they did not do, immediately, what their Queen ordered them, she had both power and will to be revenged on them, they being her subjects.

Meanwhile Moray and Argyll, in a panic as Protestants at the menace the marriage would be to their religion, told Randolph that they did not ask England for an army, 'but if Her Majesty would give them £3000 they could hold their followers together'.

When the Queen of Scots heard of this, she ordered her half-brother to meet her at Perth. But just as he was about to start, the news came that this was intended to be his last journey. Darnley and Riccio had plotted to have him murdered.

He fled to his mother's castle at Lochleven, and made public his reason. Whereupon Mary brought the charge against him that he had intended to take her prisoner and send Darnley to England.

Darnley received, in July, a fresh order to return to England. He replied, in an insolent voice, that he 'acknowledged no duty or obedience save to the Queen of Scots. . . . To return I intend not ; I find myself very well where I am, and so I purpose to keep me ; and this shall be your answer.'

'You have much forgotten your duty, sir, in such despiteful words', said the English Ambassador, and left the room, 'without reverence or farewell.'

On Saturday the 28th of July 1565, the Queen of Scotland ordered her Lord Lyon King of Arms to proclaim Henry Lord Darnley, Duke of Albany and King of Scotland. After the proclamation was made for the second time, on Monday, the new King's father threw his cap into the air, and shouted, amidst the otherwise complete silence, 'God save the King !'

Between five and six on Sunday morning, the Queen, dressed, as Randolph told Leycester, 'in the great wide mourning gown of black, with the great wide mourning hood, not unlike that which she wore the doleful day of the burial of her husband', was led into the chapel by the father of the bridegroom and the Earl of Atholl, and was married to the Waxworks King. 'God be praised', exclaimed the bridegroom's friend, David Riccio, as the King placed the ring upon his bride's finger.

Years afterwards, Moray said of her that 'she had been troubled in times past with children, young proud fools, and furious men'. But not for long. Two were soon laid in another bed than hers, and the proud, furious one was to go as far away as if he too had left her for Death. In less than two years from the time of that marriage, Mary was again to wear mourning as a bride.

# Chapter Twenty-eight

THE arrogance of the Waxworks King was by now not to be borne. His conduct was so irresponsible that he was allowed no say in the affairs of state, although he was treated, always, with the deference due to the Queen's husband. Followed everywhere by his obsequious, fawning, doting father, urging him on to further outrages, he was hated by the Council and the whole Court.

He was King in name only. At first, the Queen had given way to him in everything, excepting in allowing him to rule the kingdom. 'All honours that may be attributed by a wife', Randolph told Leycester, 'he hath it wholly and fully ; all praise that may be spoken of him, he lacketh not from herself ; all dignities that she can indue him with are freely given and granted . . . but she can as little prevail with him as against his will, as your lordship may move me to hang myself.'

On the 25th of August, the Queen of Scotland rode from Edinburgh, with Darnley, wearing gilt armour, at her side, to meet the Lords who had rebelled against her — her hope being to overcome and kill the being on whom, by now, all her powers of hatred were concentrated — (Elizabeth's image almost faded to nothing when she thought of him) — her half-brother, Moray.

She had told Randolph that she would rather lose her crown than not be revenged upon him. Later — on the 13th of October — he told Cecil : 'The hatred conceived against my Lord of Moray is neither for his religion nor yet . . . that he would take the crown from her, as she said lately to myself — but that she knoweth he knoweth some such secret

211

fact, not to be named for reverence [decency's] sake, that standeth not with her honour, which he so much detesteth, being her brother, that neither can he show himself as he hath done, nor can she think of him but as one whom she mortally hateth'.

He added that he was sure that, to have this obloquy and reproach of her removed, he [Moray] 'would quit his country for all the days of his life'.

Mary did not succeed in capturing or killing her hated brother, but he and his fellow rebels were forced to retire to the Border, then to seek refuge in England.  Soon Moray found himself in the presence of the English Queen, who had encouraged the rebellion and helped to finance it, and he was treated to the preposterous farce of being rebuked by the Queen for daring to enter her presence when he had been declared an outlaw by her good sister.

Happily, he had been prepared for this beforehand, and, after a long harangue from her on his duty — (he should, she told him, have gone straight to his Queen and complained, if he really believed her husband had plotted to murder him, instead of taking refuge in his mother's castle) — he begged her to intercede with the Queen of Scots to procure his forgiveness.

After pretending to hesitate, Elizabeth said that the Queen of Scots had so often refused her that she did not know that it would be possible to try any further mediation.  But she would consult with her Council, and tell him the result. Meanwhile, he must realise that he was in great danger, and must consider himself a prisoner.

After Moray left her presence, the Queen assured the Frenchmen, de Foix and de Maussière, who had been present (and were fully aware that she had sent £3000 to the rebels), that she had spoken the entire truth, and asked them to inform the French King.

Meanwhile, the Queen of Scots was sweeping such rebels as were left, before her.  She swore she would march to the Border — at one moment, even, that she would not rest till she reached the gates of London. De Maussière, sent from France to warn her of the dangers of her conduct, was told by her that she would sooner lose her crown than wear it at the pleasure of her rebels and Elizabeth. . . . Submit to England ? *Never !*

.        .        .        .        .

The King had now been joined by a Councillor other than his father and Riccio — a person not outwardly attractive : his portrait shows a commonplace, grim-featured face, reddish hair under a tall black Puritanical hat, and a swollen thick-set body.

Earl Morton was the son, writes Andrew Lang,[1] 'of the most accomplished and perfidious scoundrel of the past generation, Sir George Douglas, brother of Angus', who had married Henry the Eighth's sister, formerly Queen of Scotland. Lord Morton was consequently first cousin to Lady Lennox. Sir George Douglas 'alternately betrayed England, of which he was a pensioner, and Scotland, of which he was a subject'. His son inherited his gifts.

'A red-handed murderer', Lang continues, 'living in open adultery with the widow of Captain Cullen, whom he had hanged, and daily consorting with murderers . . . Morton approached the Divine Mysteries.

'His sanctimonious snuffle is audible still, in his remark to Throckmorton, at the time when Throckmorton probably saved Mary's life from the Lords' (after the death of Darnley). 'Throckmorton asked to be allowed to visit her in prison. "The Earl Morton", he wrote, "answered me that shortly I should hear from them, but the day being destined, as I did see, to the Communion, continual preaching, and common prayer, they could not be absent, nor attend matters of the world, for that they must seek the matters of God and take counsel of Him Who could best direct them." '

This admirable person affected to be deeply shocked by the manner in which the Waxworks King was treated by his wife. He was her husband, and should, therefore, have been allowed to ruin her kingdom as he pleased. He pitied his young cousin, he condoled with him on his humiliating position. 'It was a thing', he declared, 'contrary to nature that the hen should crow before the cock, and against the law of God that a man should be subject to his wife — the man being the image of God and the woman the image of man.'

This must cease ! It was time, he counselled his cousin, to emerge from this degrading position, and to force the Queen to resign the government into his hands. He — Morton — would be delighted to give him any aid in his power to bring about this desirable result.

And who, he asked, did Darnley think was responsible for this shocking treatment of him ? Why, none but Riccio, his pretended friend ! It was *he* who advised the Queen to keep him 'without revenue, and subject to herself'.[2] Darnley would never rule as King of Scotland while his false friend lived.

For some time, this virtuous man had hated Riccio. For this reason : Riccio had made a deadly enemy of Lethington, the wily and astute man, then aged about thirty, who had married Mary Fleming, the Queen's favourite Marie and her illegitimate cousin. In time, he was to become involved in more than one murder, his Queen was to save his life when it was threatened by Bothwell, and he, in his turn, was to betray her. Now, furious because he had been superseded as secretary of state by Riccio, he decided to bring about his successor's ruin by means which would entail no trouble on himself.

In a most friendly manner, therefore, Lethington strongly advised Riccio to apply for the office of Lord Chancellor, 'which', he said, 'is in Morton's hands — a man no wise fit for the place, being both unlettered and unskilful. Do but deal with the Queen to discountenance Morton as a secret favourer of Moray, and with the King to insist on his right to the Earldom of Angus, and Morton will be glad to demit to you his place as Chancellor as the price of your favour : but this place, being the chief office of the realm, can only be possessed by a Scottish nobleman.  You must therefore be naturalised as a free denizen, and have the title of an Earl, which the Queen can confer on you herself.'

*That*, he thought, should settle matters !  It did.  The former 'varlet', Riccio, swallowed the bait — hook, line, and sinker !

.         .         .         .         .

The King's conduct went from bad to worse.

'His words to all men against whom he conceiveth any displeasure, howsoever unjust it be, are so proud and spiteful that rather he seemeth a monarch of the world than he whom not long since we had seen and known as Lord Darnley', Randolph told Leycester.

His insolence to the Queen was, by now, open.  On one occasion, when drunk, at the house of an Edinburgh merchant, it was such that the Queen left the house in tears.  Then occurred some other incident — the nature of it was not specified, but may easily be guessed — that caused the Queen to 'withdraw her company from him', though a staircase connected their rooms.

And as the separation between them increased, so did the Queen's intimacy with Riccio.  As the King's conduct worsened, Riccio took his place at the Council Table, signing the King's name with a seal.  And the rage of the Waxworks King rose.

Randolph had written of the Queen's passion (possibly feigned) for Riccio on the 15th of May.  On the 19th of September he was hinting that she was Riccio's mistress, and, presently, that Bothwell was also her lover.

One night, according to himself, Darnley went to the Queen's bedroom between twelve and one.  The door was locked.  He knocked.  No answer.  At last, when he threatened to break it down, she unlocked it and stood before him.  She seemed to be alone in her room, but her husband, opening a closet, found Riccio, half dressed, cowering there.

According to him.   No one knows the truth of the story.

It was in September that he first accused her of adultery. In November, it was known that she was with child.   He had cast the shadow of bastardy on his son.


### NOTES TO CHAPTER TWENTY-EIGHT

[1] *Mystery of Mary Stuart.*
[2] Blackwood, *Life of Queen Mary.*

# Chapter Twenty-nine

LESS than two months before the King of Scotland's alleged discovery of this outrage on his honour, his devoted father was writing to his 'sweet Madge' (who was still imprisoned in the Tower for her part in arranging the marriage) 'God . . . send us a comfortable meeting.

'My Madge, we have to give God most hearty thanks for that the King our son continues in good health, and the Queen great with child. God save them all. . . . Yet for my part, I confess I want and find a lack of my chiefest comfort, which is you ; whom I have no cause to forget for all the felicity and wealth that I am in. . . . Although I do not doubt that their Majesties forgetteth you not, yet I am still remembering [reminding] them for your own deliverance to work therein as much as they can.

'I bid mine own sweet Madge most heartily farewell, beseeching Almighty God to preserve you in health and long life, and send us with our children a merry meeting.

'Your own Mathieu ; and most loving husband.'

But their Majesties' minds were employed otherwise than in making plans for the freeing of Lady Lennox. The Queen was not interested. The King could think of nothing but revenge.

That aged and sinister warlock, the Earl of Ruthven, who had been dangerously ill and bedridden for three months, was now bombarded by the Waxworks King's lamentations, entreaties, and storms of rage. Seeing a chance of ridding the country of Riccio, and of bringing back the rebel Lords from banishment, Lord Ruthven began to listen, to calculate, to plan. On his entry into the conspiracy, it grew.

Riccio was loathed : he had too much power, and it was believed that he was plotting to restore Catholicism to Scotland as the national religion.

On the 13th of February 1566, Randolph told Leycester : 'I know now for certain that this Queen repenteth her marriage, that she hateth [Darnley] and all his kin. I know that he knoweth himself that he hath a partner in play and game with him. I know that there are practices in hand contrived between the father and son to come by the crown against her will. I know that if that take effect that is intended, David, with the consent of the King, shall have his throat cut within these ten days. Many things grievouser and worse than these are brought to my ears, yea of things intended against her own person. . . . This your Lordship shall know for certain that this Queen to her subjects is now so intolerable that I see them bent on nothing but extreme mischief. . . . There is a bait laid for Signor David, that if he be caught, howsoever his mistress be offended, others will be pleased.'

For their own safety, the conspirators drew up a bond to be signed by Darnley. They 'undertook to be liege subjects to the said Prince Henry, to take part with him in all his lawful actions, causes, and quarrels, to be friends to his friends, and enemies to his enemies'. They promised to secure for him 'the crown matrimonial for his life', and that 'failing the succession of their sovereign they would maintain his right to the crown of Scotland after her death. . . . They would spare neither life, lands, goods, nor possessions in setting forward all things for the advancement of the said noble prince, and would intercede with the Queen of England for favour to be shown both to himself and to his mother.'

Darnley, in return, took full responsibility for the murder of Riccio, 'though it were in the very palace and presence of the Queen'. The signers of the bond had, however, been careful. The word 'murder' was omitted.

The Lords who signed the bond were Argyll, husband of the Queen's half-sister, Maitland, and Ruthven. In addition, Morton had been consulted, but had hesitated. Then, while he was considering the matter, the Queen deposed him as Chancellor, and, in a fury, he signed, and helped to construct the plot.

On the 6th of March, Bedford and Randolph (who had been expelled from Scotland for corresponding with the rebel Lords) told Cecil : 'The Lord Darnley, weary of bearing the name of King and not having the honour pertaining to such a dignity, is in league with certain of the Lords for a great attempt, whereby the noblemen out of their country may without difficulty be restored and in the end tranquillity ensue in that country'. They added that Cecil must have heard of certain discords that had arisen between the Queen and her husband, not only because she had refused him the crown matrimonial, but because 'he hath assured knowledge of such usage of himself as altogether is intolerable to be borne, and which, were it not over well known, we would both be very loath to think that it could be true. To take away the occasion of slander, he is himself determined to be at the apprehension and execution of him, whom he is able manifestly to charge with the crime, and to have done him the most dishonour that can be to any man, much more being as he is. We need not more plainly to describe the person. You have heard of the man.

'There are privy these : in Scotland, Argyll, Morton, Boyd, Ruthven, and Liddington. In England these, Moray, Rothes, Grange, myself, the writer hereof. . . . These are the things which we thought, and think, of no small importance . . . and knowing them certainly intended, thought it our duties to impart the same to you, Mr. Secretary, to make declaration thereof as shall seem best to your wisdom.'

The Scottish Parliament was to assemble on Monday the 11th of February, and on the following day a Bill of Attainder against the rebel Lords, including Moray, and perhaps especially with a view to Moray, was to be produced. But on the 8th the puppet King signed a safe-conduct for Moray to return to Scotland.

The Queen of Scotland seems to have received some

intimation of danger.  But she ignored it.  Perhaps by this time she despised her husband so much that she thought him incapable of action.  She forgot that there were others.

An astrologer named Damiot spoke these strange words to Riccio : 'Beware of the bastard'.  The bastard of the prediction was George Douglas, son of the Earl of Angus, and one of the chief conspirators.  But to Riccio 'the bastard' meant Moray — and he was banished — far away.

The plot was now completed and the time was ripe.  On the 4th of March the Queen opened Parliament.  This was on a Thursday.

On the Saturday of the following week, the Queen held a small supper-party in a room, not more than twelve feet square, of her private apartments.  She sat on a sofa at the supper table, and opposite her sat Riccio, wearing an evening robe of damask trimmed with fur, a satin doublet, and russet velvet hose.  His hat was on his head.  The Queen's half-sister, Lady Argyll, was her other guest, and her half-brother Lord Robert Stuart, the equerry Arthur Erskine, and her French physician were in attendance.

The night was singularly still.  No sounds were heard from outside as, in the darkness, Morton and a company of Douglases stealthily surrounded the Palace.  By eight o'clock they had taken possession of the doors, so that no one could leave or enter the Palace.  The next step was for Morton and a band of followers to seize the staircase leading to the Queen's room.

The conspirators mounted the stairs, and, soundlessly, entered the Queen's bedroom.  Suddenly, the tapestry curtain that served as door to the room in which the supper was being held was raised, and, to the Queen's surprise, her husband entered.

He sat down on the sofa beside her.  She asked him if he had had supper, but his answer seemed to stick in his throat. Instead of replying, he put his arm round her waist and kissed her.

Then the curtain stirred again, and the old warlock, Ruth-

ven, stood before her, clad in black armour as if the black ice
of death had already imprisoned him.

The Queen turned to her husband, and said one word :
'Judas!' Then, staring at the ghost in armour, she asked him
by what right and for what purpose he was there. 'Let it
please Your Majesty', he answered, 'that yonder man David
come forth of your privy chamber where he hath been too
long !'

'What offence hath he done ?' she asked. 'He is here of
my will !' then, turning on her husband, 'What means this ?'
she asked.

He was already afraid. 'Ce n'est rien', he stammered —
and, perhaps, wished that what was to be done might be left
undone. But it was too late.

'Madame,' said the ghost in armour, 'he has offended your
honour ; has offended your husband's honour ; he has caused
Your Majesty to banish a great part of the nobility that he
might be made a lord ; he has been the destroyer of the
commonwealth, and must learn his duty better.'

'Take the Queen your wife to you', he ordered Darnley.
But Darnley only stood and stared.

The Queen rose and placed herself in front of the cowering
Riccio — commanding Ruthven to go, or be committed for
treason.

By this time, the men in attendance had sufficiently
recovered from their astonishment to advance upon Ruthven
in order to throw him out. But 'Lay no hands upon me',
said the ghost, and drew his dagger.

The door of the Queen's bedroom opened, and a throng
of men, headed by Falconside and George Douglas, the
bastard of the astrologer's warning, rushed in, upsetting the
table and the lights as they came, so that the room would have
been in darkness had not Lady Argyll snatched a single candle
as it fell.

Afterwards, the Queen declared that the murderers stabbed
Riccio 'over our shoulders with whineards [whinyards], one
part of them standing before our face with bended daggs

[pistols]' . . . Ruthven, in his 'Declaration', said 'Where Her Majesty alledgeth, that night that Davie was slain some held pistols to her Majesties womb, some stroke whineards so near her crag [throat] that she felt the coldness of the iron, with many other such like sayings . . . we take God to record was nevir meant nor done ; for the said Davie receeved never a stroke in Her Majesty's presence, nor was not stricken till he was at the farthest door of Her Majesty's utter [outer] chamber'.

Ruthven lifted the Queen up and thrust her into Darnley's arms, telling him to hold her. Riccio, screaming with terror and clutching at her dress, had his little finger bent back till the pain made him release his hold. Then George Douglas seized Darnley's dagger, and stabbed Riccio over the Queen's shoulder. He was rushed away, and hurled down the staircase, his shrieks of terror and anguish reaching the Queen's ears as he was stabbed again and again. 'Madame, Madame, save me ! Save me ! I am a dead man ! Spare my life !'

He was still alive when he reached the head of the stairs ; but there George Douglas stabbed him again, with the King's dagger, saying, 'This is from the King. . .'. A few moments more, and it was all over. He had, in all, fifty-six wounds.

The porter dragged the body into his lodge and stripped it. 'This was his destiny,' he said, 'for upon this chest was his first bed when he came to this place, and there he lieth, a very niggard and mushroom knave.'

But the Queen's epitaph on him was very different. 'Poor Davy !' she said, when told he was dead, and, weeping, she collapsed on a sofa. 'Good and faithful servant ! May God have mercy on your soul !'

This does not sound like a woman mourning for her dead lover !

.    .    .    .    .

The tocsin sounded throughout Edinburgh.

.    .    .    .    .

Bothwell, Huntly, and Atholl were at supper in the Palace at the time of the murder. Hearing the tumult, they called to their followers and rushed to the Queen's rescue ; but although they threw themselves against the doors that were being held by Morton's men, they could not break them open.

There was only one thing to be done. Bothwell and his brother-in-law Huntly escaped through 'a little window where the lions were lodged'. Once out of the Palace, they could form a plan for the Queen's rescue.

Then the Provost of Edinburgh, with four hundred of the town Guard, arrived under the Queen's window. She, rushing to the window, forced it open, and called to them for help.

'Sit down', said a voice behind her. 'If you stir, you shall be cut into collops and flung over the walls.'

She was seized and torn away from the window, and her husband, appearing there, told the citizens that all was well and they had best go home.

The Queen was left entirely alone. Three months before the birth of her child, and after the horrors she had just experienced, she had no one to attend her.

When told that Riccio was dead, she had exclaimed : 'No more tears. . . . I will think upon a revenge.' Through that long night she was left alone, to think upon that revenge.

Next morning her husband rejoined her. She received him with great sweetness. She assured him that she knew *he* had no part in the murder.

The rebel Lords had feared that meeting, knowing that she would win him 'to follow her will and desire, by reason she hath been trained up from her youth in the Court of France'. They had every reason for their fear. It was an easy matter for her to get from him the names of his fellow conspirators. He betrayed them, and was, he believed, entirely reconciled to her.

He persuaded them, against their will, to allow her ladies to attend her ; and through them she communicated with Bothwell and Huntly. In the early afternoon she 'made as though she would part with her child', and the midwife and French physician who were called insisted that she must be removed from her present imprisonment.

Towards evening, the hated brother who knew her secrets entered the Palace.

It was not thus that he should have been brought before her — but with his head already severed from his body, — or, if still living, he should have been awaiting the fall of the axe. . . . But, for all her unsleeping hatred, she flung herself into his arms, and, weeping, said, 'Oh my brother, if you had been here I should not have been so unceremoniously handled'. And she gave him her Judas kiss. He knew the fate she had prepared for him — that she had willed a Bill of Attainder leading to his death to be prepared against him — but he shed tears.

On Monday morning Ruthven, Morton, and Moray met to discuss what should be done. All that is known of that meeting is that, in a letter to the Archbishop of Glasgow, the Queen said that some of the lords had 'proposed to keep her a perpetual prisoner, some to put her to death, some that she should be warded in Stirling Castle till she had approved in Parliament what they had done, established their religion, and given to the King the whole government of the realm'.

But the King told them that he 'had obtained of Her Majesty that the earls and lords should come into her presence and she would forgive all things past and bury them out of her mind'.

In the afternoon, therefore, between four and five, Moray, Morton, and Ruthven arrived in the antechamber. The Queen entered with Darnley, and they knelt to her, begging that she would pardon them and restore their estates ; to which she replied that she 'was never blood-thirsty, nor greedy upon their lands and goods'.

Morton, seeing that one of his knees was stained with the blood that was still wet upon the floor, said, 'The loss of one mean man is of less consequence than the ruin of many lords and gentlemen'.

The Queen declared she was ready to sign a bond giving them her full forgiveness. The bond was prepared, and, the Queen having left the room, Darnley took the paper, swearing to return it, signed, next day.  As this was certain, he said, he called upon them to keep the Queen a prisoner no longer.

They removed the guard — Ruthven saying that 'Whatever bloodshed followed should be on the King's head'.  Had they refused, Bothwell was fully resolved to rescue the Queen by force.

It was at midnight that she made her escape — through an underground secret passage leading into the charnel house of 'the broken tombs and demolished sepultures', among 'the bones and skulls of the ancient Kings of Scotland'.

The full moon shone upon her escape.  By her side rode the double traitor Henry Darnley.

# Chapter Thirty

IT is agreeable to know that Lord Ruthven, on his departure to Heaven in the May following the murder of Riccio, was escorted there by 'a choir of angels'. These he distinctly saw and heard (so he told the impressed onlookers) as, also, he saw 'Heaven opening to receive him'. The Earl of Morton, who was 'present at the death-bed, felt no small grief, and yet the same [departure ?] was so godly that all men that saw it did rejoice'.

Lord Darnley's departure was to be less agreeable. He had assured the Council that he 'never counselled, commanded, nor approved' the murder of Riccio. His signed declaration was posted at the Market Cross. He had signed his own death warrant. He had betrayed his fellow conspirators — the names of whom only he knew. One had been hanged as a result. And now Joseph Riccio, the brother of the murdered man, was the Queen's confidential secretary.

Wandering aimlessly in the Castle by day, 'vagabonding' by night, Darnley had no friends now but his father, his father's servants and his own. Soon he was to make another desperate mistake. 'The King', according to Knox's *History of the Reformation*, 'being now contemned by all men, because the Queen cared not for him . . . being desolate and half desperate, sought means to go out of the country ; and about the same time, by the advice of foolish cagots [hypocrites] he wrote to the Pope, the King of Spain, and to the King of France, complaining of the Queen, as not managing the Catholic cause aright. By some knave, the poor Prince was betrayed, and the Queen got a copy of those letters into her hands.'

In February 1566 that 'splendid, rash, hazardous young man, Earl Bothwell', married a twenty-year-old girl with the full eyes of a hare, a long nose, ripe-looking lips, and hair the colour of sand — Lady Jane Gordon, the daughter of that Earl of Huntly whose strange death and trial is narrated in Chapter Twenty-four. The Queen gave the stuff for the bride's dress from her own wardrobe.

Jane Gordon had been in love with another man, but fell in love with her husband after they were married. He, on his side, was infatuated with her.

Perhaps, thought the onlookers, it was only in the interests of the realm that the bridegroom spent so much time in the Queen's company. And yet . . . There was her strange, mad ride to the house where he lay wounded, in October, having been attacked by robbers. . . . There was her strange subsequent illness, that nearly led to her death — the result, it was said, of the fatigue of that ride, following the shock of the news of his wound.

This was four months after the birth of Mary's son, 'dear bought', she said, 'with the peril of her life'. He was born on the 19th of June, and the Queen told the husband who had tried to bastardise her child, 'He is so much your own son, that I fear it will be the worse for him hereafter'.

Before that birth the Queen and her husband were on most unhappy terms. According to a MS. among the Lennox papers, headed 'Some Part of the Talk between the late King of Scots and me, the Earl of Lennox, riding between Dundas and Lythkoo [Linlithgow] in a dark night, taking upon him to be the guide that night' . . . Darnley said to his father that he had often ridden that road, and Lennox replied that it was no wonder, he riding to meet his wife, 'a paragon and a Queen'. His son answered that they were not happy, and that just before the birth of their son, the Queen suggested that he should take a mistress — 'make, if it were possible, my Lord [Moray] wear horns, and I assure you I shall never love you the worse.'

What was her reason for suggesting this ? Did she hope

that Moray would kill him, and be brought to execution for it?

Lennox 'liked not the saying' but only advised his son never to be unfaithful to the Queen. His son answered, 'I never offended the Queen my wife in meddling with any other woman, in thought, let be in deed'.

This story was told by Darnley, also, to one of his servants, and it came to the ears of Moray.

In August and September 1566, the Queen made a great show of affection towards her husband. They hunted deer with Bothwell and Moray on the moors between Yarrow and Tweed. The Queen gave him a magnificent bed — that bed on which he was to lie at Kirk-o'-Fields, — and cloth of gold to make a caparison for his horse. She spoke to him in siren tones. But he, sulky because the sport was not good, answered brutally.

In September, the Queen reconciled Bothwell and Lethington. And Darnley had tried to bring about Lethington's downfall! That reconciliation brought Darnley one step nearer to the grave.

At that time, the Queen was working at affairs of state in the Exchequer House, to which large gardens were attached. It was said by Buchanan, in his *Detection*, that Lady Reres, sister of Sir Walter Scott's Magic Lady of Branksome, aunt of Mary Beaton, and a former mistress of Bothwell, let Bothwell into the garden, and so into the Queen's room, where he raped her.

But that story does not tally with Lord Lennox's later narrative, in which he wrote that even before the birth of her son, Bothwell and she were adulterers.

The Queen and her husband, 'that innocent lamb who meant so faithfully unto her as his wife', were increasingly estranged, while 'Bothwell waxed so great that he, supplying the place of the aforesaid David, was her love in such sort that she, forgetting her duty to God and her husband, and setting apart her honour and good name, became addicted and wholly assotted unto the same Bothwell. Not only for lust of body but to seek the blood of her dear husband in revenge for the death of her servant David.'

It was almost time for the Waxworks King to be gone.

This was the decision of five men, meeting together at Craigmillar. The stories about what took place there vary.

One story relates that Moray and William Maitland of Lethington (Secretary Lethington) roused Argyll from his bed, and said that in order to induce the Queen to recall Morton from banishment for his part in the murder of Riccio, they must first please her by ridding her of her husband. Huntly was then sent for, and finally Bothwell, and the five went together to the Queen's room and suggested a divorce, to which she replied that it might cast a reflection on her son's legitimacy, and that it would be better for her husband to retire to France.

Then it was that Lethington said that 'a way would be found', and that the Earl of Moray would 'look through his fingers'. (Afterwards Moray denied that anything was said in his presence 'tending to any unlawful or dishonourable end'.)

Nothing, said the Queen, must be done which would injure her conscience or honour. To which Lethington replied that if they were allowed to arrange the matter 'Your Grace shall see nothing but good, and approved by Parliament'.

# Chapter Thirty-one

DOOM speaks to us sometimes, with the hum of a gnat. We hardly feel the prick that is no sharper than that of a pin ; but it ushers in Eternity.

The words said to Mary by Lethington had been spoken in a whisper, scarcely louder than the hum of a gnat ; but through the dark corridors of the Castle that whisper floated, only half understood at first, then gathering body and meaning, until it reached the King.

He knew, now, from the fact that Riccio's murderers had been pardoned and allowed to return to Scotland, that the Queen and her friends were resolved to destroy him. That proclamation of pardon was his death sentence.

He had no friends. His arrogance, his folly, had alienated them all. During the weeks before the birth of the Prince, the King lived in separate state in the Castle, and 'vagabondised' each night. Soon the marks of that 'vagabondising', the marks of God's wrath, sealed upon him, would be seen. It was time, now, for this 'afternoon man' or night-moth, this weak, gay, proud butterfly, to be gone.

On the 15th of December 1566, the christening of the Prince was celebrated with great pomp. But where was the King ?

He who 'remained in Stirling all the time (of) the christening', Knox said in his *History*, 'never being present, kept his chamber ; his father, hearing how he was used, wrote to him to repair unto him, who soon afterwards went, without goodnight, towards Glasgow, to his father. He was hardly a mile out of Stirling, when the poison which had been given him wrought so upon him that he had very great pain and dolour in every part of his body. At length being arrived in Glasgow, the blisters broke out on him, of a bluish colour, so that the physician presently knew the disease to come by poison. He was brought so low, that nothing but death was expected, yet the strength of his youth at last surmounted the poison.'

According to George Buchanan, 'that he was poisoned, it is certainly known . . . the kind of Disease (*sic*) strange, unknown to the People, unacquainted to Physicians, especially such as had not been in Italy and Spain, black Pimples, breaking out over all his Body, grievous Sweat in all his Limbs, and intolerable Stink'.

Leaving this refreshing description of the disorder, we may ask ourselves what was its true nature.

Whilst Knox and Buchanan believed it to be due to poison, others thought it to be smallpox — which, it is true, was raging in Glasgow at the time. But the King was riding to, not from, Glasgow ; when he was seized with illness, he had only ridden a mile beyond Stirling, and the time of incubation for smallpox is from twelve to fourteen days. It is far more probable that he had been infected during those nights of 'vagabondising' and that the disease was syphilis.

According to Dr. Karl Pearson [1] 'the description of the effects of the "poison" is, in brief, closely akin to those of the acute inflammatory effects of syphilis when it first became epidemic'. Having examined the King's skull, Dr. Pearson said 'the pits [on this] must have come from some fairly serious illness. Smallpox does not give them.'

Randolph informed the British Council that 'the Queen of Scotland had the falling sickness, and the King lèpre'. (Leprosy and smallpox were, in the 16th century, confused with syphilis.) Bothwell said the King had 'roniole' or 'rognolle' — another horrible name for syphilis, which, in France of that century, was known variously as 'le gros mal', 'la grande gorre', 'la grosse vérole', 'le gros scabies', and 'la grosse rognolle'.

But Bothwell was Darnley's murderer, and we need not, necessarily, heed his testimony on the subject. However, the

present writer believes it may be true ; and if so, that is
one reason why the Queen may have withdrawn her protest
against her husband's murder.  It must be remembered that
he soon began to insist that she should return to a marital life
with him.

The Queen took the baby Prince to Edinburgh on the
14th of January 1567.  Then, suddenly, she determined to visit
the King in Glasgow.  The journey began on the 23rd, and
Bothwell rode with her to Callander, where they spent the
night, he returning to Edinburgh next morning, but leaving
his French servant Paris with her, to be the means of
communication between them.

When the King and his father heard of that approaching
visit, they were in great fear.  Lord Lennox sent one of his
gentlemen, named Crawford, to meet her on her way, and
apologise that he was unable to come in person.  He did not
attempt to hide the fact that his master feared her.[2]

'There is no remedy against fear,' said the Queen.

'Madam,' replied Crawford, 'I know so far of my master
that he desires nothing more than that the secrets of every
creature's heart were writ on their faces.'

The meaning of this was plain.  'Have you more to say ?'
she asked.  Crawford said the message was ended.

'Then hold your peace,' said the Queen.

Entering the King's room, she asked him, tenderly, what
was the meaning of a certain letter he had written to her.  How
could he ever have doubted her ?  What *could* it mean ?  Had
he a particular fear of any of the noblemen ?  (When she
mentioned Maitland, the man whom he had injured the most
deeply, he shuddered, said Froude.)  He must come with her
to Craigmillar ;  there he could take cold baths, and he would
soon be cured, and then all would be well between them.
(Craigmillar . . . the place where, it was said, a certain pact
had been signed.)

He looked at her.  Those strange eyes with a slight cast
that did but add to their fascination — those 'delicate, lively,
hazel Eies, like the Eies of a Viper' (to quote John Aubrey's

description of Francis Bacon's eyes, but the phrase describes even better those of Mary Stuart), had, said Froude, 'a strange glitter' — as if some beautiful, dangerous creature were passing behind glittering leaves.

But now she must go. He begged her to stay with him, but she had accomplished the purpose for which she had come. She had persuaded him to go with her to Craigmillar.

He sent for Crawford, and going over the conversation, word by word, asked him what he thought it meant.

Crawford said that 'he liked it not. Why should she take him to Craigmillar — that lonely, almost uninhabited spot, when she could take him to Holyrood? The King replied that he, too, had thought it strange. But he had resolved to go. Yes, he would trust himself in her hands were she to cut his throat.' [3]

Late into the night following the day when she arrived at the bedside of the man who was soon to die, the Queen sat writing a letter :

'Having departed from the place where I left my Heart, it is easy to be judged what was my Countenance, seeing I was even as mekle as any Body without ane Heart. . . .' He had said, 'that he was so glad to see me, that he believed to die for Gladness. . . . He declared unto me his Sickness, and that he would make no Testament, only leave all Things to me, and that I was the cause of his Malady, because of the Regret that he had had that I was so strange unto him. . . . And thus he said . . . "I am young. Ye will say Ye have forgiven me oft times, and yet that I return to my faults. May not any man of my age for lack of Counsel fall twice or thrice, or in Lack of his Promise," (break his promise?) "and at last repent himself, and be chastened by Experience ? If I may obtain Pardon, I protest I shall never make Fault again, and I crave no other Thing but that we may be at Bed and Board together as Husband and Wife, and if ye will not consent hereunto, I shall never rise out of this Bed. God knows how I am punished for making my God of you, and for having no other Thought but on you . . ." I trow he believed that I would have sent him away Prisoner. I answered that I would take him with me to Craigmillar, where the Mediciner and I might help him, and I not be far from my Son.

'He answered that he was ready when I pleased, if I would assure him of his Request. He desires no Body to see him . . . As for me, he would rather give his Life ere he did any Displeasure to me. And after this, he shewed me of so many little Flatteries, so carefully and so wisely . . . I had almost forgot that he said he could not doubt me, for he could not believe that I who was his proper Flesh, would do him any Evil. But as to any others that would pursue him, at least he would sell his Life dear enough ; but he suspected no Body, nor yet would not, but would love all that I loved. He would not let me depart from him. . . . Ye saw him never better, nor speak more humble. . . . And if I had not ane Proof of his Heart of Wax, and that mine were not of ane Diamond, that no shot can make break, but that which comes forth of your Hand, I would almost had Pitie of him. But fear not, the Place shall hold unto Death. Remember in Recompense thereof, that ye suffer not yours to be won by that false Race that will travail no less with you for the same. I believe they have been at School together. He has ever the Tear in his Eye ; he salutes every Body, yea, unto the least ; And Makes piteous Caressing unto them to make them have Pity on him. . . . Have you not Desire to laugh to see me lie so well, at the least to dissemble so well, and to tell him Truth betwixt Hands ? . . . I have drawn it all out of him' (she meant information implicating others). 'Ye have had the rest. We are coupled with two false Races ; the Devil sunder us, and God knit us together for ever. This is my Faith, I will die in it. Excuse I write evil, ye may guess the half of it, but I cannot mend it, because I am not well at Eyes, and yet very glad to write unto you when the rest are sleeping, since I cannot sleep as they do, and as I would desire, that is in your Arms, my dear Love, whom I pray God to preserve from all Evil, and render you Repose. I am going to seek mine till the Morne, when I shall end my Byble. . . . Advertise me what you have deliberated to do in the matter ye know (of) to the end that we may understand neitheris' (each other) 'well, that nothing therethrough be split. I am urked' (tired?) 'and ganging to sleep' (half asleep) 'and yet I cease not to scribble at this Paper in so little as rests thereof. Were it not (for) this Pockish Man . . . without him I should have a far pleasanter Subject to discourse upon. He is not over much deformed, yet he has taken very much. He has almost slain me with his Breath ; it is worse than your Uncle's, and yet I came no nearer unto him but in a Chair at the Bed-side, and he being at the other end thereat.

'Ye bade me dissemble so far, that I have obhorrence thereat ; and ye cause me to do almost the office of a Traitoress. Remember how if it were not to obey you, I had rather be dead ere I did it ; my Heart bleeds at it. . . .

'Allace ! I never deceived any Body. But I remit me altogether to your will. Send me advertisement what I shall do, and whatever thing shall come thereof, I shall obey you. Advise with yourself, if you can find out any more secret inventions by Medicine ; for he should take medicine and the Bath at Craigmillar.

'He may not come forth of the house this long time. Summa, by all that I can learn, he is in great suspicion, and yet, notwithstanding, he gives credit to my word. But yet not so far that he will show any Thing to me. But nevertheless, I shall draw it out of him, if ye will that I avow all unto him. But I will never rejoice to defame any Body that trusts in me. Yet notwithstanding, ye may command me in all things. Have no evil opinion of me for that cause, for reason Ye are the occasion of it yourself ; because, for my particular revenge, I would not do it to him. . . .

'Summa, for certainty he suspects of the thing you know, and of his life. But as to the last, how soon I speak two or three good words unto him, he rejoices, and is out of doubt.

'Now, seeking to obey you, my dear Love, I spare neither Honour, Conscience, Hasard, nor Greatness ; take it, I pray you, in good part, and not after the interpretation of your false

Good-brother' (brother-in-law, brother to Lady Bothwell) 'to whom, I pray you, give no credit against the most faithful lover that ye ever had, or shall have. See not her, whose feigned good tears should not be so much praised nor esteemed, as the true and faithful Travail I sustain for to meet the plan. For obtaining of the which against my Naturall' (Nature?) 'I betray them that may impeach (prevent?)' 'me. God forgive me, and God give you, my only Love, the hope and prosperity that your humble and faithful Love desires unto you, who hopes to be shortly an other Thing to you, for the reward of my irksome Travails.'

There was no sound in the sleeping house, excepting the faint hum of a gnat (a faint and menacing warning) and the sound of the sheets of a letter being turned, slowly, one by one.

### NOTES TO CHAPTER THIRTY-ONE

[1] Quoted in Dr. Karl Pearson's *The Skull and Portraits of Henry Stewart, Lord Darnley*. The Biometric Laboratory, University College, London.

[2] Froude, *op. cit.*

[3] Crawford's Deposition. Scotch MSS. Rolls House. Froude, *op. cit.*

# Chapter Thirty-two

BOTHWELL'S servant, Paris, after a day's ride, reached Edinburgh with the Queen's letter on the night of the 25th of January. But Bothwell was absent, and Paris must follow him to a house named St. Mary's in the Fields, or Kirk-o'-Fields, that stood just within the walls of Edinburgh. It was the property of Sir James Balfour, one of the signers of the bond.

Bothwell opened the letter, and wrote, in answer, a few words. 'Commend me to the Queen,' he said to Paris, 'and tell her that all will go well. Say that Balfour and I have not slept all night, that everything is arranged, and that the King's lodgings are ready for him. I have sent her a diamond. You may say that I would send my heart too, were it in my power — but she has it already.' [1]

After a few more words, Paris went to Maitland, who said, 'Tell Her Majesty to bring the King to Kirk-o'-Fields'.

With these messages, Paris rode through the night, arriving before the Queen had left her bed. But such was her impatience that she received him immediately. A few hours passed, then the Queen was on the road with the man who was soon to die. But he must be moved slowly, because of his condition, and it was not until the 30th that they reached the gates of Edinburgh. The King still thought he was being taken to Craigmillar.

As they reached the gates, another procession approached them, and at the head of it, Bothwell. The voice of Doom sounded in the King's ear : 'Kirk-o'-Fields is the more convenient place where the King might recover his health'. And to Kirk-o'-Fields, in spite of his remonstrances, he was taken.

It was indeed a more convenient place. 'Ane House', wrote Buchanan,[2] 'not commodious for ane sick man, nor comely for a King, for it was both ruined and ruinous, and has stood empty without any dweller in it for divers years before, in a place of small Resort, between the old falling Walls of twa Kirks, near ane few Alms-housis for poor Beggars. And that no commodious means for committing that Mischief might be wanting, there is a postern Door in the Towne Wall hard by the House, whereby they might easily pass away into the Fields.'

Everything was arranged for the King's comfort and safety. The keys of the house were given to Bothwell's groom-of-the-chamber, Thomas Nelson. (But his master had duplicates.) There was no lock to the door that led from the garden into the cellar, but that was of no account, for it could be bolted from within — so the servants were told.[3] As for the door at the bottom of the staircase leading into the King's room — there was surely no need for this. How much more practical it would be, said the Queen, if the door were taken down and made into a cover for the King's bath.

'There was nothing left', said Thomas Nelson in his Examination,[4] 'to stop the passage into the said chamber but only the portal door.'

In a small room of unspeakable stuffiness, the nightmare figure of the Leper-King, wearing a white taffeta mask to hide the disease from which he suffered, sat day-long, slept through the night, in a violet bed.

There was but little furniture: a carpet; a tall chair covered with purple velvet; a little table with a green velvet cloth; a few red velvet cushions. Here it was that the Queen sat through the days, talking with her victim. She returned to Holyrood, usually, for the night. But a little room had been arranged for her immediately under the King's, and this contained a small bed of yellow and green damask, with a fur coverlet.

She had given particular instructions as to the exact spot on which the bed was to be placed. But Paris, for some

reason, misunderstood the order. 'Fool that you are !' the
Queen said, 'the bed is not to stand there. Move it yonder to
the other side.' For it was in that room, and in the exact place
where the bed had been put, immediately under the bed of
the King, that a powder barrel was to be lighted and blow the
house and everybody in it to dust.[5]

Mary's secretary, Nau, said that the Queen, seeing Paris
after he had been dealing with the gunpowder, said 'Jesu !
Paris — how begrimed you are !' Lang, repeating the story,
says that if Mary saw Paris begrimed, it is certain that she knew
his master, Bothwell, was the murderer.

She spent two nights in that bed — Wednesday, the 5th of
February, and Friday the 7th. (For it was necessary that the
people should believe it was *she* who was the intended victim.)
But she had not, now, much longer to stay in that ruinous
place that stood among the beggars' houses, for the murder
had been planned for Saturday.

There were to be three murderers, wild youths, gentlemen
retainers of Bothwell : Hay, the Laird at Tallo, Hepburn of
Botton, and the Laird of Ormiston. . . . But then the plans
changed. Would it not be wiser, the conspirators wondered,
for the King to be killed by some *accident* — other than by an
explosion ?

Lord Robert Stuart, Abbot of St. Cross, and Mary's half-
brother, had been a boon companion of the King's. He pitied
him, and warned him. Darnley promptly betrayed him to
the Queen, as he had betrayed everyone who had ever come
to his aid, if, by so doing, he could hope to win her favour.
Stuart, knowing this had put his life in danger, found himself
in a position where, in order to save himself, he must become
the King's executioner. Darnley must be provoked to a
duel.

The Queen, on that Saturday night, sent Paris to Bothwell
with the message : 'The Abbot of St. Cross must go to the
King's room and do what the Earl knew of'. To which
Bothwell replied : 'Tell the Queen that I will speak to St.
Cross, and then I will see her'.

But the hope of a duel came to nothing, because the King was too feeble to leave his bed and fight it. So the doomed man was allowed one more night of life.

By one of those coincidences of which the Earl of Moray was a master, he was obliged, on the morning following, to tell the Queen his wife was ill at St. Andrews, and he must go to her.

On that afternoon — it was a Sunday — Margaret Cawood, the Queen's waiting woman, was married at Holyrood to one of the musicians, Sebastian. The Queen attended the wedding ; then, after an early supper, returned to her husband's bedside, saying that she intended to spend the night at Kirk-o'-Fields.

She was assiduously affectionate. . . .

.  .  .  .  .

It was after midnight that the Queen remembered she had promised to be present at the masque and ball that were to follow her maid's wedding. It was unfortunate ; for she had certainly, she told her husband, intended to remain with him. She rose, gave him her kiss, and placed a ring on his finger.

As she reached the door, she turned, and said to him, 'It was just this time last year that Davie was slain'.

Then she went out.

What was that sound ? Something was being moved in the room below, perhaps ?

Yet there was no one left in the King's house but his page, Taylor, who slept in his room, and his servants Nelson and Edward Seymour. Or so they thought.

Before sleeping — so William Drury, Marshal of Berwick, told Cecil — the King called for a cup of wine, then read the 55th Psalm : 'Fearfulness and trembling are come upon me, and an horrible dread hath overwhelmed me.

'It is not an open enemy that hath done me this dishonour, for then I could have borne it.

'It was even thou my companion, my guide, and my own familiar friend.'

There was now no sound, excepting that of the King's lips moving.

The two unseen men still waited in darkness below. And the countryside was covered with night, excepting for the light of one candle in Hamilton House.

.        .        .        .        .

The countryside had been silent for the space of an hour and a half, when there was the sound of running footsteps. Then some women in the beggars' houses heard a cry : 'Pity me, kinsmen, for the love of Him who pitied all the world'.

Silence for a moment. Then Edinburgh was violently shaken by a roar 'as if 25 or 30 cannon had been fired in a volley'.

The listening, waiting page Paris felt 'every hair of his head stand up like an awl'.

Then again there was silence.

The candle in Hamilton House went out.*

---

* The Hamiltons were enemies of Darnley and his father, and they had claims to succeed to the crown of Scotland should the Queen have no heir.

NOTES TO CHAPTER THIRTY-TWO

1 Examination of Paris. Pitcairn, *Criminal Trials*, vol. i.
2 *Detection of Mary Queen of Scots.*
3 Froude, *op. cit.*
4 Pitcairn, *op. cit.*
5 Examination of Paris. Pitcairn, *op. cit.* Froude, *op. cit.*

# Chapter Thirty-three

ALMOST before it was light, on the morning of the 10th of February, the sound of whispering was heard in the streets of Edinburgh. Small knots of people gathered together, then dispersed, as if afraid.

In a courtyard of Holyroodhouse, an excited group of servants was chattering. A man slunk through the court — Paris, going to his master's room. The talk stopped. They stared at him in silence.

In Bothwell's room the page gave way to his terror. What would happen to him? Would *he* be accused? Bothwell asked him roughly who would trouble about *him* — a mere nobody — when the lords of Scotland were involved?

The Queen of Scots had passed a peaceful night, but had awakened early. Now, as the trembling Paris entered her room, he found the curtains were closed as a sign of mourning, the widow's room was already shrouded in black, and there was no light excepting from candles. But she seemed to have borne her bereavement lightly, and now, sitting up in bed, she was being given her breakfast — a new-laid egg — by the solicitous Madame de Brêne, her governess.

She paid no attention to the terror-stricken Paris, for Bothwell came hard at his heels, and talked to her in a whisper.

The news spread through the city. According to one account, the body of the 'young fool and proud tirrane' had been left for three hours, lying under a tree, his dead page beside him, his fur-lined velvet 'nightgown' at a distance from him. He and the page had been scarcely touched by the powder.

What had happened? Had he, at last, heard another sound from those men who had waited in the room below, in darkness? Had he, knowing they had come to murder him, fled from the house, been overtaken, and 'wirried' — (strangled)?

In any case, when found, the body was carried by some of the 'rascall people' into one of the beggarly houses, and there it lay for forty-eight hours — so it was said — before the widow had it brought to the chapel of Holyrood by 'certaine souldiears . . . and vile personis, upon an auld blok of forme or tre'.

There the widow went to look at it.

She had been busy writing letters. It was certain, she told her Ambassador in Paris, the morning after the murder, that it was *her* life that had been aimed at. . . . She would rather, she said, 'lose life and all' than allow this horror to go unpunished — a deed which 'God would never suffer to ly hid'. (Did she tremble as she wrote those words?) She would punish it 'with sic rigor as sall serve for example of this crueltie to all ages to cum!'

Later on the day following the murder, Bothwell and Argyll, in their anxiety that the crime should be punished, visited the ruins. And next day, they, with Maitland, offered a reward of £2000 for whoever should denounce the murderers.

Voices were heard in the night, crying 'Bothwell hath murthered the King. . . . Bothwell. . . . Bothwell. . . .' The voices crying for vengeance on the murderer and his accomplice, the adulterous Queen, came near to the Palace, then died away again in the darkness.

As the light dawned each day, papers were seen strewn about the city, denouncing them — placards were nailed to the door of the Tolbooth — portraits of Bothwell, and the sentence 'The Queen was an assenting party, through the persuasion of the Earl of Bothwell and the witchcraft of the Lady Buccleugh' — who had been one of Bothwell's mistresses.

If he knew, said Bothwell, who were the authors of the placards, he would wash his hands in their blood.

Now, his black armour seeming the embodiment of all the darkness that overhung Edinburgh, thunder or the noise of thunder accompanying his every movement, he never left the Palace unless with fifty armed men ; and, Drury told Cecil on the 28th of February, if 'any spoke to him not assured a friend, his hand was on his dagger'.

'Upon the fifth day', wrote a contemporary,[1] 'after the murder [Darnley's], bodie was bureit at Halyruidhous, quyetlie in the night, without any kynd of solemnitie or murnyng, hard [heard] among all the personnis at Court.'

On the night, eleven months before, when, after Riccio's murder, the Queen and her husband fled among the tombs of the Kings, and over Riccio's new-made grave, she had said to him, 'Ere a twelve-month was over, a fatter than he should lie beside him'.

According to Buchanan, she kept her promise ; her husband was buried by the side of her murdered favourite. The dead boy's clothes, his horses, all his possessions, were given to Bothwell.

.        .        .        .        .

The Queen's mourning, it was said, was of a strange order.

She had forgone 'the preservation of the Corps for forty Dayes' ; but, as her champion the Bishop of Ross, writing under the pseudonym of Morgan Philippes, said, 'This was only customary for such Queenes as mourne their Husbands who were Kings. Her Grace mourneth after another Sort. She is a Prince, her husband a Private Man and a Subject.'

Besides, he was a murderer. Had not his dagger been found in Riccio's side ? She might justly have had him convicted. . . . condemned . . . executed. She did not.

This 'good gentle lady', said the Bishop, 'bemoned him a notable time, using none other than Candle light'. Then 'the closeness of the air' endangered her health, and at the urgent entreaty of her Council she left the 'continuance of this mourning . . .' and found it necessary to go out and about with Bothwell.

The morning after her husband's burial, the Queen, with Bothwell, his brother-in-law Huntly, Maitland, and a hundred other gentlemen, left Holyrood and rode to Lord Seton's house. Their presence there was blessed by that of Archbishop Hamilton.

The Queen had not been well — affected, possibly, by the news of her husband's murder. What more natural than that the days should be passed in hunting — in Bothwell's company — in archery, and in other pleasures designed to distract her mind from her loss ?

### NOTE TO CHAPTER THIRTY-THREE

[1] Thomson, *The Historie and Life of King James the Sext.*

# Chapter Thirty-four

THE agony of Lady Lennox, on hearing the news of the murder, was such that doctors had to be summoned. She was released from the Tower, and now, her face swollen and discoloured with weeping, kneeling before Elizabeth she clamoured for vengeance.

No effort had been made to trace the murderers.

Remonstrances reached Mary from the Queen Dowager of France, from her Ambassador there. Still nothing was done.

The Queen of England, on the 24th of February, wrote :
'Madam,

'My ears have been so astounded, my mind so disturbed, my heart so shocked at the news of the abominable murder of your late husband, that even yet I can scarcely rally my spirits to write to you ; and however I would express my sympathy in your sorrow for his loss, so, to tell you plainly what I think, my grief is more for you than for him. Oh, madam, I should ill fulfil the part either of a faithful cousin or of an affectionate friend if I were to content myself with saying pleasant things to you and made no effort to preserve your honour. I cannot but tell you what all the world is thinking. Men say that, instead of seizing the murderers, you are looking through your fingers while they escape ; that you will not punish those who have done you so great a service, as though the thing would never have taken place had not the doers of it been assured of impunity.

'For myself, I beg you to believe that I would not harbour such a thought for all the wealth of the world, nor would I entertain in my heart so ill a guest, or think so badly of any

246

prince that breathes.  Far less could I so think of you, to whom
I desire all imaginable good, and all blessings which you yourself could wish for.  For this very reason I exhort, I advise, I
implore you deeply to consider of the matter — at once, if
it be the nearest friend you have, to lay your hands upon the
man who has been guilty of the crime — to let no interest,
no persuasion, keep you from proving to every one that you
are a noble princess and a loyal wife.  I do not write thus
earnestly because I doubt you, but for the love I bear towards
you.  You may have wiser councillors than I am — I can
well believe it — but even our Lord, as I remember, had a
Judas among the twelve : while I am sure that you have no
friend more true than I, and my affection may stand you in as
good stead as the subtle wits of others.' [1]

On hearing that Killigrew was on his way, bearing this
letter from the Queen of England, Mary remembered her
role as desolate widow.  Rushing to Holyrood, one day before
the arrival of the emissary, she received him in a room so
darkened that it was impossible for him to see her face ; but
both her voice and words seemed, he said, full of grief. . . .
She seemed unwilling to speak of the murder — it was too
painful a subject — and discoursed mainly on the subject of
Ireland.  But she was forced to hear from Killigrew that
Bothwell was regarded by the whole world as one of her
husband's murderers, and in the end she was obliged to
promise he should be put on trial.

Even after this she continued to consort openly with him.
. . . But there were moments when she felt fear.  Why was
there that menacing and utter silence in the city — a silence
broken at night by the ghostly voices crying for vengeance ? [2]

She thought, at times, of flying to France ; but the King
and the Queen Mother had written to her that 'if she performed not her promise in seeking by all her power to have
the death of the King their cousin revenged, and to clear herself, she should not only think herself dishonoured, but to
receive them for her contraries, and that they would be her
enemies. . .'.

The dead man's father had by now accepted the widow's challenge to name the murderers. . . . He named Bothwell, two of his followers, and four foreigners : Sebastian, whose marriage had been the Queen's excuse for leaving Kirk-o'-Fields, Francis, one of Mary's personal servants, Jean de Bordeaux — and, of course, Joseph Riccio (brother of the murdered Davie).

There was now no way in which the trial could be avoided. But though Bothwell must be tried, it was impossible that he should be found guilty.  For, as Thomas Bishop, Mary's agent in England, told Melville, 'It was reported in England that Her Majesty was about to marry the Earl Bothwell, the murderer of her husband, who at present had a wife of his own, and was a man full of sin'.

The Queen sent for Moray — Bothwell being present. According to one account, he admitted his guilt, but said that 'What he had done and committed was not for his private interest only, but with the consent of others' — and, turning to Moray, he said, 'And with yours'. (This, Moray had denied most strenuously.)  He then demanded that Moray should, for the sake of his own honour, sign a bond swearing to stand by Bothwell in his defence.  Moray refused.

His life was now, therefore, in danger, and he prepared to leave Scotland.  But before leaving, he consulted with Morton and others of the Council, who assured him there was no way of preventing the marriage without violence — so extreme was the Queen's infatuation.  The Prince's life was in danger, and they were therefore resolved to put the Queen under restraint, take Bothwell, and put him to death. But he was so powerful that the only way in which this could be done was by craft.

Passing through London on his way to Italy, Moray visited the Spanish Ambassador.  'I asked him', de Silva told his King, 'whether there was any truth in the report that Bothwell was divorcing his wife.  He said this was so ; and from his account of the matter, one never heard anything so monstrous.

EARL OF MORAY

The wife, to whom he has not been married for a year, is herself the petitioner, and the ground which she alleges is her husband's adultery. I asked if he had ill-treated her, or if there had been trouble between them. He said, No. Her brother, Lord Huntly, had persuaded her into presenting the petition, to please Bothwell; and the Queen, at Bothwell's instance, had restored to Huntly his forfeited lands.

'He told me that the general expectation was, that after the divorce, the Queen meant to marry Bothwell; but he himself could not believe that a princess so nobly gifted as his sister could consent to so foul an alliance.'

.            .            .            .            .

The 12th of April was the day fixed for the trial. According to the law, the prosecution should have been allowed forty days in which to prepare the case. Fifteen only were given.

In London, Lady Lennox was besieging the Spanish Ambassador with lamentations and cries for vengeance. Her husband, in Scotland, expected at each moment to be murdered.

Meanwhile, another document was being prepared in the handwriting of Huntly, *Lady Bothwell's brother* — and this document was signed by the Queen and Bothwell. It stated that as the Queen was a widow, and in need of protection — as had been shown only too clearly by the murder of her husband — she had decided to marry once more. There were objections to a foreigner, and therefore she intended, 'for his many virtues', to marry Bothwell as soon as his divorce from 'his pretended wife' should be lawful.

This document, together with one in which Bothwell promised to marry the Queen, was put, for safety, with certain other letters, in a silver casket that had been given him by the Queen.

There was now nothing for him to fear from the trial.

The Crown should have been the prosecutor. There was

not even the slightest pretence that this was the case. Lennox was the sole accuser.

He had intended, for the safety of his life, to go to the trial of his son's murderers attended by a thousand men. But he was told he could be allowed no more than six — and those, personal servants. Knowing his danger, therefore, he absented himself.

He had asked that the trial might be postponed, in order that he might have the customary forty days in which to prepare the prosecution, and produce the witnesses. He was refused. He had asked for an early trial, he was told, and he should have it !

At that trial there was no prosecutor. There were no witnesses. The chief witness had been arrested on a charge of treason. And yet . . . One of Bothwell's companions at Kirk-o'-Fields, Black Ormiston, whispered to him, 'Fye, my lord, what deed is this ye are doing ? Your face shows what ye are. . . .'

Bothwell's counsel produced a letter from Lennox, asking for an immediate trial. The Queen had done what he asked. Why, therefore, was he complaining ? — Where was the prosecution ? — Where were the witnesses ?

There was nothing to be done but to acquit the accused.

So, at 7 o'clock that evening, the case came to a happy ending, — and Lord Bothwell, as he left the Court, 'fixed a cartel against the door wherein he offered to fight in single contest against any gentleman undefamed, that durst charge him with the murder'.

But the libels continued. They covered the walls of the city, they drifted through the streets. 'Farewell, gentle Harry. But vengeance on Mary.'

On the Market Cross a paper was found that said : 'I am assured there is none that professes Christ and His Evangel that can with any upright conscience part the Earl Bothwell and his wife, albeit she justly prove him an abominable adulterer ; and that by reason he has murdered the husband of her he intends to marry, whose obligation and promise of marriage he had long before the murder was done'.

When Mary dared to ride through the city, the women at the stalls in the Grassmarket screamed, as she passed, 'God save your Grace — if ye be guiltless of the King's death — of the King's death'.

## NOTE TO CHAPTER THIRTY-FOUR

[1] Froude. The original is in French.
[2] Froude, *op. cit.*

# Chapter Thirty-five

ON the 22nd of April, the Queen of Scots visited Stirling, for the purpose — she said — of seeing her child. But the rumours about what was supposed to be her real intent spread, and reached the ears of the Earl of Mar, in charge of the baby Prince and of the Castle. She intended, it was said, to remove the Prince to Edinburgh, where anything could happen to him, — or else give the Castle and the baby over to Bothwell. Mar foiled this plan by admitting only two ladies with the Queen.

But the seizure of the Prince — if, indeed, this had ever been planned — was not the primary reason for that journey. The plan was this : that on the Queen's return journey to Edinburgh on the 24th, Bothwell should appear with armed followers, seize her, and carry her away by force.

But this also was no longer a secret ; and Lennox, writing from the place where he hid until a ship could take him to England, wrote to his wife : 'The Queen returns this day from Stirling. The Earl of Bothwell hath gathered many of his friends. He is minded to meet her this day, and take her by the way and bring her to Dunbar. Judge ye if it be with her will or no.'

The Queen took, according to some, a tender farewell of her child, 'commending him', said Froude, 'rather needlessly to the care of the earl whose chief business was to protect him from his mother. . .'.

But William Drury, writing to Cecil from Berwick, on the 20th of May, had a different story . . . 'the prince being brought unto her, she offered to kiss him, but the prince would not, but put her face away with his hand, and did to his strength scratch her. She took an apple out of her pocket and offered it, but it would not be received by him ; but the nurse took it, and to a greyhound bitch having whelps the apple was thrown. She ate it, and she and her whelps died presently ; a sugar loaf also for the prince, but the Earl of Mar keeps the same. It is judged to be very evil compounded.'

An apple seems a strange meal for a greyhound and her whelps !

The Queen mounted her horse, and accompanied by Huntly, Sir James Melville, Maitland of Lethington, and her ordinary guard, went on her way. At Almond Bridge, two miles from Edinburgh, the Earl of Bothwell, followed by a dozen armed men, appeared suddenly, and riding up to the Queen seized her rein. The guard rushed to defend her, when, to their astonishment, the Queen, who had seemed strangely undisturbed, said that she would have no bloodshed : the Earl's followers outnumbered her guard, and rather than one man should lose his life, she would go with the Earl of Bothwell. Bewildered, the guard stood gaping, then were dispersed. Huntly, Melville, and Maitland were disarmed, and Bothwell, with the Queen and her gentlemen, started for Dunbar. They reached the city at midnight, and Huntly and Bothwell made a murderous attack on Maitland — supposedly because he was suspected of having betrayed Huntly's plan for the Queen's abduction. The Queen placed herself between him and the swords, and told Huntly that 'if a hair of Lethington's head did perish, she would cause him forfeit lands and goods and lose his life'.

The virtuous Huntly and Melville were set free next morning, but Maitland, always in danger of murder, was kept in close imprisonment. As for the Queen, she remained, and was subjected — according to herself — to the violence that rendered her marriage to Bothwell a necessity. For, according to Melville's *Memoirs* 'the Queen could not but marry him, seeing he had ravished her and lyen with her against her will', and that he had boasted he would marry her 'who would or who would not, yea, whether she would herself or not'.

Two days after the kidnapping of the Queen, Lady Both-well's case for divorce came before the Court, in which she complained of his adultery with one of her servants. The Commissioners were Protestants, Lady Bothwell a Catholic. Her divorce was pronounced on the 3rd of May, and four days afterwards her Protestant husband received from the Papal Court the decision that there had been no marriage, since there had been no dispensation for the consanguinity between them — they were fourth cousins. Archbishop Hamilton — he who had passed the night of Darnley's murder at Hamilton House (that night when a solitary candle burned, to be extinguished after two lives had been blown out) — remained mum on the subject of the dispensation he *had* granted ; for, as Hay Fleming writes, 'as far as the ability was concerned, the illegitimate Archbishop was the real head of the House of Hamilton, and a desire to advance the regal claims of that house probably explains his silence'.[1]

He had known of the murder — only the actual murderers knew more. He had encouraged the intrigue between Mary and Bothwell, for would this not lead to Mary's ruin, certain dethronement, probable death ? And the triumph of the Hamilton claims to the throne ? This he hoped to gain by her marriage. The time was not long, now, in which he must wait.

NOTE TO CHAPTER THIRTY-FIVE

[1] *Mary Queen of Scots.*

# Chapter Thirty-six

ON the 15th of May, twelve days after Lady Bothwell obtained her divorce, the Queen and the divorced man were married, at 4 o'clock in the morning, by Adam Bothwell, Bishop of Orkney, described as 'a chameleon, a sorcerer, an execrable magician, a perfect atheist'. The Queen was dressed in widow's weeds, in memory of that husband whose death had plunged her in mourning just three months before. All the Lords present in Edinburgh — even Huntly — had refused to be present at the marriage. The ceremony was performed according to the Protestant rites.

The Queen explained her marriage (to her Dominican confessor — who had warned her against it), as due to her wish to bring the feud between the two creeds to an end.

It had been slightly difficult to explain the matter to the King and Queen Mother of France. But she instructed the Bishop of Dunblane, sent to Paris for the purpose, to say that although she had found the bridegroom's 'doings rude' (rough) (in abducting and raping her), 'yet were his answer and words but gentill' ; he had been forced to that abduction by his excess of love ; and 'when we saw no esperance to be rid of him, never man in Scotland makand ane mynt (?) to procure our deliverance . . . we were compelled to mitygate our displeasure, and began to think upon what he propounded'. 'He would not agree to have the consummation of the marriage delayed . . . but as by a bravado he had won the first point, so ceased he never till by persuasion and importune suit, accompanied not the less by force, he has finally driven us to end the work begun.'

255

The French Court received her explanation with an open and cynical amusement.

The Queen of England was overwhelmed with horror at the news.

On the very day of the marriage, Mary told the French Ambassador, du Croq, that her miseries were so great she cried to Death to release her. And three days afterwards, there was a scene in which, in the presence of Bothwell and du Croq, she called for a knife to kill herself — or else, she said, 'I shall drown myself'.

Du Croq told her sternly that her marriage was inexcusable, that had he not been ordered by the Queen Mother to remain at his post he would have left immediately ; and that he refused to pay homage to Bothwell as her husband.

Bothwell would allow her to look at no one, nor would he allow anyone to look at her. He knew her, he said, too well ! She, on her side, was wildly jealous of his divorced wife — the young girl whose marriage to him had been arranged, only fifteen months before, by the Queen, who signed the contract, gave the marriage banquet and the magnificent dress of cloth of silver lined with white taffeta in which the bride appeared at the altar.

She had thought that young girl would have been forgotten. She was mistaken.

As for herself, her marriage to Bothwell was to last for only one month, before, in the presence of the rebel army, she would look on him for the last time, and, weeping bitterly, tell him she would always be true to him. In two years from that time, he would be as absent from her heart and thoughts as if he had never existed.

Yet there can be no doubt that she *had* loved him, and that that short love had brought about her ruin. He cared nothing for her. Yet in spite of her misery, her passion for him continued.

The Lords had threatened that if the marriage took place, they would crown the Prince in her stead. But they did not

MARY QUEEN OF SCOTS

move, and the Queen's next action was to command Lord
Mar to surrender to her Stirling Castle and the Prince. He
replied that without the permission of the Estate, he dared not
let the Prince leave his care.

Then the conduct of Bothwell became extremely puzzling.
He attended sermons, rode with the Queen, and, when in
public, showed her great respect.

But the anger of the people increased.

By the first week in June, the Protestant and Catholic
Lords were united in their hatred of the marriage. Various
of the Lords, including Argyll, had been about to march on
Holyrood and capture Bothwell. But Argyll's courage ebbed
away : he had been a party to that strange death at Kirk-o'-
Fields, and Bothwell's capture, were he involved in it, would
be a danger to him. He might say what he knew. So Argyll
warned the Queen.

Bothwell now knew that if he would save his life, he must
fight ; and he summoned the Borderers — for on these he
believed he could rely — to collect arms and join him at
Melrose. He left the Queen at Borthwick Castle, and went
to the encounter. But when he reached Melrose, there was
no one there. The Borderers had been persuaded by certain
of the Lords not to come to his aid.

Turning on his tracks, he joined the Queen at Borthwick,
and sent Huntly, Archbishop Hamilton, and Sir James Balfour
an urgent message bidding them to hurry to him with all the
men they could raise.

But the messenger was intercepted, and thus the Lords
knew where he had taken refuge. Morton, Hume, Lindsay,
and Mar surrounded Borthwick Castle on the night of June
the 10th. He escaped them, through a postern, into the darkness. The Lords, thinking he was still in the Castle, shouted
'Traitor, murderer, butcher', bidding him come out and
maintain his challenge. They shouted insults, also, at the
Queen, which she returned. But when they knew of Bothwell's escape, they withdrew, reaching Edinburgh at eight in
the morning. There, in the market-place, they told the

assembled crowds they had taken up arms 'to pursue their revenge for the murder of the King'.

Du Croq offered the Queen to mediate, but she answered she would come to no terms with the rebels if they intended injury to her husband.

On the 12th of June, dressed as a man, she fled, and joined her husband with such troops as they could raise, arriving at Dunbar at three in the morning. Here she was forced to borrow clothes from some woman — including a petticoat that scarcely reached below her knee. Once more Bothwell left for the Border, but returning, joined the Queen at Haddington, with 1600 men — (she had 600 with her), went with her to Seton, where they spent the night, having decided to march, next day, on Edinburgh.

Hearing this, the confederate Lords prepared for battle, the trumpets sounding at midnight on the 14th of June. Next morning they were on their way, carrying a banner on which was pictured a dead man lying under a tree, and a child kneeling at the side, with his hands raised to heaven, crying 'Judge and revenge my cause, O Lord'.

Du Croq followed this army, and when they paused for breakfast, offered them to mediate. Their answer was that there were only two ways in which a battle could be avoided. Either the Queen must leave the monster she called her husband, in which case they would again be her lieges, or Bothwell must maintain his challenge either alone or with as many seconds as he chose. They would rather be buried alive than leave the murder of the King unpunished.

The Queen was not two miles away, and her banners could be seen. Du Croq, going to her, begged her to consider what she was doing. Then Bothwell appeared, to whom du Croq bowed coldly, but refused his hand. Bothwell enquired if *he* was the object of the Lords taking to arms, and in what way he had injured them. He declared his willingness to maintain his challenge, but the Queen declared that 'The Lords must yield, or try their chances in a battle'. Terrified that her husband might be killed, she refused to allow him to fight. But Lord Lindsay, coming forward, said he was a near kinsman of the murdered man, and, kneeling, in the presence of the two armies, prayed to God to 'preserve the innocent and punish those who had shed innocent blood'. Then he was handed the great double-handed sword of Angus Bell-the-Cat, and prepared to meet the murderer. — And still the Queen restrained her husband, and still he implored her to let him maintain his challenge. She called to her army that if they were men, they would sweep the traitors from the hillside.

But, whilst waiting, the two armies had met and talked. And when the bugles sounded for the advance of the Queen's army, not a movement followed.

The Queen, in her despair, sent for one of the rebel Lords and asked if *nothing* could be done to reconcile the Lords with her husband, to which he replied that they were determined to seize him if it meant the death of them all. She entreated him to consult with them once more. He returned bearing word that if she would leave Bothwell and go with them to Edinburgh, they would protect her, and Bothwell might go where it pleased him. But she must decide without delay.

Her case was hopeless. Her men, by this time, had almost all disappeared — the rest having gone to look for food. So, with a long, despairing embrace, and the promise that she would be true to him for ever, she bade him good-bye.

At their parting — according to her secretary, Nau — Bothwell gave Mary a copy of the murder bond with the signatures. Whilst in prison at Lochleven, she said that she had 'that in black and white which would cause Lethington * to hang by the neck'.

* Maitland of Lethington.


NOTE TO CHAPTER THIRTY-SIX

This chapter and the next are taken from Froude's account, *op. cit.*

# Chapter Thirty-seven

THE Queen now entered the lines of the opposing army, and was received by Morton and Hume, who, doing her homage as Queen, told her she was now in her rightful place, among her true and faithful subjects.

At first there had been an almost entire silence from the army; but soon that changed, and a fearful cry arose from the soldiers — 'Burn the whore! Burn the murderess of her husband.'

Various of the Lords struck at the soldiers, but the shouts continued as the procession went on its way to Edinburgh, and the banner, bearing the device of Darnley's blood-stained body, was waved before her. So exhausted and faint from grief and lack of food that she could scarcely be held upon her saddle, she showed no sign of fear. 'I expected', du Croq told the Queen Dowager of France, 'that the Queen would have been gentle with the Lords, and (would have) tried to pacify them; but on her way from the field, she talked of nothing but hanging and crucifying them all. To Lindsay, riding beside her, she said, "Give me your hand, my Lord. By this hand, which is now in mine, I will have your head for this, and so assure you."'

They rode past Kirk-o'-Fields, with that terrible banner held before her. They rode through the streets of Edinburgh, so crowded that they could only move at a foot's pace and in single file. Shrieks, threats, curses, rose from all the pavements, fell from all the windows: 'Burn the whore, the murderess'. She was to spend the night at the Provost's house, at the corner of the Grassmarket. She would eat nothing — she had sworn, she said, that no food should pass her lips until Bothwell was restored to her. She asked only to be taken to her room. But the roaring crowds swarmed up the staircase and confronted her, until Maitland, who was below the window, came to her help.

She had saved his life, when Bothwell would have killed him. Now, with bitter tears, she asked him why she had been torn from her husband. He replied that the Lords were only thinking of her welfare and her honour. 'She did not know Bothwell', he told her. 'Since her pretended marriage with him, he had, again and again, assured Lady Bothwell that she was his wife, and the Queen only his concubine. He could show the Queen the letter.' (And indeed, de Silva had told his King that Bothwell, after his marriage, spent several days a week with the wife he was supposed to have divorced.)

But no — she would not hear it — she would not believe it. All she asked, she said in her desperation and ruin, was to be put with Bothwell in a ship on the ocean, to drift wherever Fate should take them. Maitland then left, and Mary was alone with her horror, her danger.

Du Croq, consulted by Maitland, said it had been easy enough to capture the Queen, the difficulty was now to know what to do with her. If she went to France, for instance, the King knew only too well that her guilt had been proved, and what she deserved. It might, of course, be a good thing if she *did* go to France. She would be shut up in a convent, Bothwell would be hanged, and the Prince would be given a French education. If the Queen of England was asked for help by the Lords, the French King would take Mary's side ; otherwise France would let them do what they liked.

Meanwhile, Mary, left alone in her room, wrote a letter to Bothwell, calling him her 'dear hart, whom she should never forget nor abandon for absens' — telling him she had only sent him from her for his safety, — begging him to take comfort.

She paid a boy to take this letter to Bothwell at Dunbar. The boy took the money, and handed the letter to the Lords ; and this letter, breaking her promise to leave Bothwell, gave them a chance of keeping her imprisoned.

At dawn, frenzied and dishevelled, she hung out of the window, shrieking, Where were her friends ? Let them come and rescue her ! There was no answer. Only that frightful banner was waved, once more, before her eyes. (It had been so placed that she could not look from the window without seeing it.) A woman, seeing her at the window, screamed insults at her. She, turning towards her with a tiger's movement, 'threatened to cause burn the town and slake the fire with the blood of its inhabitants'.

·        ·        ·        ·        ·

At midnight she was taken, secretly, to Lochleven, a little island whose lord was Sir William Douglas, Moray's half-brother.

'The hardest heart', wrote her secretary Nau,[1] 'among the most cruel barbarians would have been moved to pity at the departure of this poor Princess, who was permitted to take no other clothes than her nightdress, nor any linen. At the edge of the lake she was met by the laird and his brothers, who escorted her to a room on the ground floor.' John Leslie, Bishop of Ross, in his defence of her, declared that she was 'stripped out and spoyled of al her princely attirement, was clothed with a coarse browne cassoke'.

Lethington told Throckmorton that envoys had come from the Archbishop of St. Andrews, and that Duncan Forbes had been sent to the Lords by Huntly. She was deserted. The Queen's party, by these envoys, offered to join the Lords if they would kill the Queen.

In July 1567 she was compelled to abdicate in favour of her son, who was crowned James VI of Scotland on the second anniversary of her marriage to Darnley.

Her nights were haunted by the remembrance of a prophecy, made by a Highland woman endowed with second sight, that the Queen of Scotland would be burned at the stake — this being the punishment for husband-murderers.

Her days were filled with the fear of death. Queen Elizabeth heard — and told the Spanish Ambassador — that from a loophole in the tower which was her prison, the Queen of Scots called to a child who was wandering near by, and told him to 'tell her friends to pray to God for her soul — her body was now worth but little'.

On the 15th of August, Moray arrived at Lochleven. His Queen greeted him 'with great passion and weeping'. But by this time he knew what was the worth of those tears. She could not deduce from his 'cold, reserved' manner 'either the ill which he had conceived of her, or meant towards her'. He stayed with her for some time, but remained always with that mask upon him. After supper, however, he went to her room, and, till 'one of the clock', talked with her.

They were alone. 'Plainly, without disguising,' Throckmorton told the Queen of England, in a letter dated the 20th of August, 'he did discover unto her all his opinions of her misgovernment, and laid before her all such disorders as might either touch her conscience, her honour, or her surety. He behaved himself rather like a ghostly father unto her than like a councillor. . . . Sometimes she wept bitterly, sometimes she acknowledged her unadvisedness ; some things she did confess plainly ; some things she did excuse, some things she did extenuate.'

But Lady Lennox told the Spanish Ambassador one thing more : 'The Queen of Scots admitted to her brother that she knew the conspiracy for her husband's murder'. He left her 'in hope of nothing but God's mercy, willing her to seek to that as her chiefest refuge'.

It was no doubt in order to prevent them from falling into dishonest hands that he took charge of his sister's jewels, and from them he selected six ropes of magnificent pearls, and twenty-five huge pearls the colour 'of black muscat grapes',[2] to adorn the Queen of England, who was to be placated by being allowed to buy them for a sum which nowhere approached their cost.

The day after Moray's interview with his sister, he, who had taken on the duties of Regent, told her that 'if she practised to disturb the peace of the realm, to make a faction in it, to escape from Lochleven, or to animate the Queen of England or the French King to trouble the realm', and 'if she persisted in her affection for Bothwell', he would not be able to save her ; but that if 'she would acknowledge her faults to God ; if she would lament her sins past, so as it might appear that she detested her former life and intended a better conversation and a more modest behaviour . . . if she would make it evident that she did abhor the murder of her husband, and did mislike her former life with Bothwell, and minded no revenge to the lords and others who had sought her reformation . . . she might not only be saved, but might one day be restored to the throne'.

She now saw herself through his eyes, — saw the deformity that the noble Mary Stuart had become. Any hatred that she felt for him before was as nothing to this hatred.

. . . . .

The deposed Queen of Scots was still in close imprisonment ; but on the 1st of May 1568, she succeeded in sending letters to Elizabeth and to the Queen Mother of France imploring them for help. She had only, she said, managed to do so because the Douglas family were at dinner ; for 'their girls sleep with me'.

At the end of March, she had tried to flee from the island disguised as a laundress ; but was betrayed by the whiteness and beauty of her hands, and was recaptured. But now, the day after the writing of those letters, she succeeded in escaping . . . 'little Douglas' (William, a foundling boy of seventeen) had stolen the keys ; she landed, helped by George Douglas, and was met by a kinsman of Bothwell. Then began a wild ride across the country to a house where she would, temporarily, be safe.

As soon as Moray heard of her escape, he called together the King's party at Glasgow, and on the 13th of May the Queen's followers and those of her son met in a battle which ended in the hopeless defeat of her forces.

She fled south, riding sixty miles a day, and writing to the Queen of England, on the 15th of May, from Dundrennan, she begged for permission to visit her immediately. On the 16th of May she saw Scotland for the last time, crossing the Solway to Workington, with George Douglas and fifteen other men.

NOTES TO CHAPTER THIRTY-SEVEN

[1] *History of Mary Stuart.*
[2] Elizabeth Jenkins, *op. cit.*

# Chapter Thirty-eight

To the Queen of Scotland's utter astonishment, her 'dear sister' of England declared that 'she could not receive her in such sort as she would if she were not taxed with a horrible crime'!

Amazing! Mary had thought that all that was necessary was for her to declare her innocence and she would surely be believed. But, she told herself, if she could once gain admission to the Queen of England's presence, all would be well. She therefore sent a message to her dear sister, saying she wished to defend herself in Elizabeth's presence.

'Oh Madam,' was the reply, 'there is not a creature living who more longs to hear your justification than myself; nor one who would lend more willing ear to any answer which will clear your honour. But I cannot sacrifice my own reputation on your account. To tell you the plain truth, I am already thought to be more willing to defend your cause than to open my eyes to see the things of which your subjects accuse you. Did you but know who the persons are by whom I am warned to be on my guard, you would not think that I could afford to neglect these warnings. And, now, seeing that you are pleased to commit yourself to my protection, you may assure yourself that I will take care both of your life and honour, that neither yourself nor your nearest relations could be more concerned for your interests. On the word of a prince, I promise you, that neither your subjects, nor any advice which I may receive from my own councillors, shall move me to ask anything of you which may endanger you or touch your honour.

'Does it seem strange to you that you are not allowed to

see me ? I entreat you to put yourself in my place. When you are acquitted of this crime I will receive you with all honour : till that is done I may not ; but afterwards, I swear by God, that I shall never see person with better will, and among all earthly pleasures I will hold this to be the first.

'. . . I trust I may succeed in bringing these sad matters to an end. There is no one thing in all the world that I desire so much.

'. . . God be with you in all your good actions, and deliver you from those who bear you malice.'

It had never entered the head of the Queen of Scots that Elizabeth would insist on an impartial arbitration ; but now she was told that there was to be an enquiry into her guilt.

She fell 'into great passion and weeping'. She was ill used. The only judge was God ; she was a princess, and 'none could take upon them to judge princes . . .'. Why had she demanded to see the Queen of England ? Because 'I could and did mean to have uttered such matter unto her as I would have done for no other, nor never yet did to any. I see how things frame evil for me : I have many enemies about the Queen. If she will not help my misery herself, she can do no less than suffer me to pass to other princes.' On its being suggested that she should be removed from Carlisle, she fell into a fury. Was she, then, a prisoner, she asked ?

Knollys wrote to Cecil on the 14th of June : 'To be frank with you, there is no fair semblance of speech that seemeth to win credit with her. This cold dealing will not satisfy her fiery stomach. It is vanity to think she will be stayed by courtesy or bridled by fear from bringing the French into Scotland, or from employing all her force of money, men of war, and of friendship to satisfy her bloody appetite.'

'Put away from your mind', she wrote to Elizabeth, 'the thought that I came·hither to save my life. Neither Scotland nor the world would have refused me a refuge. I came to recover my honour and to obtain help to chastise my false accusers — not to answer these charges against me as if I were their equal, but myself to accuse them in your presence. For the cautions which you say you have received from great persons, God forbid that I should be a reproach to you ; but my cause requires haste. Let me try what other princes will do for me, and no blame will then rest with you. Restored to my throne by their hands, I will then come again to you, and defend my honour for my honour's sake, and not for any need to answer to my traitor subjects. . . . Madam, I am no equal of theirs, and I would sooner die than so, by any act of mine, declare myself.'

But the Queen of England told the Spanish Ambassador she was going to have the Queen of Scotland removed from the Border, 'whether she liked it or not'. She intended to restore her to her throne, but with the present Government. To France she was not to go.

But first, her innocence must be established.

On the 13th of July, the Queen of Scotland, in spite of 'tragical demonstrations', was taken to Bolton, and later, willy-nilly, to Tutbury, where she was placed in the care of the Earl of Shrewsbury. This was done because he had Catholic tendencies, had been in favour of her succeeding to the crown of England, and so could not be suspected of conniving at her murder. His orders were to prevent her from escaping, but 'to treat her with the honour and reverence due to a Princess of the blood royal'. But he was to remember, also, that 'besides the vehement presumption against her of the horrible murdering of her husband, other things were known . . . and these might become known to the whole world. . .'.

The enquiry into the Queen of Scotland's guilt began in late October 1568 at York. Certain letters, which had been carefully preserved — for his own safety, it was thought, by Bothwell — in a silver casket, and which had been taken from one of his servants, were to be produced as evidence of that guilt. The Duke of Norfolk, the Earl of Sussex, and Sir Ralph Sadler were in charge of the enquiry.

The Earl of Morton took his oath before the Commissioners, in December, that the casket had been forced open, on the 21st of June 1567, in the presence of himself, Lethington, Atholl, Hume, and Morton's cousin Archibald Douglas, the chief murderer of Riccio and one of Darnley's murderers.

The letters were declared by Mary's adherents to be flagrant forgeries. She was to find an ardent champion in John Leslie, Bishop of Ross.

It cannot be said that this gentleman was popular with his English brethren. From time to time, as he grew increasingly troublesome, one or another of them was placed in charge of him, in spite of their almost violent protests. The trouble seems to have been at its height in 1569.

The Bishop of Winchester, appealing to the Lord Treasurer, wrote : 'Right hon*oble*, the woman of Caanan thorow her moche importunitie obtained for her daughter deliverie from a troublesome sprite. The Griefe that groweth towardes me by a troublesome sprite causeth me to be a more importune suter to your Honor for my deliverie from soche a devellesche sprite as my house is possest withall. I praye your Honor therefore helpe me, that this devill were ridde out of my house.' Grindal, Bishop of London, was equally insistent. 'Sir, I praye you to be a meane that I be not troubled with the Bishoppe of Rosse ; he is a man of suche qualities as I lyke nothing withall. . . . Experience teacheth that none of them are reformed, which are sente to me and others : and by receivinge of them the punishment lighteth upon us. . . .

Godde keepe you.

Yours in Christe

'Edm : London. from my house at Powles this Sundaye mornynge betweene 8 and 9, immediately after the receipt of your letter.

'5 Feb : 1569.'

The Bishop of Ross was anxious to bring the world to a reasonable point of view. Well, what if the Queen of Scots *did* commit adultery ? What if she *did* commit a murder ? Let them remember King David ! Did *he* not commit a murder ? Was *he* not an adulterer ? Yet did that prevent men from singing his psalms to this very day ? And let cavillers remember, also, how highly favoured he was by Heaven !

It was, he said, owing to the 'dangerous Worlde' that the Queen of Scotland was 'enforced and constrained to take a Husband to be her comforter, her Assister, her Buckler, and her Shilde'.

It is sad to think that three years later, when the Bishop, thoroughly frightened, found himself in the Tower (at a time when Mary was considering marrying the Duke of Norfolk), he told one of Elizabeth's examiners that Mary was not fit for any husband : 'for first he saith, she poisoned her husband the French King, as he hath credibly understood ; again, she hath consented to the murder of her late husband, the Lord Darnley, thirdly, she matched with the murderer and brought him to the field to be murdered.'

'Lord !' exclaimed the recipient of these confidences, 'what a people are these, what a Queen, and what an Ambassador !'

# Chapter Thirty-nine

THE enquiry at York had been merely the blind for a host of intrigues; and soon it was moved to Westminster, where Burleigh would be able to watch over it.

The Duke of Norfolk was, or pretended to be, aghast at the criminality of the letters in the silver casket. And yet he was now playing with the idea of marrying the woman he believed to be a murderess.

The Earl of Moray was, as a result of the proceedings, in a most dangerous position. He had been induced to denounce his sister, — and she had not been condemned. He had insisted that if her guilt were proved, the Queen of England should recognise him as Regent, and the baby James as King, and that Mary should either be sent back to him or else held in England and kept for ever from becoming a danger. Elizabeth refused. Now it seemed as if Mary would be restored to the throne, and if so, his death would be certain.

The Duke of Norfolk, talking with him in the park at Hampton Court, reproached him for his denunciations and acts against his sister. But Moray declared that 'so far from not loving his sister, she was the creature upon earth that he loved the best. He never wished her harm; her own pressing was the occasion of that which was uttered to her infamy.' Had he but known it, there were only a few months left to him for earthly affection.

On the 22nd of January 1570 he, as Regent, must go on the business of the country to Edinburgh. He spent that night at Linlithgow, which then consisted of one long narrow street. Four houses away from that in which he slept, was one belonging to Archbishop Hamilton of St. Andrews, occupied by one of his retainers. A window opened onto the street, with a balcony which, when hung with drying sheets, would shield anyone hiding in the window from view. Behind the house was a garden leading into a lane.

The Archbishop had known of the proposed murder of Darnley : he had divorced Bothwell and had helped on the Queen's marriage with him — seeing in that murder and that marriage the seeds of her overthrow. While she was a prisoner at Lochleven, the Hamiltons would have urged that she should be put to death, if their claim to the throne had been allowed. Now Moray was the one being who stood between them and that claim, for once he were removed, it would be easy to dispose of the baby James.

In the Archbishop's house, James Hamilton of Bothwell-haugh, nephew of the Archbishop, waited for his victim. He had been taken prisoner in the last battle between Mary's forces and those of the rebel Lords in 1568, and would have been executed had not Moray spared his life. Now that mercy was to be repaid.

The Regent, before he left his bed, had been warned that an attempt would be made on his life. But he was used to threats, and, rising and dressing, went on his way.

It is possible that he might have passed that long narrow street, the town of his death, at a gallop ; but the street was crowded with people who wanted to look at their Regent ; to gallop would have meant danger to them, and so he rode at a foot's pace.

From behind his shroud of sheets, Bothwellhaugh fired.

The Regent put his hand to his side. He was wounded, he said. Then, dismounting from his horse, and leaning on Lord Sempill, he returned to the house in which he had spent the night.

At first no one knew from which house the shot had been fired, and in the confusion the murderer escaped, and at Hamilton Castle was received with acclamations.

The dying man, surrounded by his grief-stricken friends, told them of how he had spared his murderer's life. But he said 'he could never repent of his clemency', and, 'without speaking a reproachful word of anyone', died a little before midnight.

His sister, plunged once more into mourning, gave the murderer a pension. On the 28th of August 1571 she wrote to the Archbishop of Glasgow : 'Ce que Bothwellhaugh a faist a esté sans mon commandement, de quoy je luy scay (sais) aussy bon gré et meilleur que si j'eusse esté du conseil. J'attend les memoires que me doivent estre envoyez de la recepte de mon douaire pour fair mon estat, où je n'oublyeray le pension dudict Bothwellhaugh.'

.          .          .          .          .

Lord Pembroke and other of the English Lords believed that as it was difficult to know what to do with the Queen of Scots — it was hardly practicable to keep her a prisoner — it might even be in the cause of peace if she married the Duke of Norfolk. He, on his side, said he would 'prefer to remain unmarried, but if the Queen of Scots would accept him, he would be content to sacrifice himself for the welfare of his country'.

His own Queen did not see this proposed noble sacrifice in the same light. When she heard of it, she sent for him. She was sitting in a garden whose walls, on which fruit trees were trained, enclosed flower-beds. She asked him if he had come to give her news of an approaching marriage.

He lost his nerve immediately.

'What !' he exclaimed. 'Should I seek to marry her, being so wicked a woman, such a notorious adulteress and murderer ! I love to sleep upon a safe pillow. I count myself, by your Majesty's favour, as good a prince at home in my bowling alley at Norwich as she is, though she were in Scotland. And if I should go about to marry her, knowing as I do, that she pretendeth to the present possession of your Majesty's crown, your Majesty might justly charge me with seeking your own crown upon your head.'

But she did not believe him. She knew that, though she

would try her uttermost to save him, he would continue to seek that dangerous pillow, and, in the end, would exchange the dream of this for the reality of the headsman's block.

He now made a fatal mistake. He, who had made an enemy of Leycester by threatening to break a tennis racket over his head, and by lecturing him about his familiar conduct towards the Queen, now chose him as confidant and as go-between, begging him to induce the Queen to favour the marriage.

The Court, on progress, had arrived at Guildford. On a day of burning heat, the Queen sat on cushions in an open doorway, listening to a child playing the lute and singing, and to Leycester, who was kneeling by her side, talking  Norfolk entered unexpectedly, and Leycester, leaving the Queen, told him that he had, at that moment, been speaking of the marriage, and that she had taken this 'indifferently'.

Norfolk's intrigues now increased their scope. It had been hoped, by certain of the Council, to remove Cecil from power ; and Leycester had braved the Queen's anger by telling her that the best of her subjects saw the affairs of state so incompetently managed that either the state would 'run into danger' or Cecil must answer for that mismanagement with his head.[1]

The Spaniards blamed him for their unfriendly relations with England. But though the Spanish Ambassador had been promised, by the malcontent Lords, that he should be removed, nothing had been done.

As a revenge for the seizure of Spanish treasure-ships by the English, the Duke of Alva seized English men, ships, and merchandise in the Low Countries. Elizabeth immediately did the same to Spaniards in England, and Mary, delighted, felt certain of war. 'Tell the Ambassador', she said to his messenger, 'that if his master will help me, I shall be Queen of England in three months, and Mass shall be said all over England.'

Norfolk and Arundel were heavily involved in a treasonous correspondence with the Spaniards : suggesting to Alva that he should intercept the great English merchant fleet sailing to Hamburg, they told him that by so doing he would ensure that the citizens of London, enraged by the seizure of so great a treasure, would rise against the government, under Norfolk's and Arundel's leadership. Alva should, they advised, issue, at the same time, a proclamation declaring that the seizure of the ships was due to no hatred against England, but enmity towards those members of the Council who had succeeded in putting an end to the old-standing alliance between the countries. The Queen would then be forced to dismiss Cecil from office.

The intrigues continued, and the Spanish Ambassador, Don Guerau, was told by certain Catholics that 'at the first sign of a Spanish flag on English soil, they would rise as a man'.

The Queen of England, warned, once again, that Norfolk was plotting to marry her cousin, sent for him to sit at her table at dinner. She asked him what was the news. He said he knew of none, to which she replied, 'What ! You come from London, and can give me no news of a marriage ?' When dinner was over, she 'gave him a nip, and bade him take good heed of his pillow', and, once again, asked him what was the truth of the rumour, to which he returned evasive answers. Then she ordered him on his allegiance to put all thoughts of that marriage from him.[2]

But he was hopelessly involved, both with the Queen of Scots and with the rebellion seething underground. There was no drawing back. He left the Court without the Queen's sanction and returned to London. She sent for him peremptorily, but he replied that he had an ague, and would come to Court in four days' time, — instead of which he fled, in terror, to his estates in Norfolk. The Queen of Scots and the Spanish Ambassador urged an immediate rising, but his terror, by now, had complete hold over him, and, instead, sending a message to his co-plotter, Lord Westmorland, imploring him to make no movement or it would cost him his head, he started for the Court. He was met, and sent to the Tower.

Rumours rose and fell like the wind. The Earl of Sussex,

President of the Northern Council, sent for the Earls of North-umberland and Westmorland, both of whom were involved in the proposed rebellion. Warned by Norfolk's arrest and by a message from the Spanish Ambassador, they spoke smoothly.

The Queen ordered both to come to Court. But, at the very moment her messenger left Northumberland's house, the bells of the church rang backwards. It was the signal for the rising.

Northumberland and Westmorland might have wished to stop the rising, but it was too late. Old and young rushed to arms. The seventy-one-year-old Richard Norton, Sheriff of Yorkshire, one of the Northern Council, and Governor of Norham Castle, 'bore the cross, and a banner on which were painted the five Wounds of Christ. Seven of his eleven sons rose with him.' [3]

On the 14th of November, entering Durham Cathedral, the insurgents tore up and burned the Protestant books, threw over the Communion table, and reinstated the Catholic altars. This was repeated all over the north.

At first, Sussex did not dare to enter the fight, because sons and brothers of the insurgents were in his army, and might, as others had done at Barnard Castle, join the enemy.

The rebels held the north. Now they marched towards Tutbury, and the prisoner-Queen. But Elizabeth's army, advancing from the south, outnumbered them. The insurgents fled, without meeting them, and on the 20th of December 1569, the leaders of the insurrection escaped over the Border, and joined Mary's supporters in Scotland.

Then the revenge began : the livid, heavy fruit, blackening as the days went by, hung from the gallows-trees.

## NOTES TO CHAPTER THIRTY-NINE

[1] Froude, *op. cit.*
[2] Elizabeth Jenkins, *op. cit.*
[3] Froude, *op. cit.*

# Chapter Forty

On the 23rd of January 1571, the Queen of England visited the Bourse erected by the great city merchant Sir Thomas Gresham, who, after the death of his only son, who would have inherited it, used his vast fortune for the good of the city. Here, near to St. Paul's (which had been the meeting-place for all rogues, beggars, ghosts of ill-fortune come back from hell to some new hell of destitution), Sir Thomas built the greatest shopping centre in London.

The royal splendour and pageantry (after visiting the Bourse the Queen dined with Sir Thomas at his house in Bishopsgate) passed by the overhanging horror of the slums, by the nation of beggars, by the open gulf of horror called the Fleet Ditch.

This, said the editor of Ben Jonson's Epigrams, 'was the name given to that part of the City Ditch which extended from Fleet Lane . . . by Bridewell Walk and Holborn to the Thames at Blackfriars Bridge'.

> All that they boast of Styx, of Acheron,
> Cocytus, Phlegethon, ours have proved in one,
> The filth, stench, noise, save only what was there
> Subtly distinguished, was confuséd here. *
>     .        .        .        .        .*
>
> And for one Cerberus, the whole coast was dogs.
> Furies there wanted not : each scold was ten,
> And for the cries of ghosts, women and men,
> Laden with plague-sores and their sins, were heard,
> Lashed by their consciences, to die afeard.
>     .        .        .        .        .

\* Here comes a line too filthy to quote.

In the first jaws appeared that ugly monster
Yclepèd mud, which, when their oars did once stir,
Belched forth an air as hot as at the muster
Of all your night-tubs when the carts do cluster.

.    .    .    .    .

Between two walls, where on one side, to scar men,
Were seen your ugly centaurs, ye call car-men,
Gorgonian scolds, and harpies, on the other
Hung stench, diseases, and old filth, their mother,
With famine, wants, and sorrows, many a dozen,
The least of which was to the plague a cousin.†

By the banks of this, in the aisles of St. Paul's (the latter devoted to 'all kinds of bargains, meetings, brawlings, murders, conspiracies', as the Bishop of Durham said in a sermon after St. Paul's had been struck by lightning in 1561) and, too, in the Inns of Court, strutted, crawled, and flapped the nation of the beggars — no longer a kingdom within a kingdom, as in the time of King Henry, when they were ruled over by Puffing Dick, who according to Thomas Harman's *A Caveat for Common Cursitors*, was 'a man crafty and bold ; yet he died miserably. For, after he had commanded now fully eight years, he had the pining of the pox and the Neapolitan scurf [syphilis] and there was an end of Puffing Dick'.

Now, instead of this well-regimented nation, each beggar was a republic in himself.

Here come the 'Upright men and Rufflers', who, according to Thomas Dekker's *The Bel-Man of London*, 'walke with cudgels alike ; they profess Armes alike, though they be both out at elbows, and will sweare they lost their limmes in their Countries quarrel, when either they are lame from diseases, or have been mangled in some drunken quarrell. . . . The Palliards, or Clapperdudgeons', who 'to give cullor to their lame wandring : with Sperewort or Arsenick will they in one night poyson their leg. . .'. The 'Quire-Byrds who

---

† The above lines are part of one of Jonson's Epigrams describing 'a mad adventure undertaken by Sir Ralph Shelton and a Mr. Heyden to row down from Bridewell to Holborn'.

are such as have sung in such cages as Newgate or a County
Gaol, and having their bells given them to fly, they seek
presently to build their nests under some honest man's roofe,
not with intent to buy him any profit, but onely to put themselves into money or apparell, and then they take their flight'.
Here too come the Moone-men (the Lunatics).  'But of all
mad rascales (that are of this wing) the Abraham man is the
most phantastick . . . he swears he hath bin in Bedlam and
will talke frantically on purpose ;  you see pinnes stuck in
sundry places of his naked flesh . . . he calles himselfe Poore
Tom, and coming neer any body cryes out "Poore Tom is
a-cold".' . . . The 'Whipjackes . . . talke of nothing but
fights at Sea, piracies, drowning and shipwracks, travelling
both in the shape and name of mariners, with a counterfiet
Licence to beg. . . . These Whipjackes will talke of the Indies,
and of all countries that lye under heaven, but are indeede no
more than freshwater soldiers !'  Here come also the 'Counterfeit Cranks' (pretending epilepsy), the 'Dummerars' (counter-
feiting dumbness), the card-cheats, 'Gul-gropers' . . . ('He
that wins all', wrote Dekker, 'is the Eagle, he that stands by
and ventures is the Wood-pecker.  The fresh Gallant that is
fetcht in is the Gull.  Hee that stands by and lends, is the
Gul-groper.')  These, with their morts (the beggars' name
for women), watched the Queen go by.

Among these morts were the Glymmering Morts (glym-
mer was the beggars' name for fire) who, weeping, pretended
that their husbands, their children, their houses, all their
possessions, had been lost in a fire.

The beggars had their own language — known as the
Canting Language.  And, wrote Dekker (*Lanthorn and Candle-
light*), they 'in some wordes, retain a certaine salte, tasting of
some wit and Learnyng.  As, for example, they call a Cloake
(in the Canting-tongue) a Togeman, and in Latin Toga
signifies a Gowne, or an upper garment.  Pannem is bread,
and Panis in Latin is likewise bread. . . .'

Indeed, some of their words had a singular beauty, power
of evocation, strange echoes. . . . 'Darkeman' :  the night.

'Dewse-a-vile': the country. 'Grannam': corn. 'Glimmer':
fire. 'Gentry-mort': a gentlewoman. 'Lightmans': the day.
'Margery-prater': a henne. 'Romevile': London. 'Rome-
mort': a Queen. 'Ruffmans': the woodes or bushes.[1]

These beggars, each a universe enclosed in himself — such
'upright men' as Follentine Hylles, Ferdinando Angell, John-o
Pycons, and Sir Ginglespurre (who slept in St. Paul's, and
would say that his raggedness was caused by the death of all
the tailors from the Plague), watched the Queen go by.


### NOTE TO CHAPTER FORTY

[1] *Lanthorn and Candle-light.*

# Chapter Forty-one

THE night was lit by a thousand torches, rang with the shouts of acclamation as her people accompanied the Queen on her return to the Palace. She, coming from the banquet given by 'her merchant', as she called Sir Thomas Gresham, said to the French Ambassador, La Mothe Fénelon, 'Do not these scenes remind you in a small way of the late celebrations at Paris in honour of the public entrance of the King of France and his bride ? It does my heart good to see myself so much beloved and desired by my subjects ; I know that my people have no other cause for regret than that they know me to be but mortal, and therefore they have no certainty of a successor born of me to reign over them.'

In England, the fears of her Ministers, due to her obstinate spinsterhood, were, if anything, increased. Soon it would be too late for her to bear children, and then, said Cecil, 'she would be in danger of such as by devilish means might desire her end'. 'If God in His Goodness preserved her from murder, yet she would be in danger to lose daily the loyal duty and the love which was borne her by her subjects . . . finding no remedy to recover the affection of her people for lack of marriage and children, she would have perpetual torment in life.'

It was now too late for her to think of the Austrian Archduke. She had played with the idea of marrying him, had made him, in his own eyes, ridiculous, and the Imperial dignity was offended. In October 1570, still toying with this idea, she sent an emissary, young Mr. Cobham, on a secret mission to the Emperor, to hold before him the possibility that the marriage might still take place. The youth of the messenger had caused some surprise, for, as the French Court was told, 'if so grave and experienced a statesman as the Earl of Sussex had failed to arrange a matrimonial treaty to Her Majesty's satisfaction, it was scarcely to be expected that a beardless boy, of no weight, would be able to effect much'.

The matter had dragged on, since Lord Sussex's mission, but this was explained by the Queen's 'frequent illnesses, the wars in France and Flanders, and other impediments. But this delay, the Queen hoped, had not put an end to the suit of His Imperial Majesty's brother, and, if he would come to England now, he would be very welcome.' . . . His Imperial Majesty replied, coldly, that 'His brother was very sorry that Her Majesty had been so tardy in notifying her good intentions to him, for which he was nevertheless very much obliged, but that the Prince, not supposing that Her Majesty would have delayed her answer for three years if she had intended to accept him, had turned his thoughts on another match, and was now engaged to a Princess with whom there could be no disputes on the subject of religion ; but that he regretted he had not been accepted by the Queen at the proper time, and hoped that she would henceforth regard him as a brother'.

He then, after a few polite references to the Queen, gave the beardless boy of no account a silver vessel, and the audience was at an end.

The Queen was furious, and exclaimed 'that the Emperor had offered her so great an insult, that if she had been a man instead of a woman, she would have defied him to single combat'.[1]    One of the courtiers wrote : 'The cause of the grief and vexation of our Queen, is assuredly the marriage of the Archduke Charles with the daughter of his sister the Duchess of Bavaria, either because she had fixed her love and fantasy on him, or that she is mortified that her beauty and grandeur have been so lightly regarded by him, or that she has lost this means of amusing her people for the present, and fears that she will now be pressed by her states and her parliament not to defer taking a husband which is the principal desire of all her realm'.

As the Archduke was out of the question, the Queen dallied with the thought of marrying one of the French princes.

In 1564, the fourteen-year-old King of France's business-like mother had urged the Queen of England, then aged thirty-one, to accept him as a bridegroom. The suggestion which, surprisingly, did not meet with Elizabeth's approval, was brought forward again a little later. But now the King of France was married to another Princess.

Shortly before the marriage, the French Ambassador, being brought by Leycester into the presence-chamber at Hampton Court, 'found the Queen better dressed than usual ; and she appeared eager to talk of the King's wedding'. The Ambassador said he 'could wish to congratulate her on her own'. To which she replied that 'she had formerly assured him that she never meant to marry, but now regretted that she had not thought in time about her want of posterity. If she ever did take a husband, it should only be of a royal house, of suitable rank to her own'.

This was the opening the Ambassador waited for. The twenty-year-old Duc d'Anjou, he said, 'was the most accomplished Prince in the world, and the only person who was worthy of her alliance'. The Cardinal of Châtillon and the Vidame de Chartres echoed this opinion. But when it came to discussing the character of this thoroughly unpleasant, mincing popinjay, surrounded by painted and jewelled minions, they seemed curiously vague — and for this they had the best possible reasons.

Naturally the advantages of the marriage, as far as the realm was concerned, were considerable. The Queen would be delivered from the machinations of the Queen of Scots. The King of Spain would cease imprisoning and torturing her subjects, and the Pope would be appeased by her marriage to a Catholic.

The Queen made her usual objections. She was an old woman — she feared the Duc might already be in love with one who was younger and more fair. The French royal family were not remarkable for their fidelity to their marital vows.

'The Queen of England', wrote the harassed French Ambassador (23rd January 1571), 'is one of those who will fly when they are sought after. It is a peculiarity of the English nation who, the more you desire anything of them, the more coy they become, though what you ask is to their own advantage.'

The Queen of England was not the only proposed partner to the match who showed signs of flight. The Duc d'Anjou, also, seemed inexplicably reluctant to do his duty. First he said he would not marry her, for she was 'an old creature who had a sore leg'. Then, in February 1571, he had become even more recalcitrant. For the Cardinal de Guise, indefatigable in mischief-making, had whispered in his ear all the old scandals about his proposed bride and Leycester! He was horrified. Rushing to his mother, he complained bitterly of the trick that had been played on him. He even went so far as to say that his honour had been threatened.

For once that lady had met her match. He would not listen to reason, he was deaf to expostulations, to reminders of his filial duty. She would, the distracted woman told the French Ambassador to England, 'give half my life-blood out of my body could I alter it, but I cannot make him obedient in this matter'.

'Now, Monsieur de la Mothe,' she continued, 'we are on the point of losing such a kingdom and grandeur for my children, that I shall feel great regret. See if there be no means, as I formerly asked you, of inducing her ["the old creature with the sore leg''] to adopt one of her female relatives as her heiress, whom one of my sons could espouse.'

I do not know if this not entirely flattering suggestion reached the ears of the Queen of England.

But stay! Yet another thought. 'Would she have my son Alençon? As for him, he wishes it. He is turned sixteen, though little for his age.' (There could be no nonsense *there*! He would *have* to do what he was told. He might even, thought the Queen Mother, come to enjoy living in a Court among ancient ladies with 'Their cheeks sugar-candied and cherry-blusht so sweetly', and wearing 'nosegays of yellow hair on their furious foreheads',[2] and 'glorious borrowed gleaming bushes'.)[3]

His anxious mother pointed out that his beard was beginning to grow. Though he could not be described as actually *good-looking* (he was badly pitted by smallpox), the English Ambassador took an optimistic view.

'The pock-holes', he declared, 'are no great disfigurement of his face, because they are rather thick than deep or great. They upon the blunt of his nose *are* great and deep, how much to be disliked may be as it pleaseth God to move the heart of the beholder !'

However that might be, Monsieur de la Mothe Fénelon thought that it might be better to wait until this newly suggested suitor was a little older, for it would be unwise to give the Queen of England the idea that she was being laughed at.

By the end of February the Queen Mother, having turned her attention once more to her son Anjou, had succeeded in pestering him into saying that not only *would* he marry the Queen of England, but that he was extremely anxious to do so.

No time must be lost. She wrote, immediately, to Elizabeth, urging her to marry him instantly, *before he had time to change his mind !*

But the Queen of England continued her shilly-shallying methods. Consulting two of her ladies, Lady Clinton and Lady Cobham, whom 'she esteemed two of the most faithful of her ladies, in whom she placed more confidence than in all the ladies in the world, therefore they must on no account dissimulate with her', she enquired if they thought Monsieur was too young.

Lady Clinton assured her that 'Monsieur's youth ought not to inspire her with fear, for he was virtuous, and Her Majesty was better calculated to please him than any other Princess in the world'.

Lady Cobham was not so tactful. 'It was always happier', she remarked, 'when the couple were of the same age, or nearly the same age.' Whereupon the Queen said, sharply, that there was only a difference of ten years. (The other seven seem, for the moment, to have slipped her memory.)

The English Ambassador, Norreys, having returned from France, the Queen sent for him immediately, and questioned him closely about the Duc's appearance and general bearing. Then, seized with a wish to see him for herself, she told Leycester to arrange for him to come, incognito, to England. The Duc refused the invitation point blank, for he had been told that the Queen's ladies had been ordered to watch him ceaselessly in order to see if he appeared attracted by her.

The Queen's attitude toward the marriage varied almost from day to day. At one moment she told her ladies, who had been uttering warnings against it, that 'in truth she feared the young Prince would despise her ; and that she neither found herself in health nor inclination for a husband, and that she wished to delay the treaty till she found herself more disposed to it'.

This was repeated, immediately, to the French Ambassador, who then told Lord Leycester and Lord Burleigh 'that it would by no means be advisable for Her Majesty to trifle with the Duc d'Anjou, now matters were so far advanced, for he was not to be considered like the King of Sweden, the Duke of Holstein, or the Archduke, who were all poor princes, too far off to do her any harm ; but Monsieur was the best loved brother of a powerful King, and that he was, himself, a Duke and military leader of a very warlike nation, and so near a neighbour that in ten hours he could invade her realm ; and that she could be assured he would not brook such treatment as she had shown to the other princes'.

The Ambassador judged it more discreet, however, to say this to her advisers, rather than to the alarming woman herself. And in this he undoubtedly showed wisdom.

Negotiations for the marriage continued. Long arguments

ensued as to what form of religion the bridegroom — willing or unwilling — should profess ; and the affair dragged on — delayed, no doubt, by the Queen herself. For, as the French Ambassador was told by his spies, she was really only pretending to be willing to marry the Duc in order to stop the King of France from interfering on behalf of the Queen of Scots. He had been threatening to do so. 'Unless', he declared, 'she [the Queen of England] took means for the restoration of the Queen of Scotland to her rightful dignity, and in the meantime treated her in a kind and honourable manner, he should send forces openly to her assistance.'

The Queen of England told his Ambassador, 'Her friends have given shelter to the English rebels, and with her aid and connivance have levied war on me with fire and sword. No sovereign in Europe would sit down under such a provocation, and I would count myself unworthy of realm, crown, and the name of Queen, if I endured it.'

But to Bacon, the Lord Keeper, on the 11th of June (1570), when he begged her not to release Mary at the orders of France, vowing that if France went to war on Mary's behalf, he would kill her, she said, 'Your advice is always like yourself, who have never given me any that is not rash and dangerous ; and so far from wishing to acquire another kingdom at the price of the death of my cousin, I would rather lose my own life than consent to it'.

The path of the unfortunate Bacon was by no means smooth. His eyes, squeezed to mere slits by the pressure of the universe of fat that surrounded them, saw danger everywhere. In November of the same year, the Queen had told him, 'I have followed your advice, these two years past, in all the affairs of my kingdom, and I have seen nothing but trouble, expense, and danger. From this hour, for the same length of time, I am going to follow my own opinion, and see if I find I can do any better.'

She refused to allow any interference on the part of her Council with regard to the proposed marriage, and when Cardinal Châtillon suggested that she should consult them, replied, 'I am a Sovereign Queen, and do not depend on my Council, but they on me, who hold their lives and heads in my hands, and they dare do only what I wish'. And Parliament could only remember that when they had begged her to marry, for the sake of the succession, she had replied, 'You attend to your own duties, and I'll perform mine'.

Insulting remarks had been made about the Queen in the French Court, and these reached her ears. She said to the French Ambassador 'that it was said in France that Monsieur would do well to marry an old creature who had had the evil in her leg for the last year, which was not yet healed, and never could be cured . . . for under pretext of sending a remedy, they could send her a potion from France of such a nature, that he would find himself a widower in the course of five or six months; and that he might then please himself by marrying the Queen of Scotland, and remain the undisputed sovereign of the united realms'. She was not, she declared, 'so much shocked at this project on her own account, as she was from her regard for Monsieur, and the regal house from which he sprang'.

The embarrassed man expressed his horror, and asked the name of the person responsible, in order that 'their Majesties of France might inflict a proper punishment'. The Queen replied, angrily, that she knew the name but it was not yet time to disclose it.

But she continued to treat the Ambassador with amiability. On the 31st of July, he was able to tell the Queen Mother, 'Her Majesty filled one of her own little work baskets, which always stood in her cabinet, with beautiful apricots, and desired the Earl of Leycester to send it to him with her commendations, that he might see that England was a country good enough to produce fair fruits'. To which the grateful Ambassador replied, kissing Her Majesty's hands by proxy, that 'these fine apricots showed very well that she had fair and good plants in her realm, where I wished the grafts from France might, in good time, produce fruits even more perfect'.

She entertained him in 'a sylvan place, in the midst of

QUEEN ELIZABETH I A FEW YEARS AFTER HER ACCESSION

forests'. She sent a gentleman to him with the present of a fine stag, which she had shot with her cross-bow ; and she asked 'if he had any news from France'. She talked much of the pleasure she and the Duke would find in hunting the stag in her forests.

But alas, the proposed bridegroom had determined to seize on any pretext that would extricate him from the threatened marriage.

On the 31st of July the Queen Mother wrote to Fénelon : 'As I place particular confidence in you, I will not hide from you that the humour in which I find my son Anjou, has given me great pain. He is utterly determined not to go to England without having a public assurance for [sic] the open exercise of his religion ; and neither the King nor I can prevail on him to rely on the word of the Queen of England. . . . I would not have it mentioned, since it is possible we may work something in his mind, or in that of the Queen. If, unfortunately, matters do not succeed for my son (Anjou) I am resolved to try all efforts to succeed with my son Alençon.'

At the French Court, a severe battle followed, with alarming consequences. The Queen Mother, according to herself, 'never sobbed so much since the death of her husband ; Monsieur himself retired to his cabinet and bestowed half a day in shedding tears'. The King stormed, and said he would make anyone who interfered 'shorter by the head'.

The absurd comedy continued until January of the next year, when Elizabeth, perfectly aware that nothing would induce the bridegroom to come to England, was, in her turn, seized by religious scruples, and in order to avoid his open rejection of the marriage broke off the match on that score.

The Duc d'Alençon was immediately proposed in his stead.

NOTES TO CHAPTER FORTY-ONE

[1] Secret Memorial of de Savran for the Queen Mother of France.
[2] Nashe, *Pierce Pennilesse*.
[3] Nashe, *Christ's Teares over Jerusalem*.

# Chapter Forty-two

THE events contemporary with those detailed in the last chapter were these : as we have seen, the Queen of England was well aware that the intervention or non-intervention of France on behalf of the King's sister-in-law Mary depended largely on the possible French marriage.

The French King had reiterated that unless the lady was set free, he would take steps to force the Queen of England to release her. The negotiations for her restoration to her kingdom continued.

The Earl of Morton came to England to put forward the case for the child-King. His speech at the Commission was followed by that of the Lord Keeper, Bacon, who declared that 'If the Queen of Scotland was restored, in three months she would kindle a fire which would wrap the island in flames, and which the power of man would fail to extinguish'. If the Queen of England would recognise the Prince and support the Regent, all Scotland would instantly be at her devotion and with Scotland hers she could defy the malice of the world.

The indefatigable Bishop of Ross insisted that the Queen of Scotland's signed abdication must be set aside. What rights, he enquired, had subjects over their princes ? Morton replied, in a threatening manner, that if the Queen of England did not support the claims of the young King of Scotland, there were those who would !

The Queen of Scotland had been astonished, infuriated, and alarmed by the news that the Duc d'Anjou, who had seemed to be amongst her most persistent suitors, was about to marry her hated rival. This, she told herself, was the doing of her mother-in-law, Catherine, who had always hated her.

No help, it was evident, could be looked for from France.   To whom, then, could she turn ?

To the Pope, and to the King of Spain.

On the 1st of May 1570, a copy of Pope Pius the Fifth's Bill of Excommunication was found nailed to the door of the Bishop of London's house in St. Paul's churchyard.   It was headed thus : 'The Sentence Declaratory of the Holy Father against Elizabeth the Pretended Queen of England and those heretics adhering to her'.

Not only were 'the peers, subjects and people . . . freed from their oath and all manner of duty, fidelity, and obedience', but they were told 'that they shall not once dare to obey her or any of her laws, directions, or commands, binding under the same curse those who do anything to the contrary'.

The curse resting on the excommunicated was this : that they should never again hear human speech, that they should remain unsuccoured, for no one would dare to give them food, or the curse would fall on the giver also, that they should die unburied, and go to everlasting damnation.

A new character now appears on the scene who, for some years, had lived in London.   This windy gas-bag, full of insane plans and dangerous optimism, was, to all appearances, a most suitable tool to be used in the Queen of Scotland's plans.   He and the Bishop of Ross set to work to involve the King of Spain in these.

At the beginning of the year 1571, the Bishop wrote a letter to the Enlgish Duchess of Feria which he knew would be shown, immediately, to the King.

'The life of the Queen of Scots', he said, 'had been in great danger.   Bacon, Bedford, and Cecil had urged the Queen of England to put her to death, and this had only been prevented by the intercession of Leycester.

'A revolution in her favour might easily have been effected if the King of Spain had raised a finger, but he had given no sign, and all application to him for help had so far been received with coldness, and the Queen of Scots was now driven to entertain the question of a treaty. . . . She would rather die than be the cause of the continued oppression of the Catholics ; her party was falling to pieces, and unless the King helped her, she might consent to things which would cause her endless remorse and do fatal injury to the Christian faith. If the persecutions continued, the spirit of the Catholics would be broken, and a revolution would then be impossible. . . .

'The Catholic King perhaps thought the Queen of Scots a person of no importance, but he should remember that to her God had given by right the sovereignty of the island of Britain. Her hand so dowered was not to be despised. A marriage had been spoken of for her with the Duc d'Anjou or the Duke of Norfolk, but she was still free and at the disposition of the King of Spain if only he would take her under his protection.'

So much for the Bishop of Ross.

As for Ridolfi, who was agent to the Pope (it was he who brought a Bull excommunicating Elizabeth to England), he had so far succeeded in hoodwinking Francis Walsingham that Walsingham actually recommended him to Cecil as a suitable intermediary with the King of Spain. It is strange that Walsingham, soon to be head of the secret service — he, the spider at the centre of world-wide webs and gifted like the spider with extra visual powers, should not have divined at first the nature of the busy, buzzing fly which, in the end, was to be entangled in those nets.

He had, perhaps, *not* been hoodwinked. He may have seen in Ridolfi a person who could easily be entrapped, and who would lead other dangerous persons to their downfall.

'Tell a lie and find the truth' was his contemporaries' description of Francis Walsingham's conversations with his fellow diplomats and all suspected persons. 'He would cherish a plot some years together, admitting the conspirators to his own and the Queen's presence familiarly, but dogging them watchfully ; his spies waited on some men every hour for three years : and lest they could not keep council, he despatched them to foreign parts.' [1]

Whilst the Bishop of Ross and Ridolfi were busy trying to

involve the Pope and the King of Spain, the Duke of Norfolk wavered from side to side, varying between treachery and loyalty, hoping always that his party would induce the Queen to allow his marriage with Mary.

But the latter lady, whose will was as irresistible as fire, had no patience with his irresolution. He was told by the Bishop of Ross that she was tired of it. The Queen of England would never allow the marriage. The King of Spain was about to be asked to come to her aid, and either the Duke could fall in with her plans — in which case she would fulfil her promise and marry him — or else, if he were afraid to do so, she must regard herself as free from her engagement to him.

Terrified and irresolute, seeing that phantom crown and willing, but powerless, to seize it, the fool allowed Ridolfi to come to his house. He even discussed with him plans for the invasion of England by the Duke of Alva. He went so far as to send a message to Alva that should he land with a Spanish army he, Norfolk, would join him with English troops. But the thought of signing that message filled him with terror.

Ridolfi asked him what he had to fear. Let him think of the glittering train waiting only to rise against the Queen — forty noblemen : the Marquess of Winchester, the Earls of Worcester, Arundel, Oxford, Northumberland, Westmorland, Shrewsbury, Derby, Cumberland, Southampton ; Viscount Montague ; the Lords Howard, Abergavenny, Audley, Morley, Cobham, Clinton, Grey de Wilton, Dudley, Ogle, Latimer, Scrope, Monteagle, Sandys, Vaux, Windsor, St. John, Burgh, Mordaunt, Paget, Wharton, Rich, Stafford, Dacres, Darcy, Hastings, Berkeley, Cromwell, Lumley. . . .

Ridolfi relied, one may think, a little too much on the support of these men.

So many could scarcely have been entrusted with so dangerous a secret as that of the proposed invasion. But the Admiral of the Fleet, Clinton — according to Froude — and Shrewsbury, the warder of the lady on whose behalf the rising was to take place — these, it is probable, might have been relied on.

The Queen of Scots then wrote Ridolfi a letter which she intended should be shown to the Spanish Ambassador. She only valued her claims to the thrones of Scotland and England, she declared, for the reason that she could restore the true religion. Her own sufferings were as nothing to those of her supporters, persecuted for their faith, murdered, imprisoned, driven into exile.

She was mocked at, trifled with, and insulted with hopes of release that were never intended to be realised. She herself was daily in expectation of murder, either by poison or by open violence. A person had actually come to the house where she was kept, with orders to kill her, and she was only kept alive in order that she should be the excuse for Scotland's being plunged into the horrors of civil war. Finally she insisted on her devotion to Spain, and her faith in the success of an invasion.

Ridolfi was instructed by her to ask the Pope to grant her the annulment of her marriage with Bothwell.

The man for whose sake she had thrown away her crown, and in whose company she had wished to sail where the winds and fate should take her, was far away in a Danish prison, his spirit and body dying inch by inch. But what did she care? She had long forgotten him. Hatred reigned in his place in her heart. And perhaps the very fact that Elizabeth had saved her life more than once, the contrast between her enemy's magnanimity and her own baseness, increased that hatred. And so she demanded that annulment in order that she might marry Norfolk by whose means she hoped to satisfy that inordinate passion.

'You will explain to His Holiness', she said, 'the ill-treatment which I met with from my subject, the Earl of Bothwell. The Earl carried me, the Lord Huntly, and my secretary, to the Castle of Dunbar and afterwards to the Castle of Edinburgh. I was there detained against my will until he had procured a pretended divorce between himself and his wife, the Lord Huntly's sister, and then he forced me to marry him. I therefore entreat His Holiness to take order for my relief from this indignity, either by a process at Rome or by a commission sent into Scotland.'

Norfolk also addressed his letter, meant for the King of Spain, ostensibly to Ridolfi. As was usual with him, the letter was one mass of dissimulation, dishonesty, disloyalty.

'. . . Since His Holiness and the Catholic King may have hitherto been dissatisfied with me', he wrote, 'as having in some sort affected to be a Huguenot, you will say that I have never been disloyal to the Holy See, but have desired only to hold myself in readiness (when an occasion like the present should offer itself) to do some service to my country and the commonweal of Christendom. . . . My hope is to unite the whole island under one sovereign and to restore the ancient laws and the ancient religion. . . . If God gives me grace to conduct this enterprise to a happy end, I will then be content to do anything which His Holiness, the King of Spain, and the Queen of Scots shall ordain.

'I and my friends will adventure our lives in the cause, and I beseech His Holiness to use his influence with the Catholic King on our behalf. . . . The nobles and the people promise to take arms with myself at their head, and to adventure themselves into battle ; yet, being imperfectly provided, we cannot do all of ourselves. We ask His Majesty for money, arms, ammunition, troops, and especially for some experienced soldier to lead us ; we, on our part, providing a place where his army can land, entrench itself, and keep its stores. . . .

'In my own opinion, the most convenient post will be Harwich, where I can myself be present with the forces of the country. If Portsmouth be thought better, I will be there in strength enough, for a time at least, to hold in check the Queen of England's army.'

In receipt of this letter, Ridolfi went to the Continent, ostensibly as a servant of the Queen of England.

NOTE TO CHAPTER FORTY-TWO

[1] *Dictionary of National Biography.*

# Chapter Forty-three

Parliament was to meet on the 2nd of April 1571, and the forty noblemen mentioned by Ridolfi would therefore be in London, with their retinues, conveniently placed to rise against their Queen.

Mary tried once again to rouse the Duke of Norfolk to definite action. Now was the time, she told him, to seize the Queen of England and Cecil and, before anything could be done to rescue them, put a stop once and for all to the Anjou marriage.

Various plans had been made for her own escape. She would pretend to faint, be carried to her room, and then, dressed as a page, fly from the house through a side door while one of her ladies would lie, in her place, on the bed. . . . Or one of her ladies would go hunting disguised as her, and she, again, would be dressed as a page. There were other devices of the same sort.

.    .    .    .    .

In Brussels, Ridolfi placed his plans before the Duke of Alva. How simple they looked on paper — and they would be equally simple to execute ! Nothing could be easier than to collect eight thousand Spanish troops at Middelburg — and it would be only a night's journey to England. Six thousand would land at Harwich, the rest at Aberdeen. The east coast was as good as theirs ; the Duke of Norfolk and the Spanish Ambassador would rouse the whole nation, and the two armies, Spanish and English, would march on London, while Shrewsbury guarded his erstwhile prisoner from danger.

Unfortunately, the project did not appeal to the Duke of Alva.

'I replied', he told his King, 'that what Ridolfi proposed was full of danger ; the Earls of Westmorland and Northumberland had tried an insurrection and failed, and the Duke of Norfolk, who was to have joined them, was still in partial confinement·[because of his part in that same rising, and his attempt to marry Mary]. . . .

'I then talked the matter over with the Council. To Ridolfi . . . I said merely that he might assure the Duke of Norfolk and the Queen of Scots of Your Majesty's goodwill . . . I charged him, however, as he valued their lives to keep better guard upon his tongue ; and I have written to Don Juan Cuniga to impress on His Holiness, also, the necessity of caution. Should the Queen of England hear of what is going on she will have a fair excuse to execute them both.

'. . . I do not trust Ridolfi. He is a babbler, and has already talked over the plan with a person here who is not a member of the Council. If we land and do not succeed at the first stroke, you may be sure that the Queen of England will move heaven and earth to defend herself. She will throw herself wholly on France. She will instantly marry the Duc d'Anjou, though at present nothing is further from her thoughts, and Your Majesty may consider how you will then stand, with England, France, and Germany your enemies. No one should advise Your Majesty to run such a risk as this.

'But there is another possibility. Suppose the Queen of England dead — dead by the hand of nature *or by some other hand* [my italics] or suppose the Catholics to have got possession of her person before Your Majesty has interfered, the case is then altered. There would then be no danger from Anjou or any other prince ; and the French will no longer suspect Your Majesty of intending the conquest of England. . . .

'Your Majesty understands. The Queen being dead — naturally or otherwise — dead or else a prisoner — there will be an opportunity which we should not allow to escape. The first step must be taken by us, both for our sake and theirs,

but we may tell the Duke that these conditions being first fulfilled, he shall have what he wants. The enterprise will be as
honourable to Your Majesty as it will then be easy to execute.
So confident am I of this, that if I hear that either of these
contingencies has taken place, I shall act at once without
waiting for further instructions from Your Majesty.' (7th
April 1571.)

In short, it was proposed to 'assist' the Queen of England
'to her permanent repose'.* But where was the benefactor
who would be responsible for this longed-for blessing to be
found ?

In the Council Chamber in Madrid (to which Ridolfi was
admitted, and where the King was present). A man named
Chapin Vitelli was ready, he said, to risk his life. Let the
Council place the matter in his hands, and he would either
kill or kidnap the Queen. This would not be possible in
London, but once she went on Progress — which would be
towards the end of the summer — nothing could be easier.†
She was never accompanied by enough guards. He would
travel to England with ten or fifteen fellow conspirators and
when, as would be inevitable, she was at the house of one of the
disaffected Lords, he would pretend he had a message for her,
would be admitted to her presence, and the business would
be done.

The rising and the invasion would follow.

.        .        .        .        .

A young man named Charles Bailly, half Scottish and half
Flemish, was at the moment in Brussels. He was a fanatical
upholder of the Queen of Scots' right to the throne of England
and, as he was about to travel to London, with copies of the
Bishop of Ross's defence of his mistress, and with letters to
the wives of various nobles, Ridolfi saw in him a messenger
sent by Heaven.

He gave him a letter, therefore, addressed to the Bishop

* See also Appendix E.
† For an account of one of the Queen's Progresses see Appendix F.

of Ross, telling him the whole story of his negotiations with
the Duke of Alva and, in what must surely have been a fit of
insanity, gave him letters of the same horribly dangerous
character addressed to the Duke of Norfolk and Lord Lumley.
The letters were all in cipher but Ridolfi, leaving nothing
undone which could seal their fate, actually enclosed the key
to the cipher with the letters !

Bailly was searched at Dover, the letters were found, and
the bearer and the letters were sent, heavily guarded, to the
Warden of the Cinque Ports, Lord Cobham, then in London.

By some means, the news that a man had been arrested,
bearing papers addressed to him which, since they were in
cipher, were probably incriminating, reached the Bishop of
Ross. . . . Lord Cobham sent him the papers, sealed, with
orders to come to Blackfriars the following day and open the
packet in Lord Cobham's presence.

The Bishop was in a panic. As soon as night fell he stole
across to the Spanish Ambassador's house and, with that
gentleman's help, concocted other ciphered papers, with just
a *soupçon* here and there of minor disloyalty, but not enough
to do the writer or the recipients serious harm. With these
they enclosed a few letters from the Queen of Scots, containing
slight complaints about her treatment.

This done, the good Bishop wrote to Lord Burleigh saying
that a servant of his, bearing letters addressed to him, had been
arrested at Dover and the papers taken from him. He had no
idea whatsoever what the letters contained, but would Burleigh
be so good as to have them returned to him ? The Bishop
had no idea that Burleigh, whose spies were extremely active
and were everywhere, knew a great deal.

After the northern rebellion, a disreputable character named
Thomas Herle had been arrested. He was imprisoned in the
Marshalsea, ostensibly as a political prisoner. But he was
clever, could be useful, and *was* useful. He was, in short, a
spy in the pay of Cecil, and in this capacity had been in touch
with both the Bishop and the Spanish Ambassador. Such was
Burleigh's trust in him that he had been commissioned to find

a murderer or else a kidnapper to go to Flanders and deal with the Earl of Westmorland.

He was to prove worthy of the trust reposed in him. In order that he should gain, also, the trust of his fellow prisoners he was treated with what appeared to be peculiar cruelty ; his employer threatened him frequently with the rack, and the irons he wore were so insupportably heavy that the tender-hearted Bishop of Ross wept when he heard of them.

No sooner was Bailly sent to the same prison than this creature began to insinuate himself into his confidence. There was no one to whom Bailly could turn. He was utterly friend-less, and he was half-mad with terror. He was grateful for a friendly word. The task was easy. Bailly's new friend spoke piously of the state of religion, reverently of the sufferings of the Queen of Scots. Bailly was utterly deceived.

But although Burleigh was in possession of those letters, he still could not decode the whole cipher. Therefore the doors of the cells were left open at night. Bailly was asleep when he felt the presence of another human being, and woke to hear Herle's whisper. He had, he said, a letter from the Bishop of Ross, but he had hidden it and could not find it in the darkness. The Bishop wished to know if the Council had examined Bailly about the books found in his luggage, and about his communications with the refugees. Leaning over his victim, Herle heard a noise like that of a drum. It was the sound of Bailly's heart beating.

'What !' he cried, 'had not my lord his letters then, wherein I answered "Yes" ?'

He would say nothing more, but next morning tried to warn the Bishop. His letter was intercepted, and Burleigh knew that Herle would be of no further use to him with Bailly.

The latter was moved to an unspeakably filthy cell in the Tower, where he had 'only a little straw on the moist earth to lie upon'. He was threatened with the rack if he refused to decode the letters. He succeeded in getting a letter to the Bishop, begging him to save him — or he was 'lost for ever'.

The Bishop claimed him as his servant, and insisted on his own diplomatic privileges.

In vain. The Bishop could do nothing now but implore him to 'comfort himself in God, and remember the noble heroes who had suffered death rather than betray their masters'. The bearer of this letter took it to Burleigh.

The Lieutenant of the Tower was ordered either to obtain the code from Bailly, or to put him to the torture. He was racked, and after a few hours was seen 'staggering back to his dungeon, "scarce able to go", "discoloured and pale as ashes"'.[1] The torturers had wrung nothing from him, but they had not finished with him yet. He was told that he would be racked again, and this time more horribly.

One more hideous trick was to be played on him. A prisoner awaiting execution as a traitor — Dr. Story (whom Bailly had never seen) — was in the Tower. And now, late at night, a man came to the straw on which Bailly was lying, and said he was Story, come to administer spiritual consolation to him, through the kindness of the gaoler. . . . This pretended Story (to Bailly, a saint awaiting martyrdom) was the man Parker, the treacherous friend who had brought about the capture of Story in Flanders. He told Bailly that almost everything was known, and that if he would only decipher the letters he would be telling Burleigh nothing that he did not know already, and would, in addition, win his favour. He advised him, also, to offer to spy on the Bishop of Ross.

The wretched creature was completely deceived. He gave the cipher and everything that could possibly be wanted into Burleigh's hands — the notes about the communications between Ridolfi and Alva, the plan for the proposed invasion — everything.

The favour he had hoped to win from Burleigh was not forthcoming. He was still in the Tower, and all he had gained from his action was the scorn of his friends.

As for the Bishop of Ross, he was so ill with terror at the thought of what the rack might wring from Bailly that he barricaded himself in his house, and lay in bed for three days, refusing to eat.

Lord Burleigh was perfectly aware that the Bishop knew secrets unknown to Bailly. But how could he be made to divulge them ?

Herle was once again to prove his usefulness. He was summoned before the Council, questioned, and, as he refused to answer, was put into irons and threatened with the rack. The devoted man wrote to the Bishop, imploring his prayers and his advice. He would rather die, he said, than betray anything.

The Bishop, who seems, in some ways, to have been rather simple-minded, for all his cunning, sent a friend to visit Herle, who complained in a heart-broken manner that Bailly had mistrusted him, — 'uttering his speech in piteous forms, his irons jingling up and down by meet occasions as the fellow wept and sobbed'. He wrote again to the Bishop, 'esteeming no torment greater than unjust jealousy conceived of a true friend'.

Once more the Bishop believed him . . . and the affair ended badly. Members of the Council visited the Bishop, and he was questioned about his servant's confession and the actions of Ridolfi. They asked why certain letters that he declared had been burnt had met with this fate. He seemed unable to explain. It was difficult to know what to do with him. Since he was an Ambassador he could not be racked. (But of this he was not certain.) So, in the end, his papers and his servants were taken from him, and he was sent to the house of the Bishop of Ely, to the despair of that prelate.*

Spies were everywhere — in the prisons, at the dining-tables of the nobles. 'The rebels all expect to be in England next spring with the Duke of Alva', wrote a spy named Simson, in his Report of a Conversation at the Earl of Westmorland's Table, the 8th of October ; 'and then they will spoil the new ministers, heretics, of all they have and hang them and not leave one of them alive. They all came of Luther ;

* See Appendix G.

and the devil came to Luther by night to tell him what he should say. They say the Queen of England is no righteous Queen and ought to be put away. If the weather is fair they have news from the court of all that passes there every two days.'

.        .        .        .        .

The Duke of Norfolk's downfall came through unexpected means. He was attempting to smuggle gold into Scotland to aid Mary's supporters. The packet contained not only the money, but a letter in cipher. The bearer of the packet was not told of its contents, but thought it suspiciously heavy, and therefore opened it, and sent the whole to Burleigh. The members of the Council put in charge of the investigations were met by the Duke with fresh lies and prevarications. He was sent to the Tower, and such was his lethal folly that he wrote a note to a member of his household ordering that his ciphers should be burned. The messenger took this letter to the Lieutenant of the Tower and he gave it to Burleigh.

Two of the Duke's secretaries were seized and tortured — one, Barber, being so terrified that he confessed everything he knew. The Duke continued to lie, and accused his secretaries of having sold his life in order to save their own.

There was, by now, general consternation among the conspirators, including the Spanish Ambassador, Don Guerau, who was sent for by the Council, told that his meddling and insolence had been too much for the country, and too much for the Queen, who could no longer support his presence. He was ordered to leave England immediately. He did so in January 1572.

The Queen of Scots was told by Lord Shrewsbury that her communications with Ridolfi were known. To which she replied that she had come to England as a free Princess relying upon promises that had been repeatedly made to her, and instead of friendship and hospitality she had found a prison. The Duke of Norfolk was the Queen of England's subject, and for him she had nothing to say. For herself, she was a free Princess, the Queen of England's equal, and was answerable neither to her nor to any other person. She then ordered her secretary to tell the King of France how he had seen her treated.

The Bishop of Ross was sent for, and was told that the whole of his conduct, his speeches, his letters, were known, and that, Ambassador or no Ambassador, if he did not answer the questions put to him he 'should be made to suffer to the example and terror of all others'.

At first, while declaring his immunity as Ambassador, he swore to his innocence. He was given two days to think the matter over, and then, not knowing that the Queen had forbidden the use of the rack on him — seeing the possibility, perhaps, even of execution, he confessed. He then wrote to the Queen of Scots, telling her that all was known, and urging her to follow his example, and stop conspiring. As we have seen in an earlier chapter, he admitted to Doctor Wilson, one of his examiners, his Queen's part in her husband's murder.

The Queen of Scots, in a frenzy of rage, declared that 'the Bishop of Ross was a flawed and fearful priest, who had done as they would have him do. For herself, they should find her to be a Queen, and to have the heart of a Queen.'

Sir Thomas Smith, who was in Paris as an aide to Walsingham, told the French Council plainly that if the Queen of Scots gave any more trouble she would be dealt with.

'I was fain to declare unto them', he wrote, 'all her behaviour, her adulteries, the killing of her husband twice (it might be) with poison, and some say strangling, besides fire and gunpowder, the shameful marrying of her adulterer and murderer of her husband, who had a wife living, her deposing by the nobility and Act of Parliament. Yet the Queen's Majesty would not believe it, but had it heard again in London : and though the thing was too manifest, yet for respect that she was a Queen and her alliance, Her Majesty would not condemn her and would not absolve her.

'They seemed at last so persuaded that they could not

LORD BURLEIGH IN HIS GARDEN AT THEOBALDS

deny her evil deeds and deservings.' But they reminded Sir Thomas that she had been Queen of France, and was sister-in-law to the present King, which to some degree involved her in his fate.

The Duke of Norfolk was sentenced to death. In order to save him, two men prepared to kill the Queen and Burleigh. And yet the Queen, in spite of the danger to herself and her Minister, could not bear to sign the warrant for his execution, which should have taken place on the 21st of January. 'The Queen's Majesty', said Burleigh, 'hath always been a merciful lady, and by mercy she hath taken more harm than justice, and yet she thinks that she is more beloved in doing herself harm. God save her to His honour long among us.' 2

One Saturday in February the Queen, at last resolved that Norfolk must die, signed the order that he should be executed on Monday. But late on Sunday night she sent for her Minister and rescinded the order. The idea that he should die at her command filled her with horror. But her dangerous mercy filled her Councillors with consternation. In rescinding his death-warrant, was she not signing her own? 'The world knows her to be wise', said Lord Hunsdon, 'and surely there cannot be a greater part of wisdom than for any to be careful of their own estate, and especially the preservation of their own life. How much more needful is it for Her Majesty to take heed, upon whose life depends a whole commonwealth, the utter ruin of the whole country and the utter subversion of religion. And if by negligence or womanish pity these things happen, what she hath to answer for to God, she herself knows.'

Twice more did she sign that warrant, and twice more did she rescind it. 'God preserve Your Majesty long to reign over us by some unlooked-for miracle,' wrote Sir Thomas Smith from Paris in March, 'for I cannot see by natural reason that Her Highness goeth about to provide for it.'

It was only by the Queen's mercy and by the indomitable strength of her will that Mary was not executed at this moment. For Parliament was determined that this 'Clytemnestra', as the member for New Windsor called her, 'a killer of her husband and an adulteress', 'a common disturber of the peace of this realm', should die. 'Cut off her head and make no more ado with her', the same member advised.[3]

Another member, named Snagge, declared, 'She hath not spared her nobility, neither her bed, nor board. A sower of sedition in France, hither she came, not as an enemy but worse — as a dissembling friend, and under friendship hath sought the destruction of the Queen's Majesty.'

Thomas Norton, in his speech, made this point : 'You will say she is a King's daughter, and therefore to be spared : nay, then, spare the Queen's Majesty that is a King's daughter and our Queen'.

George Grenville, a relation of Grenville of the *Revenge*, said, 'Temeris apprehending his son and another woman in adultery cut off both their heads and then caused a coin to be made of two heads issuing out of one, for a perpetual monument of their adultery. He would have the like to be done with the Queen of Scots and the Duke, and some perpetual memory made for remembrance of the villainies of their acts.'

The Duke of Norfolk was executed on the 2nd of June 1572.

The Queen of Scots had still a little time remaining in which she must live.

NOTES TO CHAPTER FORTY-THREE

[1] Herle to Burleigh, 1st May. Froude, *op. cit.*
[2] Neale, *op. cit.* vol. 1.
[3] Neale, *op. cit.* vol. 1.

# Chapter Forty-four

THE proposed marriage between the Queen of England and the Duc d'Alençon had presented, even to the mind of his mother, certain difficulties, but the indomitable woman summoned all her strength of character and will to overcome these. Her son, she reasoned, was now (1572) twenty-one, and it could no longer be objected that he was a child.

On hearing from Sir Thomas Smith the full story of the Ridolfi conspiracy, a plot to kidnap the young King of Scotland and marry him, willy-nilly, to a Spanish princess, and of the plan for Alva to invade Harwich and rescue the Queen of Scots, she exclaimed, 'Jesus ! And doth not your mistress Queen Elizabeth see plainly that she will always be in danger till she marry ? If she marry into some good house, who shall dare attempt aught against her ?' She added that she could not recommend her son Alençon too strongly. After all, 'he is not so *very* little,' she declared, 'he is as high as you, or near so'.

'For that matter', Sir Thomas replied, 'I, for my part, make small account of height, provided the Queen's Majesty can fancy him. Since Pepinus Brevis, who married Bertha, the King of Almain's daughter, was so little to her, that he is standing in Aquisgrave [*sic*] or Moguerre, a church in Germany, she taking him by the hand, that [*sic*] his head reached not her girdle ; and yet he had by her Charlemagne, the great Emperor and King of France, reported to be almost a giant in stature.'

'It is true', said the ambitious woman, 'that it is the heart, courage and activity that are to be looked for in a man, rather than the height. But' (staring at him with her protuberant, apparently myopic, but in reality all-seeing eyes) 'have you no word of the Queen's affection in my son's way ? Can you give me no comfort ?' He was obliged to tell her that the courier, though on his way from England, had not yet arrived.

Envoys were sent to England. It was, the Queen was assured, as much for the benefit of the French Huguenots as it was for the peace of Europe that she should accept the hand of this new suitor. 'Marriage', the French envoys were instructed to say, 'was the surest bond of treaties.'

The King of France was so enthusiastically in favour of the marriage that, fearing that Leycester might stand in the way, Montmorency (one of the envoys, the other being de Foix) was ordered by their master to inform the Queen's favourite that he would receive as a reward, if he supported the plan, the hand of a Princess of France.

On Sunday the 15th of June 1572, the day after the envoys' arrival in England, Lord Burleigh brought them into the Chapel, immediately after the prayers had been read, and presented them to the Queen. She expressed great happiness at seeing them, and they, on their side, overwhelmed her with compliments. She called God to witness for her punishment 'if in her heart He saw not a true intention of bringing forth the fruits of this concord by suitable deeds : for words were no better than leaves'. 'She assured them that she was completely impartial in her dealings with Scotland.'

The parchment bearing the proposed treaty with France and the French King's signature was presented to her by the envoys, and walking to the altar, she placed her hand upon the Gospels, held by a Bishop, and swore on these to hold to the terms of the treaty, then signed this declaration at a desk of gold, held by four Earls.

Afterwards, the two envoys and the French Ambassador dined at the Queen's table, in a great banqueting hall that had been erected at Westminster in their honour. 'The top of this house', wrote Holinshed, 'was wrought most cunninglie upon canvas, works of ivie and hollie with pendants made of wicker rods, and garnished with bae, rue, and all manner of strange flowers, garnished with spangles of gold, as also beautified with hanging. . . .

'Hollie and ivie, with all manner of strange fruits, as pomegranates, oranges, pompions, cucumbers, grapes, carrets, with such other like, spangled with gold and most richlie hanged.'

The outlook, however, seemed less bright than the decorations. The Queen appeared now to be by no means enthusiastic about the marriage. The Ambassador, writing to the Queen Mother on the 22nd of June, told her that he 'had urged Burleigh and Leycester to entreat their royal mistress to give an early answer on the subject of the marriage, and grant a conference to himself and Montmorency.' 'For this cause', he continued, 'she sent for us all three on the morrow, to come to her after dinner, in private, without ceremony. We were brought by water into her garden, and found her in a gallery, where she received us all very graciously.'

She 'desired to enter into particularities, especially in the important subject of religion'. They reassured her. Everything, they declared, should be as she wished.

But then came a darker note. She enquired, 'What compensation is to be made to me, in the marriage articles, for the injury to his face from the smallpox?' 'She discussed His Royal Highness from top to toe', wrote Agnes Strickland, 'with no more ceremony than is commonly used by persons who are bargaining for the purchase of a lap-dog, a monkey, or any other animal of small account.'

They hastened to set her mind at rest on the subject of the 'injury to his face'. After he had been treated by a quack found by the Queen Mother, his face, they assured her, would be peach-smooth. Later, discussing this with the French Ambassador, Lord Burleigh, who seemed a little doubtful, enquired if the Ambassador could tell him of any person in England who had been cured by the doctor in question. 'I named two,' La Mothe Fénelon told the Queen Mother — 'one of whom is now in the city of London, and the other is a country lady, and a relation of the Countess of Bedford. In truth the said doctor is a person of great learning and much experience, and has made no difficulty of it, but said that the remedy has nothing in it that is noxious, and that it is very sure.'

But there still remained the difficulty of age. There again, the envoys assured the Queen, she need have no qualms. 'The disparity in age', they declared, 'amounted to nothing, seeing that it was only the trifling difference of nineteen years ; and as Her Majesty, from her charms of mind and person, appeared younger by ten years than she really was, and Monseigneur the Duke, in consequence of his fine manly figure and good sense, had anticipated the other nine years of his age and looked full seven and twenty years, they were placed on an equality.'

But the Queen continued her intricate courtship-dance. 'I see such extremities on both sides', Burleigh told Walsingham on the 27th of July, 'as I can make no choice. Without marriage all evils must be looked for ; by marriage without liking no good can be hoped. Therefore to God I leave it. The Queen is very irresolute.'

Walsingham, the English Ambassador to France, was, on his side, almost in despair, fearing that his Queen would listen to 'the fair words of Spain', and that the French alliance would be set aside.

'Fearful effects', the French King wrote to his Ambassador, 'would follow unless God put forth His helping hand.'

.        .        .        .        .

A terrible shadow drew nearer a — shadow that seemed as if torn from universal Night.

Then came Horror.

# Chapter Forty-five

On the 8th of June 1569 Francis de Alava, the Spanish Ambassador to France, told his King a strange story.

A certain Italian, he reported, had offered the Queen Mother to murder the Prince de Condé, Admiral Coligny, and one other of the principal leaders of the French Protestant faction — d'Andelot. These men, besides being Huguenots, were her personal enemies.

On the offer being accepted, the Italian shut himself up, for the space of six months, in a room with a German mechanic whom he had brought with him — and who constructed three figures of bronze with many joints through which daggers could pierce. The Italian cast the horoscope of the threatened men every day.

The Prince de Condé was killed in the battle of Jarnac on the 13th of March 1569, and according to the Memoirs of her daughter, Marguerite of Navarre, Catherine, being dangerously ill at the time, saw the death of her old enemy in a vision.

Three years after that time, the Duke of Alva, fighting the Protestant rebels in the Lowlands, met at first with defeat after defeat. The army of French Protestants that had come to the aid of the rebels were in a fortified town not far from Brussels.

In France, the fury of the Catholics at the ascendancy of Huguenot influence at Court, and in public affairs, grew. The King's sister, Marguerite, was about to be married to a Protestant, the young King of Navarre. The betrothal had already been celebrated with great splendour (in June 1572), and the marriage was to be in August.

Then came disaster to the Protestants in the Lowlands. Twelve hundred bodies lay in the field, and the men who had survived the battle were taken and shot by the Spaniards, or murdered by the peasants.

But an army of Huguenots was massing in France, and this army would be led to the Lowlands by Admiral Coligny, as soon as the marriage of Princess Marguerite to the King of Navarre was over. However, after the disaster to the Protestants, the leaders of the French Catholics protested to the King against any fresh help being given to the Lowlands. In vain. 'But for the King', wrote Walsingham, 'all had failed long before.'

The King had intended to send the Admiral to the Low Countries before the Princess's marriage ; but some report that had reached the Queen Mother had terrified her. She told her son that 'without the Queen of England's assistance he would not be able to bear the brunt of so puissant an enemy' ; 'without England the expedition would miscarry'. And she implored the King, 'with tears', to do nothing until the Queen of England had made up her mind about marriage with the Duc d'Alençon.[1]

Elizabeth was still irresolute. She would, and she would not, marry the boy. If she could see him, she said, perhaps she could make up her mind. Sir Thomas Smith in Paris implored that the Duc should be sent to England immediately, 'else nothing was to be looked for but continued dalliance and doubtfulness'. On the same day (the 22nd of August), Burleigh wrote to Coligny 'what God shall please to do in the cause I know not ; but I see the marriage of my lady and Queen is of more moment to the weal, both particularly of this realm, and publicly of Christendom for the benefit of religion, than I fear our sins will suffer us to receive'.

That letter was never to reach the Admiral.

.        .        .        .        .

Just before the marriage celebrations of the King's sister, the Duc d'Anjou and the Queen Mother had noticed that whenever the Admiral had had a private audience, the King appeared in a black mood, harsh towards them, both in manner and speech.

Then one day, when Anjou went to the King in his study immediately after the Admiral had left it, he was received by the King 'striding backwards and forwards furiously without a word but frequently eyeing me sideways and with such black looks and handling his dagger so ominously that I expected him to take me by the throat and stab me. . . . When he turned his back, I retired quickly toward the door, opened it, and with a shorter bow than at my entrance, made by exit.'

He went immediately to the Queen Mother, and, comparing notes, they became 'all but certain', wrote Anjou, 'that it was the Admiral who had given the King some sinister opinion of us, and we determined then and there to be rid of him'. Their only confidante was to be Madame de Nemours, who could be trusted because of her hatred of him.

The marriage ceremonies took place on the 18th of August. Four days afterwards, on Friday the 22nd, the Admiral, meeting the King coming from Chapel, went with him to the tennis court. As he was returning from there to dinner, he paused for a moment, his slippers being loose, and, turning his head, called his page.

That turn of the head saved his life temporarily. Two shots were fired from the top storey of an apparently empty house. His left arm and a finger of his right hand were shattered.

The Council was to discover, eventually, that this house was the property of the Dowager Duchesse de Guise (the house of Guise was at enmity with the Admiral); and that Madame de Nemours, the confidante of Anjou and the Queen Mother, had lodged her train there during her recent visit to Paris.

When the King heard of the attempted murder, he broke into a frenzy of rage. 'Shall I never have peace?' he shouted. And when the agitated Protestant leaders came to ask for justice, he swore that they should have it, full measure.

The Queen Mother was extravagant in her demands that the criminals should be unearthed immediately, and given exemplary punishment. The outrage was intolerable. Nobody was safe. If the crime was not punished today, it would be repeated tomorrow — 'in the Louvre — *in her bed* !'

The two would-be murderers, 'having missed one attempt so narrowly . . . considered [according to Anjou's own account] our affair until after dinner when, the King wishing to visit him [the Admiral], my mother and I determined to visit him' also 'and see the face of the Admiral'.

The Queen Mother showed a tender solicitude for the man who had so narrowly escaped death. But she and her son were decidedly uncomfortable when, the Admiral having expressed a wish to speak to the King privately, they found themselves alone with his followers, who 'whispered among themselves, passing before and behind us and not with so much respect as they should have had, as we thought, and almost as if they suspected us of having a part in the wounding of the Admiral!'

The Queen Mother, in her solicitude for the wounded man, warned the King that it would be dangerous for him to exhaust himself by talking — and in this way was able to induce the King to leave the house. She asked him at once what the Admiral had said to him. At first he refused to answer, then, bursting into a violent passion, he swore (wrote Anjou) that what the Admiral had told him was true, that the Queen Mother and Anjou were gaining control over all the affairs of state, 'and that this threatened great danger to the whole kingdom'. '"By God," he said, "since you wanted to know it, that is what the Admiral told me !"  And all this with such passion and fury that his words cut us to the heart.'

The King wished the Admiral to be taken to the Louvre, but he refused to go, saying 'only a fool would trust himself between four walls'. Nor would he accept a detachment of guards. . . . The Vidame de Chartres suggested to the King that the Admiral should be sent to Châtillon, saying that the affair was only at the beginning. But he remained in his Paris house.

'The popular quarters', wrote Roeder, in his great book *Catherine de' Medici and the Lost Revolution*, 'were so tense, the shops were closing. . . .'

The tension grew.

The King sent repeatedly, next morning, to enquire after the Admiral, who was visited, too, by the young Queen of Navarre.

The fear and suspense, as the day went on, seemed a part of the almost intolerable heat. . . .

A voice at the dining-table of the Queen Mother said that if the Huguenots did not receive justice, they would take the matter into their own hands.

After a sleepless night of increasing fear, Anjou crept, at dawn, to the room of his mother. They knew now that the Admiral must die without further delay, and as it was impossible to use any further subterfuge, he must be killed openly. But for this to be done, the King's consent must be gained.

'We decided', he wrote, 'to go to him in his study, and to send for M. de Nevers, Maréchaux de Tavannes and de Retz, and Chancellor Biraque.

'To pave the way, de Retz went to the King; and told him the truth', that not only M. de Guise (Henri, 3rd Duc, whose father had been assassinated in 1573) was involved, but also Anjou and the Queen Mother — their only aim, he declared, being to 'remove that pest from the kingdom . . . but that unfortunately the man chosen to commit the murder had missed his aim, and now the Huguenots were so desperate that they accused, not only de Guise, not only the mother and brother of the King — but the King himself. And so they were preparing to rise, that very night.'

At first, the King flew into a paroxysm of fury — swearing that he would not allow the Admiral to be touched. Then, becoming slightly calmer, but 'shaken by the danger we had shaped', he wished to know whether there was no other remedy. . . .

Then, wrote Anjou, 'we noticed a sudden extraordinary change in the King, who took our side and embraced our opinion, passing far beyond it and more criminally. . . .

'Now we had to restrain him. . . . Pacing the floor and silencing us, he said, swearing by la Mort de Dieu, that since we wished the Admiral to be killed, he consented, but that then every Huguenot must die, not one must remain to reproach him, and that we must give the command promptly. And, striding out furiously, he left us in his study.'

But he was not to be left alone. Shortly after midnight, his Doom, his mother, entered his room.

'The risk of his relenting', writes Roeder in a superb passage, 'led her to invade his last solitude. . . . But the condemned are entitled to a last solitude, and he resented her presence. He was sentenced to be haunted for life, and before the supreme ordeal began, he longed to be alone. He would never be alone again ; the relentless shapes were already upon him, and she was one of them, no longer his mother, but a presence impersonal, inexorable, looming over him for the rest of his life, no longer human.'

So afraid had she been that he would weaken, that she had advanced the signal that was to be given for the massacre by an hour and a half.

It was now between one and two in the morning.

In her fear that *he* might weaken, it had not entered her thoughts that somewhere in that indurated heart of hers there was one touch of humanity. That it would be *she*, after all, and not he, who would feel that culpable weakness.

'Now, after resting two hours,' wrote Anjou, 'when it began to dawn, the King, my mother and I went to the Portal of the Louvre, near the tennis courts, in a room commanding the Place de la Basse-cour, to see the beginning of the execution. We had not been there long and were meditating the consequences of so great an undertaking which, to tell the truth, we had not considered clearly before, when we heard a pistol shot ; where it came from or whether it hurt anyone I cannot say ; but I do know that the sound struck us all, stunning us with fear of the great disorders which were to follow. We send a gentleman in great haste to M. de Guise, commanding him expressly to return to his lodgings and, on no account to attempt anything against the Admiral ; this one order alone being enough to check everything, since nothing was to begin in the city until the Admiral had been killed. But a little later the gentleman returned and said that M. de Guise had replied that the order was too late, that the Admiral was dead, and that the execution had already begun throughout the city. And so we let the enterprise run its course.'

That enterprise was the massacre of St. Bartholomew, 24th-25th August 1572.

. . . . .

By noon next day, the red heat and the colour of the streets were as one. The red rags that had once been human beings, and that now littered the streets, numbered three thousand.

In the courtyard of the Admiral's house, the old man, flung from the window by a servant, lay like a scarlet shadow cast by the heat. As he fell, François de Guise wiped the blood from the face, then kicked it in and rode away. But later the head was 'hacked off', and there was nothing but the headless body, and, where once the head with its multitudinous thoughts had been, a multitude of flies.

The children had great fun. Some dragged the bodies of dead creatures young and small as themselves about the streets. Then, the day after the massacre, they hauled the old body from the Admiral's courtyard, cut off its hands and its genitals, and put them up for sale.[2] So, dragged along the streets, the body found refuge first at one street corner then at another — but only for a moment. Then, at last, hanging by the feet, it was exposed to view on the public gibbet at Montfaucon.

In the cemetery of the Innocents there was the miracle of the blooming of an eglantine. Vast multitudes of people

gathered to worship the sign. The tocsin sounded in praise-
giving of the wonder. Then the people knew that the flower-
ing of the eglantine was a sign from Heaven that there must
be a fresh massacre, and it was as a signal for this that the
tocsin had sounded.

.        .        .        .        .

The Queen of England was on progress, had reached
Warwick, and, leaving the Court there, had gone to spend
two restful days at Kenilworth with Leycester. She was
riding through the country lanes when news was brought to
her of the horror in Paris. She rode back to the Castle at
once, and Fénelon, who was a guest, was forbidden her
presence. It was not until four days later, when she had
reached Woodstock with her train, that she sent for him.

He passed through rows of courtiers, all dressed in black,
and preserving a complete silence. In the Presence Chamber,
the Queen stood, surrounded by her ladies and the Privy
Councillors. Again, all were in black. With a stern, sad
face, she advanced a few steps to meet him, and, in silence,
withdrew with him to a window.

Alarmed, he began to make excuses. A conspiracy against
the King's life had been discovered. Only necessary steps had
been taken.

Was the massacre of women and children a necessary step,
the Queen enquired? The Ambassador's alarm increased.
He hoped, he said, that there would be no difference in England's friendship to France. The Queen replied that she feared
a King who could give over his subjects to massacre would
be equally untrustworthy with his allies.

However, the pretence at courtship with the French Prince
continued, in a desultory fashion, until it died of sheer
inanition.

.        .        .        .        .

King Charles the Ninth had yet one year and ten months
in which he must live, crowded upon by the procession of red

ghosts. Then, in June 1574, he lay dying of haemorrhage — waking from his haunted sleep to find himself in a sea of blood.

The Queen Mother had always been addicted to witch-craft. Now, summoning her astrologers, she was advised by them to resort to one of the most appalling forms of magic, 'the Oracle of the Bleeding Head'.[3] A young innocent child was taken, and was prepared for his first Communion by the Queen Mother's chaplain. Then, on the night when the magic was to be performed, an apostate Jacobin, a Black Magician, celebrated Mass at midnight in the room of the dying King, the Queen Mother and only her most trusted attendants being present, before the image of the demon, and a transposed Crucifix. 'The Sorcerer', according to Eliphas Lévi, 'consecrated the hosts, one black and one white.' The child was brought in, was given Communion, then, on the steps of the altar, he was beheaded. 'The exorcism began', said Lévi ; 'an oracle was besought of the demon, and an answer by the mouth of the head to a secret question which the King dared not make aloud and had confided to no one. A strange and feeble voice, which had nothing human about it, was heard presently in the poor little martyr's head, saying in Latin : 'Vim patior' : 'I suffer violence'. At this reply, which doubtless announced to the sick man that Hell no longer protected him, a horrible trembling seized the monarch, his arms stiffened, and he cried in a hoarse voice : 'Away with that head ! Away with that head !' And so continued screaming till he gave up the ghost. His attendants, who were not in the confidence of this frightful mystery, believed that he was pursued by the phantom of Coligny.'

### NOTES TO CHAPTER FORTY-FIVE

[1] The Duc d'Alençon was by now the Duc d'Anjou, owing to the death of the late King, his brother, and the accession of the hitherto Duc d'Anjou to the throne. But in order to avoid confusion, I still refer to the new Duc d'Anjou as d'Alençon.

[2] Roeder.

[3] Lévi, *History of Magic*.

# Chapter Forty-six

THE French courtship of the Queen of England had, as we have seen, dawdled along until, in 1575, it disappeared in the distance. But only for a while. Three years later it reappeared on the horizon, owing to the fact that Alençon had taken up arms in the Netherlands, and must, somehow, be dislodged — for, as the Queen's message to his adversary, demanding a cessation of fighting, declared, 'she would not allow these countries to be reduced to servitude by him [Don Juan] nor yet be possessed by the French'.

Alençon's adventure had not been backed, *officially*, by the King ; but when the Spanish Ambassador protested, the King refused to order the return of his brother, and when the Ambassador reminded him that he was responsible for the conduct of his subjects, he answered that though he would dislike a quarrel with Spain, he would dislike even more a quarrel with his brother.

The Frog Prince, Alençon, meanwhile (the Queen of England had christened him 'My Frog', and wore, always, a jewelled frog in her bosom as a compliment to him) had been performing as intricate a dance as the object of his courtship. Inheriting from his mother an almost insane ambition, he was capable of committing any deed in order to further it. At the time when Elizabeth's coolness towards him had injured his pride, his mother had suggested a marriage with a Spanish Princess, in order to diminish the power of the Guise faction. While considering this, he considered, also, the suggestion made by the Duc de Guise (whose power he was required to diminish) to join with him and the Queen of

JAMES VI OF SCOTLAND AGED EIGHT

Scots' party in Scotland, seize Edinburgh and Dumbarton Castles, kidnap the young King, smuggle him into France and, holding him there as hostage, demand that Mary should be set at liberty.

In furtherance of this last-named plan, the Comte de Retz, going to Scotland on business, carried secret messages to the Guise faction there. But, as he passed through London, the Queen sent for him and told him she was perfectly aware of his machinations. He had come to unsettle England, and serve the cause of a wicked woman 'whose head should long since have been struck from her shoulders'. He might do his worst, but the Queen of Scotland should never be freed, even if it cost the Queen of England her crown and her life.

The Queen of Scots' afflictions were at this time increased by the loss of her beloved aunt and mother-in-law, to whom she had been touchingly reconciled.[1] On the 9th of March (1577) after Lord Leycester had dined with Lady Lennox at her house in Hackney, she unfortunately became violently ill as soon as he had left the house, and died almost immediately.

Alençon now came to the conclusion that his ambition would best be furthered by a marriage with the Queen of England. Therefore he renewed his courtship, which the Queen appeared to welcome. But when Mendoza, the Spanish Ambassador, excused himself for not having come to Court on the plea that he thought the Queen would be too busy with preparations for her wedding to receive him, she replied, 'An old woman like myself has something else to think of besides marrying ; the hopes I gave that I would marry Alençon were given for the purpose of getting him out of the Netherlands States ; I never wished to see them in the hands of the French'.

In January 1579, Alençon's 'chief darling' Jean de Simier, Baron de St. Marc, arrived at the English Court. Lively, suave, and flattering, he delighted the Queen, who called him 'my monkey' while he, in letters to her, signed himself 'à jamais le singe votre'.

He was lodged at Greenwich, in a house surrounded by gardens and known as the Pavilion. But, although he was not actually in the Palace, the Queen's obvious pleasure in his company was such that a fresh scandal was started about her : it was said that he used love potions, and that the Queen admitted him to a far too great intimacy, and to her presence at the most unsuitable hours.

Such, by now, was Alençon's ardour, that he could not be restrained by his brother's advice from coming to England, heavily disguised. Entering Simier's room, while that gentleman was still asleep, he was luckily prevented from rushing into the Queen's bedroom in order to kiss her hand, and it was not until she was fully arrayed that they met.

She was immediately charmed with him — or said that she was — and thirteen days and nights of courtship followed — the Frog Prince, on his side, being, according to himself and Simier, so deeply in love that the night before he left England was passed in despairing sighs and moans, and he rose at dawn to speak of the Queen's divine beauty and to swear that he could not live without the hope of seeing that loveliness again. He wrote four letters to her from Dover, three from Boulogne, wiping, he said, the tears from his eyes. He kissed her feet, he was her faithful slave, and so on.

But though Alençon was delighted with England, England was not delighted by him. A large part of the nation objected strongly to the marriage ; and in September a secretly printed tract was disseminated through the country. It was called *The Discovery of a Gaping Gulf Wherinto England is like to be Swallowed by another French marriage, if the Lord forbid not the banns by letting Her Majesty see the sin and punishment thereof!* A man named John Stubbs, whose sister was the wife of the leader of the Puritans, was the author. In this work, Stubbs raged against the Catholic religion, accused the French royal house of being 'rotten with disease, sealed with visible marks of divine vengeance upon their carcases for their manifold cruelties'.[2] It declared also that the French desired the marriage, above all, at this time when childbirth would be a

terrible danger to the Queen who might well expect death
(she was forty-six).

The Queen was, not unnaturally, furious. The French,
with whom she wished to remain on terms of friendship, and
their Prince, her guest, had been grossly insulted. The city
authorities and the bishops were ordered to read to those for
whom they were responsible a long proclamation, in praise of
the Queen's government and her devotion to the Protestant
faith. Stubbs and the printer and Page, the publisher, were
arrested, and were condemned to have their right hands cut
off, and to imprisonment. The printer was pardoned, but
Stubbs and the publisher underwent their punishment. On
the scaffold Stubbs, as his right hand was hacked off, raised his
hat from his head with his left hand, cried 'God save the
Queen !', and fainted. The publisher, says Sir John Neale,
'lifted his bloody stump ; "I have left there a true Englishman's hand", he cried, and went away very stoutly and with
great courage'.

The scene was watched in entire silence.

In October the Queen decided to ask the advice of the
Council on the subject of the marriage, and a violent struggle
began — lasting, one day, from eight in the morning till seven
in the evening. It was now only too evident that a large part
of the Council and her people were utterly opposed to it.
But though it might be thought that the last thing the Queen
wanted was to marry her Frog Prince, when a deputation from
the Council visited her, one morning, to advise her against
the marriage, she burst into tears, and cursed the folly that had
made her consult them, and so deprive the kingdom of a child
born of her body and the line of King Henry. Leycester,
Walsingham, and Knollys were in deep disgrace, and strongly
upbraided by her.

It was then that Simier and the French Ambassador, suspecting that her love for Leycester was the original cause
of the Queen's hesitation, told her something she had not
known.

Leycester had been married, for over a year, to her hated

cousin Lettice, the widowed Countess of Essex. And, himself married, he had tried to prevent her marriage. Moreover, his marriage had been kept secret from her, which was an insult to her both as Queen and as a woman.

The Queen's fury was terrifying. It mattered nothing to her that she had declared, over and over again, that she would never marry him.* He had betrayed her love for him, had made a mock of her.

The Court was at Greenwich, and the Queen immediately ordered Leycester to be arrested, and sent to a tower built by Henry the Eighth in the Park — and called by him, in the days when he loved Anne Boleyn, the Tower Mireflore, the Tower of the Wondrous Flower, because she had stayed there.[3] It was in this tower that Leycester was to be imprisoned until she could have him sent to the Tower of London.

But the Earl of Sussex, the Lord Chamberlain, implored her to see reason. It would be an irremediable blot upon her reputation. And at last she, knowing Sussex's utter devotion to herself, knowing too that he detested and distrusted Leycester, with whom he had more than once quarrelled in her presence, saw that it was only for her sake that he appeared to be trying to save his enemy, and she relented — Leycester then went to Wanstead. His wife was ordered not to dare appear in the Queen's presence.

The long dream was over. But while the sun, after rising in splendour, and performing his daily task, may hide in a night that Argus himself cannot penetrate, the Queen in her grandeur might not know such healing darkness. The eyes were everywhere. Her nights were watched by her ladies, every movement, action, expression, was studied and reported.

As for Leycester, the noise of whispering voices was like the sound of the sea-sorrow, at first far away, then coming nearer until he feared to be overwhelmed by the waves.

He wrote to Burleigh : 'I perceave by my brother of Warwyke, your Lordship hath found the like bitterness in Her Majesty toward me that others (too many) have acquainted

* See also Appendix G.

me not a lyttle, having so faythfully, carefully, and chargeably
served Her Majesty this twenty yeres, as I have done. Your
Lordship is witness, I trust, that in all her services I have been
a direct servant unto her, her state, and crown, that I have not
more sought myne owne particular profit than her honour.

'Her Majesty, I see, is grown into a very strange humour,
all things considered, toward me . . .

'And as I carryed myself almost more than a bondsman
many a yere together, so long as one dropp of comfort was
left of any hope, as you yourself, my Lord, doth well know,
so being acquitted and delyvered of that hope, and by both
open and pryvate protestations and declarations dyscharged,
methinks it is more than hard to take such an occasion to
beare so great displeasure . . .

'I have lost both youth, liberty, and all my fortune reposed
in her ; and, my Lord, by the tyme I have made an even
reckoning with the world, your Lordship wyll not give me
much for the remainder of my twenty yere's service ; but I
trust styll, she that hath been so gracious to all, wyll not only
be grievous to me . . .'

This letter is dated the 12th of November 1579, and must
have been written soon after the Queen heard of his marriage.

Simier left England at the end of November. But his
master's courtship of the Queen was not at an end. The Frog
Prince returned to the English Court at the end of October
1581, having tried to do so in May, but having been prevented
by storms at sea.

Burleigh received this letter from the Queen : 'Let me
know what you wish me to do'.

In July, the Queen had written a grieved letter to her
suitor, telling him that 'though her body was hers, and
she could not marry him, her soul was wholly dedicated to
him'.

This did not seem entirely satisfactory. And yet — the
affair was not hopeless. On the 22nd of November, as the
Queen and Alençon were walking, side by side, in the gallery
at Greenwich, with Leycester and Walsingham behind them,

the French envoy Mauvissier joined them.    Whereupon the
Queen said to him, 'Write this to your master : The Duke will
be my husband.'    With this, she turned to the Duc, kissed him
on the lips, and taking a ring from her finger, she placed it on
his.    She then ordered the whole Court to assemble, and told
them that the Duc was to be their future master.

But a fresh disappointment was to follow.    For in the
course of the night she seemed to have changed her mind again,
and next morning said to him, 'Two more such nights would
bring me to my grave'.

She told Leycester and Hatton that she intended to prevent
the marriage by asking the King of France for concessions
which it would be impossible to give.    On Hatton enquiring
how she would extricate herself if the King *did* give her what
she asked, she replied, 'With words, the coin most current with
the French', and added, 'When the field is large and the
soldiers cowards there are always means of creeping out'.

Meanwhile, the Court Balls, the banquets in honour of the
Queen's future bridegroom increased in splendour.    But none
of the dances performed — neither Nobody's Jigg, Solomon's
Jigg, the Galliard, the Brawle, the Capriole or Goat's Leap,
nor the Canary, derived, according to A. Sieveking, from
the aborigines of the Canary Islands . . . a ballet composed
for a masquerade, where the dancers were dressed like the
Kings and Queens of Mauritania, or else as savages in plumage
of different colours — could rival in the swiftness of their
gyrations those of the Queen's pre-nuptial dance !

Dazzled, if bewildered, the King congratulated her and
himself.    But Walsingham enquired privately of the Duc's
secretary and the French emissary Pinant (who was in England
to arrange the marriage settlements) the sum the King would
require as damages if the marriage did not take place — which
seemed more than likely, as the Queen had asked for the
return of Calais among other things.

Leycester, back in favour, was by now thoroughly
frightened by the news of the growing anger in Paris (for the
French Court was beginning to understand the situation only

too clearly). He suggested raising £200,000 as a bribe to Alençon to go away, peaceably, and with no resentment. But this suggestion offended the Queen, who said that if Alençon weighed money in the scales with her affections, he should have neither affections nor money !

Still, anything to be rid of him ! But unfortunately he refused to go. He was entreated to think of his honour. He was told that he was urgently needed in the Netherlands (from which the Queen had been so anxious to dislodge him). This had no effect. The Queen changed her mind again and offered him limitless sums, declaring her deep sorrow that honour must come before love. He said that he saw, now, that she felt no love for him. But he had her letter, her word, her ring, and he would *never* leave England until she was his wife. He was warned that he had better go before New Year's Day, or he would have to give the Queen a New Year's present. Even this had no effect.

The Queen told Burleigh she would not marry him to be Empress of the Universe. Burleigh now implored him, openly, to leave. The Duc replied that he 'had only meddled with the Netherlands in order to marry the Queen, and if the Queen would not marry him, he would desert the Netherlands and would complain to every Prince in Christendom of the way in which he had been treated. His brother the King would avenge him.' Burleigh could do nothing with him.

The Queen told him she could not marry a Catholic. He replied that so great was his love for her that he would even turn Protestant for her sake. The Queen offered to be a sister to him. He answered that his passion for her caused him anguish. He had run a thousand risks for her — had defied the whole of Catholic Europe, and rather than leave England without her he would prefer that they both perished.

'You must not threaten a poor old woman in her own kingdom,' said the Queen. 'Passion, not reason, speaks in you, or I would think you mad.' And she begged him not to use such terrible words.

'No, no, Madame, you mistake,' he cried. 'I meant no hurt to your blessed person. I meant only that I would sooner be cut in pieces than not marry you, and so be laughed at by the world.'

And he burst into tears.

The Queen lent him her handkerchief to wipe them away, and the absurd scene came to an end.

'The tricks which the Queen is playing to get rid of Monsieur', said Mendoza, 'are more than I could describe.'

She induced the Prince of Orange to send messenger after messenger imploring the Duc to return immediately. She bribed his attendants to tell him that should he allow the Netherlands to escape him, he could never show his face again. She told Pinant that Mendoza was at her feet, entreating for an alliance between Spain and England.

At last, driven to distraction, Alençon allowed himself to be harassed into leaving — but not before he had extricated from the Queen a promise of money to hire a German army (she gave him £30,000, with bills for £20,000 extra) and not before he had succeeded in getting her to promise that Leycester and Howard should accompany him to Holland, and, above all, that he might return to England and claim her as his bride. This promise she gave, and told him to address his letters to his wife the Queen of England.

Together with the whole Court, she accompanied him to Canterbury, with every sign of devotion, and of sorrow. Three of her warships guarded him to the Netherlands, and Leycester, Howard, Hunsdon, and other courtiers, a hundred gentlemen, and three hundred serving-men, were his attendants.

The Queen seemed sunk in grief at this forced farewell. 'I would', she told the Spanish Ambassador, 'I had my Frog swimming in the Thames instead of the marshes of the Netherlands.'

Alas, they were never to meet again — for on the 10th of June 1584, her Frog Prince died.

She wept every day for three weeks, and refused to transact

any business. 'Melancholy doth so possess us', said Walsing-ham, 'that both public and private causes are at a stay for a season.'

She was, she told the French Ambassador, a forlorn widow. But that astute diplomat declared, 'She is a Princess who can act any part she pleases'.

NOTES TO CHAPTER FORTY-SIX

[1] See Chapter Fifty.
[2] Neale, *Queen Elizabeth*.
[3] Elizabeth Jenkins, *op. cit.*

# Chapter Forty-seven

In 1580 the country had been disturbed — indeed terrified — by several grave portents.

Why, for instance, the people asked themselves, had the great bell at Westminster tolled, in April, when nobody was near ? Why were the thunderstorms in June so violent ? But that was not all. Still more puzzling and serious was the fact that Alice Perin, aged eighty, had given birth (to quote a paragraph from Mr. Evelyn Waugh's *Edmund Campion*) 'to a prodigy with a head like a helmet, a face like a man, a mouth like a mouse, a human body, eight legs, all different, and a tail half a yard long, while in the same year another monster was reported from Stowe that was both male and female, with mouth and eyes like a lion'. And the people of Somersetshire were terrified by the apparition of three companies of sixty men each, sombrely attired in black, marching across the sky.

All these phenomena were plainly warnings. But against *what* ?

It is difficult, at this distance of time, to guess what they portended. It is possible that the eighty-year-old Mrs. Perin's disconcerting offspring was a plain indication that Heaven would frown on the proposed marriage of the Queen, considered by some as at a dangerous age for marriage — (she was forty-seven) — one that boded ill for any child that might be born — (after all, the Duc d'Alençon was a Catholic !). The apparitions darkening the sky may have been intended as a warning that the black-clothed Jesuits would soon darken the land — indeed, had already begun to do so. But then again, as they were seen at a time when the Duc d'Alençon and his train had come once more to the English Court, they may have been Frenchmen. One cannot tell.

A Papal Bull against the Queen had been launched in 1570 (it was afterwards modified). In the following year, in spite of the Excommunication, the Queen had refused to allow the 'invasion of her Catholic subjects' conscience' — to quote Sir John Neale [1] — 'by extending the compulsory attendance at Church to compulsory attendance at communion'. For she who, in a prayer composed by her, and written in her own hand in her little prayer book, had prayed 'Give to me, the Queen, thy counsels, that I may judge thy people in justice and thy poor in understanding' did indeed try to judge in justice ; she was indeed averse to religious persecution — at least at the beginning.

In the Parliament of 1581, however, with the rumours of the building of the Happy Armada, and the arrival of the Jesuits, it was proposed to show the Pope 'how little his curses can hurt us', and the English Catholics 'how little his blessings can save them from that punishment which we are able to lay upon them'. The Bill that was, in the end, to be known as 'the Act to retain the Queen's subjects [in other words the Catholics] in their due obedience' was brought forward.

The Queen still set her will against the ill-treatment of Catholics. And yet 'By its main provision', says Sir John Neale, 'whoever withdrew the Queen's subjects from their natural obedience, or converted them *for that intent* to the Romish religion, were to be adjudged traitors, as were those who willingly allowed themselves to be thus withdrawn or converted. Those significant words "for that intent" made the approach political and secular : as a modern scholar expressed it, "the law refrains from plainly defining conversion to Catholicism as treason, it was rather conversion accompanied by withdrawal of allegiance which was condemned".'

The Queen's insistence on clemency — 'her bishops', she told the Spanish Ambassador, Mendoza, 'were a set of knaves, and she would not countenance the ill-treatment of her

Catholic subjects' — her retention of the principle that 'consciences are not to be forced' were a grief to many of her Councillors. 'Her Majesty', wrote Bacon, 'not liking to make windows into men's hearts and secret thoughts, except the abundance of them did overflow into overt and express acts or affirmations, tempered her law, so as it restraineth only manifest disobedience, in impugning and impeaching advisedly and maliciously Her Majesty's supreme power, and maintaining and extolling a foreign jurisdiction.'

As Sir John Neale remarks, a little earlier than the passage quoted above : 'It [the Bill] directed its greater severities against recruitment for the fifth column'.

But it was possible, of course, to misunderstand intentions. . . . A little care, a little tact, and you had the Catholics where you wanted them.

Mendoza wrote to the King of Spain, 'the leading Catholics of the country, unless they would forget God, and profess the errors which are here established . . . will not only lose lands, liberty, and perhaps life, but through these laws now passed through Parliament, they may leave tainted names to their children. . . . They feel as men the shame of figuring before their descendants as traitors to their Prince, yet they see also that these rigorous and unjust laws may be the means of extirpating the Catholic religion out of the land, unless the execution of them be prevented. It is to effect this purpose that the heretics have pressed them on the Queen. They have made her believe that the Catholics will not be contented with liberty of worship, but desire a change of sovereigns. They have pretended that her life is in danger, the independence of the country threatened, with other lies and fictions.'

In spite of the Queen's detestation of cruelties in the name of religion, the most ghastly horrors had been enacted long before the passing of the 1581 Bill. In 1568, a priest in whose trunk 'several books against infant baptism, with other dangerous papers' had been found, was sentenced. 'He stood in the pillory three several days at Rochester, his ears were cut off, his nose slit, and his forehead branded with the letter R.

He was condemned to perpetual imprisonment, and died, some months after.' Not without the suspicion that he had poisoned himself.

The present writer is not surprised that, according to the prayer for the Queen's recovery from a dangerous illness in the same year, 'God had abashed her soul with divers troubles and terrors of mind'.

The priests who came to England, their mission being to bring back souls to the Catholic faith, knew they were almost certainly going to an unspeakable death. One of the greatest of these martyrs, the Blessed Edmund Campion, wrote — the letter was addressed, possibly, to John Bavand, his old tutor — these words : 'When I was in Rome, did you not spend your entire self on me ? On one from whom, to your knowledge, there could be no repayment, one just embarking from the world ; in some sort a dying man. It is a work of high compassion to bury the dead. . . . You were munificent to me as I went to my rest in the sepulchre of religion. . . .' [2]

He arrived in England on St. John the Baptist's Day, 1580.

'I cannot long escape the hands of the heretics,' he wrote, '. . . I am in apparel to myself very ridiculous' (he was travelling disguised as a jeweller). 'I often change it, and my name also. I read letters sometimes myself, that in the front tell news that Campion is taken, which noised in every place where I come, so fills mine ears with the sound thereof, that fear itself has taken away all fear. My soul is in my own hands ever. . . .'

He was captured at last, in the hiding-place known as the Priest's Chamber — a hole hollowed out in the wall — in the house of a Mrs. Yates who had sheltered him, where he had preached and said Mass. On the 22nd of July 1581, he was brought into London, dressed in his disguise, his velvet hose, his cap with a feather, and on that cap was affixed a placard with the words 'Campion, the seditious Jesuit'. His feet were tied under his horse's belly, his arms pinioned behind him — and so, through threatening shrieking crowds, he rode to the Tower. He was thrown into the cell called 'Little Ease' —

a hole at one end of the torture chamber, sunk in complete darkness, and so built that he could neither stand nor lie at full length.

For four days he remained there. Then, on the fifth, brought out of the darkness into a blinding light, he saw two faces that he had known in his early youth — those of the Queen and Leycester. They had shown him kindness, and now, remembering him, were determined, if it were possible, to save him.

The Queen asked him if he acknowledged her as his lawful sovereign. The sentence against her sovereignty, contained in the Papal Bull, had been relaxed. He said that he did so acknowledge her. To further questions he replied that he would pay her Majesty what was hers, but to God he must give what was God's.

The Queen, when he was sent back to the Tower, ordered that he should be well treated. Burleigh saw to it that he was not. On the 31st of July he was questioned as to his allegiance, and as to the houses that had sheltered him. He would not confess, and was racked on two successive days.

One of the men in charge of the torture chamber, Thomas Norton, wrote to Walsingham, on the 27th of March 1582 : 'None was put to the rack that was not first by manifest evidence known to the Council to be guilty of treason, so that it was well assured beforehand that there was no innocent tormented. Also none was tormented to know whether he was guilty or no : but for the Queen's safety to know the manner of the treason and the accomplices.

'Nor was any man tormented for matter of religion, nor asked what he believed of any point of religion, but only to understand of particular practices against the Queen for setting up their religion by treason or force. . . .'

In face of this monstrous hypocrisy, what can be said ? Of what treason was Campion guilty ?

'The Queen', said Froude, 'was still eager to save Campion. He was promised pardon and liberty if he would consent to appear once in church. When kindness failed' (one can imagine what Froude would have had to say had a clergyman of the English Church been asked to betray his faith) 'torture was again tried, but nothing more could be wrung from him ; and the Council then determined to bring him and the other priests to trial. Some delay was necessary, for the last racking had dislocated his limbs, and he could not at once be moved.'

At his trial, on the 20th of November, at Westminster Hall, the Father was unable to raise his broken arm to testify, so two of the priests accused with him raised it for him.

'We are charged with treason,' he said. 'We are no traitors. We are Catholics, and what is that to the purpose ? We persuaded the people — but what then ? We seduced no subject from his allegiance. We have nothing to do with their allegiance. We are men dead to the world, and we travailed for the salvation of souls. We touched neither State nor policy. We had no such commission. We were told that if we would attend church and hear sermons we should be released, and it is therefore impossible that we could have committed treason. Our religion and our religion only is our crime.'

But for that crime they were to suffer the traitor's death.

'At length,' wrote Froude, 'on the 1st of December, Campion . . . was brought with Sherwin and Bryant [two other priests] out of the Tower. They had suffered their last miseries there, and Little-Ease, and the scavenger's daughter, and the thumbscrew, and the rack, and the black cells, and the foul water, were parted with for ever. Peace at any rate, and after one more pang, a painless rest lay now before them. The torture chamber brought one blessing with it — Death had ceased to be terrible.'

The priests were tied to hurdles, and dragged through the streets. The crowd was enormous. Sir Francis Knollys, Lord Charles Howard, and Sir Henry Lee were present with official pardons should the condemned men consent to hear a Protestant sermon and to acknowledge that the Pope had no power to depose the Queen.

Campion reiterated that he died for religion, and not for treason. He then prayed for 'Your Queen and mine, to whom I wish a long quiet reign and all prosperity'. Because of that prayer he was allowed to hang until he was dead, and it was only then that he was mutilated, disembowelled, and quartered. After Campion's death, Mendoza told his King it was seen that they had torn away his nails.

The Duc d'Alençon was at that time at the English Court, and the Protestants were in terror that the Queen would marry him. 'It was considered', wrote Froude, 'that the punishment of the Jesuits during his stay in London would quiet the apprehension of the country.'

.     .     .     .     .

In the year 1586, a sadist of the most horrible description, Richard Topcliffe, then aged fifty-two, was described as being one of Her Majesty's servants, and for two years previously was regularly employed by Lord Burleigh — 'but in what capacity', says the *Dictionary of National Biography*, 'does not appear'. One imagines as a torturer.

Wearing court dress, and with a sword hanging at his side, he would examine the prisoners. 'He was old and hoary and a veteran in evil', wrote Father Gerard.[3]

According to the *Dictionary of National Biography*, this monster 'boasted that he had a machine at home, of his own invention, compared with which the common racks in use were child's play'.

'Because the often use of the rack in the Tower was so odious, and so much spoken of by the people', wrote a contemporary, this ghastly travesty of a human being was allowed — indeed encouraged — to torture priests in his own house 'in such sort as he shall think good'.[4]

This infamous man wrote to the Queen about Father Robert Southwell, the Jesuit, author of *The Burning Babe*, that he 'kept him very straitly in his strong chamber at Westminster, and if Her Majesty wishes to know anything in his heart, then shall he be made to stand against the wall, his feet standing upon the ground, and his hands as high as he can reach against the wall. . . .' ('The torture', according to the Catholic Record Society, 'consisted in hanging the victim by the hands, the weight of the body doing the work of the rack.')

'It will', this obscene creature told the Queen, 'be as though he were dancing a "trick" or "figure" at trenchmore.' The Queen gave her permission for it to be done. At his trial, Father Southwell said he would rather have endured ten deaths than pains so exquisite. One priest, Christopher Bayles, was for nearly twenty-four hours in this unspeakable torture.

Such was the horror and wrath caused by the treatment of Southwell that even the Protestants protested, and the letters to the Privy Council were of such a nature and so many that Burleigh had the author of the torture imprisoned on the charge of having exceeded the powers given him. But the imprisonment was for a short time only : it was but used as a blind.

On the 21st of October 1591, a seminary priest was given over to imprisonment in Topcliffe's house, to be subjected to any torture that he could devise. After unspeakable torments invented and applied by Topcliffe during the intervening months, the hideous execution of this priest and others took place on the 21st of February in the following year.

It was a freezing day, and Topcliffe's victim was forced to stand in his shirt for nearly two hours while Topcliffe plagued him to recant. In this he was unsuccessful. Then, 'before the cart was driven away, his shirt was pulled off his body, so that he hung stark naked, whereat the people muttered greatly, and the other sheriff [one presumes Topcliffe was the first] named Massam, said to the officers, "You play the knaves. They be men. Let them be used as men."' He ordered that they should hang until they were dead. In the case of Father Fenn, the first sheriff prevented this ; but the other priests were dead before they were mutilated.

The monster of cruelty was also a lewd liar. He told one of his victims, Father Pormont, who swore to it at his trial —

that he had 'used very secret dealings with the Queen, and had seen her bare above the knee'. And that she had said to him, 'Be not these the armes, legges, and body of King Henry ?' To which he answered 'Yea'.

He said, too, that 'she gave him for a favour, whyte lynnen hose wrought with whyte sylke', and that he was 'so familiar with her, he may take her away from any company, and that she (is) as pleasant with every one that she doth love'. He declared that 'He doth not care for the Council, for that he hath due authority from Her Majestie'.

Mr. Topcliffe was essentially a business man. In 1594, he sued one of his accomplices, Thomas Fitzherbert, complaining that this gentleman had promised him £5000 'if he would persecute his [Fitzherbert's] father and uncle to death, together with Mr. Bassett' (whoever he might be). But Mr. Fitzherbert resisted the claim because, he said, Mr. Topcliffe had not fulfilled the conditions, for the two elder Fitzherberts had died unassisted to their repose by Mr. Topcliffe ; and as for Mr. Bassett, he 'was in prosperity'.

It was thought by the authorities that if a case so curious was brought by one of Her Majesty's servants, the character of the servant in question might be misunderstood ! So 'the matter was put over for secret hearing'. But when Mr. Topcliffe made some remarks unflattering to the Lord Keeper and some of the Council, this did not go as well as he had hoped, and he was imprisoned in the Marshalsea for contempt of Court — only for a few months, however. He was soon out again, spying, torturing, and presiding at executions. And such was his business capacity that in the end he gained possession of Fitzherbert's family property in Derbyshire.

His activities were many. Amongst these was the seduction of Anne Bellamy, the daughter of the family which pitied and fed Babington when he was in hiding. Mr. Topcliffe did this in order to be enabled to arrest Southwell, and that she might be a witness against, and bring about the death of her parents, brothers, and the friends who had trusted her — twenty-six persons in all.

From the embraces of Topcliffe she went, most suitably, to those of Nicholas Jones, the underkeeper of the Gate House. 'She was a monstrous creature', wrote Father John Gerard,[5] 'and thought nothing of bartering away her own father's life, and Father Southwell's too' — (she was a witness for the prosecution of the latter).

As for her brothers : 'One of these two young men, Thomas', wrote Father William Weston,[6] 'was tortured in the Tower of London and died on the rack, though the heretics gave it out that he had strangled himself. The second, Jerome, was condemned to death at the same time as Anthony [Babington] and the other accomplices, and was executed. Their mother was shut up in the Tower. There, after a few months, she died, wasted with sorrow and with the squalor and filth of her imprisonment. If one thinks only of this present life, her end was miserable : but, as I see it, it was glorious : no less than a martyr's and no different from it.'

## NOTES TO CHAPTER FORTY-SEVEN

[1] Neale, *op. cit.*, *1559–1581*.
[2] Original MSS. in Campion's hand at Stonyhurst. Simpson's translation.
[3] *John Gerard*, translated from the Latin by Father Philip Caraman, S.J.
[4] Letter addressed to Father Robert Parsons, 3rd August 1592.
[5] *John Gerard, op. cit.*
[6] Translated by Father Philip Caraman, S.J.

# Chapter Forty-eight

In the late summer of 1583, a terrible omen, a comet of great beauty, appeared over London. What did it foretell but the death of someone great in the land?

The Queen was at Richmond when it was seen, and all her Court was filled with fear. But she, 'with a courage answering to the greatness of her state, ordered a window to be opened, and walked towards that strange light, saying "Jacta est alea" — the dice are thrown'.[1]

England was, indeed, once more menaced with invasion, the plan being that the Duc de Guise and his brother, later the Duc de Mayenne, would attempt to land in Rye Harbour, while Spanish forces landed in Ireland.

But would it not, Henri de Guise and his brother wondered, be better to have Elizabeth murdered even before the invasion? Later in the year, a young man, Francis Throckmorton, a nephew of the late Ambassador to France, Sir Nicholas, who was involved in the plot, was captured and tortured. He endured the horrors of the first racking, but at the second, wrung by agony, he confessed the whole plot — the proposed invasion, the fact that the Queen of Scots and Mendoza, the Spanish Ambassador, were fully implicated (the Throckmorton family were amongst Mary's staunchest adherents). 'Nay,' the poor wretch cried, 'I have betrayed her who was dearest to me in the world.' All he longed for, he said, was death. This was granted him.

The fury against the Queen of Scots grew.

As for Mendoza, he was told that the Queen would no longer endure his conduct, and that he must leave England within fifteen days. Though he was an Ambassador, he was told, he was lucky that the Queen had not had him chastised. A Court preacher accused him, before the Council, of having conspired at the Queen's murder.

'The insolence of these people', the Ambassador wrote to Secretary Idriaquez, 'so exasperates me that I desire to live only to be revenged upon them. I hope to God the time will soon come, and that He will give me grace to be an instrument in their punishment. I will walk barefoot over Europe to compass it. His Majesty, I am certain, will send them the answer which they have deserved.' And he wrote to the King, 'God has made Your Majesty so great a prince that you cannot overlook such insolence, though they offer you all the world to forgive them'.

Mendoza became Spanish Ambassador in Paris, where Babington consulted him in 1585.

In 1585, England being evidently on the brink of war with Spain in the Netherlands, Walsingham judged that it was more than ever necessary to watch for Catholic plots. It would be as well, he thought, to find a way in which the Queen of Scots might believe she was corresponding secretly with her adherents in letters which, unknown to her, would be read by him.

The Queen of Scots was, by this time, in the charge of Sir Amyas Paulet, at Chartley. A cask of ale was sent, each week, for the Queen's ladies and secretaries, from a Burton brewer. Nothing was easier than to bribe the brewer, and insinuate, by one of the spies employed by Walsingham, and posing as a fervent adherent of Mary's, that it would be as well for the Queen's secretary to search the cask on its arrival. And there, sure enough, was a little box of wood containing a letter from the Queen's representative in Paris, Morgan. What an admirable device ! Letters could obviously reach the Queen in this way, and be answered by her in the utmost secrecy. She sent for all the letters to her that had been held at the French Embassy since the Throckmorton Plot of 1583.

Among these were many letters in cipher from Morgan, Paget, the Archbishop of Glasgow. All these secret letters, received and sent by Mary, were, of course, read and copied by Walsingham's secretary.

The plot had succeeded beyond Walsingham's hopes.

'Monsieur l'Ambassadeur,' said the Queen of England to the French Ambassador, 'you have much secret communication with the Queen of Scotland, but, believe me, I know all that goes on in my kingdom. I myself was a prisoner in the days of the Queen my sister, and am aware of the artifices that prisoners use to win over servants and obtain secret intelligence.'

The Queen of Scots was now almost in sight of her freedom — but that freedom was to come through death. Soon others besides Walsingham were working towards that end.

There was a young man named Anthony Babington, of Dethick in Derbyshire. He was rich, and it is said that he had been a page in Lord Shrewsbury's household, when the Queen of Scots had been put into his charge, and had fallen under her enchantment.

Though known to be a Catholic, he was admitted at Court — Elizabeth resolutely refusing to exclude any because of their religious beliefs. Now, among disaffected young men in the English Queen's own household, he looked for, and found, fellow conspirators.

The actual instigator of the plot to kill the Queen of England was a priest named John Ballard, who had arrived in England, dressed as an officer in blue velvet with a feathered cap, under the name of Captain Fortescue.

Ballard consulted Mendoza, who told King Philip, on the 13th of August, that six of the Queen's own attendants had sworn to kill her, and were waiting only till a way had been found for the Queen of Scots to escape, and till the Prince of Parma, or a fleet from Lisbon, was ready to invade England.

Babington's fellow conspirators were Charles Tilney, one of the Queen's gentlemen pensioners; Edward Abington, son of her Under-Treasurer ; Jones, son of the Master of the Wardrobe ; Dunn, of the First Fruits Office ; Robert Barnwell, an Irishman visiting the Court — and several other young men about the Palace, Chidiock Tichbourne, Edward Charnock, Edward Windsor, Sir Thomas Gerrard, and Thomas Salisbury. All these owed the Queen gratitude. There was only one that did not — John Savage.

The Queen was the first who would be assassinated ; then the turn would come of Walsingham, Hunsdon, and Sir Francis Knollys.

Such was the conspirators' mad folly that they went so far as to tell the Queen of Scots — the one person in the world who, for her own sake, should have known nothing — of the plot. Paget wrote to her that a rebellion might be at hand, and that the Prince of Parma might land at Scarborough or Newcastle. He was so insane as to send Babington to her, with the key of a cipher. It is true that he warned her not to communicate with Ballard, but added, to Curle, her secretary, 'There be many means in hand to remove the beast that troubles all the world'. (14th June.)

A few days later he wrote to her that 'there were many good members attending upon opportunity to do the Queen of England a piece of service which, if it pleased God to lend assistance, he trusted would quiet many things'.

These communications were, of course, read by Phillips, Walsingham's secretary, who was then at Chartley under the pretence of helping with the household accounts.

The Queen of Scots had sworn she was innocent of the Parry attempt on Elizabeth. . . . But now what would she answer ? There could be no mistake about it : those letters meant that the murder of her cousin was intended.

'We attend', wrote Phillips, 'her very heart at the next.' (14th-24th July.) They had it.

She wrote to Babington ; as though she were already his Queen, she addressed him as 'Trusty and well-beloved' ; she gave him most lengthy advice as to her own rescue — told the conspirators to 'consider and consult together if, as it is possible, they cannot execute their particular purpose [her rescue] it will then be expedient to proceed with the rest of the enterprise. If the difficulty be only with myself, if you cannot manage my rescue because I am in the Tower, or some other place too strong for you, do not hesitate on that account. Go on for the honour of God.'

Walsingham by now knew almost everything. He knew that Babington was not to be one of the actual murderers, because he was to be in charge of the Scottish Queen's escape. . . . He knew that twelve or fourteen young gentlemen met at supper every night, and that the murderers were to be found among these. Feather-witted, and feather-capped, blown this way and that, alternately, by vainglory and fear, they were so incredibly rash as to have their portraits taken in a group, that the saviours of England might be so immortalised. That picture was shown to the Queen of England. She recognised the conspirators.

Babington now found it necessary for him to go to Paris to consult Mendoza. As a passport must be procured through Walsingham, he went to Walsingham's house and applied to one of the secretaries, Pooley (who had helped to decipher his letters, but whom he believed to be disaffected), and asked to be presented to Walsingham.

This being done, he promised Walsingham to act as a spy among the refugees. Delighted, Walsingham gave him interview after interview, each drawing the net still more tightly round him. During one of these visits, he had a long talk with Pooley, actually showed him the Queen of Scots' letter, and assured him that he would soon see the invasion of England and the murder of Elizabeth.

Happy in the knowledge that he would soon receive his passport, Babington spent his evenings at suppers given by him and his fellow conspirators. In the flashing summer weather they had no feeling that their doom was approaching, until one night in August the news reached them that a servant of Ballard's, who knew much — or everything — was a government spy.

Then the braggart and coward Babington decided to save himself by betraying his companions. He wrote to Pooley, telling him to inform Walsingham on his behalf that there was a conspiracy, and that he was prepared to tell all he knew.

A terrifying silence ensued. Babington might already have been dead. . . . Hour by hour his terror increased.

Next morning, Ballard, alias Captain Fortescue, was arrested, while in a tavern with several of his fellow conspirators.

Babington, in his terror, flew to Savage, who had not been present at the arrest, and cried, 'What remedy now?' 'No remedy now', was the answer, 'but to kill her presently' (immediately). 'Very well, then go you unto the Court tomorrow, and execute the fact.' 'Nay,' was the reply, 'I cannot go tomorrow, for my apparel is not ready.'

Babington flung money at him, told him to buy clothes and to kill the Queen without further delay. He then sent a further message to Walsingham, who replied that he might come in a day or two.

That night he had supper with some of the Walsingham household. A piece of paper was handed to one of these, and, managing to look over the man's shoulder, he saw that it ordered him to be watched.

Making some excuse, he fled from the supper table, leaving, such was his fear, his cloak and sword behind. Rushing to such of his fellow conspirators as he could find, he told them that all was lost. They fled to St. John's Wood (then a forest), disguised as labourers; they then hid in a barn at Harrow. It was days before they were found and brought to London.

The bells of the City of London rang, bonfires were lit as if the country had known some great victory.

The Queen apparently suggested to her Council the necessity of adopting 'some new device' to make the horrors her would-be murderers were to suffer more appalling, and to fill anyone who thought of emulating them with terror. But

Burleigh told the Queen 'that the punishment prescribed by the letter of the law was to the full as terrible as anything new that could be devised, if the executioner took care to protract the extremity of their pains in the sight of the multitude'.

That care was taken, in the case of the first batch to be executed on the 20th September 1586. On the following day, owing to the attitude of the crowds, the rest were allowed to hang till they were dead before being cut down.

·          ·          ·          ·          ·

The terror in the outlying countryside at the danger from which the Queen had so narrowly escaped was great. Rumours flew like birds.

Mr. Thomas Ward, the Dogberry of Honyton, seems to have been especially diligent in spreading fears and rumours, and succeeded in terrifying the Mayor of Exeter almost out of his wits, so that in his fright he wrote to Lord Burleigh and consulted Her Majesty's Council as to what steps he must take to combat the disasters that had overtaken the kingdom.

Having got it into his noddle that the Queen of Scots was 'fledd' (of the truth of this he was assured by a Mr. Howard), Mr. Ward sent orders right and left that the highways and byways must be searched for her, 'under pain of death'. His weathercock mind then turned in a different direction, with the result that he sent out a Hue and Crye, to be carried by horsemen, galloping over the countryside. 'Her Majestyes City of London by the enemies is sett on fyre.' 'For Mr. Turlett of Ansten broughte this from the Bell, the 1st of Februarie.' The Hue and Crye must be sent 'from towne to towne, to make your armor and artillery in readyness, and that with all speed, upon paine of death.

'Hast ! hast ! hast !

'Thomas Warde, Constable to Honyton.'

Eventually, on the 8th of February 1587, Philip Gawdy in a letter to his father said there was 'much uncertayne newes touching the Queene of Skottes. In that she should have hidd herself in the topp of a chymney, and so by that meanes not being founde that they should have made presently great search for her and then she might have escaped.'

She had not. But that longed-for delivery was soon to come.

### NOTE TO CHAPTER FORTY-EIGHT

[1] Malcolm, *Manners and Customs of London.* Elizabeth Jenkins, *op. cit.*

# Chapter Forty-nine

THE English government knew, now, that war with Spain was inevitable. And before it could break out, the dangerous Mary must be disposed of.

Murder was the obvious, most sensible way in which to accomplish this. But at first the Queen of England was inexplicably sensitive on this point. So a free 'Association' must be formed (1584) calling on all patriots to swear 'to protect their own Queen's person, and to revenge to the uttermost all such malicious actions and attempts against Her Majesty's most Royal Person', both upon the guilty persons, and also 'by all forcible and possible means [to] pursue to death every such wicked person, by whom or by whose means, assent, or privity any such invasion or rebellion shall be in form aforesaid denounced, to have been made, or such wicked act attempted, or other thing compassed or imagined against Her Majesty's person'.

In addition, 'Every such person by or for whom any such act shall be executed, and their issues, being any wise assenting or privy to the same, shall be excluded and disabled for ever to have a claim . . . on the said Crown of the realm'.

Could the matter have been put more plainly? Would *nobody* have the tact to understand what was wanted, and to do it?

It will hardly be believed that the Queen of Scots had the bad taste to offer to put her hand to the bond.

The offer was refused, with some coldness. At the same time a Bill was introduced in Parliament for the punishment of 'Jesuits, seminary priests, and such disobedient persons'. All those of English nationality who remained in England after forty days were to be proceeded against as traitors ; whilst English students and priests on the Continent were to return to England immediately, renounce their faith, and take the Oath of Supremacy, or they, too, would be treated as traitors.

The House of Commons was deeply shocked by a fiery outburst on this subject from the new member for Queen-borough, Kent, Dr. William Parry, who actually went so far as to declare the Bill was 'full of blood, danger, and despair to English subjects, and pregnant with fines and forfeitures, which would go to enrich not the Queen, but private individuals'.

His outraged fellow members handed him over to the Serjeant-at-Arms, but to their astonishment the Queen had him released next day, and so the session came to an end.

Parry was a most mysterious character. It is more or less certain that he was an English spy, but that makes his speech in Parliament strange. In 1580 he was corresponding with Burleigh and wrote, on the 1st of May, 'I do find my credite and favour to be such with the best of the English and Scottish nations in Rome and Paris (by the hope conceaved of my redy-ness and abilyty to serve theym) that I doubt not within a few monethes to be well able to discover the deepest practises'.

Burleigh had had such trust in him — at that time — that when his young nephew Anthony Bacon visited Paris, he sent him with a special introduction to Parry.

In July 1582, Parry had gone to Paris on a secret mission. But he was already distrusted by the English refugees. To dispel the distrust he became reconciled to the Church, and, in the winter, went to Rome on what he described as 'a dangerous and not very honourable mission'. He was, in fact, hoping to get from the Church, and, if possible, from the Holy Father himself, a signed paper applauding his resolution to murder Elizabeth.

He approached the Cardinal of Como, by letter. The Cardinal's reply was not quite what he had hoped. Still, he wrote to Burleigh from Lyons : 'If I be not deceaved I have shaken the foundation of the English semynary in Rheims, and utter overthrowen the credite of the English pensioners in Rome'.

Owing to the correspondence with the Cardinal of Como, he seems to have reinstated himself in the trust of Paget and Morgan (Mary's agents in Paris), who presented him to the Papal Nuncio, Ragazzoni, whom he promptly asked to forward to the Pope his request for a plenary indulgence for 'An important enterprise, full of danger'. 'And I undertake it', he wrote, 'for the public good and the peace of the whole of Christendom, for the restitution of the Kingdom of England to the Apostolic See, and for the liberation of the Queen of Scotland, the only true and undoubted heiress of the Crown of England, from her long and weary sufferings.'

The Legate was, unfortunately, perfectly aware of Parry's character. Writing to the Cardinal of Como, enclosing Parry's application, he said, 'the writer is all too well known. Here, his reputation is certainly bad.' Still, as no actual mention was made of the proposed murder, the Cardinal, in his reply to the Legate, said 'No harm is done in giving him confidence *as long as he does not pass to something else*'.

This letter was written on the 30th of January 1584, and on the same day the Cardinal sent Parry the plenary indulgence for which he had asked; but it was worded as vaguely as Parry's request.

So certain had Parry been that he would receive the indulgence, that he did not even wait in Paris till it arrived, but returned to England, and, asking for an audience of the Queen, assured her that a plot had been formed to murder her.

The stories about what happened at the audience differ. According to Froude, 'The Queen', Parry said, 'told him no Catholic who would live as a loyal subject should be troubled either for religion or for the supremacy' (he had apparently pleaded for leniency towards them); 'but her manner was cold and stern, and "he departed with fear"'.

Having received the plenary indulgence, he showed it to Burleigh, saying it was the answer to his offer to murder the

Queen. Here, at last, he declared, was Burleigh's supreme opportunity to involve the Church of Rome in the scandal of attempted murder.

He had hoped for a reward. He got one that was unexpected.

His interview with the Queen, his production, to Burleigh, of the plenary indulgence, were before he took his seat in Parliament as member for Queenborough. Now his speech on the subject of the ill-treatment of Catholics, and the fact that he knew a great deal too much, were to lead to his ruin. His continued existence, like that of the Queen of Scots, was undesirable.

A trap was laid for him.

He had been asked to spy on Edmund Neville (a relation of the exiled Earl of Westmorland). He urged Neville, as he had urged Paget and Morgan, to murder the Queen.

Neville was arrested. All was known, he was told, about his communications with Parry. His only hope of saving himself was by denouncing Parry, and divulging all he knew. Filled with terror, he did so — Leycester and Sir Christopher Hatton taking his statements. That night, Parry and his accuser were brought face to face at Walsingham House, and Parry was sent to the Tower, charged with 'plotting to encompass the murder of the Queen', though according to himself he had warned her of the plot of Morgan and Paget.

What was the truth ? Had he, indeed, plotted her death, or was he, as has been suggested, 'playing a double game, acting as *agent provocateur* ?' All that we know is that he was incurably twisted, and an incurable optimist. 'Skulking about the Palace Gardens,' said Froude, 'he saw the Queen continually, and again and again endeavoured to screw his courage to the striking point ; but he was made of the wrong material, and he found, or made, excuses for delay. Once, when he was about to stab her, he was appalled by her likeness to Henry VIII.'

In any case, his death was assured.

At his trial a confession signed by him was produced.

Whereupon he had the presumption to say that this was wrung from him by the threat of torture !

*Torture !* The Court could hardly believe their ears ! The outraged Lord Hunsdon swore that the word had never passed his lips. Torture ! Perish the thought ! No ! All he had said was, 'If you will willingly utter the truth of your-self it will do you good : if you will not, we must then proceed in ordinary course to take your examination'. Yet now he was accused of threatening the rack !

Parry was now exactly where Burleigh wanted him. What was Parry to do ? Actually the confession was, from point of view, true — for he had (whether acting as *agent provocateur* or not) plotted treason and the Queen's assassina-tion. What use would it be to plead that he was spying for Burleigh, was an *agent provocateur* ? Who would testify to the truth of this ? Not Burleigh. No, he was no longer useful, he knew too much, he made blunders in act and in speech. And now he was to be made to pay for his twistings, his half-lies, his subterfuges, and for the only good deed, as far as we know, that he did in all his life — his speech in Parliament.

'I appeal', he cried, 'to the Queen's own knowledge, and to my Lord Treasurer's and Master Secretary's.'

In vain. There was no escaping his fate.

'I never meant to kill her,' he cried to Hunsdon. 'I will lay my blood upon Queen Elizabeth and you before God and the world.'

He was executed on the 2nd of March 1585, and swearing to the end that he was innocent, 'was turned from the ladder and after one swinge was cast down : when his bowelles were taken out, he gave a great groane'.

# Chapter Fifty

THE marriage in 1568 between the Queen of Scots' gaoler, the sixth Earl of Shrewsbury (a widower), and his thrice-widowed, brassy, marigold-haired, self-complacent, furious-tongued, intriguing Bess Cavendish, 'Bess of Hardwick', had been, at first, extremely happy. Addressing her as 'My dear None' (Nun ?), one letter spoke of his joy in 'possessing one that I know loves me so dearly', and told her he had reminded his son Gilbert 'how happy he is to have a mother like you'.

'My swetehart,' he wrote to her, 'Your true and faithfull zeale you beare me is more comfortable than anything I can thynke upon, and I give God thanks dayly for his benefits he hath bestowed on me, and greatest cause I have to gyve him thanks (is) that he hath sent me you in my old yeares to comfort me withall. . . .

'I thank you for your fat capon, and it shall be baken and kept cold and untouched tyll my swetehart come ; guesse who it may be. . . . Farewell my swete true none and faithefull wyfe.'

Lady Shrewsbury addressed her husband always, at that time, as 'My jewell'.

Alas, when eleven years had passed, Lord Shrewsbury felt less gratitude for the comfort that had been sent to him in his 'old yeares'. Lady Shrewsbury, whatever her faults — and these seem to have been intolerable — was a woman whose genius for building was as great and as instinctive as that of the bees for building their gold combs — Hardwick Hall, built by her orders, is one of the greatest beauties of England — and Lord Shrewsbury, when not being railed at, was largely forgotten in the excitement of giving rein to her art.

But the presence of that siren-voiced mistress of discord,

the Queen of Scots, may have had its effect on the domestic
life of the house in which she was kept prisoner. It was
probably at the end of 1568 when she was placed in Lord
Shrewsbury's charge. At first she and the wife of her gaoler
were inseparable.

'The Queen', wrote Lord Shrewsbury, 'continueth daily
resort unto my wife's chamber, where, with the Lady Leviston
and Mrs. Seaton, she useth to sit working with her needle,
in which she much delighteth, and in devising of works ; and
her talk is altogether of indifferent and trifling matters without
ministering any sign of secret dealing and practice.'

Unhappily, as the familiarity grew, so did the discord.
She was to remain with Lord and Lady Shrewsbury for fifteen
years, and long before the end of that time husband and wife
were scarcely on speaking terms.

To the discomfort brought about by the two ladies was
now added the friendship of Mary's sleepless enemy, her
mother-in-law Lady Lennox, who, frightened by her belief
that Elizabeth would soon die, and that she would find herself
the hated accuser of the new Queen, hastened to become her
daughter-in-law's alleged adherent. (This did not prevent
her from continuing her vituperation against Mary at the
English Court.)

The reason given by Lady Lennox for this sudden love of
her daughter-in-law was the consummate devotion in which
both mother and grandmother held Mary's son, the King of
Scotland. Mary's 'most humble and loving mother and
Aunt Margaret Lennox' was 'as fearful and as careful as Your
Majesty of him, so that the wicked Governor [Morton]
should not have power to do harm to his person'.

The price extracted by Mary for the reconciliation was
that Lady Lennox should write her letters expressing her
grief to think of the wrong she had done her dear daughter-
in-law by the accusations she was induced to make against her
by Elizabeth and her Council.

Elizabeth, hearing rumours that mother-in-law and
daughter-in-law were reconciled, asked Lady Lennox if this

were true. 'I asked Her Majesty if she could think so,' wrote Lady Lennox to Burleigh (10th September 1574), 'for I was made of flesh and blood, and could never forget the murder of my child : and she said, Nay, by her faith she could not think that ever I could forget it, for if I would, I were a devil.'

Lady Lennox asked the Queen for a safe-conduct to go to her house at Settringham, where she wished to go with her son Charles because she had been warned of a plot to kidnap the eight-year-old King James. Unhappily, she was — according to herself — taken ill, en route, at Lady Shrewsbury's house ; and, while she remained in bed for six days, her son Lord Charles (Darnley's brother), and Lady Shrewsbury's daughter, Elizabeth Cavendish, were much thrown together and fell in love.

The three Janus-faced ladies, Lady Shrewsbury, Queen Mary, and Lady Lennox, arranged a marriage between them, which was to be kept secret from Elizabeth. But it became known. . . . And Lord Charles was in the line of succession ! This led to another sojourn in the Tower for Lady Lennox.

As soon as her daughter was safely married to Lord Charles, Lady Shrewsbury's temper towards her royal charge changed. And her temper was matched — although it took a quite different direction — by that of Lord Shrewsbury. This grew steadily worse. The look of reproach and bewilderment in his eyes, the melancholy of his long face (whose parti-coloured beard was like thin Spanish moss) were soon to be changed for a look of anger. No longer had he a lost appearance — that of one wandering in a forest. Instead, he had the energetic appearance of one seeking out an enemy.

His son Gilbert, writing to his stepmother in 1575, said, 'My lord . . . is very often in exceeding choler of slight occasion ; a great grief to them that loves (sic) him to see him hurt himself so much'.

On the 10th of February 1581, he told his servant Bawdwyn that he was 'most quiet when I have the fewest women about me', and that he had refused to take two servants recommended to him as 'I have too many spies in my house already'.

He quarrelled with Gilbert Talbot and his wife (a daughter of Lady Shrewsbury's marriage to Sir William Cavendish) because of their affection for Lady Shrewsbury, whom he accused, at Court, of calling him beast, knave, and fool, to his face, and of mocking and mowing at him.

He felt persecuted. His ex-chaplain, Corker (described by Lord Shrewsbury as 'so perilous a caterpillar in the Commonwealth'), accused him of favouring the Queen of Scots.

An inn-keeper of Islington, named Walmesley, was in the habit of telling his guests that 'The Earl of Shrewsbury had gotten the Scottish Queen with child, and that he knew where the child was christened'.

It is probably true that, as her husband said, Lady Shrewsbury 'scolded like one from the Bank' (a London slum). But I think her main fault was coarseness. Her heart was warm : she could love — as is shown by her tender love for her little grandson, the child of Gilbert and Mary Talbot. His parents, writing to her on the 1st of August 1577, said 'George is very well, I thank God ; he drinketh every day to La [Lady] Grandmother ; rideth to her often, yet within the Court ; and if he have any spice, I tell him La Grandmother is come and will see him ; which he then will quickly hide, or quickly eat, and then ask where La Ganmode is'.

Alas ! Twelve days later, his grandmother, writing to Lord Burleigh, said : 'It pleased God of His goodness yesternight a little before supper to visit suddenly my dearest Jewel under God next to my Sovereign, with mortality and sickness. And that it hath pleased God of His goodness to take that sweet babe from me ; he surely was a toward child.'

Lady Shrewsbury loved another grandchild dearly — the orphaned Arabella Stuart, child of her daughter Elizabeth and Darnley's younger brother. Her portrait when she was aged two shows a dignified fat-faced little child in an embroidered jacket, holding a doll as bright as a flower-garden buzzing with the bee-winged summer lights.

Poor 'Arbell' — poor 'sweet jewell', as her grandmother called her ! Her life should have been one of caution, but it was not. Yet who could foretell that she would die mad ?

When she was ten, there was an intrigue to marry her to her cousin James. Then, when she was seventeen, a more dangerous plot arose : it came to the ears of Burleigh that arrangements were being made to marry her to Rainuto, son of the Duke of Parma. And it was thought that the Duke laid claim to the English throne.

Burleigh wrote to Lady Shrewsbury, warning her. To which she replied :

'. . . My good Lord, I was at the first much troubled to think that so wicked and mischievous practices should be devised to entrap my poor Arbell and me, but I put my trust in the Almighty, and will use such diligent care as I doubt not but to prevent whatsoever shall be attempted by any wicked persons against the poor child. I am most bound to Her Majesty that it pleased her to appoint your Lordship to give me knowledge of this wicked practice, and I humbly thank your Lordship for advertising it : if any such like hereinafter be discovered I pray your Lordship I may be forewarned. I will not have any unknown or suspected person to come to my house. Upon the least suspicion that may happen here, anyway, I shall give advertisement to your Lordship. I have little resort to me : my house is furnished with sufficient company : Arbell walks not late ; at such time as she shall take the air, it shall be near the house, and well attended on : she goeth not to anybody's house at all : I see her almost every hour in the day : she lieth in my bedchamber. If I can be more precise than I have been, I will be. I am bound in nature to be careful for Arbell : I find her loving and dutiful to me. . . . I would rather wish many deaths than to see this or any such like wicked attempt to prevail.' (1592.)

But by that time Lord Shrewsbury, and the Queen of Scots, and almost everybody with whom Lady Shrewsbury could and did quarrel, were dead. And perhaps she had mellowed — had even learnt her lesson.

It was a different matter in 1584, when Lord Shrewsbury and the Queen of Scots were alive, and there were a thousand matters to pick quarrels about. Then, not only the ex-chaplain Corker and the inn-keeper Walmesley spread scandals : Lady Shrewsbury was most active in doing so. Complaint was made to her Sovereign, and finally, according to Queen Mary, 'the said lady upon her knees, in the presence of the Queen of England and some principals of her Council, denied to her the shameful bruits by herself spread abroad about me'.

.        .        .        .        .

Amongst Burleigh's papers at Hatfield was a letter, seemingly addressed to Queen Elizabeth by her cousin Mary — which, if indeed it is in Mary's handwriting, satisfied two hatreds. As illiterate as it is horrible, it seems impossible for Mary, of the great utterance, to have written it. I give it for what it is worth : *

'According to what I promised you, and you have since desired, I declare to you now with regret that such things should be brought into question, but very sincerely and without any anger which I call my God to witness that the Countess of Shrewsbury said to me about you what follows, as nearly as possible in these terms ; to the greater part of which I protest that I answered rebuking the same lady for believing or speaking so licentiously of you, as a thing which I did not at all believe — knowing the disposition of the Countess and by what spirit she was then urged on against you : Firstly that one to whom you said you had made a promise of marriage, before a lady of your chamber, had lain many times with you with all the licence and familiarity which husband and wife can use to one another. But that undoubtedly you were not as other women and for this reason all those who desired your union with the Duke of Anjou "Duc d' Alençon", (considering that it could not be consummated) were foolish ; and that you

---

* I have been forced to amend the punctuation and, in some places, the grammar, as otherwise it is quite unreadable.

would never wish to lose the liberty of making love and gratifying yourself with new lovers, regretting this, said she, that you would not content yourself with master haton [Hatton] and another of this kingdom. On account of the honour of the country, that which vexed her most was that you not only compromised your honour with a foreigner named Simier going to find him at night in the chamber of a lady whom the Countess greatly blamed in this affair, where you kissed him and indulged in divers unseemly familiarities with him. But also you revealed the secrets of the Kingdom, betraying your own Councillors to him. That you had disported yourself with the same dissoluteness with the Duke his master who had been to find you one night at the door of your chamber where you had met him with only your night-dress and dressing gown on and that afterwards you had let him enter, and that he remained with you nearly three hours. As for the said haton [Hatton] that you ran him hard, showing so publicly the love that you bore him that he himself was constrained to withdraw from it ; and that you gave a box on the ear to kiligrcw for not having brought back the same haton after he had been sent to recall him having departed in anger for some insulting words you had said to him because of certain gold buttons which he had on his coat. That she had worked to bring about a marriage between the said haton and the late countess of Lennox her daughter but that for fear of you he dared not consent ; that even the Count of Oxford dared not reconcile himself with his wife for fear of losing the favour which he hoped to receive by becoming your lover. That you were lavish towards all such people and those who lent themselves to such practices, as for one of your chamber Gorge to whom you had given three hundred pounds a year for having brought you the news of the return of hatton ; that to all others you were very ungrateful and niggardly and that there were only three or four in your kingdom to whom you had ever been generous. She advised Me, while laughing unrestrainedly, to place my son in the ranks of your lovers as a thing that would be of my very great advantage to me and would put Monsieur the duke out of the running, (in which he would be very disadvantageous to me if he continued) And when I answered to her that that would be taken for unfeigned mockery, she replied to me that you were as vain, and thought as highly of your beauty as if you were a goddess of heaven ; And that she would become responsible for making you believe it readily and for receiving my son in that humour. That you took such great pleasure in flatteries beyond all reason that you were told for example that at times one dared not look at you because your face shone like the sun ; that she and all the other ladies of the Court were constrained to use such flatteries, and that in her last visit to you she and the late Countess of lenox while speaking to you dared not look at one another for fear of bursting out laughing at the tricks she was playing on you.' . . . Her 'daughter Talbot' had declared that 'she would not for anything in the world be in your service near your person seeing that she would be afraid you would do to her as you did to her cousin Shedmur whose finger you had broken, making those of the Court believe that it was a candlestick which had fallen on it ; and that to another serving you at table you had given a violent blow on the hand with a knife, and, in a word to these last points and common gossip you were played and imitated by them as in a comedy. . . .'

There is much more of the same sort. The letter ends thus :

'For God's sake be certain of [trust] her who wishes to serve you and can do so from my bed compelling my arm and my sufferings to satisfy and obey you.'

Marie R.

The letter does not strike me as one which would be pleasing to the recipient.

# Chapter Fifty-one

WHEN it became necessary to proceed against Mary, the central figure of the conspiracies, the first thing to do, obviously, was to seize her papers, prevent her from hiding or destroying any proofs against her, and prevent her from communicating with her secretaries or confidential servants. But it was difficult to know how to effect this.

Sir Amyas Paulet, her custodian at Chartley, near Stafford, suggested to his Queen in 1586 that his charge should be taken hunting, stopped on the way, and charged with complicity in the Babington plot, that she should be taken, guarded, to a house in the neighbourhood while he, returning to Chartley, would ransack her rooms, and seize all letters, notes and, papers of every kind, and would separate her secretaries Nau and Curle, and imprison them.

He was ordered to perform this immediately, as the secretaries were needed to give evidence in London.

The Queen of Scots was still unaware of the discovery of the plot and the capture of Babington and his fellow conspirators ; she was in the highest spirits. Babington would surely arrive at any moment to rescue her ! She was therefore enchanted when, on a lovely August morning, the kindly Paulet suggested they should ride to Sir Walter Aston's park at Foxall, nine miles distant, and kill a buck. With most of her train, including her two secretaries, they set off. They had almost reached the gates of Foxall, when they saw a company of horsemen, waiting in the road. . . . It was, it *must* be, Babington, come, as she had so long waited for him to do. . . . But no. As they approached the waiting men, the leader of the band, riding up to her, saluted her and produced an order from the Queen of England.[1] Nau and Curle were to be arrested, and the Queen of Scots was to be taken to Tixall.

All hope was gone. She knew, now, that all had been discovered. And the fires broke from her nature, in wild curses against the Queen, against the messenger. Were not her servants men ? she shrieked. Let them draw their swords like men, and fight for their Queen. But they were but a handful, and easily overcome. She was taken to Tixall, and Curle and Nau were carried as prisoners to London.

Sir Amyas Paulet rode back to Chartley, searched the Queen's rooms, and took from their hiding-places her papers and letters — many of the latter from English nobles and knights hailing her as their future Queen. These would be placed before the Council, who would understand for the first time the full scope of the lady's underground activities.

She remained at Tixall for a fortnight, then was taken once more to Chartley. As she left Tixall, she saw a number of beggars staring at her, and cried, 'I have nothing for you. I am a beggar as well as you ; all is taken from me'.

On her arrival, she was told that Barbara Mowbray, one of her maids and the wife of Curle, had borne a premature child as the result of shock. Going to her bedside, the Queen —always generous to her servants — swore that she would take upon herself any blame imputed to Curle. (She was to forget that promise.) Then, as there was no priest to baptise the child, she took it upon her knee and, sprinkling water upon its face, said, 'Mary, I baptise thee in the name of the Father, of the Son, and of the Holy Ghost'.

Returning to her desolate rooms, looking at the broken locks, the emptiness, she said to Sir Amyas, 'Some of you will be sorry for this. Two things cannot be taken from me — my English blood and the Catholic religion, which I will keep till my death.'

.        .        .        .        .

Thomas Morgan, as already related, had written, from Paris, at the time of the last conspiracy, a letter he knew would be seen by Mary, in which he said, 'There be many means in hand to remove the beast that troubles all the world'. But in spite of this, and many other evidences that Mary knew Elizabeth's death was plotted, Elizabeth still dreamed of forgiving her, of saving her — as we shall see in the next chapter.

But there was no answer to the Queen of England's letter promising forgiveness if she would confess. And Paulet now said he could not be responsible for the Queen of Scotland if she remained at Chartley. . . . The Council sat day after day at Windsor, but the Queen, her old Chief Minister told Walsingham, was 'variable as the weather'.[2]

She was obliged to consent that her cousin should be tried, but would not decide where the trial should take place. The Tower was suggested. The Queen would not hear of this. Hertford Castle? Too near London. Fotheringay? Too far. Grafton, Woodstock, Northampton, Coventry, Huntingdon? Too weak in defence, or too small for the occasion. 'So with weariness of talk', Lord Burleigh declared, 'Her Majesty left off all till a time I know not when.'

But the Council said, 'The death of Mary is the life of Elizabeth, or the life of Elizabeth is the death of Mary'. And the trial was certain.

Four years before this time, knowing that her own murder was intended — and that Mary was an accessory — Elizabeth had commanded Beale (Clerk to the Council, and Walsingham's brother-in-law) to say these words to the Queen of Scots : 'However she is bold with men who can judge of things outwardly, she ought to beware how she dallied with God'.

. . . . .

The place of the trial had at last been decided, and through the fox-coloured autumn woods leading to Fotheringay, the twenty-six carts containing the Queen of Scots' luggage lumbered. The Queen herself was to follow. She seems to have had no intimation of danger.

The day after the arrival of the Commissioners who were to try her, Sir Walter Mildmay, accompanied by Paulet, entered the Queen of Scots' presence, bearing the Queen of England's letter, which stated that it was regrettable that the Queen of Scotland was so void of conscience as to deny what had been proved, for she thus made it inevitable that she must be brought to trial. She was 'required to answer the noble persons sent to try her, as if she were in the Queen of England's presence'.

The Queen of Scotland, having read the letter, said that she found it strange that Her Majesty should write her a command, and require her to answer as if she were a subject. She was born a Queen. She would neither prejudice her royal rank, nor her royal blood, nor the rights of the son who would succeed her, nor set so poor a precedent for other princes as she would do should she submit to so great an indignity. She knew nothing of the laws of England, nor who could be her peers and therefore competent to try her. She had no counsel, and her papers and secretaries had been taken from her. She had done the Queen of England no injury, either by deed or thought, nor could anything be proved against her. She had come to England for protection, only to be kept as a prisoner. The laws of England had not protected her, and she would not answer to them.[3]

Sir Walter Mildmay left her presence and was succeeded, in a few hours' time, by Burleigh and the Chancellor, who told her that neither her imprisonment nor the fact that she was Queen of Scotland exempted her from obeying as a subject. The Commission had been sent to try her, and if she persisted in her refusal to appear before them, she would be tried in her absence.

She reiterated that she was no subject, but a Queen, and would suffer a thousand deaths before she acknowledged herself a subject. If the Queen of England would acknowledge that she was her next of kin, and the rightful heir to succeed her, then she, on her part, would own that England had a claim on her. Otherwise, she, who had been detained in England against her will, and as a prisoner, owed England nothing. As for the trial, she would answer to the Parliament of England, before which she had always wished to prove her innocence, but to none other.

'We then', said Burleigh, 'will proceed tomorrow in the cause, though you be absent and continue contumacious.'

'Search your conscience,' she replied. 'Look to your honour. God reward you and yours for your judgment against me.'

But by the next day, she had changed her mind. She knew the strange enchantment she cast over every man who had ever come into her presence — with the exception, perhaps, of John Knox. She had seen the names of many of her friends on the Commission. So, next day, when the Commissioners met to try her, she decided to appear before them.

In the Chamber of Presence, a Chair of State with a canopy, representing the throne, had been placed at one end of the room. On each side of this were benches. The Chancellor, Burleigh, and nine Earls — Worcester, Oxford, Kent, Derby, Rutland, Cumberland, Warwick, Pembroke, Lincoln, on the right — on the left were thirteen Barons — Zouche, Abergavenny, Stafford, Grey, Morley, Lumley, Sturton, Sandys, Wentworth, Mordaunt, St. John of Bletsoe, Compton, and Cheyney.

Below these, on either side, were the Privy Councillors, Hatton, Walsingham, Crofts, Sadler (who, says Froude, 'had held Mary Stuart in his arms when she was a baby'), Mildmay, and Sir Amyas Paulet. In front of the Earls sat the two Chief Justices, Wray and Anderson, with the Chief Baron, Manwood ; and on the other side, four of the Judges. Popham and Egerton, the Attorney and Solicitor-General, sat at a small table before the Chair of State.

A chair for the Queen of Scotland was placed in the middle of the room, facing the company.

She entered, wearing her usual long grey dress. She looked round the room, then seated herself. The Chancellor rose to his feet, and, addressing the room, said that 'the Queen, having been advertised to her great sorrow, that the Queen of Scots had conspired the destruction of herself and the state, had sent them to hear the charges against her, and to ascertain her defence'.

She rose, and declared that the Queen of England had promised her protection. She had come to England to seek this, only to be held prisoner. She was no English subject, but a Queen, and therefore answerable to no earthly tribunal. She did not come before them as a criminal; but having heard that certain things were to be alleged against her, she had come to refute them.

She was told that every person in England, no matter of what degree, was answerable to the English laws when they were broken.

Judge Gawdy then opened the case for the Crown. Giving the details of the Babington plot, he accused the Queen of Scots of being an accessory before the fact, of having approved and abetted it.

The Queen of Scotland did not know exactly how much had been discovered against her. She said, therefore, that Babington was quite unknown to her. She had neither spoken nor written to him, nor had she ever received a letter from him. As for plotting harm to the Queen, she neither plotted it herself nor knew it had been plotted by others. She demanded that she should be shown what evidence they had against her.

They produced the letters written by Babington to her, and read them over.

'It may be that Babington wrote those letters,' she replied, 'but let it be proved that I received them. If Babington or others affirm it, I say that they lie openly.'

They produced Babington's confession, Savage's, Ballard's. She showed no signs of confusion, but continued her denials.

Then came the answer she had written to Babington. It was not hers, she declared. Peradventure it was in her cipher, but she had neither written nor dictated it. Nothing was easier than to counterfeit a cipher. And, turning to Walsingham, she enquired, might it not, perhaps, have been *his* work.

Only a few of the Commissioners knew exactly how the plot had been discovered — the story of that useful cask. Therefore, rising to his feet, Walsingham replied : 'I call God to record that as a private person I have done nothing unbecoming an honest man, nor as I bear the place of a public person have I done anything unworthy my place. I confess that being very careful of the safety of the Queen and realm, I have curiously searched out the practices against it. If Ballard had offered me his help, I should not have refused it.'

(Not Ballard, but the gallant, swaggering, feathered popinjay Babington had offered his help, hoping, though in vain, to save his own skin by betraying his comrades.)

The Queen of Scots saw possibilities in this last sentence of Walsingham's. He must not, she said, be angered against her. Of course, when rumours of his tortuous behaviour had reached her, she had not believed them. She would no more credit them than she would believe slanders against herself. Then, 'Do not believe', she cried, 'that I have consented to the Queen's destruction.' And, bursting into tears, 'I would never make shipwreck of my soul by conspiring the destruction of my dearest sister'.

The Judges produced the confessions wrung from Nau and Curle. Why, she asked, produce the confessions and not the men ? They, facing her, would be forced to acknowledge the truth. What was Curle ? Only a toy in the hands of Nau ! And (remembering the hatred of the English people towards her uncle) Nau had been secretary to the Cardinal of Lorraine. Anyone could bribe or terrify him into swearing falsely. Certainly, having been unjustly held prisoner in England, she had sought help from anyone who would be likely to give it. (The mere fact, she thought, that she could admit so much *must* make them believe the rest of her statements.)

Then : 'All majesty', she said, 'and all safety of Princes fall to the ground if they depend on the writings and testimony of secretaries. I delivered nothing to them but what nature delivered to me, that I might at length recover my liberty.

I am not to be convicted but by my own word or writing. If they have written anything which may be hurtful to the Queen my sister, they have written it without my knowledge ; let them have the punishment. Sure I am if they were here they would clear me of blame.'

Burleigh spoke of her correspondence with Mendoza, Paget, and Morgan. She had done no more, she said, than she had warned the Queen of England she would do — ask for help from the Catholic Powers. She had never plotted the murder of the Queen. Nor could she be shaken in her denials that she knew nothing of either Ballard or Babington.[4]

The Court then rose.

On the following day she reiterated her denials. She was questioned again, about her correspondence with Mendoza, her intrigues with the King of Spain. At the end of Burleigh's speech, to which she had listened with no sign of confusion, she asked, once more, to be brought before Parliament or into the presence of the Queen of England, then, rising to her feet, she left the room.[5]

The proceedings had seemed to her almost as a play in a theatre, of which she was a spectator only. Paulet said that she asked him, afterwards, 'who this lord was, and that lord was, seeming extremely curious'. She said that 'English history was a bloody one, but had no meaning in her speech to reach to her own cause'. 'She was utterly void of all harm.' [6]

During the second day of the trial, 'a few hasty lines scribbled at midnight' from Windsor reached the Commissioners. They were ordered to proceed no further until they had returned to London with the notes of the trial.

NOTES TO CHAPTER FIFTY-ONE

[1] Froude, *op. cit.*
[2] Neale, *op. cit.*, vol. 2.
[3] Narrative of Proceedings, 11th October. Froude, *op. cit.*
[4] Froude, *op. cit.*
[5] Froude, *op. cit.*
[6] Froude, *op. cit.*

# Chapter Fifty-two

BEFORE the trial of the Queen of Scots, Elizabeth had driven her Council to distraction by changing her mind every day on the subject of the wording to be used. Now, as Parliament was about to sit, she drove them to further distraction by remaining at Richmond.

Letters, messages, orders, were delayed. 'These hard accidents', said Burleigh, a victim at the time of that unfortunate 'grief in the foot' to which he was subject, 'happen by her Majesty's being so far from here.' Worn out by pain, he must yet take extra journeys practically in the middle of the night. 'I came home', he wrote, after having been forced to travel to Richmond, 'after daylight, as also I passed through the city and Southwark afore daylight — which served me to small purpose, for though I came (to the Palace) about 8 A.M., yet Her Majesty did not stir from her bed afore 10 A.M.' And in another letter, 'I cannot but utter my opinion, long before daylight, for I have been up since 5 A.M.'.[1]

Parliament opened on the 29th of October 1586, and there was a general demand that Mary Stuart — 'the principal conspirator and very root from which all other lewd weeds do spring' — should be put to death — and that immediately — the eighty-year-old Sir Ralph Sadler praying 'God, for His mercy, to put it into Her Majesty's heart to take away this most wicked and filthy woman . . . who from the beginning hath thirsted for this crown, is a murderer of her husband . . . and is a most detestable traitor to our Sovereign and enemy to us all'. He added that 'If the Queen's Majesty do not justice upon her, assuredly it will be thought and said that either Her Majesty loveth insecurity — regarding nothing the wealth and quiet of this Realm and subjects — or else, plainly, that she is afraid to do it'.

On the 12th of November, a deputation of Lords and Commons arrived at Richmond to demand the death of Mary. Being received by the Queen, the Speaker read the petition. It stated, 'She is only a cousin to you in remote degree. But we be sons and children of this land, whereof you be not only the natural mother but the wedded spouse. And therefore much more is due from you to us than to her alone.' 'Either we must take her life from her without your direction, which will be to our extreme danger by the offence of our law ; or else we must suffer her to live against our express oath' (the Oath of Association), 'wherewith no Act of Parliament or power of man whatsoever can in any way dispose.'

The Queen replied, 'As I came to the throne with the willing hearts of subjects, so do I now, after twenty-eight years' reign, perceive in you no diminution of good will, which, if haply I should want, well might I breathe but never think I lived.[2]

'And now, albeit I find my life hath been full dangerously sought and contrived by such as no desert procured it, yet am I therefore so clear from malice . . . that I protest it is and hath been my grievous thought that one, not different in sex, of like estate, and my near kin, should be fallen into so great a crime. Yea, I had so little purpose to pursue her with any colour of malice that it is unknown to some of my Lords here — for now I will play the blab — I secretly wrote her a letter upon the discovery of treasons, that if she would confess them, and privately acknowledge them by her letters unto myself, she never should need be called for them unto so public question . . .

'. . . Were there no more dependency upon us, but mine own life were only in danger, and not the whole estate of your religion and well doings ; I protest . . . I would most willingly pardon and remit this offence. Or if by my death other nations and kingdoms might truly say that this Realm had attained an ever prosperous and flourishing estate, I would (I assure you) not desire to live, but gladly give my life to the end my death might procure you a better Prince. And for your sakes it is that I desire to live ; to keep you from a worse. For as for me, I assure you I find no such pleasure in it that I should much wish it, nor conceive such terror in death that I should greatly fear it. And yet I say not but, if the stroke were coming, perchance flesh and blood would be moved with it, and seek to shun it.

'I have had good experience and trial of this world. I know what it is to be a subject, what to be a Sovereign, what to have good neighbours, and sometimes evil-willers. I have found treason in trust, seen great benefits little regarded. . . .

'. . . In this late Act of Parliament you have laid an hard hand on me — that I must give direction for her death, which cannot but be most grievous ; and an irksome burden to me.

'. . . And even now could I tell you that which would make you sorry. It is a secret ; and yet I will tell it you (although it be known I have the property to keep counsel but too well, often times to mine own peril). It is not long since mine eyes did see it written that an oath was taken, within few days either to kill me or to be hanged themselves ; and that to be performed ere one month was ended.'

('The Lord Treasurer', said a marginal note on the MSS., 'stood up to verify it.') 'Hereby', continued the Queen, 'I see your danger in me, and neither can nor will be so unthankful or careless of your consciences as to take no care for your safety.'

After saying that in so weighty a matter she must 'with earnest prayer beseech His Divine Majesty so to illuminate mine understanding and inspire me with His Grace, as I may do and determine that which shall serve to the establishment of His Church, preservation of your estates, and prospect of this Commonwealth under my charge', she declared that 'whatever any Prince may merit of their subjects, for their approved [proved] testimony of their unfeigned sincerity,

either by governing justly, void of all particularity, or suffering of any injustices done (even to the poorest), that do I
assuredly promise inviolably to perform, for requital of your
so just deserts'.

She rose and stepped down from the Cloth of Estate, 'they
most affectionately praying unto God for her long and happy
reign over them, she for the same yielding great thanks'.
And so departed.

According to Burleigh 'her speech drew tears from many
eyes'.

On the 24th of November, a delegation from both Houses
arrived again at Richmond and was addressed by the Queen.
'. . . Since now', she said, 'it is resolved that my surety cannot be established without a Princess's head, I have just cause
to complain that I, who have in my time pardoned so many
rebels, winked at so many treasons, and either not produced
or altogether slipped them over with silence, should now be
forced to such a proceeding, against such a person.

'. . . I was not simply trained up, nor in my youth spent
my time altogether idly ; and yet, when I came to the Crown,
then entered I first into the school of experience, bethinking
myself of those things that best fitted a King — justice, temper,
magnanimity, judgment. As for the two latter, I will not
boast. But for the two first, this may I truly say : among my
subjects I never knew a difference of person, whose right was
one ; nor never to my knowledge preferred for favour what
I thought not fit for worth ; nor bent mine eyes to credit a
tale that first was told me ; nor was so rash to corrupt my
judgment with my censure ere I heard the cause. I will not
say but many reports might (by) fortune be brought me by
such as must hear the matter, whose particularity might mar
the right ; for Princes cannot hear all causes themselves. But
this dare I boldly affirm ; my conduct went with the truth
of my knowledge.'

Parliament assembled again on the 2nd of December,
when the Lord Chancellor announced that the Proclamation
against Mary would appear under the Great Seal of England.

It was proclaimed throughout the country, to the joy of the people : bonfires were lit in the streets, the air was loud with the noise of bells because the hated woman was to die.

The Parliament was adjourned once more until the 15th of February 1587 — weeks of anguish for the Queen of England. For still she hoped to find some way by which her cousin's life might be spared. On the 7th of December, giving audience to the French emissary de Bellièvre, who had been sent to England to plead for that life, she said, 'I have been compelled to come to the resolution I have taken, because it is impossible to save my own life if I preserve that of the Queen of Scots ; but if your Ambassadors can point to any means whereby I may do it consistently with my own security, I shall be greatly obliged to you, never having shed so many tears at the death of my Father, of my Brother the King, or of my sister Mary, as I have done for this unfortunate affair'.

Then, some days later, she said to him, 'I gave you several days to consider some means by which I could, without being in danger of losing my own life, preserve hers ; and having heard nothing from you on that point, and I not having found any other expedient, I am not at liberty to be cruel against myself, and His Majesty should not consider it just that I who am innocent should die and that the Queen of Scots who is guilty should be saved'.

The Queen of England wrote to her cousin warning her that Parliament had passed sentence on her.

Mary's reply to this letter contained these passages :

'Now, since I have been, on your part, informed of the sentence of your last meeting of Parliament, Lord Buckhurst and Beale having admonished me to prepare for the end of my long and weary pilgrimage, I beg to return thanks, for my part, for these happy tidings. . . .

'I will accuse no one ; nay I pardon, with a sincere heart, every one, even as I desire every one may grant forgiveness to me, God the first. But I know that you, more than any one, ought to feel at heart the honour or dishonour of your own blood, and that, moreover, of a Queen and the daughter of a King.

'Then, Madame, for the sake of that Jesus to whose name all powers bow, I require you to ordain, that when my enemies have slaked their black thirst for my innocent blood, you will permit my poor desolated servants altogether to carry away my corpse, to bury it in holy ground, with the other Queens of France, my predecessors, especially near the late Queen my mother ; having this in recollection that in Scotland the bodies of the Kings, my predecessors, have been outraged, and the Churches profaned and abolished ; and that as I shall suffer in this country I shall not be given place near the Kings your predecessors, who are mine as well as yours ; for according to our religion, we think much of being interred in holy earth. As they tell me that you will in nothing force my conscience nor my religion, and have even conceded me a priest' [that was not so] 'refuse me not this, my last request, that you will permit me free sepulchre of this body when the soul is separated, which, when united, could never obtain liberty to live in repose, such as you would procure for yourself — against which repose, before God I speak, I never aimed a blow ; but God will let you see the truth of all after my death.

'And because I dread the tyranny of those to whose power you have abandoned me, I entreat you not to permit that execution be done on me without your own knowledge, not on account of the torment, which I am most ready to suffer, but on account of the reports' [presumably that she was a suicide] 'which will be raised concerning my death, without other witnesses than those who would inflict it, who, I am persuaded, would be of very different qualities from those parties whom I require (being my servants) to be spectators and withal witnesses of my end, in the faith of our Sacrament, of my Saviour, and in obedience to His Church. And after all is over, that they may carry away my poor corpse (as secretly as you please) and speedily withdraw, without taking with them any of my goods, except those which, in dying, I may leave to them . . . which are little enough for their long service.

'One jewel * that I received of you, I shall return to you with last words, or sooner if you please.

'Once more I supplicate you to permit me to send a jewel and a last adieu to my son, with my benediction, for of my blessing he has been deprived, since you sent me his refusal to enter the treaty whence I was deprived by his wicked Council ; this last point I refer to your favourable consideration and conscience, as the others ; but, in the name of Jesus Christ, and in respect to our consanguinity, and for the sake of King Henry VII, your grandfather and mine, and for the honour of the dignity we both held, and of our sex in common, do I implore you to grant these requests. . . .

'To conclude, I pray God, the just Judge, of His mercy, that he will enlighten you with His Holy Spirit, and that he will give me His grace to die in the perfect charity I am disposed to do, and to pardon all those who have caused, or who have co-operated in my death. Such will be my last prayer to my end, which, I esteem myself fortunate, will precede the persecution' [of the English Catholics] 'which, I foresee, menaces this isle, where God is no longer seriously feared and revered, but vanity and worldly policy rule and govern all — yet I will accuse no one, nor give way to presumption. — Yet, while abandoning this world and preparing myself for a better, I must remind you, that one day you will have to answer for your charge, and for all those whom you doom, and that I desire that my blood and my country may be remembered in that time. For why ? From the first days of our capacity to comprehend our duties, we ought to bend our minds to make the things of this world yield to those of eternity !

---

* This was probably the diamond ring which Elizabeth sent her as a token of amity. 'It was', said Melvil, 'an English custom to give a diamond, to be returned at a time of distress, to recall friendship.' The description of the celebrated ring is curious. Two diamonds were set in two rings and, when laid together, formed the shape of a heart. Elizabeth sent one to Mary and kept the other.

'From Fotheringham [Fotheringay] this 19th December
1586

> Your sister and cousin
> > Prisoner wrongfully

> > > Marie (Royne).'

Fourteen years before that time, Elizabeth had said to
Fénelon, 'There seems to be something sublime in the words
and bearing of the Queen of Scots that constrains even her
enemies to speak well of her'. That sublimity of utterance
remained with her till the end. Reading this letter, it seems
inconceivable that the writer should have been the author of
the low and infamous scandal letter that has been ascribed to
her.

Leycester told Walsingham, 'there is a letter from the
Scottish Queen that *hath wrought tears*, but, I trust, shall do no
further herein ; albeit *the delay is too dangerous*'.

Every day brought rumours of new perils. In January
the Council announced that a fresh plot to murder the Queen
had been discovered in which the French Ambassador,
l'Aubespine, and the brother of the English Ambassador to
France were involved. It was rumoured that the Spanish
Fleet were at Milford Haven, the Scots had invaded England,
the north of England had rebelled.

There was no help for it. The Queen of Scots must die.


### NOTES TO CHAPTER FIFTY-TWO

[1] Neale, *op. cit.*, vol. 2.
[2] Neale, *op. cit.*, vol. 2.

# Chapter Fifty-three

IT was thought, by many, that there might be certain objections to 'a hangman touching the head' of a Queen of Scotland, the ex-Queen of France. Her son might protest. But James did not care. His mother was nothing to him (although at last he was forced by his subjects whose weathercock minds now veered round to Mary's side to simulate fury because her death was threatened). But in a letter to Leycester, dated the 15th of December, he wrote 'How fond (foolish) and inconstant I were if I should prefer my mother to the title, let all men judge. My religion ever moved me to hate her course, although my honour constrains me to insist for her life.'

The insistence in question was not very strong. Shambling of gait, uncouth of person and visage, he was never fond (in the modern sense of the word) excepting of most unworthy persons and under most unworthy circumstances. He was constant to nothing excepting his determination to inherit the English crown. His terrible pre-natal experiences had unmanned him : he could not bear the sight of a sword. He was known to cry in the presence of grooms and other servants at the thought that he might not be Darnley's son, but a bastard. He was, however, a mass of great learning.

He had no reason to love his mother, who had called upon God to curse him, and who had disinherited him in her will (which had been found, at Chartley, and sent to him). He was, at last, forced to intercede for her life.

At one moment, the French Ambassador believed that her life would be spared. She would be sent to the Tower, where she would live as a Carmelite nun (with two women only to wait on her), and seen by the outer world through a grating.

Now, at Fotheringay, she was told that Parliament had pronounced sentence on her, and that if she would not plead for pardon she must die. She replied that she died for the cause of religion, and that she thanked God for so great an honour. She was assured that she was not to die for the cause of religion, but for having plotted to kill the Queen of England and to seize the crown. She continued to swear that she had never once plotted the Queen's destruction.

The Commissioners left her for a while to consider if she would repent and ask for pardon. Then, as when they returned they found her still contumacious, they said that this being so, she would no longer be treated as a Queen, and her Cloth of State, with the royal arms of Scotland, would be taken from her.

She replied that she was an anointed Queen ; nobody could deprive her of her Queenship, and as a Queen she would die. They had, she said 'no more right over her than a highwayman over an honest magistrate whom he might meet in a wood. God would avenge her. English Kings had been murdered, and she was of their blood.'

Her custodian ordered her women to remove the canopy over the Chair of State. They refused, cursing him, so his own servants tore them down. Where the Arms of Scotland had been, she hung a Crucifix.

For the first time, her gaoler seated himself in her presence, and did not bare his head.

In a letter to the Pope, she wrote begging him, since her Almoner might not be allowed to come to her, that he would himself grant her absolution. She was coming, she said, like the Prodigal, to Christ, offering her blood at the foot of the Cross. She begged him to take her son into his care, and save him from damnation as a heretic. But, if he remained in his heresy, she bequeathed her rights to the English crown to the King of Spain.

This letter was dated 23rd November (3rd December).

.          .          .          .          .

Mary's brother-in-law, the King of France, was only shocked at the *manner* in which it was proposed to put her to death. Why could the English not have shown more *tact*? The woman could easily have been poisoned, throttled, smothered with a pillow. Who would have cared? Nobody. But to 'offend all the sovereign princes and Kings in the world . . .' (by) 'subjecting a sovereign Queen to that from which God has by special privilege exempted Kings, who cannot be judged except by Him' — that was a very different matter !

It was obviously better that she should be murdered. The Archbishop of Canterbury was enthusiastic for the idea, and, according to Beale, 'was sent to Mr. Secretary Walsingham to persuade him. One Wingfield (as it was thought) should have been appointed for this deed ; and it seemed that Her Majesty would have it done so rather than otherwise, pretending that Archibald Douglas, the Scottish Ambassador, had so advised her. . . .'

Leycester was also in favour of the plan. But unfortunately 'both the Secretaries misliked thereof', as did the Queen of Scots' two custodians, as we shall see.

On the 1st of February, the Queen of England, finding no escape from doing so, signed the warrant for the execution, and giving it to Secretary Davison, ordered him to take it to the Lord Chancellor for the Great Seal to be affixed. But, as he was leaving the room, she complained violently that Sir Amyas Paulet and his fellow custodian Sir Drue Drury had not found some way of putting her to death without the order for the death being signed. Davison was, she said, to go immediately to Walsingham and write a letter to that effect, to be signed by both.

The letter ran as follows :

'To Sir Amice Poulet,
'After our hearty commendations, we find, by speech lately uttered by Her Majesty, that she doth note in you both a lack of that care and zeal of her service that she looketh for

at your hands, in that you have not, in all this time, of yourselves, without other provocation, found out some way to
shorten the life of that Queen, considering the great peril she
is subject unto hourly as long as the said Queen shall live.
Wherein, besides a kind of lack of love towards her, she noteth
greatly that you have not that care of your own particular
safeties, or rather of the preservation of religion and public
good, and prosperity of your country, that reason and policy
commandeth, especially having so good a warrant and ground
for the satisfaction of your conscience towards God, and the
discharge of your credit and reputation towards the world,
as the Oath of Association which you have both so solemnly
taken and vowed, and especially the matter wherewith she
standeth charged being so clearly and manifestly proved
against her.   And therefore she taketh it most unkindly towards her, that men professing that love towards her as you
do, should, in any kind of sort, for lack of the discharge of
your duties, cast the burthen upon her, knowing, as you do,
her indisposition to shed blood, especially of one of that sex
and quality, and so near to her in blood as the said Queen is.
These respects, we find, do greatly trouble Her Majesty who,
we assure you, has sundry times protested, that if the regard
of this danger of her good subjects and faithful servants did
not more move her than her own peril, she would never be
drawn to assent to the shedding of her blood.   We thought
it very meet to acquaint you with these speeches lately passed
from Her Majesty, referring the same to your good judge-
ments ;   and so we commend you to the protection of the
Almighty.

'Your most assured friends,

Francis Walsingham
William Davison

'at London
  Feb : 1 1586.'


It was now late at night, so the writers of this letter decided
to postpone sending it and the Warrant until next day.   Early

next morning, the order reached Davison from the Queen, that if the Great Seal had not been affixed to the Warrant he was to wait to do so until he had seen her.

Obtaining an immediate audience, he was asked by the Queen why he had been in such a hurry to have the Warrant sealed.

He replied that he had but obeyed her orders and asked if he was to proceed in the matter. She said yes, but once again lamented passionately that she had not been spared the necessity of making this cruel decision. He protested that the decision must be *hers*. Whereupon she ended the audience.

Davison now feared for his own safety, foreseeing clearly that she had every intention of putting the blame upon him ; and, not daring to send the Warrant without knowledge of the whole Council he, accompanied by Hatton, consulted Burleigh, who was in bed with 'a grief in his foot'. It was decided to call a meeting of the Council for next day. At this, a letter was signed ordering the custodians to proceed, immediately, with the preparations for the execution.

Arriving at Fotheringay with this, Beale was told immediately by Paulet and Drury, of the strange letter they had received, suggesting they should 'suffer their charge to be violently murdered by some that should have been appointed for the purpose'.

The matter was then discussed thoroughly by Beale, Paulet, Drury, and Shrewsbury, but, according to Beale, they remembered the end of Edward the Second and Richard the Second, and 'it was not thought convenient or safe to proceed covertly, but openly'. It seems fairly certain that if they *had* allowed her to be murdered, they would have then been used as scapegoats.

The two custodians wrote, therefore, the following letter :

'To Sir Francis Walsingham, $K^{nt}$,
'Sir,

Your letters of yesterday coming to my hands this present day at five in the afternoon, I would not fail, according to your directions, to return my answer with all possible speed, which shall deliver unto you, great grief and bitterness of mind, in that I am so unhappy to have lived to see this unhappy day, in the which I am required, by direction from my most gracious Sovereign, to do an act which God and the law forbiddeth. My good livings and life are at Her Majesty's disposition, and am ready to lose them this next morrow if it shall so please her, acknowledging that I hold them as of her most gracious favour. I do not desire them, to enjoy them, but with her Highness's good liking ; but God forbid that I should make so fowle a shipwracke of my conscience, or leave so great a blott to my posteritie, or shed blood without law and warrant ; trusting that Her Majesty, of her accustomed clemency, will take this my dutiful answer in good part (and the rather, by your good mediation) as proceeding from one who will never be inferior to any Christian subject living in duty, honour, love and obedience towards his Sovereign. And thus I commit you to the mercy of the Almightie.

'Your most assured poore friends

A. Paulet.

D. Drury.

'Your letter coming in the plural number, seems to be meant as to Sir Drew Drury, as to myself, and yet because he is not named in them, neither the letter directed unto him, he forbeareth to make any answer, but subscribeth in heart to my opinion.'

The Queen, on reading this letter, broke into a fury, exclaiming against the 'daintiness', 'the niceness of these precise fellows', and the 'perjury of him' (Paulet) and others 'who had failed to fulfil the oath they had taken when they signed the Oath of Association'.

Davison's fears for his own safety were not allayed.

# Chapter Fifty-four

ON Tuesday, the 7th of February 1587, a servant entered the apartments of the Queen of Scots, and told her that Beale, with the Earls of Shrewsbury and Kent and the High Sheriff of Northampton, had arrived at the Castle, and that they wished for an audience.

She sent for her ladies and most of her servants, then the Commissioners arrived in her audience chamber. They told her that the Queen of England had no longer been able to resist her subjects' demand for the Queen of Scotland's execution, and that she must prepare to die next morning.

She had spent most of her long imprisonment under the roof of Lord Shrewsbury, and it was with a trembling voice that he read the death-warrant. The Queen crossed herself, and answered, 'In the name of God, these tidings are welcome, and I bless and pray Him that the end of all my bitter sufferings is at hand. I could receive no better news, and thank the Almighty for His Grace in allowing me to die for the honour of His Church, the ancient Catholic and Romaine religion.'

She placed her hand on a Bible which lay on a table near her, and took a solemn oath that — 'I have never either desired the death of the Queen, or endeavoured to bring it about, or that of any other person'.

She asked only that her Chaplain, who had been kept from her, should be allowed to return to her during the hours before her death, and that the execution might not take place next morning, so that she might have more time to prepare her soul.

But both requests were refused her, and her Chaplain was ordered to keep to his room lest, said the fanatical Earl of

Kent, he should administer to the dying woman 'the Papistical Extreme Unction'. She was, instead, told that an Anglican Dean would attend her. She refused this offer with indignation.

A large part of her last night was spent in writing letters.

Her apothecary promised to deliver two diamonds, concealed in a melted drug, to Mendoza — one diamond being for the Ambassador, the other for his King — together with a message to the King of Spain that she was a martyr for her faith, that she begged him to reward her servants for their long devotion, and that it was her dying prayer that, although she would not see the triumph of the true religion, he would invade and conquer England, and then reward Cecil, Leycester, Walsingham, Huntingdon, Paulet, and Secretary Wade for their treatment of her.

This letter having been written, she spent the rest of the night with eyes wide open, while her ladies prayed silently.

At eight o'clock next morning the Provost Marshal knocked at the outer door leading to her apartments. There was no answer, for the Queen, kneeling at her *prie-Dieu*, was reading aloud the prayers for the dying. Alarmed, he went in search of the Sheriff, and together they went to the outer door, which was now open. And standing in the doorway was the prisoner Queen, robed as for a feast.

She had discarded the long grey dress which was her usual costume, and wore instead black velvet and satin. A long veil covered her coils of false hair ; round her neck was a gold crucifix, and jewelled Paternosters were attached to her girdle. In her hand was held a crucifix of ivory.

As she went on her way, leaning on the arm of an officer of the guard, she saw Andrew Melville, the master of her household, kneeling in tears. 'Melville,' she said to him, 'you should rather rejoice than weep that the end of my troubles is come. Tell my friends I die a true Catholic. Commend me to my son. Tell him I have done nothing to prejudice his Kingdom of Scotland ; and so, good Melville, farewell.'

She kissed him, then asked where was her Chaplain, and why were not her ladies present ? *

Kent said that her Chaplain had been ordered to keep to his room, and that as for her ladies, he said, with innate delicacy, that he had feared that they might scream or faint, or that 'they would not stick to put some superstitious Popery in practice, if it were but *dipping their handkerchiefs in Your Grace's blood*' (the italics are mine).

'My Lords,' said the Queen, 'I will give my word that, although I shall be dead, they will do no such thing.' 'The Queen', she said, 'would never deny so slight a request.' Weeping, she added, 'You know I am cousin to your Queen, of the blood of Henry the Seventh, a married Queen of France, and anointed Queen of Scotland'.

After some argument, she was allowed to choose six of her people to accompany her. She chose Andrew Melville, her physician, her surgeon, her apothecary, and two of her ladies : Barbara Mowbray, the young wife of her secretary Curle whose new-born child she had baptised, and Elizabeth Kennedy.

About three hundred nobles and knights stood behind a rail in the great hall, beyond which was the scaffold, covered in black, a black cushion on which she was to kneel, and a chair. The axe leant against the rail, and two masked figures stood on either side, behind the scaffold.

The Queen looked round her, smiled, and with absolute calm mounted the scaffold.

The sentence condemning her to death was read.

'Madam,' said Lord Shrewsbury, 'you hear what we are commanded to do.'

'You will do your duty,' she said, and was about to kneel and pray when the Dean of Peterborough walked up to her. 'Madam,' he said, with a deep bow, 'the Queen's most excellent Majesty . . .' Overcome, perhaps, by the scene, by the Queen of Scots' absolute calm, he repeated this phrase four times.

* She wished them to be with her at her death.

But at the fourth repetition, the Queen interrupted him, saying, 'Mr. Dean, I am a Catholic. It is useless to attempt to move me, and your prayers will avail me nothing.'

'Change your opinion, Madam,' said the Dean, who had by now recovered his power of speech. 'Repent of your sins, settle your faith in Christ, by Him be saved.'

'Trouble not yourself further, Mr. Dean,' said she ; 'I am settled in my own faith, for which I mean to shed my blood.'

Lord Shrewsbury said, 'I am sorry, Madam, to see you so addicted to Popery'.

'That image of Christ you hold there', said the Earl of Kent, 'will not profit you if it be not engraved on your heart.'

To this insolence she made no answer but, turning her back on the Dean, knelt in prayer. But she was not to pray or to die undisturbed. The Dean, accompanied by the crowd, chanted an extempore prayer. The Queen paid no attention but spoke, in Latin, the Penitential Psalms, and prayed for the Holy Father.[1]

Her ladies came to disrobe her. She took the crucifix from round her neck ; the ladies hung her veil upon the rail of the scaffold.

Then, as the black robe was lifted from her, she was seen to be clad entirely in the colour of blood. In this red velvet underclothing, she knelt to die.

The executioner, horrified at the spectacle or at his task, first struck the back of the Queen's head. Her neck was unsevered.[2]

A groan came from her open mouth. The second time he struck, the axe, though it brought floods of blood from the doomed woman's neck, did not sever it. At the third stroke, the head rolled from the body, across the scaffold. The wig was detached, and the watchers saw that the head was that of an old woman, with short grey hair.

At first, the watchers were so horrified they were rendered speechless. But then the chief executioner held up the head and cried 'God save the Queen !'[3] The Dean of Peterborough said, 'Amen ! Amen ! So perish the Queen's enemies.' And the Earl of Kent muttered, 'Such end happen to all the Queen's and Gospel's enemies'.

According to Zweig, the dead woman's lips continued to move for nearly a quarter of an hour.

Then, as the head and body were about to be carried away, it was seen that the Queen's little dog had hidden beneath her petticoat, and was 'embrued with her blood'. It would not leave its dead mistress, but came and lay between her head and shoulders. At last it was carried away and washed.

.          .          .          .          .

London gave itself up to rejoicing. Bonfires were lit in the streets, the noise of bells ringing and cannons being fired was like that of a storm at sea.

But the Queen of England could neither eat nor sleep for grief. And the men who had sent off the warrant for her cousin's execution were to experience her full fury. She raged at Burleigh ; Davison was tried in the Star Chamber and sentenced to an enormous fine, and to imprisonment in the Tower during the Queen's pleasure.[4] Thus the Queen hoped to appease the anger of the Scots. He remained in prison for eighteen months, until after the defeat of the Armada. But the Queen was not ungenerous. His fine was remitted, and he retained the office of Secretary until his death.

### NOTES TO CHAPTER FIFTY-FOUR

[1] Froude's account says that 'she prayed for the Church she had been ready to betray [this is wholly unfair], for her son whom she had disinherited, for the Queen whom she had endeavoured to murder. She prayed God to avert His wrath from that England which she had sent a last message to Philip to beseech him to invade. She forgave her enemies whom she had invited Philip not to forget, and then, praying to the Saints to intercede for her with Christ, and kissing the Crucifix and crossing her own heart, "Even as thy arms, O Jesus," she cried, "were spread upon the Cross, so receive me into thy mercy and forgive my sins".

'She rose ; the executioners came to her, and begged her to forgive them.

' "I forgive you," she said, "for now I hope you shall end all my troubles." '

[2] Zweig, *The Queen of Scots*.

[3] Zweig, *op. cit.*

[4] Neale, *op. cit.*

# Chapter Fifty-five

THE last years of Leycester's life, until the time of England's triumph over the Armada, were years of acute misery.

His great friend, his colleague in the rebellion of the Protestant Dutch against Spain, William of Orange, was murdered on the 10th of July 1584 by a youth named Balthazar who, having hidden behind a pillar, fired poisoned bullets into him as he came from his dining-room. Balthazar was executed with the most hideous torments.

Nine days after the shock of Orange's murder Leycester's little son Robert, aged about four, died, and Leycester was accused by his enemies, in pamphlets, of having had him murdered by his nurse because he was a hunchback. There is no record of his deformity, and his father loved him tenderly.

In answer to Vice-Chamberlain Hatton's letter of condolence, which contained the phrase 'go on in your high and noble labours in the comfort of Christ. . . . Of men's hearts you enjoy more than millions which, on my soul, do love you no less than children, or brethren. Leave sorrow, therefore, my good lord, and be glad in us which much rejoice in you.' Leycester replied, 'I must confess to have received many afflictions within these few years, but not a greater, next to Her Majesty's displeasure ; and if it pleased God I would the sacrifice of this poor innocent might satisfy ; I mean not towards God (for all are most sinful and wretched in His sight ; and therefore He sent a most innocent lamb to help us all that are faithful), but for the world.

'The afflictions I have suffered may satisfy such as are offended, or at least appease their long, hard conceits : if not,

SIR CHRISTOPHER HATTON

yet there is a blessing for such as suffer : and so there is for those that be merciful. Princes (who feel not the heavy estate of the poor afflicted) . . . seldom do pity according to the true rules of charity — and therefore comfort. . . . I beseech the same God to grant me patience in all these worldly things, and to forgive me the negligence of my former times, that have not then been more careful to please Him, but have run the race of the world. . . .'

He was soon to fall into deep disgrace with the Queen.

In the autumn of 1585 she found herself faced with the necessity of sending forces to help the Dutch Protestants in their rebellion against Spain. The atrocities in the Netherlands had been appalling. Strype's *Annals of the Reformation* (Vol. II, Part 2) gives this hideous account 'of an English gentleman present when the Spanish spoiled Antwerp' in 1576. (Strype thinks the writer was Dr. Thomas Wilson, an agent of Elizabeth — he who was so astonished by the *volte-face* and general antics of Mary Queen of Scots' former apologist, the Bishop of Ross.)

'I refrain to rehearse the heaps of dead carcasses which lay at every trench they entered ; the thickness of which did in many places exceed the height of a man — I forbear also to relate the infinite numbers drowned in the new town. I list not to reckon the infinite number of poor Almains, who lay burnt in their armour. Some, their entrails scorched out, and all the rest of the body free. Some, their heads and shoulders burnt off, so that you might look down into the bulk and breast, and take there an anatomy of the secrets of nature. Some, standing upon their waists, being burnt off by the thighs, and some, no more than the very top of the brain taken off by fire, while the rest of the body did abide unspeakable torments. . . .'

The Queen did not want war with Spain. She had wished, as we have seen at the time of the Alençon comedy, to keep the French out of the Netherlands, and to do so the Spanish sovereignty must be maintained. For this reason, when at Christmas 1575, the Netherlands sent an embassy to England, offering to make Elizabeth their Queen if she would give them protection, she refused categorically.

In the autumn of 1585, however, she contemplated sending Leycester with an army to the Netherlands to join the insurgents against the Duke of Parma, and she sent Drake to the Azores with thirty-six ships to establish a base there from which he could harry, chase, and plunder the King of Spain's ships, to pillage the Spanish treasures, after an English cornfleet had been taken by the Spaniards. 'Neither', says Sir John Neale, 'constituted a formal act of war.'

Leycester, after many delays caused by the Queen's hesitation, was about to set out for the Netherlands when it came to the Queen's ears that Lady Leycester, her hated cousin Lettice, had arrived in London, prepared to follow her husband. 'It was told Her Majesty', his steward told him, 'that my ladie was prepared presently to come over to your excellencie with such a trayne of gentilwommen, and such riche coaches, lytters, and syde-saddles, as Her Majestie had never suche, and that there should be such a courte of ladies, as should far passe Her Majestie's Court heare.'

The Queen flew into a violent passion. She told Leycester he was only going to Flanders for his own ostentation. 'She used', wrote the Spanish Ambassador, Mendoza, in Paris, 'the most scandalous words to him, and ended by saying that he was a traitor, as was all his stock. . . . She called Walsingham a rogue for having incited Alençon to go to the Netherlands.'

In a fury, she said she would send another, or no one. She was calmed by Burleigh, Hatton, and Walsingham, who told her, quite untruly, that the news about Lady Leycester's preparations was false.

Then her rage died down, but she said she was ill, and Leycester must remain near her, for she felt her death approaching. 'She used very pitiful words to me', he told Walsingham, 'of her fear she shall not live, and would not have me from her. . . . I did comfort her as much as I could, only I did not let her know how far I had gone in preparation . . .'

Next day she felt better, but four days afterwards her illness returned. On the 26th of September, Walsingham told Leycester that '. . . unless God give Her Majesty another mind, it will work her and her subjects' ruin . . .'. To which Leycester replied, 'It was one of the strangest dealings in the world : [he] was weary of life and all'.

Her changes of mind were such that Walsingham was worn out.

Eventually Leycester and his army set out on the 22nd of October. His task was begun under impossible conditions. The promised army had been sent over without stores, without food, without money. The soldiers who had been sent to garrison Flushing remained for ten days in open boats, sometimes even without food. For a week after this, they took refuge in a church at Middelburg, their clothes, rotted by the rain, falling off them. At Flushing, when eventually they arrived, they were refused either bread or clothing by the citizens, excepting for money. And they had none.

The New Year opened disastrously. On the morning of the 1st of January, before Leycester was dressed, the sound of trumpets reached him from the courtyard.

This heralded the arrival of a delegation which had come 'to offer him . . . with many good wishes for Her Majesty's sake, the absolute government of the whole provinces [sic] . . . and to proclaim the same immediately'.

Leycester accepted the offer. This he did without one word of warning to his Queen. 'In so doing', writes Sir John Neale, 'violating his instructions, jeopardizing his sovereign's policy, and — perhaps most galling of all — making a mockery of the eloquent pamphlet, published in several languages, in which she declared her desire for peace, and her intention to seek neither territory nor authority in the Netherlands.'

It was not until the beginning of February that the news reached England. The Queen's fury was unbounded. She was particularly enraged because he had allowed himself to be addressed as 'Your Excellency'. On hearing this, he ran into even greater danger by telling Walsingham that 'I refused a title higher than Excellency . . .'.

She sent Sir Thomas Heneage to the Netherlands, with these instructions (after referring to Leycester twice as 'a creature of our own') : she ordered Leycester to 'make an open and public resignation in the place where he accepted the same absolute government'.

Heneage took, also, a letter from the Queen to Leycester ; it is dated the 11th of February : 'How contemptuously we conceive ourselfe to have been used by you, you shall by this bearer understand, whom we have expressly sent unto you to charge you withall. We could never have imagined, had we not seen it fall out in experience, that a man raysed uppe by ourselfe, and extraordinarily favoured by us above anie other subject of this land, would have in so contemptible a sort broken a commandment, in a course that so greatly toucheth us in honour, whereof, although you have shewed yourselfe to make but little account, in most undutifull a sort, you may not therefor thinck that wee have so little care of the reparation thereof as we mynd to passe so great a wronge in silence unredressed. And therefor, our expresse pleasure and commandment is, that all delayes and excuses layd apart, you do presently, upon the dutie of your allegiance, obey and fulfill whatsoever the bearer hereof shall direct you to do in our name : whereof fayle you not, as you will answer the contrarye at your uttermost perill.'

In early March, Leycester's brother, Lord Warwick, wrote to him, 'Our mistress's extreme rage doth increase rather than in any way diminish, and she gives out great threatening words against yourself. Make the best assurance you can for yourself. Trust not her oath, for that her malice is great and unquenchable. Repose your trust in God, and let this be a comfort to you, that you were never so honoured in your life among all good people as you are this day.'

The Queen swore, 'I will let the upstart know how easily the hand which has exalted him can beat him to the dust'.

She would not send him money, she would not send him troops. She raged at Burleigh when he tried to find excuses for him. Then, when her old counsellor offered to resign, she called him a 'presumptuous fellow'.

Next morning she had changed again, and the Council persuaded her to send troops and money. Soon, Raleigh was able to tell him, 'You are again her sweet Robin'.

But on the 17th of March 1586, he told Burleigh of his feeling that he had been publicly disgraced : 'How great a grief it must be to an honest heart and a true, faithful servant, before his own face, to a company of very wise and grave councillors who had conceived a marvellous opinion before of my credit with Her Majesty, to be charged with a manifest and wilful contempt . . . matter enough to have broken any man's heart. . . . Although I must say to your lordship for discharge of my duty, I can be no fit man to serve here ; my disgrace is too great, protesting to you, my lord, that since that day I cannot find it in my heart to come into that place where by my own sovereign's letter, I was made to be thought of her so lewd a person . . . My heart is broken ; although this far I can quiet myself, that I know I have done Her Majesty as faithfull and as good service in these countries as ever she had done her since she was Queen of England.'

He told Walsingham that he wished the Queen would order him to the other side of the world, where he might serve without offending her sight again.

Did he write thus from wounded affection ? Wounded pride ? A sense of unjust treatment ? He knew that she had never forgiven his marriage, and the end of the long dream in which she would always be young, always beloved.

But she changed from day to day. When she was walking in the garden, she was told that he was ill, and was begged to send one of her physicians (Dr. Goodrowe) to him. Whereupon she was 'much moved' and said she was sorry that Leycester had need of him. Of her anger with him she said, 'You know my mynd. I may nott endewre that my man should alter my commyssen, and the authoritye that I gave him, uppon his owne fancies, and wythought me.'

At last his letters to the Queen touched her heart. He had written, indeed, most movingly. . . . 'Most gracious lady, consider my long, true and faithful heart toward you, and let not this unfortunate place here bereave me of that which above all the world I esteem, which is your favour and your presence. I see my service is not acceptable, but rather more and more distresseth you. . . .

'But if ever spark of favour was in Your Majesty toward your old servant, let me obtain this my humble suit, protesting before the Majesty of all Majesties that there was no cause under heaven but His and yours could have made me take this absent journey from you in hand.'

In her softened mood, she wrote to him, 'Rob, — I am afraid you will suppose by my wandering writings that a midsummer moon hath taken large possessions of my brains this month, but you must needs take things as they come into my head, though order be left behind me'.

He sailed for England in his flagship on the 23rd of November 1586, followed by a Dutch embassy of five. The States had complained to the Queen about Leycester, in highly abusive letters. They had accused him, among other things, of turning his troops into brigands, to prey upon the poor Dutch peasants. For two months, she would not receive the embassy — did not, indeed, until the 7th of February 1587, the day before the execution of the Queen of Scots.

The first interview was extremely alarming to the envoys. The Queen said they had spread reports that she was trying to make peace behind their backs. 'Princes', she told them, 'transact business in a certain way, and with a princely intelligence, such as private persons cannot imitate. Among us princes we are not wont to make such long orations as you do, but you ought to be content with the few words that we bestow upon you, and make yourselves great thereby.'

The second interview was equally terrifying : 'I had intended', she told the envoys, 'that my Lord of Leycester should return to you. But that shall never be. He has been treated with the grossest ingratitude, he has served the Provinces with ability, he has consumed his own property there, he has risked his life, he has lost his near kinsman Sir Philip Sidney whose life I should be glad to purchase with many millions, and, in place of all reward, he receives these venomous letters, of which a copy has been sent to his sovereign, to blacken him unto her.'

Soon everybody was in disgrace. 'The Lord Treasurer', the Secretary told Leycester, 'remaineth still in disgrace, and behind my back, Her Majesty giveth out very hard speeches of myself. . . . And if Her Majesty could be otherwise served, I know I should not be used. . . .'

As for the Lord Treasurer : 'Why Her Majesty useth me thus strangely, I know not. To some she saith that she meant not I should have gone from the Court ; to some she saith, she may not admit me, nor give me contentment. I shall dispose myself to enjoy God's favour, and shall do nothing to deserve her disfavour. And if I be suffered to be a stranger to her affairs, I shall have a quieter life.'

. . . . .

The past years had been full of grief and disaster for Leycester. He was in his fifties, old according to the span of life of that time ; he was worn out, and already had the illness from which he was to die.

On the 23rd of September 1586, an ambuscade was prepared by Sir John Norreys and others to intercept the Spanish troops who were about to force their way into the city of Zutphen with provisions for many months of siege until it could be relieved.

There had been a heavy fog ; this lifted suddenly and the Queen's forces found themselves only a few paces from the Spanish forces, six times their number. Sir John Norreys — 'Black Norreys' — son of the Queen's old friend the 'Crow', and another of the commanders, Sir William Stanley, had, for about a month, disliked each other. But now Sir John shouted across to Stanley, 'There hath been ill-blood between us. Let us be friends together this day, and die side by side, if need be, in Her Majesty's cause.'

Stanley shouted in reply : 'Living or dead, I will stand or lie by you in friendship'.

Philip Sidney saw that another officer, Pelham, had insufficient armour. He threw across to him his own steel thigh-pieces, and so came to his death. For he was, Leycester wrote, wounded 'with a musket shot upon his thigh three fingers above his knee, a very dangerous wound, the bone being broken in pieces'.

When he was brought a cup of water, he asked that it should be given to another of the wounded, a private soldier who was groaning with thirst as he was carried away.

'O Philip,' Leycester said to his nephew, 'I am sorry for thy hurt' ; and, according to Stowe, Sir Philip answered, 'O my Lord, thus have I done to your honour and Her Majesty's service'. Sir William Russell coming to him, kissed his hand and said with tears, 'O noble Sir Philip, there was never man attayned hurt more honourably than ye have done, nor any served like unto you'. The fighting continued for over an hour, Sidney leading the charge against the Spaniards though his thigh was crushed. He would not leave the field until two thousand Spaniards came from the city, so that the victory was theirs.

It was thought that he might recover ; but eleven days after the battle, he died in the arms, not of the unworthy woman who had inspired some of the greatest lyrics in the language, but of his wife.

On the 6th of October Leycester had been appointed one of the Commissioners to try Mary Queen of Scots. He sailed for England with Drake in his flagship on the 23rd of November. It was almost a year since he had seen the Queen.

He went to Bath, in the hope of being cured of the mortal illness which had seized upon him, but on the 6th of July 1587 he returned to the States, in the vain hope of restoring some order there.

After so much misfortune he could not foresee the triumph over the Armada — those last days of his life in which, once more, he had the friendship of his Queen, as when they were young and had thought that happiness lay before them.

## NOTE TO CHAPTER FIFTY-FIVE

The information contained in this chapter owes much to Mr. Frederick Chamberlin's *Elizabeth and Leycester*.

# Chapter Fifty-six

ON a day in June 1588, the Lord Treasurer received the following letter :

'Rt honourable and my very good lord,
   '. . . At our being at sea we had divers intelligences ; but specially, one of most importance, which is a hulk, which came from St. Lucar six weeks past, and on her way homewards saw this day . . . a great fleet of ships which came from Lishbourne, having the wind northerlie and so coming to the westwards ; which the skipper and his company judge to be the great fleet that the King of Spayne hath made ready : for that they saw so many as they could not number them. . . .
   'It is to be looked for that either we shall heare of them very shortly, or else they will go to the Groyne, and there assemble themselves, and make their full rendez-vous. . . .
   'Thus humblie taking my leave of your good lordship, I dailie pray to God to bless Her Majestie and to give us Grace to feare Him.   So shall we not need to doubt the enemie, though they be many.
   'From aboard her Majesty's good shipp The Revenge, ryding in Plymouth Sound.
   'This VII day of June 1588
      'Your good lordship's very ready to be commanded :
                                                      Fr. Drake.'

Then came a pause.   Then an English pirate showed that he loved England more than his life.
   According to John Smith, the founder of Virginia, this man, whose name was Fleming, was 'as much saught for as

any pirate of the Queen's reign, yet such a friend to his country, that discovering the Spanish Armada, he voluntarily came to Plymouth, yielded himself freely to the Lord Admirall, and gave him notice of the Spaniards coming ; which good warning came so happily and unexpectedly that he had his pardon, and a good reward'.

'At length off the Lizard', wrote Camden, the English 'descried the Spanish ships, with lofty turrets, like castles in front like a half moon, the wings thereof spreading out about the length of seven miles, sailing very slowly, though with full sales, the winds being, as it were, tired with carrying them, and the ocean groaning with them.'

'This Navie', according to the account of one prisoner, 'was esteemed by the King himselfe to containe 32000 persons, and to cost him every day thirty thousand ducats. . . .'

'The generall of this mightie Navie', says Hakluyt, 'was Don Alonzo Perez de Guzman, duke of Medina Sidonia, Lord of St. Lucar, and Knight of the Golden Fleece. Don Martinez de Ricalde was Admirall of the Fleete.

'Francis Bovadilla was Chiefe Marshall. . . . Likewise Martin Alarcón was appointed Vicar Generall of the Inquisition, being accompanied by more than a hundred Monkes, to wit Jesuits, Capuchines, and friars mendicant. . . .

'There were 124 very noble and worthy gentlemen, which went voluntarily of their owne cists and charges, to the end they might scc fashions, learne experience, and attaine unto glorie. Amongst whom was the Prince of Ascolo.*

'Many potentates, princes, and honourable personages hied themselves : out of Spaine the Prince of Melito called the Duke of Pastiano and taken to be the sonne of Pergames de Silva, but in very deed accounted among the number of King Philip's base sonnes. Also the Marques of Burgrave, one of the sonnes of Archduke Ferdinand and Philippa Welsera, Vespasian Gonzaga of the family of Mantua, being for chivalry a man of first renowne, and therefore Vice-roy in Spaine. Item John Medices base sonne unto the Duke of

* By report — the illegitimate son of the King.

Florence.   And Amadas of Savoy, the Duke of Savoy his base sonne, with many others of inferior degrees.'

The Spanish royal standard floated at the fore of the Commander-in-Chief's ship; at the main was a flag on which was painted a crucifix between the figures of Our Lady and St. Mary Magdalen.   Hundreds of banners fluttered from the whole fleet — each ship bearing the flag of its province, Naples, Andalusia, those of the nobles and Knights, and those of the Saints to whom the ships were dedicated.

The appearance of the crews and their officers was as gallant as that of the ships they manned.   Some of the sailors wore armour ;   others quilted coats (mainly of white and green) as a protection against the cannon.   The nobles wore white satin or camlet beneath their armour, ruffs, gold lace, and silk stockings.

Almost eighteen months before this time, Admiral Sir William Winter (he of the unaccountable inspiration, amounting almost to monomania, that bade him, twenty-four years previously, attack the French ships arriving at Scotland) wrote to the principal officer, 'Our ships doth [sic] show themselves like gallants here.   I assure you it will do a man's heart good to behold them.'

This huge advancing procession was first seen, off the Lizard, by an English fishing-boat that, with great daring, circled round it, counting the numbers.   The Spaniards pursued them, but the boat escaped and vanished.   Then fire on fire, from end to end of the coast, warned England of her danger.

The English Fleet awaited the enemy.

'On Sunday the 21st of July 1588 * the English ships that were come out of Plymouth had recovered wind of the Spaniards two leagues to the westward of Eddystone, and about 9 of the clock in the morning, the Lord Admiral sent his pinnace, named the Disdain, to give the Duke of Medina

---

* A Relation of Proceeding, B.M. Cotton. Julius. F. X pp. 111-17. No date, title, signature, or endorsement.   A neat, clerkly, contemporary writing.

defiance, and afterwards in the Ark bare up with the Admiral of the Spaniards [sic] wherein the Duke was supposed to be, and fought with her until she was rescued by divers ships of the Spanish army. In the meantime Sir Francis Drake, Sir John Hawkyns, and Sir Martin Frobisher [sic] fought with the galleon of Portugal wherein Don Martinez de Ricalde, vice-admiral, was supposed to be. The fight was so well maintained for the time, that the enemy was constrained to give way and to bear up room to the eastward, in which, bearing up, a great galleon, wherein Don Pedro de Valdes was captain, became foul of another ship which spoiled and bare overboard his foremast and bowsprit, whereby he could not keep company with their fleet, but being with great dishonour left behind by the Duke, fell into our hands. . . .

'This Monday being the 22nd of July, the Spaniards abandoned the ship that the day before was spoiled by fire, to the which His Lordship sent the Lord Thomas Howard and Sir John Hawkyns, knight, who together, in a small skiff of the Victory's went aboard her — where they saw a most miserable sight — the deck of the ship fallen down, the steerage broken, the stern blown out, and about 50 poor creatures burnt with powder in most miserable sort. The stink in the ship was so unsavoury, and the sight within board so ugly, that the Lord Thomas Howard and Sir John Hawkyns departed and came unto the Lord Admiral to inform His Lordship in what case she was found.'

'The two and twentie of July [1] Sir Francis Drake espied Valdez his shippe, whereunto hee sent forth his pinnasse, and . . . sent him word that he should yeeld himselfe. Valdez for his honor's sake caused certaine conditions to be propounded unto Drake : who answered Valdez that he was not now at leisure to make any long parley but if he would yeelde himselfe he should find him friendly and tractible : howbeit if he had resolved to die in fight, he should proove Drake to be no dastard.

'Then Valdez with 40 or 50 noblemen and gentlemen came on board Sir Francis Drake's ship. . . .

'Valdez comming unto Drake and humbly kissing his hand protested to him that he and his had resolved to die in battell, had they not by good fortune fallen into his power, whom they knew to be right curteous and gentle, and whom they had heard by generall report to bee most favourable to his vanquished foe : insomuch that he sayd it was to be doubted whether his enemies had more cause to admire and love him for his great, valiant, and prosperous exploites, or to dread him for his singular felicitie and wisedom, which ever attended upon him in the warres, and by the which he had attained unto so great honour.   With which Drake embraced him and gave him very honourable entertainment, feeding him at his owne table, and lodging him in his cabbin . . .

'The same day was set on fire one of their greatest shippes, being . . . the shippe of Michael de Oquendo Vice-Admirall of the whole Fleete, which contained great storre of gunne powder and other warre like provision.   The upper part only of the shippe was burnt, and all the persons therein contained (except a few) were consumed by fire.

'. . . On Tuesday (the 23rd of July) . . . was the most furious and bloodie skirmish of all, in which the Lord Admirall of England continued fighting amidst his enemies' Fleete, and seeing one of his Captaines afarre off, hee spake unto him in these wordes : oh George, what doest thou ?   Wilt thou now frustrate my hope and opinion conceived of thee ?   Wilt thou forsake mee nowe ?   With which wordes hee being inflamed, approached foorthwith, encountered the enemie, and did the part of a most valiant Captaine. . . .'

The Armada made for Calais.   But this was to be no refuge.

On the 27th of July, the Queen was informed, '. . . it was resolved some exploit should be attempted the night following by fire, which was performed, and what distress came thereof we know not'.

Sir William Winter was amongst the sallors who had counselled this.

'Sir Henry Palmer', he told Walsingham, 'was assigned to bear over, presently, in a pinnace for Dover, to bring away such vessels as were fit to be fired, and materials apt to take fire. . . . About 12 of the clock that night, six [actually there were eight] ships were brought . . . and going, in a front, having the wind and tide with them, and their ordnance being charged, were fired; and the men that were the executors, so soon as the fire was made, they did abandon the ships, and entered into the five boats that were appointed for the saving of them. This matter did put such terror among the Spanish army that they were fain to let slip their cables and anchors; and did work, as it did appear, great mischief among them by reason of the suddenness of it, we might perceive that there were two great fires more than ours, and far greater and huger than any of our vessels that we fired did make.'

The enormous apparitions of what had once been the pride of Spain lumbered into the open ocean, harried by their enemy. The ocean rose against them, a hurricane swept them before it, a universal darkness descended from the skies. 'For months afterwards', wrote Roeder, in a superb passage, 'phantom vessels were sighted off the coast of Ireland, of Scotland, of Denmark, roaming aimlessly in search of a Spain that had vanished in the general vertigo.'

Some of the galleons were wrecked off the Irish coast. The bodies of the drowned were swallowed by the sea or drifted to land. The body of the young Prince of Ascolo, reputed to be Philip's son, floated through those mist-white waters like a swan — sailing onward in a doublet and breeches of white satin, with stockings of russet silk.

NOTE TO CHAPTER FIFTY-SIX

1 Hakluyt, vol. iv.

# Chapter Fifty-seven

IT was some time before England knew that the Armada was utterly defeated, was in full flight to the north, past the Dutch coast. The Queen received two letters from Drake saying that he believed the ships had only gone to Denmark to refit, and begging her not to dismiss the forces.

On the contrary, fresh forces arrived at Tilbury, and on the 24th of July 1588 the Queen appointed Leycester Lieutenant and Captain General of the Queen's Armies and Companies, awaiting the attack at Tilbury.

According to 'the Churchwarden's "accompt"' at Lambeth, it had been 'a pleasant sight to behold the soldiers as they marched towards Tilbury, their cheerful countenances, corregious wordes and gestures, dauncing and leaping wheresoever they came, and in the campe their most felicitie was to hope to fight with the enemie, where oft times rumours ran of their foes' approach, and that present battell would be given them, they were as joyfull at such newes as if lustie giants were to run a race'.

On the 9th of August, the Queen arrived to review her troops.

Next day, as she was sitting at dinner with Leycester in his tent, the news was brought her that Parma and his army had embarked, and that the invasion of England must be expected at any moment.

It was customary for a monarch to be surrounded by guards, to avoid the danger of assassination. But the Queen, reviewing her troops, had for her only guards four men and two boys.

First came the Earl of Ormonde, bearing the great sword

of State, then a page dressed in white velvet, carrying the Queen's silver helmet with its white plume ; then a second boy, also dressed in white velvet, and leading by a white strap the Queen's charger.

The Queen wore a silver corslet over her white velvet dress, and held a truncheon in her hand. Leycester rode on her right, his stepson Essex on her left. Both wore armour. Behind them walked Sir John Norreys, the son of the Queen's old friend the 'Crow'.

Elizabeth's speech to the soldiers — they numbered from four to five thousand (Camden was incorrect in saying they amounted to 23,000)—ran thus :

'My loving people,
'We have been persuaded by some that are careful of our safety, to take heed how we commit ourselves to armed multitudes, for fear of treachery : but I assure you, I do not desire to live in distrust of my faithful and loving people. Let tyrants fear. I have always so behaved myself that under God, I have placed my chiefest strength and goodwill in the loyal hearts and goodwill of my subjects ; and therefore I am come amongst you, as you see, at this time, not for my recreation and disport, but being resolved, in the midst and heat of the battle, to live or die amongst you all ; to lay down for God, for my kingdom, and for my people, my honour and my blood, even in the dust. I know I have but the body of a weak and feeble woman ; but I have the heart and stomach of a King, and of a King of England too, and think it foul scorn that Parma or Spain or any Prince of Europe, should dare to invade the borders of my realm ; to which, rather than any dishonour should grow by me, I myself will take up arms, I myself will be General, Judge, and Rewarder of every one of your virtues in the field.

'I know already for your forwardness you have deserved rewards and crowns ; and we do assure you, on the word of a Prince, they shall be duly paid you. In the meantime, my Lieutenant General shall be in my stead, than whom never

Prince commanded a more noble or worthy subject ; not doubting but that by your obedience to my General, by your concord in the camp and your valour in the field, we shall shortly have a famous victory over these enemies of my God, of my Kingdom, and of my People.'

So spoke the woman who had once said to the Archbishop of St. Andrews (after the death of the Scottish regent Morton), 'I am more afraid of making a fault in my Latin than of the Kings of Spain, France, Scotland, the whole house of Guise, and all their confederates. I have the heart of a man, not of a woman, and I am not afraid of anything.'

The speech was received with thunderous cheers.

There were, for Elizabeth and Leycester, a few short weeks in which, perhaps, they relived their youth. But death was soon to take possession of the man (old before his time, whose beauty and pride of bearing had long since deserted him), and of the Queen's heart. On the 7th of September a spy, writing to Spain 'advices from England',[1] said, 'For the last few months, he' (Leycester) 'has usually dined with the Queen, a thing they say, such as has never been seen in this country before'. And in the same letter, the King of Spain's correspondent said he had 'seen the Earl going all through the city accompanied by as many gentlemen as if he were a King and followed by his household and a troop of light horse'.

He was 'going from a country house of his [at Wanstead] to St. James, and was quite alone in his coach. He had gone there a few days before on horseback, even more splendidly accompanied, and showed every appearance of health, as if he would have lived for years.' . . . But that look of health was transitory. In a last desperate effort to regain it, he travelled to Buxton. He was not to reach it.

On the 29th of August, at a place near Thame in Oxford, he wrote to his Queen :

'I most humbly beseech Your Majesty to pardon your old servant to be thus bold in sending to know how my gracious

Lady doth and what ease of her pain she finds, being the chiefest thing in the world I do pray for, for her to have good health and long life. For my own poor case, I continue still your medicine and it amends much better than any other thing that hath been given me.

'I am hoping to find perfect cure at the bath. With the continuance of my wonted prayer for Your Majesty's most happy preservation, I humbly kiss your foot — from your old lodging at Rycott' (this is a reference to the fact that she stayed there on her journey to Woodstock, with her gaoler Bedingfield, after the Wyatt rebellion and her release from the Tower) 'this Thursday morning by Your Majesty's most faithful and obedient servant,

R. Leycester.'

On Wednesday, the 4th of September, at ten in the morning, he died.

Ten days after his death, it was reported she was so grieved that for some days she shut herself in her chamber alone, and refused to speak to anyone until the Treasurer and the other Councillors had the door broken open.

For, although her heart was now alone for ever, that solitude must be endured amongst the exulting crowds, on her return from the Service of Thanksgiving for the defeat of the Armada — the shouts of rejoicing and of loving loyalty towards the Queen, the thousands of flags. For was she not married to her kingdom ?

After her death, in the little box covered with pearls in which she kept her rings, and that stood beside her bed, a letter was found on which, under the direction, she had written

'His last Letter'.

.        .        .        .        .

Lady Leycester did not repine unduly. Within a year of her husband's death, she married Sir Christopher Blount, who had been Leycester's Master of the Horse in the Netherlands.

At the time of the marriage, she was forty-nine and he twenty-four years old.

Both her son, Essex, and Blount, her new husband, were executed after the Essex revolt.

This old rag of an outworn splendour, this old traitor to the heart, this mother of the beloved of that singing flame Sir Philip Sidney, lived until she was ninety-four. At the age of ninety-two, she could be seen, every morning, walking from her house in Drayton Bassett, 'for a full mile'.[2]

### NOTES TO CHAPTER FIFTY-SEVEN

[1] C. E. S. P. Simancas, 10. 420.
[2] Chamberlin, *Elizabeth and Leycester.*

# Chapter Fifty-eight

THE summer sun shone as brilliantly as ever on Queen and courtier, in her Progresses ; but there were moments now when she felt a little cold, as if age had chilled her hot blood. What could that shadow be, that stood between her and the sun ? — a shadow lonely in his state (though all the world should come to him) as she was in hers.

The shadow of Death ? — Death coming to beings beloved by her, as, soon, he would come to her ? He had played with her, when she was a little child, in the heat of the day. Then that shadow had gone again. . . . Now it seemed as if he had returned, and watched her silently. But why ? Her heart was already in his keeping.

Now, in 1597, as she sat at her writing-table, with the two silver cabinets in which she kept her paper, and which she used as writing-boxes, she thought of the happy visit, five years before, she had paid to that dear familiar friend to whom she was now writing — that friend whom she was in the habit of calling 'My Crow' because of the blackness of her hair and the darkness of her complexion — and to that friend's husband, Lord Norreys, son of the Henry Norreys executed as one of Queen Anne Boleyn's supposed paramours.

Lord Norreys, grown old, had met the Queen at the door of his house, and greeted her by saying that, although he was past the age of martial deeds, 'my house, my armour, my shield, my sword, the riches of a young soldier, and an old soldier's relics, I should here offer to Your Highness, but my four boys have stolen them from me, vowing themselves to arms'. ('My helmet now shall make a hive for bees.')

Of those four sons, Sir John Norreys was then commanding the English forces in France, Sir Edward was serving in the Netherlands, the other two in Ireland.

'The rumour of their deaths', the old man continued, 'hath so often affrighted the Crow, my wife, that her heart hath been as black as her feathers. I know not whether it be affection or fondness [foolishness] but the Crow thinketh her own birds the fairest, because to her the dearest. What joys we both conceive, neither can express ; suffice it they be as your virtues, infinite. And although nothing can be more unfit to lodge Your Majesty than a Crow's nest, yet shall it be most happy to us that it is, by Your Highness, made a phoenix nest.'

It was summer then, and the sun was warm. Years ago.

And now, in her handwriting beautiful and elegant as the marks made by the waterfly on smooth waters, she was writing a letter to Sir John's mother telling her of the Queen's grief for her.

He who, when in France, had 'brought off a small handfull of English from a great armfull of enemies, fighting as he retreated, and retreating as he fought', transferred to Ireland, 'where supplies, sown thick as promises, came up thin in performances, so slowly were necessities sent unto him', found that he must 'fight with left-handed foes . . . who could lye on the coldest earth, swim through the deepest water, run over what was neither earth nor water, I mean bogs and marshes . . .'.

(Surley boy, on the shore, wringing his hands and weeping, 'like to run mad for sorrow', watching, with his followers, their defenceless wives and children massacred on the blood-stained island. . . . The light of the rising sun on the soldier's brow, like the mark of Cain.) *

'The news reached him [Norreys] that a great lord of the opposite party was preferred over him to be made lieutenant of Ireland. Then, this working soul broke out the case of his body, as wanting a vent for his grief and anger, and, going up into his chamber, at the first hearing of the news, he suddenly died, Anno 1597.'

* See Appendix H.

'Mine own dear Crow', wrote the Queen.

'Although we have deferred long to represent unto you our grieved thoughts, because we liked full ill to yield you the first reflections of our misfortunes, whom we have always sought to cherish and comfort, yet knowing now that necessity must bring it to your ears, and nature consequently must raise many passionate workings in your heart, we have resolved no longer to smother either our care for your sorrow, or the sympathy of our grief for his death ; wherein, if society in sorrowing work any diminution, we do assure you, by this true messenger of our mind, that nature can have stirred no more dolorous affection in you, as a mother for a dear son, than the grateful memory of his services past hath wrought in us, his sovereign, apprehension of the miss of so worthy a servant.

'But now that nature's common work is done, and he that was born to die hath paid his tribute, let that Christian discretion stay the flow of your immoderate grieving, which hath instructed you, both by example and knowledge, that nothing of this kind hath happened but by God's providence, and that these lines from your loving and gracious sovereign serve to assure you that there shall ever remain the lively character of you and yours that are left, in valuing rightly all their faithful and honest endeavours.

'More at this time I will not write of this subject, but have despatched this gentleman to visit both your lord and to condole with you in the true sense of our love, and to pray you, that the world may see that what time cureth in weak minds, that discretion and moderation help you in this accident, where there is so opportune occasion to demonstrate true patience and moderation.'

Ripeness is all. . . .

Blanche Parry, old and blind, — she who had once learned necromancy from her cousin, Dr. Dee, had died, in 1590. . . . She had been with the Queen since the latter was a child, had lived with her during the terrible days following Admiral Seymour's execution — in the still more terrible days when, in the time of Queen Mary, she had kept Death at bay.

The foxy astute Walsingham, longing for death because of the pain that consumed him, — he, too, had gone to his peace.

In the winter of 1591 Sir Christopher Hatton, the kindly, loyal, rather foolish person who, her Vice-Chamberlain for many years, then her Lord Chancellor, had truly loved her, died at Ely House, whose rent, paid to Bishop Cox (to whom the house had belonged, but from whom the Queen had wrested it, by means of threats), was a red rose for the Gatehouse and garden, to be paid each Midsummer Day.

The extravagance laid on Hatton through his high offices was great, and at his death he owed the Queen fifty-six thousand pounds.

'When he could not raise money, the Queen probably reproached him with her kindness. But she was in despair at his death. He was the Keeper of the Queen's conscience, and when she reproached him it sank to his heart.'

It is, indeed, said that he died of a broken heart. Accused of being a mere mushroom of the Court, 'that sprang up at night and sank again at his noon — it broke his heart that the Queen (who seldom gave *boons*, and *never forgave due debts*) vigorously demanded the payment of some arrears, which Sir Christopher did not hope to have remitted, but did only hope to be forborne . . . and this cast him into a mortal disease. The Queen afterwards did endeavour what she could to recover him, bringing, as some say, cordial broths unto him with her own hands; but all would not do. Thus no pullies can draw up a heart cast down, though a Queen herself set her heart thereto.

'He was reputed to be a man of pious nature, a great reliever of the poor, of singular bounty and munificence to students and learned men (for which reason those of Oxford chose him as their Chancellor of their University), and one who in the execution of the office of Lord Chancellor could satisfy his conscience in the constant integrity of his endeavours to do all with right and equity.'

In a Jesuit pamphlet that was found, written by Father

Parsons, under the name of Andrew Philopater, it was said that Hatton 'departed very unwillingly from his life on the very day that the edict against the Jesuits and seminary priests was published, which he was said to have resisted as long as he lived and would never have assented to, partly because, being a more moderate man, he would not have approved such cruelty, partly because he differed so heartily from Cecil and the Puritans, to whom Cecil showed patronage, nor would he that they should be increased to oppressing of the Catholics. Hence arose that suspicion of poison for his removal which was written in divers letters from England.'

(And yet — he was foremost in the prosecution of Parry, the only member of Parliament who was brave enough to oppose the Bill against Jesuits and seminary priests ; and he said to Ballard 'thy religio Catholica ?   nay, rather it is diabolica'.

But he may, of course, have been acting against men whom he truly believed to be would-be murderers.)

Five years later, in 1596, Lord Hunsdon, 'who neither was wise nor seemed wise', 'being sick to death, saw come to him, one after another, six of his companions, already dead.   The first was Dudley, Earl of Leycester, all on fire ; the second, secretary Walsingham, also in fire and flames ;   Puckering [the Lord Keeper] so cold and frozen, that touching Hunsdon's hand, he thought he should die of cold.   Then came Sir Christopher Hatton, lord chancellor, Heneage, and Sir Francis Knollys, all flaming, and standing round Hunsdon's bed told him to prepare to join them, with Cecil, who was, as yet, alive.'

Lord Hunsdon affirmed on oath that he saw these, sent word to Cecil of the message they had delivered for him, and in a few hours died.[1]

The shadow had fallen.   Soon the Queen would be alone.


NOTE TO CHAPTER FIFTY-EIGHT

[1] This story was quoted by Dr. Johnson in 'Purgatory proved by Miracles'.

# Chapter Fifty-nine

ON the 10th of May 1591, Her Majesty paid a long visit to the Lord Treasurer at Theobald's — involving him, of course, in the usual gigantic expense, and his household in the inevitable worry.

Finding him (according to Harrison's *Journal* of the 21st of that month) very melancholy, she 'caused to be delivered to "the disconsolate and retired Sprite"' (for she was in the habit of addressing him, in affectionate raillery, as 'Sir Spirit', or 'Sir Sprite') '"the eremite [hermit] of Theobald's, a charter giving him leave to retire to his old cave, and abjuring desolations and mournings to the frozen seas and deserts of Arabia Petraea". Amongst the shows there presented [at Theobald's] was a conference between a gentleman usher and a post [courier ?] pretending to deliver letters from the Emperor of China. At her departure yesterday, she knighted Mr. Robert Cecil, the Treasurer's younger son, whom some expected to be advanced to the Secretaryship ; but in the Court it is said that the Knighthood must serve for both.'

There the Court was wrong. Business-like, snub-nosed, slightly deformed Sir Robert, so satisfactory a son to his father, so worthy a recipient of his father's maxims and counsels, was soon to succeed his parent as the Queen's chief secretary. Lord Burleigh had every cause to be satisfied with his children's advancement in life, brought about by his ceaseless care and forethought.

The Lord Treasurer bore, one supposes, the ten days during which Her Majesty untiringly cheered his spirits, with his usual patience. But he was beginning to feel his age, — was becoming a little testy. And in five years from that time

(on the 13th of March 1596), according to Harrison's *Elizabethan Journal*, 'The old Lord Treasurer, upon some pet,
would needs away against her [the Queen's] will on Thursday
last, saying that her business was ended ; and that he would
for ten days go take physic. When the Queen saw it booted
not to stay him, she said he was a froward old fool.'

His cruelty, too, had begun to grow on him. A month
before that time (on the 11th of February), 'Five men called
Nixen, Pepper, Ellis, Johnson, and Anglesey, that had counter-
feited the hands of the Lord Treasurer and others of the
Council, were sentenced today in the Star Chamber. The
first three are sentenced to stand in the pillory and lose their
ears, and be branded on the forehead with an F and condemned perpetually to the galleys. Johnson suffereth the same ;
but Anglesey, inasmuch as he wrote the names fearing lest
Johnson would stab him, to the pillory and imprisonment
only. The Lord Treasurer moveth that since such burnings
die out in a short time, they should be scarified on the cheeks
with the letter F by a surgeon, and that some powder be put
there to colour it so that it would never vanish ; but the
others' [I suppose the Judges are meant] 'made no reply to
this.' [1] Used as they were to perpetrating the most horrible
cruelties, this suggestion apparently disgusted even the most
hardened.

The year 1596 was one in which, watching her Lord
Treasurer's increasing feebleness, Elizabeth, also, was made
aware that old age spares not even a Queen.

The Bishop of St. David's preached before the Court, on
Good Friday, a most unhappy sermon ! 'Taking as his text
the lines "O teach us to number our days, that we incline our
hearts unto wisdom", the Bishop went on to speak of some
sacred and mystical numbers, as three for the Trinity, three
times three for the Heavenly Hierarchy, seven for the Sabbath,
seven times seven for a Jubilee, and, lastly, seven times nine
for the Grand Climacterical.' [2]

This was too much. The Queen would, in September,
reach the age referred to !

The Bishop could not but be aware, 'for the pulpit standeth vis-à-vis to her Closet', that he had gone too far, so hastened to 'retire upon . . . more plausible numbers', such as the Number 666, 'with which, said he, he could prove the Pope to be Anti-Christ; also of the fatal number 88, which being so long before spoken of as a dangerous year, yet it hath pleased God not only to preserve her but to give her a famous victory against the united forces of Rome and Spain'.

But then, falling once more, unfortunately, under the spell of his own eloquence, he ended with the following prayer, as if spoken by Her Majesty in person :

'Oh Lord, I am now entered a good way into the climacterical year of mine age, which mine enemies wish and hope to be fatal unto me.'  And he ended the prayer with these words : 'Lord, I have now put foot within the doors of that age in which the almond tree flourisheth, wherein men begin to carry a calculation within their bones, the senses begin to fail, the strength to diminish, yea all the powers of the body decay.  Now therefore grant me grace that though mine outward man thus perish yet my inner man may be renewed daily.  So direct me with Thy Holy Spirit that I may daily wax elder in godliness, wisdom being my gray hairs and undefiled life mine old age.'

The Queen, opening the door of her closet, instead of giving him thanks 'or good countenance', told him that he would have done better 'to keep his arithmetic to himself !' '"But I see", said she, "the greatest clerks are not the wisest men."  With which the Queen went away discontented, and the Lord Keeper hath commanded him to keep his house.'

The sermon, however, had told on her, and although next day she ordered his release, and 'rebuked one of her ladies who spoke scornfully of him, she said she "thanked God that neither her stomach nor strength, nor her voice for singing, nor fingering for instruments, nor lastly her sight was any whit decayed".  And to prove the last before the Courtiers, she produced a little jewel that hath an inscription of very small letters.  She offered it first to my lord of Worcester and

then to Sir James Crofts to read, and both protested bona
fide they could not.  Yet the Queen herself did find out the
posy and made herself merry with the standers-by upon it.'

But the wrinkles were falling, faster and faster, soundless
as snowflakes.  And now there were no mirrors in the Palace.


### NOTES TO CHAPTER FIFTY-NINE

1 Harrison, *Elizabethan Journal*.
2 Harrison, *op. cit.*

# Chapter Sixty

In the year before the Armada, a new favourite had risen to power — Robert Devereux, Earl of Essex, the son of the Queen's hated cousin, the Countess of Leycester.

Essex's mother, Lady Leycester, and his sister Penelope, were of an equal unpleasantness, false, sly, arrogant, and alternating between insolence and cringing. We must be grateful to Penelope for inspiring some of the most wonderful love-lyrics in our language, addressed to her under the name of Stella by Sir Philip Sidney. Great men have loved unworthy women, then as now.

Essex shared their insolence, and, to some degree, their falsity. From one angle, one might see his nature as that of a born gigolo — (but with this fault, not as a rule possessed by gigolos, that he totally misunderstood the character of the old, great woman on whom he battened). But he had, also, a noble side. He was fantastically brave, and he *could* be loyal — though not to his benefactress, — only to his friends. He had great beauty of person.

Essex accepted every bounty from his Queen. When aged twenty-four, in spite of his huge properties, he owed £23,000, and in a letter to the Queen's Vice-Chamberlain, — meant, of course, to be repeated to her — he said 'the Queen had given him so much, he dared not ask her for more'.

For years brother and sister carried on a secret correspondence with King James of Scotland, Lady Rich being the actual writer. She called herself by the name of Rialta, King James was named Victor, the Queen, in insolent mockery, Venus, and Essex the Weary Knight, because, his sister said, he was 'exceeding weary, accounting it a terrible thrall that he now lives in, and wishes the change'. . . . In other words, he wished for the death of his benefactress. Essex seems, indeed, to have been unhappy — or at least discontented — at Court. An undated letter from him is quoted in Maud Stepney Rawson's *Penelope Rich and her Circle* : 'Dear Sister, because I will not be in your debt by sending you a footman, I have directed the bearer to you to bring mee news how you do. I am melancholy, merry, sometimes happy, and often discontented. The Court is of so many humours as the rainbow hath colours. The time wherein we live is more inconstant than women's thoughts, more miserable than old age itself, and breedeth both people and occasions like myself, that is, violent, desperate, and fantastical. Myself for wondering at other men's adventures, have no leisure to follow the ways of mine own heart, but by still resolving not to be proud of any good that can come, because it is by the favour of chance ; nor do (I) throw down my mind a whit, for any ill that shall happen, because I see that all fortunes are good or evil, as they are esteemed. . . .

Your brother that dearly loves you

R. Essex.'

Reading that letter, it is possible to pity him.

Elizabeth's affection for her young cousin has been, probably, vastly distorted. It was not, the present writer believes, an unpleasant infatuation of an old, vain woman for a young man. The lonely Queen, constantly mourning secretly for her childless state — that state that not only left her alone, but threatened dangers to her kingdom — saw in him, perhaps, the son that she might have had.

She loved the sight of youth, and she loved children. Of the latter there are pathetic instances, such as that of which Richard Brakebury wrote to Lord Talbot : [1]

'If I should write how much her Majesty this day did make of the little lady your daughter, with often kissing, which Her Majesty seldom useth to any, and then amending with pins, and still carrying her with Her Majesty in her own barge, and so unto the privy lodgings and so homeward . . .

you would scarce believe me. Her Majesty said (as true it is) that she is very like my Lady her grandmother. She behaved herself with such modesty as I pray God she may possess at twenty years old. . . .' She was kind, too, to little Lady Arabella Stuart (this may have been partly to instil fears into the child's cousin King James, as to the succession). The little girl being then not quite twelve years old, the Queen sent for her to Court, gave her a place at her table when she dined in public, and gave her precedence above all the Countesses.

On the 25th of August 1587, the French Ambassador l'Aubespine told, in his despatch, that the Queen had called the attention of his wife, who had dined with her a few days previously, to the child. 'After dinner, the Queen being in a lofty grand hall with Madame l'Aubespine de Chasteauneuf, and all the countesses and maids of honour near her, and surrounded by a crowd of gentlemen, Her Majesty asked the ambassadress "if she had noticed a little girl, her relation, who was there?" and called the said Arabella to her. Madame de Chasteauneuf said much in her commendation, remarked how well she spoke French, and that she "appeared very sweet and gracious".

"'Regard her well", replied the Queen, "for she is not as simple as you may think. One day, she will be even as I am, and will be lady-mistress ; but I shall have been before her."'

That kindness may, of course, have been partly for reasons of policy. But the kindness was there.

Unfortunately, her Majesty's love of youth did not always extend to her maids of honour, whom she would, from time to time, reward for services ill-performed with a buffet.

But to return to Essex.

In 1589 Don Antonio, the titular King of Portugal, was at the English Court, asking for the Queen's aid in expelling the Spaniards from Portugal, and restoring him to his kingdom.

The youth of England had not forgiven the Armada, and

the final plea of Parliament, on dissolving, was that it might please the Queen to send an expedition against Spain. She replied that she was too poor to bear the burden herself, but her brave subjects were welcome to fit out an armament for the liberation of Portugal from the Spanish yoke, provided they would do it at their own expense. She promised to lend them ships of war.

In consequence, Drake and others sailed from Portsmouth to Lisbon on the 18th of April — the Queen having subscribed £6000. But the Queen did not know that the discontented Essex had slipped away from Court and joined the fleet. She sent orders for his return, but it was too late.

According to Strickland, he was the first to leave the boats, and wading through the sea, up to his shoulders, joined in the attack on the Castle of Peniche. After the surrender of the Castle, Sir John Norreys, general in charge of the expedition, 'advanced as far as to take the suburbs of Lisbon ; but the King of Morocco failing to send his promised aid, the Portuguese being languid and unenthusiastic, and the ammunition on the ships being insufficient, the expedition failed'. But Essex, advancing to the gates of Lisbon, 'beat a thundering summons there, and challenged the Governor to come out and encounter him in single combat'. There was no response.

He showed an equal bravery at the battle of Zutphen, in which Sir Philip Sidney was mortally wounded, and at the siege of Rouen.

.        .        .        .        .

At home, Her Majesty was showing an increasing irritability to those in attendance upon her. 'Her Highness', Mr. Fenton wrote to Sir John Harington, 'spake vehemently, and with great wrath, of her servant Lady Mary Howard forasmuch as she had refused to bear her mantle at the hour her Highness is wont to air in the garden, and on small rebuke, did vent such unseemly answer as did breed great choler in her mistress. Again, on another occasion, she was not ready to carry the cup of grace during the dinner in the privy chamber, nor was she attending the hour of her Majesty's going to prayer ; all of which doth now so disquiet her Highness, that she swore she would no more show her any countenance, but out with all such ungracious, flouting wenches ; because, forsooth, she hath much favour and marks of love from the young earl' [Essex had by this time returned to Court] 'which is not so pleasing to the Queen, who doth still exhort all her women to remain in the virgin state as much as may be. I adventured to say, so far as discretion did go, in defence of our friend . . . which did nothing to soothe her Highness's anger, who said "I have made her my servant, and she will now make herself my mistress ; but in good faith, William, she shall not, and so tell her ". . . .

'It might not be amiss to talk to this poor young lady to be more dutiful, and not absent at prayers and meals : to bear her Highness's mantle, and other furniture, even more than all the rest of the servants, to make ample amends by future diligence, and always to go first in the morning to her Highness's chamber, forasmuch as such kindness will much prevail to turn away all former displeasure. She must not entertain my lord the earl in any conversation, but shun his company ; and, moreover, be less careful in attiring her person, for this seemeth as more done to win the earl than her mistress's good will.

'If we consider the favours shown her family, there is ground for ill-humour in the Queen, who doth not now bear with such composed spirit as she was wont, but since the Irish affairs seemeth more froward than commonly she used to bear herself towards her women ; nor doth she hold them in discourse with such familiar matters, but often she chides them for small neglects, in such wise as to make these fair maids cry, and bewail in piteous sort, as I am told by my sister Elizabeth.'

.        .        .        .        .

The Queen's temper, under the harassments to which she was subjected, had not improved. But though the maids of honour 'bewailed in piteous sort' at moments, they were, at others, given to a most unsuitable 'joyosity'. Indeed, poor old Sir Francis Knollys was so disturbed by the way in which 'some of the Ladyes and Maydes of Honour us'd to friske and hey about in the next roome, to his extreme disquiet at nights, though he had often warned them of it [that] when they were all at their revells, (he) stripps off to his shirt, and so with a payre of spectacles on his nose, and Aretine in his hand, comes marching in at a posterne doore of his owne chamber, reading very gravely, full upon the faces of them. . . . He often traverst the roome in this posture above an houre.'

Lord Essex's attention was diverted from the maids of honour — though only temporarily — by his marriage in 1590 to the widowed daughter of Walsingham : (the latter had died, recently, from 'carnosity and tympany' — and, possibly, from overwork and disappointment that his services were so poorly rewarded).

Only seven years before, in 1583, the Queen had been displeased by the lady's marriage to Sir Philip Sidney, that 'Deare Astrophel that in the ashes of thy Love livest againe like the Phoenix'. That love had been given to the unworthy Penelope Devereux, sister of Essex ; but after she was married to Lord Rich, this — perhaps affectionate — marriage with Walsingham's daughter was arranged.

Sir Henry Sidney, in a letter to the father of the bride, said that he 'most utterly agrees in the proposed marriage of their children, and had hoped by this means to have obtained some small suit of Her Majesty, for he might have received a great sum of money for the goodwill of his son's marriage. . . . As the Queen will not be moved to reward him, he therefore will detail all his services, in the two high offices he has held, Lord Deputy in Ireland, and Lord President of Wales. He has twice been Lord Deputy. He returns to Court and goes to his great and high office in Wales, a happy place of government ; for a better people to govern, or better subjects, Europe holdeth not. (He had) Various other employment of high character to his great charges, in which he neither won nor saved. He has not so much ground as will feed a mutton. His wife was a lady in Court. When he left her to go to Newhaven, she was a full fair lady, in his eyes the fairest. When he returned, he found her as foul a lady as the smallpox could make her, which she did take by continually nursing Her Majesty in that sickness, so as now she liveth solitarily. . . .' He, Sidney, 'at ten years of age, was Henchman to King Henry VIII, and was put to that sweet Prince his son, Prince Edward : he was his companion and playfellow, who died in his arms. He has three sons, one (Sir Philip) of excellent good proof, the second of great hope, the third not to be despaired of. He is now fifty-four years of age, toothless and trembling, £5000 in debt, and £30,000 worse than he was at the death of his dear King and Master, King Edward VI. He prays for blessings on the match between their dear children. He sends a buss to their sweet daughter, and craves from Walsingham a blessing on the young Knight, Sir Philip.'

Not only Sir Francis Walsingham suffered from disappointment.

Sir Philip, as we have seen, died of a wound received at the battle of Zutphen, at which Essex was present. The news of Essex's marriage to the widow was received with a burst of fury. But, as John Stanhope, a gentleman of the Privy Chamber, told Lord Talbot, 'God be thanked (she) doth not strike *all* she threats'.

### NOTE TO CHAPTER SIXTY

[1] Lodge, *Illustrations of British History.*

THE SECOND EARL OF ESSEX

# Chapter Sixty-one

THE European wars were breeding a new occupation for the younger sons of landed families — that of professional soldier. And these young men found a natural leader in the rash, spendid, swashbuckling Essex, who wrote of them: 'I love them for mine own sake, for I find sweetness in their conversation, strong assistance in their employment, and happiness in their friendship. I love them for their virtue's sake and for their greatness of mind. . . . I love them for my country's sake, for they are England's best armour of defence and weapon of offence. If we may have peace, they have purchased it ; if we must have war, they must manage it.' [1]

As soon they were to do.

A Spanish army had landed in Brittany — constituting a great threat to England. From there, a second fleet could advance upon her.

But it was against the Queen's judgment that an expedition was sent (in August 1591), whose purpose was to aid the new King of France, the Huguenot Henri of Navarre, in his siege of Rouen.

Essex had implored the Queen, on his knees, for two hours, to be allowed to accompany the expedition. She had refused, understanding his rash and foolhardy character. But she was, at last, over-persuaded by Burleigh, and she let him go.

He had a magnificent bravery ; but he did also treat the campaign as if it were the Field of the Cloth of Gold — riding through a hundred miles of enemy country, heedless of risk, gallivanting and flaunting, to his meeting with the King, in orange velvet sprinkled with precious stones. The infantry, which he had left, unoccupied, at the base, had at last to be summoned to his aid. Then, writes Sir John Neale, 'he closed a foolish escapade with a purposeless bravado that cost him the life of his brother'.

The expedition was to have lasted two months. One had already passed.

The Queen was furious. He was ordered home. He sent Sir Thomas D'Arcy to implore her to allow him to remain. His return, he said, would cover him with dishonour. He must first avenge his brother. But the Queen remained firm.

He was tireless in his indiscretions. Before sailing, he knighted twenty-four of his followers, telling them that they should not suffer because they had been prevented from covering themselves with glory. This also angered the Queen, who when she learned of it said, 'His lordship had done well to have built his almshouses before he had made his Knights'.

But his stay in England was for a few days only. The Queen was persuaded to allow him to return to France, and her forces to remain there.

From France, he wrote to her : 'Most fair, most dear, and most excellent Sovereign, The two windows of your Privy Chamber shall be the poles of my sphere, where, as long as Your Majesty will please to have me, I am fixed and immoveable. When Your Majesty thinks that heaven too good for me, I will not fall like a star, but be consumed like a vapour by the sun that drew me up to such a height. While Your Majesty gives me leave to say I love you, my fortune is as my affection, unmatchable. If ever you deny me that liberty, you may end my life, but never shake my constancy, for were the sweetness of your nature turned into the greatest bitterness that could be, it is not in your power, as great a Queen as you are, to make me love you less.'

But the siege of Rouen went on and on, and still the city did not fall. Essex challenged the Governor to fight a duel, or in a tournament. But the Governor answered that his position forbade him to fight. The Queen said the enterprise was 'rather a jest than a victory'.

In January she ordered him home. As he left the shore, he

kissed his sword. The rest of the troops remained. And still Rouen did not fall.

.        .        .        .        .

At home, the dislike between Essex and Sir Robert Cecil grew. When Walsingham died, Essex had tried to induce the Queen to restore the disgraced Davison to the secretaryship. She refused, and, giving no one the place, relegated the duties to Burleigh. Then, whilst Essex was at Rouen, she made Sir Robert Cecil a member of the Council, and part-secretary with his father.

Essex was the friend of two young men — Anthony Bacon (born in 1558), and his brother Francis (born in 1561), — Francis, with the 'tall black hat and staff',[2] the 'delicate lively hazel eie, like the eie of a viper',[3] a heart as cold, and a mind as brilliant and hard as a diamond, had an ambition as strong as his dislike of his cousin Sir Robert Cecil — (their mothers were sisters). That dislike was equalled by Essex's detestation of Cecil, and Cecil's cold, watchful hatred of him.

Essex's arrogance grew ; but with it went a certain generosity and wish to aid his friends. He was determined to procure the Attorney-Generalship for Francis Bacon. It was given to Edward Coke, the Solicitor-General.

Essex wrote to Bacon : 'The Queen hath denied me your place for you, and hath placed another. . . . You have spent your time and your thoughts in my matters ; I die if I do not somewhat towards your fortune ; you shall not deny to accept a piece of land which I will bestow upon you.' At first Bacon would not accept this, but in the end, he said : 'I can be no more yours than I was. . . . And if I grow to be a rich man, you will give me leave to give it back to some of your unrewarded followers.'

Here we see Essex at his best — generous and indeed noble. But he had another side. Sulking like a spoiled baby, lying in bed and pretending to be ill when the Queen would not let him have his own way, he was, in spite of these childish devices, a relentless enemy.

A year before he wrote that letter to Francis Bacon, he brought — in order to show the Queen his brilliance as a detective, and in order to satisfy his hatred against one of the Court doctors — that poor old man to the horrible death prescribed for traitors.

Dr. Lopez was a Portuguese Jew. He seems to have worked as a spy against Spain for Walsingham and Burleigh. Alan Gordon Smith, in *William Cecil, the Power behind Elizabeth*, wrote that 'he played the usual game of Parry and the rest, plotting and counterplotting with such bewildering complexity that anyone, happening by chance upon some suspicious clue, might be led to entirely wrong conclusions'.

Essex had suggested to Lopez that he should bring any information that came his way, to him ; but every time that he went to the Queen with a secret divulged by Lopez, it was only to find that she knew it already and was laughing at him. It was obvious that Lopez was laughing also !

Then, one night, the Doctor was so unfortunate as to visit two Portuguese friends, and, according to Harrison, 'making merry with them, he began to inveigh against the Earl of Essex, telling them with some secrecies, how he had cured him, and of what disease, with some other things that did disparage his honour'.

They went straight to the favourite.

Then a Portuguese named Tinoco, recently arrived in England, told Sir Robert Cecil of certain things which, wrote Harrison, 'should be made known to the Queen for the sake of her person'.

He was, he said, in the pay of the King of Spain, and had been ordered by the King to 'try to win Dr. Lopez, the Portuguese Jew that is Her Majesty's physician, and endeavour to draw a letter from him, promising to do him service ; he was to remind Lopez that he had daughters, and that they should not want good marriages'. Lopez was to be asked to take especial note of any secret preparations of the army. The King had sent Dr. Lopez 'a jewel of great value'.

On the 24th of January 1594, Dr. Lopez was called before the Lord Treasurer, Sir Robert Cecil, and the Earl of Essex — the latter being 'at great enmity with him, and having long sifted matters against him'. But the Cecils, father and son, knew better than to believe those matters.

Lopez was entirely innocent. They knew only too well that he was innocent — for was he not their spy ? After this first hearing, before Essex had had time to go to the Queen, Sir Robert arrived and 'related to the Queen that there was no matter of malice, for in the poor man's home were found no kind of writings of intelligences of which he was accused, or otherwise that hold might be taken of him'.

But he was committed to the care of Essex's steward, at Essex House. The Queen, however, called Essex a rash and temerarious youth, to enter into a matter against the poor man which he could not prove, and whose innocence she knew well enough ; 'but malice against Dr. Lopez, and no other, hatched this matter ; which displeaseth her much, and more for that her honour is interested' (involved).[4] Essex, in a fury, retired to his room, slamming the door violently, and there remained, sulking, for two days, refusing to see anyone but the Lord Admiral. He then set to work.

There were certain Portuguese adventurers in London, who would say or do anything if threatened with the rack, or promised a reward. Essex contacted these.

He now had the 'evidence' he wanted. Lopez had, he declared, been in the pay of the King of Spain for seven years. 'I have discovered', he wrote to Anthony Bacon, 'a most desperate and dangerous treason. The point of (the) conspiracy was Her Majesty's death. The executioner should have been Dr. Lopez ; the manner poison. This I have so followed as I will make it as clear as the noonday.' Injured vanity had been added to his hatred of the old man.

The Doctor was sent to the Tower.

It would have been fatal to divulge the dealings that Burleigh had long had with the accused man. — Burleigh knew perfectly well that he had no motive for the Queen's murder —

indeed, that he stood to lose everything by it.   But the same was true of Parry.

It was infuriating to the Cecils to have to pretend that Essex had been right, when, as a matter of fact, they had many reasons for thinking that he was wrong.[5]   But there was nothing to be done.   It was regrettable, but the Doctor would have to be disembowelled.   And he was.

Sir John Neale says that he may or may not have been guilty.   It seems that he *did* offer to poison the Queen, if paid a large sum by the King of Spain ;  but he may have been acting as *agent provocateur*.   Sir John thinks that the Queen still doubted his guilt, for she ordered the Keeper of the Tower to refuse to surrender him for execution.   But he adds, 'What happened afterwards is a mystery.   According to a later story, Essex by a trick managed within two months to get Lopez out of the Tower where the Queen's protection covered him, and was thus able to bring him to the scaffold.'

One does not know what happened to the two daughters who 'should not want good marriages'.

### NOTES TO CHAPTER SIXTY-ONE

[1] Neale, *op. cit.*, vol. 2.

[2] Pope-Hennessy, *London Fabric.*

[3] Aubrey, *Brief Lives.*

[4] Harrison, *op. cit.*

[5] Smith, L. B., *English Treason Trials and Confessions in the Sixteenth Century.   Jour. Hist. Ideas.* XV (1954), pp. 471-98.

# Chapter Sixty-two

IN August 1595, a month after four Spanish galleys had swooped down on Cornwall and burnt Penzance, Drake and Hawkins sailed upon that last tragic voyage to the Spanish Main, the adventure from which they were not to return.

The Queen and her Ministers were warned that Spain was preparing a new Armada. Therefore, before the end of the year, she was urged to send a fleet to harry the Spaniards in their own ports. She was contemplating doing so, when the news came that Spaniards from the Netherlands were besieging Calais.

With the enemy at the gates of England, all thought of attacking Cadiz had to be put aside. 'As distant as I am from your abode,' she wrote to Essex, 'yet my ears serve me too well to hear that terrible battery that methinks sounds for relief at my hands. Go you, in God's name.'

But on the day following, Calais fell.

The Queen turned her thoughts once more to Cadiz. The vast expense that would be involved caused her to hesitate ; but in the end she decided to send an expedition, — the navy commanded by Lord Howard of Effingham, the army by Essex. The Queen sent the latter a letter, and with this the prayer : 'Most Omnipotent and Guider of all our world's mass ! that only searchest and fathomest the bottoms of all hearts and conceits, and in them seest the true original of all actions intended. . . . Thou, that didst inspire the mind, we humbly beseech, with bended knees, prosper the work and with best forewinds guide the journey, speed the victory, and make the return the advancement of Thy fame, and surety to the realm, with least loss of English blood. To these devout petitions, Lord, give Thou Thy blessed grant. Amen.'

Sir Robert Cecil sent, together with the Queen's missives, this ridiculous and blasphemous letter : 'No prayer is so fruitful as that which proceedeth from those who nearest in nature and power, approach the Almighty. None so near approach His place and essence as a celestial mind in a princely body. Put forth, therefore, my Lord, with full confidence, having your sails filled with her heavenly breath for a forewind.'

Essex's enemy Sir Walter Raleigh, — that 'tall, handsome, and bold man', now aged forty-four, was among his companions on the expedition.

The English fleet was sighted by the garrison of Cadiz at the end of June 1596. On reaching the city, the order being given to land, Essex, in his joy, threw his hat into the sea, and Raleigh's answer to the Spanish cannon was loud fanfare after fanfare on the trumpets.

In fourteen hours the siege was over, and the English entered the city. The Duke of Medina Sidonia — the admiral of the Armada, now governor of Andalusia — hurried to the city. 'This is shameful,' he wrote to his King. 'I told you it was necessary to send me men and money, and I have never even received an answer. So now I am at my wits' end.' But he was able to lay one salve to his pride. The West Indian fleet, consisting of fifty ships with merchandise worth eight million crowns, was in the inner harbour. Essex had ordered it to be taken, but before this could be done the Duke had the whole fleet destroyed by fire. And, it was said, for the first time since the defeat of the Armada eight years before, a faint reflection of a smile seemed to pass over his face.

The gallantry and humanity of Essex filled even the Spaniards with admiration : churches and priests were spared, and three thousand nuns were escorted to the mainland with great courtesy.

The English remained in Cadiz for a fortnight. Essex had wished to fortify the town and then await the Queen's wishes. This was not allowed. He then advised that the

SIR WALTER RALEIGH

army should march into the interior of Spain. This also was disallowed. His final suggestion was that the Fleet should put to sea and seize the returning West Indian treasure ships. This, again, was vetoed. So the English forces returned home.

In the case of Essex, his homecoming was unhappy. It was true that he was worshipped as a hero by the populace, but the Queen was by no means pleased with him. She had found £50,000 for the expedition — and what had she got in return? Only a demand for more money! Essex had missed seizing the treasure fleet in Cadiz harbour. And what was the meaning of these rumours of treasures looted from the Spaniards? The Fleet had brought back rich hostages. The Queen said that their ransoms were to be paid to *her*: to which Essex replied that this would mean depriving the soldiers of their prize money. It was owing to their incompetence, the Queen replied, that the prize was not larger.

She was annoyed, too, by his excessive popularity, and by the fact that he had been compared, in a sermon preached at St. Paul's, to the greatest generals in history.

But then came a revulsion in his favour. If Essex's advice had been taken, the West Indian treasure fleet that arrived at the Tagus only two days after the English had left would have been taken with twenty million dollars. The Queen then turned on his accusers, and made his uncle, Sir William Knollys, Privy Councillor and Comptroller of the Household.

Lord Burleigh and his son were thoroughly alarmed at this increase in favour, and the former thought it prudent to take Essex's side at the next Council, on the subject of the ransoms. Whereupon the Queen stormed at him : 'My Lord Treasurer, either for fear or favour you regard my Lord of Essex more than myself. You are a miscreant.'

The old man, now very white and bent, and troubled with his 'grief in the foot', crept away. 'My hand is weak!' he told Essex. 'My mind is troubled!' He was, he lamented, 'between Scylla and Charybdis', and 'my misfortune is to

fall into both. . . . Her Majesty chargeth and condemneth
me for favouring you against her ; your Lordship contrari-
wise misliketh me for pleasing of Her Majesty, to offend you.'
Perhaps it would be best to 'shun both these dangers by
becoming an anchorite . . . whereto I am meetest for my
age, my infirmity, and daily decaying estate!'

A month after Essex sailed for Cadiz, the Queen had given
Sir Robert Cecil the title of Chief Secretary. (He had been
this, in all but name, for five years.) With the giving of this
title, a plague of ladies descended upon him. Most insistent
in her importunities was, perhaps, his aunt Lady Russell. This
unescapable lady — for such she was, in spite of Sir Robert's
wiliness — had always some axe for him to grind, usually an
axe belonging to somebody else. A Dean wished for a
Bishopric. A neighbour longed for a knighthood. She
desired her nephew to 'yield the best favour to a godly and
honourable nobleman, the Earl of Kent, to be in the Earl of
Huntingdon's place'. (But then came a note of caution : 'I
would not have it known to proceed from me, because he is
a widower and I a widow'.)

It was possible for Sir Robert, receiving with apprehension
the almost ceaseless flow of letters from his aunt, to gain from
the signature some idea of the weather ruling in that lady's
mind : 'Your desolate wronged aunt'. 'Your loving aunt,
poor but proud.' 'Your aunt that ever deserved the best.'
'Your honest, plain-dealing aunt.'

Lady Russell's incurable interest in the affairs of others led
to the danger of perpetual visits. On hearing that there had
been some dispute between her nephew and Sir William
Knollys, she wrote : 'If you will have me come to court to do
you any good offices, who have ever a natural instinct to be
honest and natural in the hour of trial, *howsoever it be deserved*
[the italics are mine], let me know your mind, and then, so
you procure [*sic*] Her Majesty and my Lord Chamberlain
that I may have a convenient lodging within the house, I
will come when you desire. Otherwise, upon the least wet
of my feet and legs by long clothes or cold, my pate is so

subject to rheum that my hearing will be so bad as that I am fit for no company or other places than my own cell.

'Your Aunt that ever deserved the best.

E. R.

Dowager.'

But trying as was Lady Russell, she was nothing to Lady Cobham. Lady Russell's strong suit was a Cassandra-like gift of foreboding mixed with a strong sense of being unappreciated; Lady Cobham's was a temper so violent that the Cecil family 'clapped on all their sails' at her approach.

Lady Cobham, with Lady Raleigh, Lady Northumberland, and Essex's sister Lady Rich, were busy plotting to advance the claims of the King of Scotland to succeed to the crown of England. Lady Cobham was particularly anxious to involve Sir Robert in the intrigue, and, in pursuit of this aim, paid him incessant visits. When unable to avoid these, he would yet slip from her grasp with the agility of an eel, 'for sometimes he spoke of King James with respect, and afterwards, in a long time again, he would never so much as speak of him'.

Lady Cobham was nonplussed. But there came a letter from Scotland which caused her to suspect, not only that he had been corresponding the whole time with the King, but that he had actually written in that correspondence things highly unflattering to herself. 'She is in such a passion', Lord Henry Howard told a Scottish correspondent, that she said 'to my worthy nephew, the Lord Thomas Howard, who is her Counsellor at these straits', that if her intrigues came to the Queen's ears — and she had thought, for some days, that the Queen looked at her strangely, — not only would she denounce Sir Robert to Her Majesty, but, as well, 'she threatened to break the neck of that weasel (which was her own term) that had disgraced her'.

# Chapter Sixty-three

WHILE the weasel in question was in imminent danger of dissolution, his father was considering his errors in strategy. Had he been wrong, he wondered, to ignore, to make no use of his wife's nephews, the Bacon brothers. Was it possible that Essex's rise to power might be, in part, due to their cleverness? And if so, would it be too late to draw them away from Essex to himself? Few men are untouched by the thought of gain. Anthony, he supposed, would be the easiest to approach, and Lady Russell, their aunt and his sister-in-law, should be sent to sound him. She arrived, with warm messages offering advancement and friendship. But Anthony's devotion to Essex was fanatical. Nor had he forgotten those years of early youth in which he and his brother had been ignored, nor his hatred for his cousin Robert. His aunt was amazed at his revelations of the latter's conduct. When he told her that Robert had 'denounced [sic] a deadly feud against him : "Ah, vile urchin !" exclaimed the formidable woman, "is it possible ?" Her nephew laughed, and quoted the Gascon proverb, "Bran d'âne ne monte pas au ciel".'

Francis Bacon was, as his uncle guessed, adviser to Essex. The Queen, he told his patron, must not think of him as 'a man of a nature not to be ruled, that hath the advantage of my affection, and knoweth it ; of an estate not grounded for his greatness ; of a popular reputation ; of a militar dependence' [sic]. For 'I demand whether there can be a more dangerous image than this represented to any monarch living, much more to a lady and of her Majesty's apprehension'. No. He must work to obliterate these fears from her mind.

He must 'take all occasion, to the Queen, to speak against popularity and popular courses vehemently, and to tax it in all others'; but his speeches were to be speeches only, for he must, in fact, remain the people's idol, because 'as to a popular reputation', that was 'a good thing in itself, and that, well gained, is one of the best flowers of your greatness both present and to come'. Most important of all, he must avoid arousing in her the suspicion of his 'militar dependence'. For 'herein I cannot sufficiently wonder at your Lordship's course . . . for her Majesty loveth peace'.

Francis was not the only member of the Bacon family to give the Favourite advice. Old Lady Bacon, from Gorhambury, interested herself in his affairs. The report of his misdeeds averted her attention, temporarily, from the delighted contemplation of the eternity of hell-fire being prepared for persons who had displeased her, and the disgraceful shortcomings of her elder son and his servants. She was more than a little frightened of Francis, and therefore directed her diatribes against him to her son, Anthony. 'Surely I pity your brother,' she wrote (because of his debts) — 'but so long as he pitieth not himself but keepeth that bloody Percy . . . yea as a coach companion and bed companion — a proud, profane, costly fellow, whose being about him I verily fear God doth mislike and doth less bless your brother in credit and otherwise in his health — surely I am utterly discouraged. . . . That Jones never loved your brother indeed, save for his own credit, living upon your brother and thankless though bragging. . . . It is most certain that till Enny, a filthy wasteful knave, and his Welshmen one after another — (for take one and they will still swarm ill-favouredly) — did so lead him in a train, he was a towardly young gentleman, and a son of much good hope in godliness. . . . I will not', she declared, 'have his cormorant seducers and instruments of Satan to him committing foul sin by his countenance, to the displeasing of God and His godly fear.'

Lady Bacon now decided to warn Lord Essex against cormorant seducers. Scandalised by the rumour that he was engaged in an intrigue with a married lady, she wrote admonishing him. The lady was 'unchaste and impudent, with, as it were, an incorrigible shamefacedness'. She was an 'unchaste gaze and common byword'. 'The Lord, by His Grace, amend her.' Or, better still, 'cut her off before some sudden mischief'. Essex, in return, wrote the old lady — soon to fall into a gibbering cackling madness — a letter of much sweetness, denying the rumour, and saying 'I live in a place where I am hourly conspired against, and practised upon. What they cannot make the world believe, that they persuade themselves unto ; and what they cannot make probable to the Queen, that they give out to the world. . . . Worthy Lady, think me a weak man, full of imperfections, but be assured I do endeavour to be good, and would rather mend my faults than cover them.'

It is sad that the nobility and sweetness of nature shown in his letters to others never appeared in those to his Queen. He resented, one supposes, his chained condition, tied to this magnificent mummy, with her old sandal-wood body wrapped in cerecloths of glory — a mighty death in life.

.        .        .        .        .

It was believed that a new Armada was about to attack the Isle of Wight. Therefore Essex, with Raleigh and Lord Thomas Howard under him, was ordered to take a fleet and a powerful armed force to Ferrol, and to destroy everything they found there. It seemed at the moment as if Essex was to be reconciled with his enemies. In celebration of this, he gave a dinner-party at his house for Robert Cecil and Raleigh, and, going to the Queen, begged her to admit Raleigh (in disgrace for seducing and then marrying one of her maids of honour) to her presence. She did so, and gave him his former position as Captain of the Guard. Raleigh had a suit of silver armour made, in which, glittering like a star, he stood in the antechamber.

The expedition to Ferrol was a failure from the beginning It was caught in a storm, and the ships were scattered. Refitted·

the fleet started again.  Then Raleigh disobeyed orders, and advanced to attack Ferrol before Essex and the rest of the fleet could arrive to support him.  Asked why he did not court-martial Raleigh, the, in some ways, very gallant Essex replied, 'Had he been my friend, I should have done so'.  Then the Spanish treasure fleet escaped and, while the English fleet was occupied elsewhere, the fleet from Ferrol sailed for England, and was only prevented by a storm from attacking Falmouth.

The Queen was furious.

On his return, Essex behaved like a spoilt child because the Lord Admiral, Howard, had been created Earl of Nottingham, which, with his office, gave him precedence over Essex.  The latter stayed away from the Council ; he stayed away from Court ;  he stayed away from the celebrations on Queen's Day — the anniversary of her succession, the entry into the fortieth year of her reign.  At last the Queen ended his sulks by creating him Earl Marshal, which gave him precedence over the Lord Admiral.

He seems to have spent much of his time, during this period, in philandering with the maids of honour — Lady Mary Howard, and his 'fairest Brydges' — to the grief of Lady Essex and the annoyance of the Queen.

Then, one day, when the question of a new Lord Deputy for Ireland was being discussed in Council, by the Queen, Essex, the Lord Admiral, Robert Cecil, and good Windebank, Clerk of the Signet — long since freed from his torments with Sir Robert's elder brother — Essex persistently contradicted the Queen, and finally, with an insolent gesture, turned his back on her.  She immediately boxed his ears.  'Go and be hanged,' she cried.  Whereupon, to the amazement of the other men, he with a loud oath seized his sword, and shouted at the Queen : 'This is an outrage.  I would not have borne it from your father's hands.'  The Lord Admiral restrained him.  The Queen remained immovable.  There was a moment of utter silence.  Then the rooms near the Council Chamber heard the sound of flying footsteps.

# Chapter Sixty-four

APPALLED, the Court had waited to hear the fate of the young fool who had drawn his sword on the Queen. But the amazing woman showed no sign of what was happening in her mind. The affair might almost have taken place in a dream. He was not sent to the Tower, but retired to his house at Wantage. From there, he wrote the Queen the only letter she ever received from him that held some trace of the nobility in his nature — this mingled with unworthy flattery. 'Madam, when I think how I have preferred your beauty above all things, and received no pleasure in life but by the increase of your favour towards me, I wonder at myself what cause there could be to make me absent myself one day from you. But when I remember that Your Majesty hath by the intolerable wrong you have done both me and yourself, not only broken all laws of affection, but done against the honour of your sex, I think all places better than where I am, and all dangers well undertaken, so I might retire myself from the memory of my false, inconstant and beguiling pleasures. . . . I was never proud, till you sought to make me too base. And now, since my destiny is no better, my despair shall be like my love was, without repentance. . . . I must commend my faith to be judged by Him Who judgeth all hearts, since on earth I find no right. Wishing you all comforts and joys in the world and no greater punishment for your wrongs to me, than to know the faith of him you have lost, and the baseness of those you shall keep,

'Your Majesty's most humble servant
R. Essex.'

440

In August 1598, Burleigh died. Ten days after the death of her old wise Councillor the Queen received a new and terrible blow. There came the news that an army in Ireland, marching under the generalship of Sir Henry Bagenal to relieve the fort on the Blackwater, had been attacked by the rebel Tyrone. The army was annihilated, and the general killed.

The Court was filled with dismay. But to one man it brought joy in the midst of his appalling death agony: King Philip, dying by inches, his soul in all the odour of sanctity, his corrupted body eaten by worms as if he were already in the grave; King Philip, whose dying body had been lifted to the oratory so that the last sight on which his eyes should rest would be the high altar. His prayers had been answered; he was indeed beloved by Heaven, and here was the sign that this was so. The heretics were at last defeated, the Queen of England and her wickedness punished.

For fifty days he had lain in torment. But now Heaven claimed him. The torment was over. He lay at peace, in his grandeur, his holiness; his wickedness, his bewilderment ended.

On hearing of the disaster in Ireland, Essex went immediately to Whitehall to ask that his services should be used. But the Queen did not receive him. 'He hath played', she said, 'long enough upon me, and now I mean to play awhile with him, and stand as much upon my greatness as he hath upon his stomach' (*i.e.* pride). Once again, he wrote her a long letter, to which she replied, verbally, 'Tell the Earl that I value *myself* at as great a price as *he* values *himself*'. To which he replied, 'I do confess that, as a man, I have been more subject to your natural beauty than as a subject to the power of a king'. This unpleasant letter caused the Queen to receive him; but she made it clear that she had not forgiven him.

The Lord Keeper Egerton remonstrated with him. 'Let policy, duty, and religion enforce you to yield, and submit to your sovereign, between whom and you there can be no proportion of duty.' To which he replied: 'I have been content to do Her Majesty the service of a clerk, but can never serve her as a villain or a slave. But, say you, I must yield and submit. I can neither yield myself to be guilty, or this imputation laid upon me to be just. . . . Nay more : when the vilest of all indignities are done unto me, doth religion enforce me to sue ? . . . What, cannot princes err ? Cannot subjects receive wrong ? . . . Let Solomon's fool laugh when he is stricken ; let those that mean to make their profit from princes' (for of course he had made none) 'show no sign of princes' injuries.'

In September, Essex was gravely ill. The Queen sent her doctors to him, and forgave him. On his recovery, he begged again to be sent to command the army in Ireland. 'The Court', he said, 'is the centre, but methinks it is the fairer choice to command armies. . . . I have beaten Knollys and Mountjoy in the Council, and by God I will beat Tyrone in the field.' For the Queen's sake, he said, he would have thought danger a sport and death a feast.

The Queen approved his wish, and he left for Ireland on the 27th of March 1599.

In order that he might have his friends about him, he wished the Earl of Southampton, who had been in disgrace for seducing and then marrying a maid of honour, to be General of the Horse, and his stepfather Sir Christopher Blount Marshal of the Army. The Queen allowed the second appointment, but refused the first.

From the moment he landed, he plunged into disaster.

He disobeyed the Queen's orders about Southampton, and gave him the appointment. The Queen ordered Essex to dismiss him immediately. Again, he disobeyed. He had been ordered to march against Ulster. Instead he started war in Leinster. He had been told to confer knighthoods only as a reward for some great deed. He promptly knighted an official who was in disgrace and had been recalled.

The campaign in Ulster should have been undertaken in June. The month passed by, and Ulster remained untouched. In July, having taken a single castle, Essex returned to Dublin.

On the 19th of July, the Queen rebuked Essex for his

disobedience, and ordered him to march immediately against Ulster. . . . 'In order to plant your garrisons in the North and assail that proud rebel [Tyrone] we command you to pass thither with all speed.' Before this letter reached him, he was pursuing a fresh will-o'-the-wisp.

The Queen ordered him to attack Tyrone immediately. 'After', she wrote, 'you shall have certified us to what form you have reduced things in the North . . . you shall with all speed receive our warrant, without which we do charge you, as you tender our pleasure, that you adventure not to come out of that kingdom by virtue of any former license whatever.'

One day she met Francis Bacon, and taking him aside, asked him what view he took of the state of affairs in Ireland, and of the conduct of the Lord Deputy. To which he replied : 'Madam, if you had my Lord of Essex here with a white staff in his hand, as my Lord of Leicester had, and continued him still about you for society to yourself, and for an honour and ornament to your attendance and Court in the eyes of your people, and in the eyes of foreign ambassadors, then were he in his right element. For to discontent him as you do, and yet to put arms and power into his hands, may be a kind of temptation to make him prove cumbersome and unruly. And therefore if you would send for him, and satisfy him with honour here near you, if your affairs — which I am not acquainted with — will permit it, I think were the best way.'

It was Bacon's first step downwards — or upwards.

The Queen then sent a terrifying letter to the Lord Deputy : 'We require you to consider whether we have not great cause to think that your purpose is not to end the war'.

Essex seems, by now, to have been a little mad. Bent on his own destruction, he had accepted a secret message from Tyrone, suggesting that they should enter rather into a truce than a battle, and that if Essex would be guided by Tyrone, the latter would make him the greatest man that England had ever known. They met, as Essex thought, in secret.

But there were two hidden eavesdroppers at their meeting-place. . . . Here, according to the Winwood Memorials, are the particulars of 'Tyrone's Propositions, 1599' :

1. That the Catholic religion be openly preached.
2. That the churches be governed by the Pope.
3. That Catholic churches be restored.
4. That Irish priests, prisoners, be released.
5. That they may pass and repass the seas.
6. That no Englishmen be churchmen in Ireland.
7. That a university be erected upon the Crown lands.
8. That the governor be at least an earl, and called viceroy.
9. That the Lord Chancellor, Treasurer, Counsel of State, Justices of Law, Queen's Attorney, Queen's Sergeant, etc., be Irishmen.
10. That all principal Governors of Ireland, as Connaught, Munster, etc., be Irish noblemen.
11. That the Master of Ordnance be an Irishman, and half the soldiers.
12. That no Irishman shall lose his lands for the fault of his ancestors.
13. That no Irishman shall be in ward, but that the living during the minority shall be to the younger brothers or sisters.
14. That all statutes prejudicing the preferment of Irishmen in England or Ireland shall be repealed.
15. That neither the Queen nor her successors shall enforce any Irishman to serve her.
16. That O'Neale, Odonnel, Desmond, and their partakers shall have such lands as their ancestors enjoyed two hundred years ago.
17. That all Irishmen shall freely traffic as Englishmen in England.
18. That all Irishmen shall travel freely.
19. That they may use all manner of merchandise wheresoever.
20. That they may use all manner of trades.
21. That they may buy all manner of ships and furnish them with artillery.

Spedding, in his edition of the *Life and Letters of Lord Bacon*, asks, 'Now can any one believe that Essex came over from Ireland [as he was soon to do] intending to lay these propositions fairly before Queen Elizabeth, and hoping to persuade her that the man who had consented to entertain them was the man to do her work with rebels ?'

There is, however, no reason to think that Essex did intend to lay them before her, nor is it by any means certain that the document is genuine. But it is certain that Tyrone proposed a truce, 'to be concluded', says Lytton Strachey, 'for six weeks, to continue by periods of six weeks until May Day, and not to be broken without a fortnight's warning. Essex again agreed. All was over. The campaign was at an end.'

In his despair at being ordered to remain in Ireland, and in his general sense of failure, Essex had written to the Queen : 'From a mind delighting in sorrow ; from spirits wasted with travail, care, and grief ; from a heart torn in pieces with passion ; from a man that hates himself and all things that keep him alive, what service can your Majesty reap ? Since my services past deserve no more than banishment and proscription into the most cursed of all countries, with what expectation and what end shall I live longer ? No, no, the rebel's pride and successes must give me means to ransom myself, my soul, I mean, out of this hateful prison of my body. And if it happen so, your Majesty may believe that you shall not have cause to mislike the fashion of my death, though the course of my life may not please you. From your Majesty's exiled servant, Essex.'

He now decided, however, neither to die nor to remain exiled ; but, once again, to disobey her and to come to England. For he could not, he told himself, have lost his hold over her. Once he was in her presence, she would feel her old affection.

He arrived on the 28th of September 1599. The Court was at Nonesuch, in Surrey. Sir Christopher Blount had warned Essex that if he should carry out his original plan of leading a small army from Wales to London — to throw Cecil from power — it would lead to civil war. Better, he said, to take only a few hundred followers, and bring about a *coup d'état* at Court. But now he put aside all thoughts of violence.

On the way to Nonesuch, he met Lord Grey of Wilton,

an adherent of Cecil, who was on his way to Court.  One of Essex's followers, Sir Thomas Gerrard, begged him to allow Essex to arrive first, 'that he may bring the first news of his return himself'.  But Lord Grey, on a fresher horse than that of Essex, reached the Court first, and went straight to Cecil.

The Queen was being dressed.  Cecil sent her no word of what had happened, but sat and waited.

At ten o'clock Essex reached the Palace, and, without waiting to wash or to change his clothes, rushed, unannounced, through the presence chamber, the privy chamber, into the Queen's bedroom. . . . The magnificent ruin stood before him — Carthage and Palmyra in disarray — the sunset-coloured wig, and all the tires and towers, and crowns, fallen away.

# Chapter Sixty-five

IT was impossible to read the Queen's mind. She was, he thought, delighted to see him. She told him, laughing, to change his clothes, and let her continue dressing. Returning, he talked with her for an hour and a half, and came down to dinner thanking God that after so many storms abroad he had found a sweet calm at home. But he had mistaken her. She began to ask frightening questions, and his replies angered her. Presently she declared that he must explain his conduct to the Council.

At eleven o'clock that night he received the Queen's message : he was ordered to keep to his chamber.

At two o'clock next day, he was brought before the Council. Rising as he entered the Council Chamber, they then reseated themselves, while he remained standing, to hear the charges the Secretary brought against him : 'His disobedience to Her Majesty's instructions in regard to Ireland — his presumptuous letters written to her while there — his making so many idle knights, his contemptuous disregard of his duty in returning without leave. And, last, his over-bold going to Her Majesty's presence in her bedchamber.'

The Queen said she would 'pause and consider his answer'.

A few days afterwards, he was sent to York House, under the care of the Lord Keeper, and the Court moved to Richmond.

The Queen's anger fell on everyone connected with the fallen favourite. Sir John Harington, the Queen's godson, was, as he said, 'almost wrecked on the Essex coast'. The Queen was angry because he was one of the 'idle knights' created by the Lord Deputy, and because he had accompanied

Essex on his return to England. When he presented himself before her for the first time since his return, she said, frowning: 'What! Did the fool bring you too? Go back to your business.' He told a friend that she was like an angry lioness 'such, indeed, as left no doubt whose daughter she was. She chafed much, walked fastly to and fro, looked, with discomposure in her visage, and, I remember, she catched my girdle, when I kneeled to her, and swore "By God's Son, I am no Queen! — that man is above me! Who gave him command to come here so soon? I did send him on other business." It was long before more gracious discourse did fall to my hearing, but I was then put out of my trouble, and bid "go home". I did not stay to be bidden twice. If all the Irish rebels had been at my heels, I should not have made better speed, for I did now flee from one I both loved and feared.' 'I came to court', he told another correspondent, 'in the very heat and height of all displeasures. After I had been there but an hour, I was threatened with the Fleet. I answered poetically "that coming so late from the land-service, I hoped I should not be pressed to serve her Majesty's fleet in Fleet Street". After three days, every man wondered to see me at liberty, but though, in conscience, there was neither rhyme nor reason to punish me for going to see Tyrone, yet if my rhyme had not been better liked than my reason, when I gave the young lord Dungannon an Ariosto, I think I had lain by the heels for it. But I had this good fortune, that after four or five days the Queen had talked of me, and twice talked to me, though very briefly. At last she gave me a full and very gracious audience, in the withdrawing-chamber, at Whitehall, where, herself being accuser, judge, and witness, I was cleared and graciously dismissed. What should I say? I seemed to myself like St. Paul, rapt up to the third heaven, where he heard words not to be uttered by men, for neither must I utter what I then heard. Until I come to heaven, I shall never come before a statelier judge again, nor one that can temper majesty, wisdom, learning, choler, and favour better than her Highness.'

Essex was by now gravely ill ; but the Queen found this difficult to believe. He had pretended illness too often.

The grief-stricken Lady Essex sent the Queen a jewel : it was returned. On the next Sunday, she arrived at the Palace, dressed in black — her whole attire being under £4 in value — and went to Lady Huntingdon's room, to beg her to intercede with the Queen that she might visit her husband, who she believed was dying. Lady Huntingdon did not dare see her, but sent a message that she would tell the Queen of her plea. Lady Essex received the answer 'that she must attend Her Majesty's pleasure by the Lords of the Council, and come no more to Court'.

Meanwhile, the Court rang with the sounds of tilts and tourneys, watched by the Queen, who, on the 19th of November 1599, gave Lord Mountjoy her glove.

The French Ambassador Boissise, who had been instructed by his King to intercede for Essex, if this were possible, wrote, on the 21st of November : 'I waited upon the Queen yesterday, in the house of a gentleman near Richmond, where she was enjoying the pleasures of the chase. . . . She was not sorry that I should see her hunting equipage and her hunting dress, for in truth she does not appear with less grace in the field than in her palace, and, besides, she was in a very good humour. . . . The Privy Council have gravely considered the case of the Earl of Essex, and it was determined, without an opposing voice, "that he has well and faithfully served" (the Queen) "and that even his return, although it was contrary to the orders of the Queen, yet it hath been done with a good intention." They have communicated their decision to the Queen, but she is not satisfied with it. She holds a Court every day and says "that she will allow the present tournament in commemoration of her coronation to continue, that it may clearly appear her Court can do without the Earl of Essex". Many consider that she will continue a long time in this humour ; and I see nobody here who is not accustomed to obey ; and the actions of the Queen are never mentioned but in terms of the highest respect.'

On the 28th, the Ambassador wrote : 'The Earl of Essex is not much mentioned at Court ; he is still confined, and I do not perceive that his liberation is an object of much consideration'.

Essex refused to eat, and drank excessively, thereby increasing his fever. Sending for eight doctors, he spoke of making his will. He was then allowed by the Queen to walk in the garden, and there was some talk of his being permitted to return to his own house, for both the Lord Keeper and his wife were ill. His sisters Lady Rich and Lady Northumberland, dressed in black, came to Court to implore the Queen to allow him to be moved as soon as this was possible.

'My Lady Essex', Rowland Whyte wrote, 'rises almost every day as soon as light, to go to my Lord Treasurer and Sir John Fortescue, (on behalf of her lord) for to this Court she may not come.'

Essex received the Communion on the second Sunday in December, and Lady Essex, allowed to see him, found him so despairingly ill that he could only be moved from his bed by lifting him in the sheets. It was thought he was dying.

On the 13th of December, the French Ambassador told his King that a warrant had been made out, committing Essex to the Tower, and that this had been brought twice to the Queen, who had refused to sign it.

In an audience granted him, the Ambassador entreated the Queen to consider duly which would be the most expedient ; to persist in the punishment of the Earl of Essex, and lose, by so doing, one of her best servants and ministers, and prolonging a dangerous and hazardous war in Ireland ; or, being satisfied with a moderate punishment, to make the Earl more careful and more capable, therefore, of doing her services, and by this means put an end to the war, and save her country. . . . 'She heard me patiently, and then said, but not without emotion, "that she entreated your Majesty not to judge of the facts, without being well informed ; that the Earl had so ill conducted himself in his charge, despising the orders and regulations which he had received from her, that Ireland was in great danger, — that he had conferred with the chief of the rebels, without preserving the honour or the dignity of the Crown, and that he had, at last, returned to England, against her express commands, and had abandoned the army and the country to the mercy of her enemies,— which were acts that deserved punishment, which she had not yet inflicted, for the Earl was well lodged in the house of one of his friends, where he had a good chamber, and a gallery to walk in". She said she would consider thereafter what she ought to do, but she begged your Majesty to retain your good opinion of her.'

The illness of Essex was, at last, so serious that the Queen sent her own physician, Dr. James, to him, with a verbal message, which she spoke with tears in her eyes, telling him to 'comfort himself, and that, if it were not inconsistent with her honour, she would have come to visit him herself'.

He appeared to be dying, and the Queen had him moved from his own room to the Lord Keeper's, and allowed Lady Essex to stay with him all day, leaving only at night.

On the 19th of December, all the bells in London tolled, for it was said that he was dead. And a few days after, on Sunday, prayers were said for him in all the churches in London.

But at about this time, there was a new change in the Queen's mind, and she ceased to enquire for news of his health. It had, perhaps, been instilled into her mind that, once again, he was feigning illness.

Christmas was kept at Court with great splendour. 'Almost every night', wrote Rowland Whyte, 'her Majesty is in presence, to see the ladies dance the new and old country-dances with tabour and pipe.'

It had been decided to bring Essex before the Star Chamber, and Lady Essex had, therefore, been forbidden to visit him. However, after receiving a properly humble letter from him, begging that he might not be brought to the Star Chamber, the Queen granted his plea. — But, soon after, he being now on the way to recovery, and able to walk in York Garden, she was angered because his wife, mother, Lord Southampton, and other friends, had waved to him from a window overlooking the garden.

It was now that his friends prepared for him his final downfall.

His sister Lady Rich, not knowing that her odious letters to the King of Scotland, mocking at the Queen's vanity, and calling her Venus, had come into Cecil's hands, wrote her a letter of the most insolent flattery, which contained, also, a sinister hint about the Queen's relations with Essex : 'Early did I hope this morning to have had mine eyes blessed with your Majesty's beauty ; but seeing the sun depart into a cloud, and meeting with spirits that did presage by the wheels of their chariot some thunder in the air, I must complain and express my fears to the high majesty and divine oracle, from whence I received a doubtful answer ; . . . that words directed to the sacred wisdom should be out of season, delivered for my unfortunate brother, whom all men have liberty to defame, as if his offence was capital, and he so base, dejected a creature, that his life, his love, his service to your beauties and the state, had deserved no absolution after so hard punishment, or so much as to answer in your fair presence, who would vouchsafe more justice and favour than he can expect of partial judges, or those combined enemies, that labour on false grounds to build his ruin, urging his faults as criminal to your divine honour, thinking it a heaven to blaspheme heaven'.[1]

The effect of this illiterate and odious letter was anything but that which Lady Rich had anticipated. She was ordered to confine herself to her house, and the Queen spoke of bringing the matter before the Star Chamber, and of sending her to the Tower.

Essex was allowed to go to his own house in March 1600, in charge of a keeper. But in May an ambitious printer or his ill-advised friends published a tract he had written in 1598, called by him his 'Apologie', together with Lady Rich's insolent letter. And at the same time, Essex's intemperate letter to the Lord Keeper Egerton, written at the time when his ears were boxed, found its way into print. Essex, in despair, wrote the Queen a frenzied letter : 'As if I were thrown into a corner like a dead carcass, I am gnawed on and torn by the basest creatures upon earth. The prating tavern-haunter speaks of me what he lists ; the frantic libeller writes of me what he lists ; they print me and make me speak to the world, and shortly they will play me upon the stage. The least of these is worse than death, but this is not the worst of my destiny ; for you, who have protected from scorn and infamy all to whom you once showed favour but Essex . . . have now, in the eighth month of my close imprisonment, rejected my letters and refused to hear of me, which to traitors you never did. What remains is only to beseech you to conclude my punishment, my misery, and my life.'

Angered by the slander on her that he had been con-demned unheard, the Queen, on the 5th of June, had him brought before a special Commission.

Kneeling before the Council, with a bundle of papers which he held, at times, in his hand, at others placed in his hat, he defended himself against the charge of treason. 'I should do God and mine own conscience wrong if I do not justify myself as an honest man.' And, placing his hand over his heart, he said, 'This hand shall pull out this heart when any disloyal thought shall enter it'.

The examination, beginning at nine in the morning, lasted till eight at night ; sometimes he knelt, sometimes stood, or leaned against a cupboard, until the Archbishop of Canterbury, out of mercy, had a stool brought to him.

The feeling in the country against Cecil and Francis Bacon had grown, — the people believing that they were largely responsible for Essex's disgrace. Certainly it was noticed at Court that the Queen's anger against him seemed to have increased every time that Bacon was in her presence. He had written her a strange letter, containing this passage : 'My life hath been threatened, and my name libelled, which I count an honour. But these are the practices of those whose despairs are dangerous, but not yet so dangerous as their

hopes, or else the devices of some that would put out all your
Majesty's lights, and fall on reckoning how many years you
have reigned.'

But perhaps, when writing that, he had not Essex's ruin
in mind. He had felt, he said, a year or two before that time,
like a hawk anxious to perch upon the hand of the Queen,
but unable to fly, because he was 'tied to another fist'.

Certainly, the day after Essex appeared before the Commission, Bacon said to the Queen : 'You have now, Madam,
obtained the victory over two things which the greatest
princes cannot at their wills subdue ; the one is over fame —
the other is over a great mind. For surely the world is now, I
hope, reasonably satisfied ; and for my lord, he did show
that humiliation towards your Majesty, as I am persuaded he
was never in his life more fit for your Majesty's favour than
he is now.' And he added an earnest entreaty that he should
be forgiven.

The Queen seemed moved, and ordered him to give a
written account of the proceedings.

.    .    .    .    .

Sir Robert Cecil, at about this time, knew a temporary
release from the importunities of his aunt Lady Russell, as
that lady was busy preparing for the marriage of her daughter
Anne, one of the Queen's maids of honour, to Lord Herbert.

'Mrs. Anne Russell', according to Whyte, 'went from
court upon Monday last with eighteen coaches ; the like
hath never been seen among the maids of honour. The
Queen in public used to her as gracious speeches as have been
heard of any, and commanded all her maids to accompany
her to London ; so did all the lords of the court. Her Majesty
is to be at the marriage.' 'My lord Cobham prepares his house
for Her Majesty to lie in, because it is near the bride's house.
There is to be a memorable mask of eight ladies ; they have
a strange dance, newly invented ; their attire is this :—each
lady hath a skirt of cloth of silver, a rich waistcoat, wrought
with silks, and gold and silver, and their hair about their

shoulders curiously knotted. The maskers are my Lady Dorothy, Mrs. [Miss] Fitton, Mrs. [Miss] Carey, Mrs. [Miss] Bess Russell * etc. These eight dance to the music Apollo brings ; and there is a fine speech which mentions a ninth, much to her honour and praise.'

The wedding was at Blackfriars ; the bride met the Queen at the waterside, and six knights carried Her Majesty in a litter to the house of Lady Russell, with whom she dined, then, at nightfall, went through the house of Dr. Puddin, who presented her with a fan, to that of Lord Cobham, with whom she supped. The masque was performed after supper, Mary Fitton being the leader, and after the first dance, the eight masquers chose eight other ladies with whom to dance.

'Mrs. Fitton', wrote Whyte, 'went to the Queen and wooed her to dance. Her Majesty asked the name of the character she personified ; she answered "Affection". "Affection !" said the Queen ; "affection's false" ; yet Her Majesty rose and danced.'

* Bess Russell died less than a fortnight after her sister's wedding.

NOTE TO CHAPTER SIXTY-FIVE

Strickland, *op. cit.*

# Chapter Sixty-six

ESSEX was summoned to York House on the 26th of August 1600, and was told 'that it was Her Majesty's pleasure to restore him to liberty, save of access to Court'. His plea that he might be allowed to kiss the Queen's hand before going to the country, was answered by the message 'that though Her Majesty was content that he should remain under no guard, save that of duty and discretion, yet he must in no sort suppose himself to be freed from her indignation; nor must he presume to approach her court or person.

Lady Rich continued under well-deserved restraint.

The Queen appointed Lord Mountjoy, the lover of this unpleasant young woman, to be Lord Deputy of Ireland in Essex's stead; and Francis Bacon, on hearing of this, said, 'Surely, Madam, you cannot make a better choice, unless you send over my Lord Essex'.

'Essex!' she exclaimed. 'When I send Essex back into Ireland, I will marry you. Claim it of me!'

There were festivities at Court; the Moorish Ambassador visited her at Oatlands.

But the Queen suffered from a carefully disguised melancholy.

Sir Robert Sidney wrote to Harington the following sad account :

'I do see the Queen often; she doth wax weak since the late troubles, and Burleigh's death doth often draw tears down her goodly cheeks; she walketh out but little, meditates much alone, and sometimes writes, in private, to her best friends. Her Highness hath done honour to my poor house in visiting me, and seemed much pleased at what we did to please her.

QUEEN ELIZABETH I

My son made her a fair speech, to which she did give most gracious reply. The women did dance before her, whilst the cornets did salute from the gallery, and she did vouchsafe to eat two morsels of rich comfit-cake, and drank a small cordial from a golden cup. She had a marvellous suit of velvet [a train], borne by four of her first women attendants in rich apparel ; two ushers did go before, and at going up stairs she called for a staff, and was much wearied in walking about the house, and said she would come another day. Six drums and six trumpets waited in the court, and sounded at her approach and departure. My wife did bear herself in wondrous good liking, and was attired in a purple kyrtle fringed with gold, and myself in a rich band and collar of needle-work, and did wear a goodly stuff of the bravest cut and fashion, with an under-body of silver and loops. The Queen was much in commendation of our appearances, and smiled at the ladies, who, in their dances, often came up to the step, on which the seat was fixed, to make their obeisance, and so fell back into their order again.

'The younger Markham did several gallant feats on a horse before the gate, leaping down and kissing his sword, and then mounting swiftly on the saddle, and passed a lance with much skill. The day well nigh spent the Queen went and tasted a small beverage, that was set out in divers rooms where she might pass, and then, in much order, was attended to her palace, the cornets and trumpets sounding through the streets. One knight, I dare not name, did say "the Queen hath done me more honour than some that had served her better" ; but envious tongues have venomed shafts, and so I rest in peace with what hath happened, and God speed us all, my worthy knight.'

The Queen told Francis Bacon, one day, 'that Essex had written to her some dutiful letters, which had moved her ; but after taking them to flow from the abundance of his heart, she found them but a preparative to a suit for renewing his farm of sweet wines' — a monopoly she had granted him in the past.

She answered his petition by saying she would 'enquire into its annual value' — which is believed to have amounted to £50,000 — adding that 'when horses become unmanageable it was necessary to tame them by stinting them in the quantity of their food'. But Essex, deeply in debt, repeated his suit. He was told the monopoly was, for the future, to belong to the Crown.

This meant, for Essex, entire financial ruin. And he seems to have been, by now, on the verge of madness. Harington, who visited him, described his furies as such that 'The man's soul seemeth tossed to and fro like the waves of a troubled sea . . .'. 'His speech of the Queen became no man who hath mens sana in corpore sano.'

It is not known, for certain, how much of that speech was repeated to the Queen ; but Raleigh said 'that the expression of Essex that the Queen was cankered, and that her mind had become as crooked as her carcase cost him his head, which his insurrection had not cost him, but for that speech'.

He was now on the verge of actual treason — a treason not confined to words. Essex House became the centre for all the malcontents in London ; and Lady Rich and Essex's stepfather were tireless in urging him to complete his ruin.

In the autumn of 1599, Raleigh had written to Sir Robert Cecil : 'Sir, I am not wise enough to give you advice ; but, if you take it for a good counsel to relent towards this tyrant, you will repent it when it shall be too late. His malice is fixed and will not evaporate by any of your mild courses ; for he will ascribe the alteration to Her Majesty's pusillanimity, and not to your good nature, knowing that you work but upon her humour, and not out of any love towards him. The less you make him, the less he shall be able to harm you and yours. And if her Majesty's favour fail him, he will again decline into a common person.

'For after-revenges, fear him not. . . .

'Lose not your advantage. If you do, I rede your destiny. . . .

'Let the Queen hold Essex while she hath him. He

will ever be the canker of her estate and safety. Princes are lost by security and preserved by prevention. I have seen the last of her good days and all ours — after his liberty.

'Yours W. R.'

It was thought, by some of Essex's adherents, that Raleigh intended to kill Essex with his own hand, if no other way could be found of getting rid of him.

The intimates of Essex were now urging immediate action. But what was to be done ? Should they march on the Court ? Raise the City on Essex's behalf, and overthrow the Secretary and his power ?

Cecil, on his side, knew that something must be done. Therefore, on Saturday the 7th of February 1601, a messenger arrived at Essex House, commanding Essex to appear before the Council. This was believed by Essex and his adherents to be the prelude to his being sent to the Tower. He declared to the messenger that he was too ill to come. And his friends, crowding round him, decided that next day Cecil should be thrown from power.

Sunday morning saw the guard strengthened at Whitehall, and Sir Charles Danvers, in panic, dashed to Essex House with the warning that it was no longer possible to take the Court by surprise. Essex must fly, immediately, to Wales, and raise a rebellion there. By ten in the morning, a crowd of three hundred had gathered in the courtyard, when a knocking was heard at the gate, and the Earl of Worcester, the Lord Keeper Egerton, the Lord Chief Justice, and Sir William Knollys, entering the house, said they had been sent to ask the meaning of this assembly, and to say that if it arose through any grievance, the cause should be examined and justice given. The noise from the crowd was such that it was impossible for their words to be heard, so Essex took them to the Library, where the crowd pursued them, shouting, 'Kill them ! . . . Away, my Lord ! They abuse you ! They betray you ! You lose time.' Essex told the Councillors to remain where they were, and he would return, and go with them to the

Queen. He was swept through the door and into the street
by the mob yelling 'To the Court ! To the Court !'

There were not enough horses, so they were forced to
walk. Down the Strand the mob rushed, waving their
weapons, and in front of the rebels walked Sir Christopher
Blount, shouting to the people of London that they must rise.

Then came the news that Essex had been proclaimed a
traitor.

The people watched from doorways and windows.

The rebels reached St. Paul's at noon, and still the people
watched, and did not join them. Essex walked on, shouting,
as he went, that there had been a plot to murder him, and
that the succession to the throne had traitorously been sold
to the Infanta of Spain.

And still the people watched in silence.

By the time he reached Cheapside, he knew, says Lytton
Strachey, that all was lost. And still he walked on, the perspira-
tion pouring down his face. In Gracechurch Street he paused,
and went into the house of his friend Sheriff Smith, but Smith,
saying that he must consult the Lord Mayor, left the house,
and when Essex came out he found that many of his adherents
had gone, while the Queen's force had increased. Then he
resolved to return to Essex House, but soldiers were awaiting
him at Lud Gate, and chains barred the way. The rebels
charged, a page was killed, others mortally wounded, and
Blount received a wound. Going down to the river, Essex
reached his house by boat, to find the Councillors had gone.
He started to barricade the house, but before he could do so
the Queen's soldiers arrived under the command of the Lord
Admiral, and Essex, surrendering, was taken to the Tower.

.     .     .     .     .

At his trial, Essex swore that Raleigh had resolved to
assassinate him. And he repeated his accusation against Robert
Cecil that he had sold the Crown to the Spanish Infanta — a
charge that Cecil, who had been listening behind a curtain,
swore, on his knees, was a lie.

Essex's old friend Francis Bacon was in charge of the prosecution, — Bacon, who wrote, 'Love as if you were sometime to hate, and hate, as if you were sometime to love. . . .' Coldly, and with inexorable logic, he brought his accusations. 'I call forth', said Essex, 'Mr. Bacon against Mr. Bacon', and he told how Bacon had helped him write letters to the Queen. 'These digressions', Bacon answered, 'are not fit, neither should be suffered' ; adding that the letters were harmless. 'I have spent more time', he said, 'in vain studying how to make the Earl a good subject to the Queen and State than I have done in anything else.' 'To take secret counsel, to execute it, to run together in numbers, armed with weapons — what can be the excuse ? Warned by the Lord Keeper, by a herald, and yet persist. Will any simple man take this to be less than treason ?'

Essex said, 'If I had purposed anything against others than my private enemies, I would not have stirred with so slender a company'. To which Bacon replied : 'It was not the company you carried with you, but the assistance you hoped for in the city, which you trusted unto. The Duke of Guise thrust himself into the streets of Paris, on the day of the barricadoes, in his doublet and hose, attended only with eight gentlemen, and found that help in the city, which (God be thanked) you failed of here. And what followed ? The King was forced to put himself into a pilgrim's weeds, and in that disguise to steal away to escape their fury. Even such', he said, turning to the Peers, 'was my Lord's confidence too ; and his pretence the same — an all hail and a kiss to the city. But the end was treason, as hath been sufficiently proved.'

Essex and Southampton were found guilty.

In the Tower, Essex fell into a despair that verged on insanity. He must make, he said, a full confession to the Council. To them, he said he was a miserable sinner, grovelling heart-broken before the Judgment Seat of God. His furious denunciations of his co-conspirators poured in a constant stream. They were all traitors — his stepfather, his sister, Sir Charles Danvers. His sister, he said, was particularly

infamous. Not only was she a traitress, she was an adulteress.
. . . 'She must be looked to, for she hath a proud spirit.'
'I know my sins unto Her Majesty and unto my God. I must
confess to you that I am the greatest, the most vilest and most
unthankful traitor that has ever been in the land.'

But this grovelling was not to save him.

On the 21st of February 1601, he was beheaded in the
courtyard of the Tower. It was the duty of the Captain of
the Guard, his old enemy, Sir Walter Raleigh, to be present
at the execution; but there was some murmuring amongst
the few onlookers, and he withdrew.

On the morning of the execution the Queen was playing
the virginals. When the news was brought to her that the
execution had taken place, there was complete silence in the
privy chamber, excepting for the sound of the virginals.

The Queen continued to play.

# Chapter Sixty-seven

NOTHING had happened — only the fall of some bright star, a change in the Queen's mind. 'She is quite disfavoured and unattired', wrote her godson Harington, 'and these troubles waste her much. She disregardeth every costly cover that cometh to the table, and taketh little but manchet and succory pottage. Every new message from the city disturbs her, and she frowns on all her ladies. I had a sharp message from her, brought by my lord Buckhurst, namely thus, — "Go, tell that witty fellow, my godson, to get home ; it is no season to fool it here". I liked this as little as she doth my knighthood, so took to my boots, and returned to my plough, in bad weather. I must not say much, even by this trusty and sure messenger, but the many evil plots and designs have overcome all her Highness's sweet temper. . . .

'She walks much in her privy-chamber, and stamps with her foot at ill news, and thrusts her rusty sword at times, into the arras, in great rage. My lord Buckhurst is much with her, and few else, since the city business, but the dangers are over, and yet she always keeps a sword by her table. . . . So disordered is all order, that her Highness hath worn but one change of raiment for many days, and swears much at those that cause her griefs in such wise, to the no small discomfiture of all about her, more especially our sweet lady Arundel, that *Venus plus quam venusta*.'

On the 17th of March 1601, Sir Christopher Blount, the former Lady Leycester's third husband, and Sir Charles Danvers were beheaded ; but Southampton's death sentence was commuted to imprisonment, in which he remained till her death.

The days were sunk in melancholy.

Then, in the autumn of that stricken year, the Queen made what was, perhaps, the greatest speech of her long reign.

On the 30th of November, at three in the afternoon, she received a number of members of the House of Commons in the Council Chamber at Whitehall. These had come to give her thanks for granting their petitions that the ills arising from the giving of monopolies (such as that for sweet wines that had been given to Essex) should cease. Through the Speaker, the House had been told that 'she understood that divers patents . . . were grievous to her subjects and that the substitutes of the patentees had used great oppression'. She had 'never assented to grant anything that was *malum in se*'. 'I cannot express unto you', he said, 'the apparent indignation of Her Majesty towards these abuses. . . .'

Now, to her thankful members, she said : 'I do assure you there is no prince who loves his subjects better, or whose love can countervail our love. There is no jewel, be it of never so rich a price, which I set before this jewel : I mean your love. For I do esteem it more than any treasure or riches ; for that we know how to prize, but love and thanks I count invaluable. And, though God hath raised me high, yet I count the glory of my crown, that I have reigned with your loves. This makes me that I do not so much rejoice that God hath made me to be a Queen, as to be a Queen over so thankful a people. Therefore, I have cause to wish nothing more than to content the subject ; and that is a duty which I owe. Neither do I desire to live longer days than I may see your prosperity ; and that is my only desire. And as I am that person that still yet under God hath delivered you, so I trust, by the almighty power of God, that I shall be His instrument to preserve you from every peril, dishonour, shame, tyranny, and oppression ; partly by means of your intended helps' (they were granting her subsidies) 'which we take very acceptably, because it manifesteth the largeness of your good loves and loyalties unto your sovereign.

'Of myself I must say this : I never was any greedy, scraping grasper, nor a strait, fast-holding prince, nor yet a waster. My heart was never set on any worldly goods, but only for my subjects' good. What you bestow on me, I will not hoard it up, but receive it to bestow on you again. Yea, mine own properties I account yours, to be expended for your good ; and your eyes shall see the bestowing of it all for your good. Therefore, render unto them, I beseech you, Mr. Speaker, such thanks as you imagine my heart yieldeth, but my tongue cannot express.'

Till now, the members knelt, but the Queen said, 'Mr. Speaker, I would wish you and the rest to stand up, for I shall yet trouble you with longer speech'. They rose to their feet, and she continued : 'Mr. Speaker, you give me thanks, but I doubt me I have a greater cause to give you thanks than you me, and I charge you to thank them of the Lower House from me. For, had I not received a knowledge from you, I might have fallen into the lapse of an error, only for lack of true information.

'Since I was Queen, yet did I never put my pen to any grant but that, upon pretext and semblance made unto me, it was both good and beneficial to the subjects in general, though a profit to some of my ancient servants who had deserved well at my hands. But the contrary being found by experience, I am exceedingly beholden to such subjects as would move the same at the first. And I am not so simple as to suppose, but that there be some of the Lower House whom these grievances never touched, and for them, I think they spake out of zeal to their countries and not out of spleen or malevolent affection as being parties grieved, and I take it exceeding gratefully from them, because it gives us to know that no respects or interest had moved them, other than the minds they have to suffer no diminution of our honour and our subjects' love unto us. The zeal of which affection, tending to ease my people and knit their hearts unto me, I embrace with a princely care, for above all earthly treasure I esteem my people's love, more than which I desire not to merit.

'That my grants should be grievous to my people and oppressions privileged under cover of our patents, our kingly dignity shall not suffer it. Yea, when I heard of it, I could give no rest unto my thoughts, until I had reformed it. Shall they, think you, escape unpunished that have thus oppressed you, and have been respectless of their duty, and regardless of our honour ? No, I assure you, Mr. Speaker, were it not more for conscience' sake than for any glory or increase of love that I desire, these errors, troubles, vexations and oppressions, done by these varlets and lewd persons, not worthy the name of subjects, should not escape without condign punishment. But I perceive they dealt with me like physicians who, ministering a drug, make it more acceptable by giving it a good aromatical savour, or when they give pills do gild them all over.

'I have ever used to set the Last Judgment Day before mine eyes, and so to rule as I shall be judged to answer before a higher Judge, to whose judgment seat I do appeal, that never thought was cherished in my heart that tended not unto my people's good. And now, if my kingly bounties have been abused, and my grants turned to the hurt of my people, contrary to my will and meaning, and if any in authority under me have neglected or perverted what I have committed to them, I hope God will not lay their culps and offences to my charge ; who, though there were danger in repealing our grants, yet what danger would I not rather incur for your good, than I would suffer them still to continue.

'I know the title of a King is a glorious title ; but assure yourself that the shining glory of princely authority hath not so dazzled the eyes of our understanding, but that we well know and remember that we also are to yield an account of our actions before the great Judge. To be a King and wear a crown is a thing more glorious to them that see it, than it is pleasant to them that bear it. For myself, I was never so much enticed with the glorious name of a King or royal authority of a Queen, as delighted that God hath made me His instrument to maintain His truth and glory, and to defend this Kingdom (as I said) from peril, dishonour, tyranny and oppression.

'There will never Queen sit in my seat with more zeal
to my country, care for my subjects, and that will sooner with
willingness venture her life for your good and safety, than
myself. For it is my desire to live nor reign no longer than
my life and reign shall be for your good. And though you
have had and may have many princes more mighty and wise
sitting in this seat, yet you never had nor shall have any that
will be more careful and loving.

'Shall I ascribe anything to myself and my sexly weakness ? I were not worthy to live then ; and of all, most unworthy of the mercies I have had from God, who hath given
me a heart that yet never feared any foreign or home enemy.
And I speak it to give God the praise, as a testimony before
you, and not to attribute anything to myself. For I, oh Lord !
what am I, whom practices and perils past should not fear ?
Or what can I do ? That I should speak for any glory, God
forbid.

'This, Mr. Speaker, I pray you deliver unto the House,
to whom heartily recommend me. And so I commit you all
to your best fortunes and further counsels. And I pray you,
Mr. Comptroller, Mr. Secretary, and you of my Council,
that before these gentlemen go into their countries, you bring
them all to kiss my hand.'

So spoke the old Queen, with the night falling around
her.

# Chapter Sixty-eight

On the 4th of August 1598, 'Sir William Cecil, Knight of the Order of the Garter, Lord Burleigh, Master of the Wards and Liveries, High Treasurer of England, famous Counsellor to the Queen's Majesty all her raigne, and likewise had been to Edward VI; who for his singular wisdom was renowned throughout all Europe, departed this mortall life at his house by the Strand'.

His last years had been filled with grief.

In 1582, his son-in-law, William Wentworth, died, after a few hours' illness, of the plague. The Lord Treasurer was to have attended on the Queen at Hertford, but when, returning to his country house, he found his son-in-law newly dead, he sent to the secretary Walsingham, to make his excuses to the Queen. He, in reply, reported the Queen as saying 'she had as just cause to be grieved for the public, as his lordship for his part'. And that 'the taking away a man of his virtue and hope, in this corrupted age, was an argument of God's displeasure towards us'; he ended with this prayer : 'The Lord give us grace to make our own profit thereof; and send your lordship patience to bear this cross, laid upon you, in that Christian course that becometh you'.

'The Queen, as well, sent Mr. Manners, the Earl of Rutland's son, to the lord treasurer, with great sorrow, to comfort him from herself.' [1]

The dead man's wife, who was with child, died five months after him (in April 1583). The Queen sent an affectionate message of condolence ; then, after a time, sent, by Walsingham, to ask Burleigh, in order to take his mind from his sorrow, to return to work. The message ran : 'That as she was pleased, for a time, to permit him to wrestle with nature, not doubting but that wisdom and religion had wrought in him, ere this, that resolution that appertained to a man of his place and calling ; so now she thought, that if the health of his body might so permit, he should do better to occupy himself in dealing in public causes, than by secluding himself from access, to give himself over a prey to grief. And particularly that she would be glad of his advice on a matter of weight, concerning an offer lately made unto her by the Scots Queen, sent to Court from the Earl of Shrewsbury.'

Then, in 1588, that death was followed by that of his own beloved wife, with whom he had lived, in great happiness, for forty-three years. Of that death, he wrote : 'There is no cogitation to be used with an attempt to recover that which can never be had again ; that is, to have my dear wife to live again in this mortal body, which is separated from the soul, and resteth in the earth dead, and the soul taken up to heaven, and there to remain in the fruition of blessedness unspeakable, until the general resurrection of all flesh ; then, by the almighty power of God (who made all things of nothing), her body shall be raised up, and joined with her soul, in an everlasting unspeakable joy, such as no tongue can conceive.

'Therefore my cogitation ought to be occupied in these things following : To thank Almighty God for his favour, in permitting her to have lived so many years together with me ; And to have given her grace to have had true knowledge of her salvation by the death of His Son Jesus. . . .

'And, too, of her many charitable deeds whereof she determined to have no outward knowledge while she lived. . . .'

Her charities were great, and included yearly sums to be given for the feeding of the destitute in the prisons.

The old wise counsellor had fallen into an incurable melancholy, from which the Queen tried in vain to rouse him. In 1583, the year after his son-in-law's death, he begged Her Majesty that he might be allowed to leave her service and retire into private life — his reasons being that he had heard rumours that she was displeased with him, and, also, that he had 'received some hard words in the Council'.[2] To these troubles had been added that 'unhappie griefe in the foote', the gout.

The Queen wrote to him, with her own hand, the following letter.

'Sir Spirit,' (for this was her playful and affectionate way of addressing him) 'I doubt I do misname you. For those of your kind (they say) have no sense. But I have of late seen an *ecce signum*, that if an ass kick you, you feel it so soon. I shall recant you from being *Spirit* if ever I perceive that you disdain not such a feeling. Serve God, fear the King, and be a good fellow to the rest. Let never care appear in you for such a rumour : but let them well know, that you rather desire the righting of such error, by making known their error, than you to be so silly a soul, as to foreshadow that you ought to do, or not freely discover that you think meetest, and pass of no man so much, as not to regard her trust, who putteth it in you.

God bless, and long may you last. Omnino. E.R.'

(Endorsed by the Lord Treasurer : 'Received 8 May, 1583'.)

Now, as he lay waiting for death, by an open window under which spread the glittering sea of gillyflowers, so much prized by him, he, sleeping a little, then waking to be given 'physique made of the red or Clove Gilloflower', that gives 'so gallant a tincture to a Syrope', or 'that Comfortable Cordiall to cheer the Heart', made of Conserve of Gilliflowers, musk, a spoonful of cinamon water, syrup of gilliflowers, and ambergreece — or a little cup of Gilliflower Wine, made of 'red Gilliflowers put into Sack, with Sugar Candy and Ambergreece' — perhaps these, and the sight and odour of that glittering sea of flowers, were of some comfort to the old man on whom the cares of state had lain so heavily, and whose happiness was gone.

('Old, old, Master Shallow.')

Sir John Harington recorded her great anxiety and solicitude for the dying old man. Lady Arundel was sent by her, every day, 'with enquiries as to his state, and bearing an excellent cordial for his stomach, which Her Majesty gave her in charge, and said that she did entreat Heaven daily for his longer life, else would her people, nay herself, stand in need of Cordials too'. 'The Lord Treasurer's distemper', wrote Harington, 'doth marvellously distemper the Queen, who saith "that her comfort hath been in her people's happiness and their happiness in his discretion"; neither can we find, in ancient record, such wisdom in a prince to discover a servant's ability, nor such integrity to reward and honour a prince's choice.'

The Queen often came to visit him, and when the servants brought him cordials or food, she would insist on giving it him with her own hands.

At one moment he felt well enough to write his son Robert a letter : 'I pray you diligently and affectionately let Her Majesty understand, how her singular kindness doth overcome my power to acquit it, who, though she will not be a mother, yet she sheweth herself, by feeding me with her own princely hand, as a careful norice [nurse] ; and if I (ever) may be weaned to feed myself, I shall be more ready to serve her on the earth ; if not, I hope to be, in heaven, a servitor for her and God's church.

'And so I thank you for your partridges.

> 'Your languishing father
> 'W. Burleigh.'

'10 July 1598.

'P.S. Serve God *by serving the Queen*, for all other service is indeed bondage to the devil.'

He was aged seventy-six.

'On the day of his death', we are told, 'at 7 in the morning, he fell into a convulsion, like the shaking of an ague. "Now", quoth he, "the Lord be praised ; the time is come"; and then, calling for his children, he blessed them and took his leave of them, commanding them to "serve God and love one another". He also prayed for the Queene that she might live long, and, at last, die in peace.

'He languished, till four of the clock, sometimes wanting, sometimes having, speech.

'During which time he often said "O what a hart is this, that will not let me die ! Come, Lord Jesu ! One dropp of death, Lord Jesu !" — and so lay praying to himself, as we might hear him speak softly.

'In which extremity you must imagine the wailing of his children and friends, servants (being twenty in the chamber), every one praying and devising, what to give him, if it were possible, to hold his life in him.

'. . . Then, lying still, the standers by might hear him say softly to himself, "Lord, receive my spirit !" "Lord, have mercy on me !" which were the last words he was heard to speak.'[3]

So died 'the youngest, the oldest, the gravest, the greatest counsellor in Christendom'.[4]

## NOTES TO CHAPTER SIXTY-EIGHT

[1] Strype.
[2] *Desiderata Curiosa.*
[3] *Ibid.*
[4] *Ibid.*

# Chapter Sixty-nine

[This chapter owes much of its information to Agnes Strickland's
*The Life of Queen Elizabeth*.]

AFTER the death of Essex, 'Green wounds scarce abide the
toucher's hand', the Queen said to a lady who, seeing her sunk
in deep melancholy, asked what troubled her. 'She sleepeth
not so much by day,' said a letter from Court, 'neither taketh
rest by night. Her delight is to sit in the dark and sometimes
with shedding of tears to bewail Essex.'

.        .        .        .        .

The antiquarian Lambarde, having been received by the
Queen in her privy chamber at Greenwich for the purpose of
receiving from him his *Pandecta* of the Tower Records, she,
turning over the pages, said, when she came to the reign of
Richard II, 'I am Richard the Second. Know ye not that?'
(She was thinking of the play about Richard II which Essex
had performed immediately before the rising.)

'Such a wicked imagination', said the old man, 'was
determined and attempted by a most unkind gentleman —
the most adorned creature that Your Majesty ever made.'

'He that will forget God', said the Queen, 'will also forget
his benefactress.' Speaking of the past of England, she said,
'In those days, force and arms did prevail, but now the wit of
the fox is everywhere on foot, so as hardly one faithful or
virtuous may be found'.

Her state varied from day to day. At one moment there
were rumours in the city that the Queen was dead; and she,
hearing these, said, 'Dead but not buried. Dead but not
buried.'

Sometimes it seemed as if she would recover from her
melancholy; and we remember the great phrase uttered by

her at her Coronation : 'Time hath brought me hither, and Time must still be my friend'.

'We are frolic at Court,' the Earl of Worcester told Lord Shrewsbury, 'much dancing in the Privy Chamber before the Queen's Majesty, who is exceedingly pleased therewith . . . Irish tunes are at this time most liked ; but in winter "Lullaby", an old song of Mr. Byrd's, will be more in request, as I think.' [1]

The world had fallen into winter, and the strawberry paths of the Palace gardens were white with frost as they had been, in spring, with the dew. And the cold, almost like that of death, had invaded the heart and veins of the Queen. The deaths of ladies about the Queen (The Countess of Nottingham — the daughter of Lord Hunsdon, Lady Peyton of the Tower, Lady Skolt, and Lady Heyward) seemed like leaves falling, and added to the Queen's melancholy.

Once Lord Sempill, looking through the window of a room in the Palace, saw the old Queen dancing to the sound of a pipe and tabor, leaping into the air like a tall thin flame with, as sole companion apart from the musicians, Lady Warwick, who for forty years as girl, wife, and widow, had been her faithful servant.

When she made her last journey from Hampton Court, as she passed through Kingston, an old man cried, 'May you live to an hundred years !'

The old Queen looked pleased and Lord Sempill, seeing this, said, 'Some preachers pray she may live as long as the sun and the moon'.

But her melancholy grew.

On the 27th of December 1602, Harington wrote to his wife : 'Our dear Queen, my royal godmother, and this state's natural mother, doth now bear show of human infirmity too fast for that evil which we shall get by her death, and too slow for that good which we shall get by her releasement from her pains and misery. I was bidden to her presence; I blessed the happy moment, and found her in a most pitiable state. She bade the Archbishop ask me if I had seen Tyrone. I replied, with reverence, "that I had seen him with the Lord Deputy" [Essex]. She looked up, with much choler and grief in her countenance, and said "Oh ! Now it mindeth me that you were *one* who saw this man *elsewhere*", and hereat she dropped a tear, and smote her bosom. She held in her hand a golden cup, which she oft put to her lips, but in sooth her heart seemeth too full to lack more filling. . . . She made me come to the chamber at seven o'clock.

'Her Majesty enquired of some matters which I had written ; and as she was pleased to note my fanciful brain, I was not unheedful to feel her human, and read some verses ; whereat she smiled, once, and was pleased to say, "When thou dost feel creeping Time at thy gate, these fooleries will please thee less. I am past my relish for such matters. Thou seest my bodily meat doth not suit me well. I have eaten but one ill-tasted cake since yesternight."

'She rated most grievously, at noon, at some who minded not to bring up certain matters of account. Several men have been sent to, and when ready at hand, Her Highness hath dismissed in anger ; but who, dearest Moll, shall say "Your Highness hath forgotten"?'

Lady Southwell, one of the Queen's ladies (sister-in-law to the martyr Robert Southwell, the poet of the 'Burning Babe'), kept a record of the strange, fairy-tale atmosphere of her mistress's last days. That record is now at Stonyhurst.

'Her Majesty', she wrote, 'being in very good health one day, Sir John Stanhope, vice-chamberlain and Sir Robert Cecil's dependent and familiar, came and presented Her Majesty with a piece of gold of the lightness of an angel, full of characters, which he said an old woman in Wales had bequeathed to her (the Queen) on her deathbed ; and thereupon he discoursed how the said testatrix, by virtue of her piece of gold, lived to the age of 120 years, and in that age having all her body withered and consumed, and wanting nature to nourish her ere she died, commanding [sic] the said piece of gold to be carefully sent to Her Majesty, alleging [sic] further, that as long as she wore it at her body, she could not die. The

Queen in confidence took the said gold, and hung it about her neck . . .

'Though she became not suddenly sick, yet she daily decreased of her rest and feeding, and in these fifteen days she fell downright ill, and the cause being wondered by my Lady Scrope, with whom she was very private and confident, being her near kinswoman, Her Majesty told her (commanding her to conceal the same) that she saw one night her own body, exceeding lean and fearful, in a light of fire.'

This vision was at Whitehall, a little before she departed for Richmond, and was testified by another lady, who was one of the nearest about her person, of whom the Queen demanded, 'Whether she was not wont to see sights in the night?' telling her of the bright flame she had seen.

'Afterwards, in the melancholy of her sickness, she desired to see a *true* looking-glass, which in twenty years before she had not seen, but only such an one as on purpose was made to deceive her sight, which true looking-glass being brought her, she presently fell exclaiming at all those flatterers which had so much commended her ; and they durst not after come into her presence.'

No longer was that face which, in youth, had been beautiful, painted ; and the great Queen saw her humanity under the former trappings of glory.

On the 14th of January 1603, having had a cold which lasted for two days, she was warned by the astrologer Dee to 'beware of Whitehall'. She travelled to Richmond Palace, saying that this was 'the warm winter-box to shelter her old age'.

.      .      .      .      .      .

At first she seemed better ; but on the 28th of February her illness returned.

Her cousin Robert Carey, afterwards Earl of Monmouth, was summoned to Court. 'I found the Queen ill-disposed,' he wrote in his *Autobiography*, 'and she kept her inner lodging ; yet, hearing of my arrival, she sent for me. I found her in one of her withdrawing chambers, sitting low upon her cushions. She called me to her ; I kissed her hand, and told her it was my chiefest happiness to see her in safety and in health which I wished might long continue. She took me by the hand, and wrung it hard, and said, "No, Robin. *I am not well*" ; and then discoursed to me of her indisposition, and that her heart had been sad and heavy for ten or twelve days, and in her discourse she fetched not so few as forty or fifty great sighs. I was grieved, at the first, to see her in this plight, for in all my lifetime before I never saw her fetch a sigh, but when the Queen of Scots was beheaded. Then, upon my knowledge, she shed many sighs and tears, manifesting her innocence that she never gave consent to the death of that Queen. . . .

'This was upon a Saturday night, and she gave command that the great closet should be prepared for her to go to chapel next morning.

'But Sunday morning came, and the Court long expected her coming.

'After eleven o'clock, one of the grooms [of the closet] came out, and bade make ready for the private closet, for she would not go to the great. There we stayed long for her coming ; but at the last she had cushions laid for her in the privy chamber, hard by the closet door, and there she heard the service. From that day forward she grew worse and worse ; she remained upon her cushions four days and nights at the least. All about her could not persuade her either to take sustenance, or to go to bed.'

'The Queen', said another of her courtiers, 'had fallen into a state of moping, sighing, and weeping melancholy ; and being asked by her attendants "whether she had any secret grief ?" she replied "that she knew of nothing in this world worthy of troubling her". . . .

'On Wednesday, the Lord Admiral, her cousin, was summoned. Kneeling beside her, where she sat among her cushions, kissing her hands, he begged her with tears to take a little sustenance. She allowed him to feed her with a little broth, but when he implored her to go to bed, she refused, and said, "If he were in the habit of seeing such things in his bed as she did when in hers, he would not persuade her to go there".'

After Cecil and the rest of the Council left her presence, the Queen said to her cousin, 'My lord, I am tied with a chain of iron about my neck. I am tied, I am tied, and the case is altered with me.'

'At last she was carried to bed, almost by force, but left it almost immediately and returned to her cushions and lay there, "in a manner insensible"', the French Ambassador told his King, 'not speaking above once or twice in two or three hours, and at last [she] remained silent for four and twenty, holding her finger almost continually in her mouth, with her rayless eyes open, and fixed upon the ground, where she sat on cushions, without rising or resting herself, and was greatly emaciated by her long watching and fasting'.

She was again put to bed 'almost by force'.

Her ladies were seized with terror, imagining witchcraft ; for one had seen the phantom of the Queen drifting down the long corridors.

According to Lady Southwell, 'Lady Guildford, then in waiting upon the Queen, leaving her in an almost breathless sleep in her Privy Chamber, went to take a little air, and met Her Majesty, as she thought, three or four chambers off'. Lady Guildford returned, in terror, to the Queen's room, to find that she had seen an apparition only. For the Queen lay there, '. . . still in the same lethargic, motionless slumber in which she had left her'.

'The Queen kept her bed for fifteen days', wrote Lady Southwell, 'besides the three days she sat upon a stool ; and one day, when, being pulled up by force, she obstinately stood on her feet for fifteen hours.'

On the 23rd of March, she, having been restored to bed, said, 'I wish not to live any longer, but desire to die'.

'She made signs', wrote Carey, 'for her Council to be

called, and by putting her hand to her head, when the King of Scotland was named to succeed her, they all knew he was the man she desired should reign after her.'

The Archbishop of Canterbury knelt by her side ; '. . . he began to pray, and all that were by did answer him. After he had continued long in prayer, the old man's knees were weary ; he blessed her, and meant to rise and leave her. The Queen made a sign with her hand . . . meaning that she wished him to continue his prayers.' This he did, 'with earnest cries to God for her soul's health, which he uttered with that fervency of spirit, that the Queen, to all our sight, much rejoiced thereat . . .'. But 'by this time it grew late, and every one departed, all but the women who attended her'.

The long journey was almost at an end.

She who was born on the eve of the Nativity of Our Lady, died on the 24th of March, the eve of the Festival of the Annunciation.

The Queen fell into a deep sleep, and drifted far, far away from the land she had loved so well.

It was at about three in the morning that it was found she had 'sayled so far that she came at last to the place where she found no night at all, but a continual light and brightnesse of the Sunne, shining clearly upon the huge and mightie Sea'.

### NOTES TO CHAPTER SIXTY-NINE

[1] Anecdote quoted by James Pope-Hennessy in *London Fabric*.

# Dr. Dee

MANY years after Dr. Dee had foretold the date auspicious for the Coronation, the Queen received, in the privy gardens at Greenwich, this old man who 'delivered her Majesty the heavenly admonition and her Majesty took it thoughtfully.— Only the Lady Warwyck and Sir Robert Cecill his Lady were in the garden with Her Majestie'.[1]

The old man was Dr. John Dee.

John Aubrey, the great-grandson of his cousin 'Will Aubrey', wrote of Dr. Dee: 'He had a very fair, cleare rosie complexion; a long beard as white as milke; he was tall and slender; a very handsome man. . . . He wore a Gowne like an artist's gowne, with hanging sleeves and a slitt; a mighty good man he was.'

His had been an extraordinary career. A highly distinguished scientist, mathematician, and astronomer (he was a Fellow of Trinity College, Cambridge), he was also the principal alchemist of England, believing it possible to transmute base metal into gold, and to discover the philosopher's stone. John Aubrey wrote that 'Arthur Dee, his sonne, a Physitian at Norwich and intimate friend of Sir Thomas Browne, M.D. told Mr. Bathurst that (being but a Boy) he used to play at Quoits with the Plates of gold made by Projection in the Garret of Dr. Dee's Lodgings in Prague'.

In 1580, he put together descriptions of lately discovered countries for the Queen, at her request, and his calculations facilitated the adoption of the Gregorian Calendar in England in 1583.

But 'in those darke times', as Aubrey wrote, in his character of Dr. Dee's fellow mathematician, Thomas Allen, 'astrologer, mathematician, and conjurer were accounted the same things'. Thomas Allen (like Dr. Dee) 'had a great many Mathematical Instruments and Glasses in his Chamber, which did also confirme the ignorant in their opinion, and his servitor (to impose on Freshmen and simple people), would tell them that sometimes he should meet the Spirits coming up his stairs like Bees'. . . . And, too, when visiting a friend, he 'happened to leave his Watch in the Chamber windowe. (Watches were then rarities.) The maydes came in to make the Bed, and hearing a thing in a case cry Tick, Tick, Tick, presently concluded that that was his Devill, and tooke it by the String with the tongues [tongs] and threw it out of the windowe into the Mote (to drowne the Devill). It so happened that the string hung on a sprig of an elder that grew out of the Mote, and thus confirmed them that twas the Devill. So the good old gentleman gott his watch again.'

But Dr. Dee was not as lucky as Mr. Allen. The mob broke into his house at Mortlake, and wrecked all his mathematical instruments.

Dr. Dee had been in the confidence of the Queen from the reign of her sister Mary, when she narrowly escaped a charge of witchcraft. (He had been presented to her, in her early girlhood, by Sir William Cecil.) She would often send for him, as when, alarmed by the appearance of a comet, she summoned him to Windsor, where he spent three days in explaining it to the Queen, or as when he was sent for to consult with her doctors about her toothache. When he was dangerously ill at Mortlake, the Queen sent two of her own physicians to attend him, and, as well, sent Lady Sidney, with 'pithy' and comforting messages from the Queen, and 'divers rarities' from the Queen's table.

Supposed by the mob, as we have seen, to be a wizard, he defended himself, in his Preface to Sir Henry Billingsley's first English translation of Euclid's *Elements* (1570), from the charge of witchcraft, declaring that arithmetic 'next to theologie is most divine, most profound, most subtle, most commodious, and most necessarie'. Quoting Plato, he affirmed that 'it lifts the heart above the heavens by invisible lines'.

He invented the paradoxical compass, predicted the invention of the telescope, and, indeed, suggested that perspective glasses should form a part of the Army's equipment. In 1580, he was constantly at Muscovy House, drawing charts for the captains Charles Jackson and Arthur Pett for their north-east journey to Cathay.

'Young Mr. Hawkins, who had been with Mr. Drake', came, according to the Doctor's Diary, 'to me at Mortlake', in 1581, and, two years after, on the 23rd of January (1583), 'Mr. Secretary Walsingham came to my house where by good luck he found Mr.

Awdrian Gilbert, and so talke was begunne on the North West Straights discovery', and on the following day 'Mr. Awdrian Gilbert and John Davis went by appointment to Mr. Secretary, to Mr. Beale his house, where only we four were present, and we made Mr. Beale secret of the North-West passage, and all charts'.

Such was Dr. Dee's fame that the 'Emperor of Muscovia, upon report of the great learning of the mathematician, invited him to Mosco, with offer of two thousand pound a yeare, and from Prince Boris one thousand markes, to have his provision from the Emperor's table, to be honourably received, and accounted as one of the chief men in the Land'. Alas for him ! He did not accept the offer.

In 1582, or 1583, a terrible zombie-like figure, a medium inhabited by an evil spirit, came into this good old man's life. Dressed always in black, and wearing always a skull cap to hide where his ears had been shorn away, this creature followed him like his shadow — a shade ever growing in length.

Edward Kelley, the medium, against whom the charge had been brought of digging up a recently executed criminal's corpse in order to question the dead — this was the being who was to help bring Dr. Dee to his ultimate ruin. He became Dee's inseparable companion, in England and abroad — and the thief of Dee's discoveries.

Certain difficulties, we understand from Eliphas Lévi's *Transcendental Magic*, attended the questioning of the Dead. And as the authorities were stubbornly opposed to the digging up of corpses, it was probably wiser to do so when invisible — and this desirable state could be brought about, according to the *Grimorium Verum* [2] by 'the interment of seven black beans with the head of a dead man, to be buried face upwards and watered with brandy'.

So far, so good. But as for the actual questioning : it must be preceded by a blood sacrifice, a fast of fifteen days, with 'a single unsalted repast after sundown. It should consist of black bread and blood, or black beans and milky and narcotic herbs.' [3] In addition, the questioner must 'get drunk every five days after sundown on wine in which five heads of poppies and five ounces of pounded hempseed have been steeped for five hours, the infusion being strained through a cloth woven by a prostitute'.

Above all, the ceremony *must* take place in a sufficiently gloomy place ; and a censer must be swung with incense made of 'camphor, aloes, ambergris, and storax, mixed together with the blood of a goat, a mole, and a bat ; four nails taken from the coffin of an executed criminal ; the head of a black cat which has been nourished on human flesh for five days ; a bat drowned in blood ; the horns of a goat . . . and the skull of a parricide'.

A good deal more of the same kind was needed ; and one formula of evocation 'consists only in these words "Dies Mies Jeschet Boenedoesef Douvema Enitemaus"'. Lévi says, 'We make no pretence of understanding the meaning'.

Taking all things into consideration, as the purpose of evoking the Dead was to gain a fortune, I cannot but think that it would have been cheaper, and less trouble, to become a member of the Stock Exchange. But we must remember that in the 16th century there *was* no Stock Exchange.

The sinister creature Kelley was to take all the credit due to Dee. He professed to have produced 'nearly an ounce of the best gold' from about an ounce and a quarter of mercury.

Burleigh, on hearing this, quickly took this pretended great alchemist under his protection. Kelley was knighted. And when he was at Prague, Dyer, the Queen's agent, received a letter from the Lord Treasurer urging him to beg 'Sir Edward Kelley to come over to his native country and honour Her Majesty with the fruits of such knowledge as God has given him'. (Dyer, who had been Dee's almost lifelong friend, had, of course, deserted him for Kelley.)

But there must have been awkward moments for the latter — as when the Lord Treasurer suggested that the alchemist should 'send Her Majesty as a token a good round sum of money, say enough to defray the expenses of the Navy for the summer'. Not only that, but he asked (the 18th February 1591) for 'a prescription for the elixir of life'.

In an undated letter, the Lord Treasurer wrote : 'Many say if you come not, it is because you cannot perform what has been reported of you. . . . I am expressly commanded by Her Majesty to require you to have regard of her honour. . . . Be assured of worldly reward. You can make your Queen so happie . . . surely as no subject she hath can do the like.' (For Elizabeth's greed for money, always great, was growing on her.) . . . 'Good Knight, let me end my letter conjuring you, in God's holy name, not to keep God's gift from your natural countrie, but rather helpe make Her Majestie a glorious and victorious power against the mallyce of hers and God's enemies.'

But the good Knight remembered his experiences in the stocks, and the shearing of his ears. He was in Prague, and in Prague he intended to remain. He had now been created a Baron of his semi-adopted country, but at one moment he seems to have been put in prison there, for Philip Gawdy, writing to his brother from 'my L of Shrewsbury's house' (December 1593), said 'Kelley is delivered out of prison and restored to his former estate, and maketh gold as fast as a hen will crack nuttes'.

The gentle Dee said of him only that he did 'injure me unkindlye'.

Dee had been promised many benefits by the Queen. . . . That he should be Provost of Eton . . . Chancellor of St. Paul's. None of these promises were kept. One by one, all his hopes faded.

Long after the Queen's death, when, in his destitution, and persecuted by the mob, he begged to be tried for witchcraft, King James paid no heed ; he was nearly eighty ; he had no money left ; and now there was no one left with whom he could speak, excepting his daughter Katherine, and the Archangel Raphael, who came to visit him.

The Archangel tried to comfort him. The old man had been hoping that money would come from the Emperor Rudolf. It did not come. But the Archangel said, 'Let it go. . . . The Emperor of all Emperors will be thy comfort'.

On a hot day in July, when he was staying at the Three Keys, in King Street, Westminster, the Archangel came again to visit him, and told him that 'his perishing bodily form shall be restored and made sound, for he is shortly to go on a long journey to friends beyond the sea . . . he is to have long life. . . . And instead of living in want, or beholden to those who love him not, he shall be provided for where he shall be able to do God service. He shall enjoy fame and memory to the end.'

'But', said his biographer, Charlotte Fell Smith, 'the old man thought he would like to take Katherine his daughter with him. What would he do without her ?'

It was not yet quite time for that long journey. The time came in 1608.

## NOTES TO APPENDIX A

[1] Dr. Dee's Diary.          [2] Professor E. M. Butler, *Ritual Magic*.
[3] Eliphas Lévi, translated by A. E. Waite.

# Witchcraft in Elizabethan England

IT was singularly unfortunate that Lord Robert Dudley's name should be associated with necromancy, since, at the time of the Queen's accession, the peril from witchcraft was already such that Bishop Jewel felt constrained to preach a sermon in her presence, denouncing the evil, and demanding its punishment by death.

'The horrible using of your poor subjects', declared the Bishop, 'enforceth thereof. It may please Your Grace to understand that this kind of people, within these last few years, are marvellously increased within your realm. These eyes have seen most evident and manifest marks of their wickedness. Your Grace's subjects pine away even unto death, their colour fadeth, their flesh rotteth, their speech is benumbed, their senses are bereft. Wherefore your poor subjects' most humble petition unto your Highness is that the laws touching such malefactors may be put into execution. For the shoal of them is great, their doings horrible, their malice intolerable, the examples most miserable. And I pray God they never practise further than the subject.'

But they did, and in the first year of the reign.

'Black magic', wrote Eliphas Lévi in his *History of Magic*, 'may be defined as the art of inducing artificial mania in ourselves and in others ; but it is, also, and above all, the science of poisoning.'

The people believed that a good magic existed. But that consisted of a wise use of the powers of Nature, or was founded on fancy, and had nothing to do with black magic.

It was imagined, for instance, that if 'the small blew leaves of the periwinkle, beaten into powder with earthworms, be put in the fyre, it shall be turned into blew colour'.[1] Or if the little blue flowers of the herb vervaine be put into a dove-house, 'all the doves shall be gathered there ; and if the powder thereof be put in the sunne, it shall appeare that the sunne be blew'.

Such was the innocent country magic, that harmed no one.

The black science seemed to have existed from the beginning of time.

Montague Summers, in *Witchcraft and Black Magic*, declares (p. 73) that 'the blood-maniac Commodus (A.D. 180–192) and the hag-ridden Caracalla (A.D. 214–217) offered human sacrifices to devils, sought oracles from familiar spirits, and companioned with the fraternity of sorcerers'. And that 'St. Clement, St. Augustine, Eusebius . . . were of opinion that sorcery and the worship of the devil were the chief reasons for the Deluge . . . Cham (Ham) having revived the forbidden science'.

Drop after drop of water gathering, moving until in their multitudes they formed mountains, gaining a diabolical force, taking on an appalling life, engendered by the will to destroy. Mountains of water gathering. . . . Or the body of a man melting, small drop by drop. . . .

King Duffius of Scotland fell into a strange sickness, in which he dwindled away, day by day, night by night, as if he were a man of wax and the days and nights a fire. One day, a passer-by heard from a girl's lips some mysterious words, meant to be unheard. Whereupon, 'some of the Guard being sent, found the lass's mother with some Hags, such as herself, roasting before a small moderate Fire, the King's picture made of Wax. The design of this horrid Act was that as the Wax by little and little did melt away, so did the King's body. . . . The Waxen Image being found and broken, and those old Hags being punished by death, the King did in that moment recover.' [2]

Many years later, another King of Scotland was to be subjected to the same attempt. 'Anny Samson' (evidence given at her trial) 'affirmed that she, in company with nine other witches, being confined in the night beside Prestonpans, the Devil their master being present, standing in the midst of them, there a body of wax, shaped and made by the same Anny Samson, wrapped within a linen cloth, was first delivered to the devil ; which, after he had pronounced his verdo, delivered the same picture to Anny Samson, and she to her nearest marrow, and so everyone round about, saying 'This is King James the Sixth, ordered to be consumed at the instance of a nobleman, Francis Earl of Bothwell'. [3]

Persons of high position were involved in the cult. Dame Alice Kyteler, for instance, in 1324. Her rank saved her from the flames, but the Bishop of Ossory was able to burn those who were accused

with her. . . . Hags black as the secret places of Hell. . . . Ladies
like the brightness fallen from the air. Personages with long
whispering trains and glittering crowns like the reflection of flames.
Such were among the devotees of the Devil.

The Duchess of Gloucester had been arraigned on the charge of
witchcraft and sentenced to imprisonment for life in the reign of
Edward the Third. In France, in the time of Elizabeth, Catherine
de' Medici was reputed to be a sorceress,[4] and her sons, the Kings of
France, consulted witches.

Strangest of all, is the history of the evil Bishop of Parma. In
1061 he (to whom the Emperor had promised his support) usurped
the name of Pope Honorius the Second, and marched against Rome.
He was defeated and condemned by all the prelates of Italy and
Germany. He made, however, a second attempt which was foiled,
and he then sank into obscurity. It was then, says Lévi, 'that he
decided to become the high priest of sorcerers and apostates, in
which capacity, and under the name of Honorius II, he composed
the *Grimoire* that passes under his name'. (The first edition was
published in 1629.) This is full of the most horrible blasphemies.

'The doctrine of this *Grimoire*', says Lévi (p. 300), 'is the same
as that of Simon and the majority of the Gnostics : it is the substi-
tution of the passive for the active principle.'

On the second page of the book, there are two circular magical
seals. . . . One of the meanings — there are several, and of great
complication — is that 'Heaven and Hell are each the reflection of
each ; that which is above is as that which is below'.

In the Prologue to the *Grimoire*, the Anti-Pope says : 'Until
this present, the Sovereign Pontiffs have alone had the charge of
evoking and commanding Spirits. His Holiness Honorius II, being
moved by his pastoral care, has deigned benignly to communicate
the science and power of evocations and of empire over spirits to
his venerable Brethren in Jesus Christ, with the conjurations which
must be used in each case. . . .'

'Here, in all truth', writes Lévi, 'is the pontificate of Hell, that
sacrilegious priesthood which Dante seems to stigmatise in the
raucous cry uttered by one of his princes of perdition : "Pope
Satan, Pope Satan : Aleppe". Let the legitimate pontiff continue
as prince of Heaven ; it is enough for the Anti-Pope Cadalus to be
the sovereign of Hell.'

One of the conjurations in the *Grimoire* begins with this verse :

O Lord, deliver me from the infernal terrors,
Exempt my spirit from the sepulchral larvae ;
To seek them out I shall go down to Hell unaffrighted,
I shall impose my will for a law upon them.

In 1303, the Bishop of Chester was accused to the Pope of worshipping the Devil (the horned god) in the form of a sheep.[5] And John Knox was known by those who held him in but small affection, to have been seen in animated conversation with the Foul Fiend in the churchyard of St. Andrews Cathedral.[6] Indeed the Scots seemed particularly addicted to the cult, for, many years after the death of Knox, in the reign of Charles the Second, not only were Scottish Bishops cloven-hooved, but they cast no shadows !

.        .        .        .        .

Though black magic and witchcraft may not be identical in technique, their object is the same — to worship the power of Hell and to spread its kingdom upon earth.

As recently as 1934, in a case in which a black magician, the late Aleister Crowley, sued Messrs. Constable and Miss Nina Hamnett for libel — (it is unnecessary to say that he lost his case) — the following horrible evidence was given by the plaintiff :

After saying 'the forces of good were those that had constantly oppressed me, I saw them daily destroy the happiness of my fellow men', he added that his magical experiments began in a flat in Chancery Lane. 'I had two temples, one white . . . one black, a mere cupboard in which stood an altar, supported by the figure of a negro standing on his hands. The presiding genius of this place was a human skeleton . . . which I fed from time to time with blood, small birds, and the like. . . . The idea was to give it life, but I never got further than causing the bones to become covered with a viscous slime. . . .' 'I expect', said Crowley, 'that was the soot of London.'

Reading this evidence, it is easy to understand the terror inspired by the witches — even by their daily habits, by those meals at which they, according to Bodet, 'before taking their repast, bless the table, but with blasphemous phrases, hailing Beelzebub as the Lord and protector of all things'.[7] (Beelzebub, the Lord of Flies.) The Witches' Feast, whereat, according to the same authority, everything was black — the bread, the wine, the torches (these were dipped in resin or pitch which gives a blue flame).

Round the table on which this bread and wine were spread, lit by those blue lights — round the Chief, disguised as a black goat and displaying the sacred bread on his horns, gathered the witches — the blackened, charred-looking, hollow faces (like a hole dug by desperate hands down into the depths of Hell), the hair like a whistling wind — and their familiars, Inges, Tewhit, Jamarra, Great Tom Twitt, Jeso, Prickear, Elemanzar, Pyewacket, Peck-in-the-Crown, Griezel Greedigut [8] — toads, cats, hares . . .

If any harmless magic were practised by such witches as these, it would be of the kind mentioned by Albertus Magus in his spell 'To raise a Rainebow', in which 'yf . . . (a) serpent be burned and the ashes of it put in ye fyre, anone shall there be a raine-bowe with a horrible thunder'.

Sometimes, however, the Devil would appear in a very different guise. He was seen, in France, as a gay gallant, wearing a plumed hat. And a butter-woman going to market was met by him in the guise of a gay young sprig walking in the budding lanes of spring.

.        .        .        .        .

In the first year of Elizabeth's reign, Sir Anthony Fortescue, a member of a famous Catholic family, was, with certain accomplices, charged with casting the Queen's horoscope. He was acquitted for lack of evidence, but three years later was implicated in 'an infamous design which involved the Ambassadors of Spain and France'. Two 'conjurors' employed by Sir Anthony, aided by a 'wicked spryte' drawn from the depths of Hell, had discovered that the Queen was about to die.

But worse was to come. In 1578, the Queen's subjects were appalled to learn that a wax image of her, intended to cause death, had been found in the house of a priest known to be a magician.[9] And in 1584, 'Auld Birtles, the great devel, Darnally, the sorcerer, Maud Two-good, enchantress, the auld witch of Ramsbury' were tried for their confederacy against Her Majesty, since 'they have diverse and sundry times conspired her life'.

As the danger to the Queen and her subjects grew, the latter wondered why there were not more executions. It is not difficult to tell a witch. One infallible test is to try to cut the hair of the accused. For instance, on the 4th of December 1599, a crone called Anne Kerke was brought before Sir Richard Martin, who immediately commanded the sergeant to pull ten or twelve hairs from her head and try to cut them.

Not only did the scissors turn round in the sergeant's hand, but the edges were so battered, so jagged as the result of their encounter with the hair, that they were useless ever after. The sergeant threw the hair into the fire, but the fire, after turning as blue as if 'the small blue leaves of the periwinkle' had been thrown into it, 'flew from it, and the hairs remained unbrent'.

Anne Kerke was hanged.

Apart from those who undoubtedly did try to communicate with the forces of evil, the harmless, the poverty-stricken, the old, the ugly, were frequently arraigned, and it is pleasant to record that children were particularly active in getting these hanged. In 1591, a little girl of ten, Joan, the eldest daughter of Sir Robert Throckmorton, succeeded in getting a whole family executed on the charge of bewitching her.

This amiable child was addicted to throwing fits during which she 'screeched long and loud'. One day, Gammer Alice Samuel, nearly eighty years of age, ugly and poverty-stricken, came to the house ; whereupon, seeing her long, craggy, crazy, bearded face, the colour of grey boulders covered with lichen, and her empty goat's eyes, this infant exhibitionist denounced her. 'Did you ever see one more like a witch than she is ? Take off her black thumbed cap, for I cannot abear to look at her !'

The old woman was so dumbfounded she could find no words. But nothing was done against her until the child's doctor, at his wits' end, since she yelled incessantly, and no ostensible cause could be found for this phenomenon, asked if she had been bewitched.

By this time, several sisters of the afflicted infant, envious, no doubt, of the attention lavished on her, had been seized with fits of shrieking, and declared that Gammer Alice had bewitched them also. Old Lady Cromwell (Oliver's stepgrandmother) was so overcome, when visiting the stricken parents, by the sight of the children twisting themselves into knots, and by the sound of their unceasing screams, that she bearded the witch and, after a violent struggle, succeeded in tearing a lock of grey hair from her head.

That very night the heroic woman was tormented by appalling dreams, awoke yelling, and for the next fifteen months spent her time in alternate screechings and faintings until, worn out by her exertions, she died.

Gammer Alice, dazed and mazed by denunciations, yelled

exhortations to confess, and by the children's howls and contortions, confessed at last that she entertained three familiars, Pluck, Catch, and White, had sold her soul to the Devil, and that she had killed Lady Cromwell and cast a spell upon the children.

The martyred infants then remembered the existence of John Samuel, the crone's husband, and accused him, together with their daughter. So the whole family was hanged.

In 1597, the three children of a gentleman named Starkie, living in Lancashire, succeeded in getting a man named Hartley, whom they accused of being a witch, executed.

These children had become addicted, about three years before, to the usual screamings and contortions, and their father consulted Hartley, who, at first, seemed successful in his treatment. But then the symptoms began again, accompanied by the phenomena ascribed to the presence of witches — the Struwwelpeter-like rising of the hair on the head, the flashing flight of hares over the green baize grass — so swift that they must clearly be spirits ; the sudden lighting of blue-flamed candles, where no means of lighting could be found. So Hartley was accused of 'meaning the children a mischiefe'. For he would 'kisse them if he could, and therewith breathe the Devil into their bodies'.

He was hanged ; but the children, not content with this by no means inconsiderable triumph, continued shrieking.

At last Mr. Darrell, who had been of help to another victim of witchcraft, and a second preacher, Mr. More, came to the house and confronted the children, who immediately redoubled their yells, the Fiend causing them also to 'scorn the preachers'. For when these called for the Bible, the children stopped screaming and fell, instead, into shrieks of laughter, saying, 'Reach them the bibble-babble, bibble-babble, bibble-babble' — with, according to the chronicle, 'many other scorning and filthy speeches'.

Maddened by the noise, aghast at the power of the Fiend and the depravity of the children, the preachers exhorted the former to depart and the latter to repent. With what result ? Only reiterated yells of 'bibble-babble, bibble-babble'.

But the preachers were not to be worsted ; and next morning, at seven o'clock, the possessed persons, who by this time numbered seven (as the children had been joined in their pursuits by all the maids in the house), were laid out on beds, in a row, screaming and twisting.

The preachers continued their exhortations until three in the afternoon, all seven sufferers 'roaring and bellowing in extreme and fearful manner. . . . There was such struggling and striving between those praying and the devil . . . labouring who should be the loudest, till the preachers' voices were spent and no strength almost left in them.'

But in the end the preachers were triumphant, and the sufferers declared that the spirit had passed out in the shape of some ugly creature, 'a crow's head, or an urchin [hedgehog] or a foul ugly man with a hump on his back'.

One naughty vain little girl (Mr. Starkie's eldest daughter, aged fourteen) had been very strangely affected. . . . 'Come on, my lad,' she yelled to her possessing spirit. 'Come on and set my partlet on one side as I do on the other. . . . Thus, my lad, I will have a fine Smocke of silke, it shall be finer than thine, I will have a Petticoat of silke not redde but of the finest silk that is, it shall be guarded and a foote high : it shall be laid on with gold Lace : it shall have a French Bodie, not of whalebone, for that is not stiff enough, but of horne, for that will hold it out, it shall come low, to keepe in my belly. My lad, I will have a French farthingale, it shall be finer than thine ; I will have it low before and high behind, and broade on either side, that I may laye mine arms upon it. My lad, thy Gowne is of crimson satten, but mine shall be of blacke wrought Velvet, it shall be finer than thine. I will have my Sleeves set out with wire, for stickes will breake and are not stiffe enough. I will have my Periwinkle so fine, finer than thine. I will have my cap of black Velvet with a flews (?) of golde, and my haire shall be set with Pearls, finer than thine. I will have my Partlet sette with a ribater and starched with blew Starch ; and pinned with a row or two of Pins. My lad, I will have a Brisk (?) of whalebone, it shall be tyed with two silke Points, and I will have a drawn wrought stomacher imbroidered with golde, finer than thine. I will have my Hose of Orringe colour, this is my request, and my corke shoes of red Spanish leather, finer than thine. I will have a Skarf of red Silke, with a gold Lace about the edge. I will have a Fan with a silver Steele and a glasse set in it, finer than thine. My lad, thou must bring me a paire of Gloves of the finest Leather that may be, with two golde laces about the thumbe, and a fringe on the toppe with flews and redde silke underneath, that I may drawe them through a golde Ringe, or else I will none of them.' [10]

Finer than thine.   Finer than the Fiend in all his glory.

.          .          .          .          .

It was not, however, safe to trifle with the Fiend.   For some-times he himself meted out condign punishment to the offenders. He tore the heart out of the bosom of old Lady Hatton, at the ex-piration of the contract she had made with him.   And in 1563, the very day after a naughty, blasphemous little girl, Dennis Benfield, aged twelve, had told her school-fellows that 'God is an old doting fool', she, on her way back from London, where she had been shopping, was pursued by a wind (which, for some reason best known to himself, the Foul Fiend had chosen as a garment) with the result that she turned completely black, was deprived of speech, and was buried that very night, far from her home.

Throughout the reign, the Fiend was particularly active ; and his activities took many forms.   He even went so far as to inspire two youths, named Kniveton and Light, to shout the refrain 'Fallen-tida, dilleo' in church on Candlemas Day 1583, and this they per-sisted in doing in spite of all efforts to stop them.   They were brought before the Recorder, Sir William Fletewode, who reported to Sir William Cecil (by now Lord Burleigh), 'I do suppose that they are descended from the blood of Nero the tyrant.   I never knew of such tyrannical youths.'

Not, it is true, with these descendants of Nero, but certainly with witches and necromancers, it was supposed that Lord Robert Dudley was involved.   For did not he, and did not the Queen, consult, not once, but frequently, the learned Dr. John Dee, the scientist, believed by the people to be a witch ?

### NOTES TO APPENDIX B

[1]  *The Secrets of Albertus Magus.*
[2]  Buchanan, *History of Scotland*, I, p. 245.
[3]  Pitcairn, *op. cit.*, vol. I, pt. iii, p. 246.
[4]  Lévi, *op. cit.* (p. 391).
[5]  Margaret Murray.
[6]  Rogers, *Scotland Social and Domestic*, p. 276.   Murray.
[7]  *Discours des Sorciers.*
[8]  Summers, *History of Witchcraft.*
[9]  Calendar of State Papers.
[10]  'Discourse concerning the certain possession and dispossession of certain persons in Lancashire', Harrison, *op. cit.*

# Cecil's deplorable son, Thomas

As though cares of state hung not heavy enough, during the years 1561 and 1562, on Sir William Cecil, he was plagued by the constant ill-behaviour of his eldest son Thomas, then in Paris in the charge of his tutor, Mr. Windebank.

Reading Sir William's notes for the guidance of his younger and more satisfactory son, his exhortations to the distraught Windebank, I think there can be little doubt that he was the original of the old, wise counsellor so much prized by the King of Denmark and Queen Gertrude, so much hated by Prince Hamlet.

The turns the irresponsible behaviour of the youthful Thomas would take were unpredictable.

'Good Windebank', the afflicted parent wrote on the 24th of March 1561, 'if there be left any spark of a recovery of a good name to my son, attempt all your cunning.' Writing on the same day to the son in question, he ended his letter by signing himself 'your father of an unworthy son'.

By the 2nd of April the following year, writing to the unfortunate tutor, he declared : 'Windebank, I am here used to pains and troubles, but none creep so near my heart as doth this of my lewd son. I am perplexed what to think. The shame that I shall receive to have so unruled a son grieveth me more than if I had lost him by honest death. Good Windebank, consult with my dear friend Sir Nicholas Throckmorton, to whom I could have referred the whole. I could be best content that he would commit him secretly to some sharp prison. If that shall not seem good, yet would I rather have him sent away to Strasburg, if it could be possible, or to Lorraine, for my grief will grow double to see him until some kind of amends. If none of these will serve, then bring him home, and I shall receive that which it pleaseth God to lay on my shoulders : that is, in the midst of my business, for comfort a daily torment. If ye shall come home with him, to cover the shame let it appear to be by reason of the troubles there. . . . I am so troubled as well what to write I know not.'

Sir Nicholas Throckmorton, consulted, was, of course, delighted to meddle and to advise. On the 26th of April, he wrote advising the unhappy father of this unworthy son to 'send some letters to [his son] to check his inordinate affection with which he is transported towards a young gentlewoman abiding near Paris, which the writer and Mr. Windebank by their admonitions had tried to dissuade him from, but in vain. She is a maid, and her friends will hardly bear the violation of her.' Sir Nicholas would have sent him hence to see other parts of France, 'but for the troubles here, which increase daily. The plague is very rife in Paris. It would be possible for his dear friend to recall this unsatisfactory son to England, giving as an excuse the troubles in Paris and the prevalence of the plague.'

Sir Nicholas, good-naturedly, hoped that his friend would 'judge of his passion as fathers do when they censure their sons' oversights, committed when most subject to folly and lost to reason'; and he begged him 'not to measure his son by himself, but respite him as other young men'. At the same time, he warned his friend 'not to delay in this matter'.

Nine days later, Windebank informed Sir William that 'Mr. Thomas's means for money was that he would have sold all his apparel together with Windebank's. . . . Mr. Thomas has come to an extremity of evil meaning.'

'P.S. There must be great heed taken that by friendship Mr. Thomas have not money either from England or from Antwerp.'

A second letter, written on the same day, declared that Windebank 'could do no good either by reasoning and counselling amicably or by threatening'.

However, Windebank at last succeeded in getting Mr. Thomas to a place eight leagues from Paris, where he could not find 'the means to continue his accustomed haunts, by reason that there are no horses nor money to be got', because Windebank had warned his friends not to lend him any.

But worse was to come. On the 8th of June, Windebank, driven, by this time, almost out of his mind by worry, told the English Ambassador: 'In his conversation with Mr. Cecil, he certainly gathers a promise of marriage to the Nun; but whether it is made before witnesses he does not confess. . . . If made without witnesses, it was no matter ; if made with them, the matter might be prevented if he would plainly tell it.' To which the youth had replied, despondently, that 'it could not be remedied but by God's help'.

(The scandal ! The son of Sir William Cecil, a prop of the Reformed Church, concerned in the abduction of a Nun !)

Continuing his revelations, Mr. Thomas said the Nun 'had desired him to bring some of his countrymen to be witnesses, which he refused, but promised [to marry her ?] on his word. He also saith her younger brother knew of the matter, and, consequently, more of her friends, who determined to have her from the Abbey ; and sending word to know if she was ready, she said she could not, trusting to the promise Mr. Cecil had made to her.' (The phrase about being ready is obscure in its meaning.)

Taking all this into consideration, Windebank did not see how Mr. Cecil could stay in France or indeed anywhere excepting in his own country, for fear that the Nun's friends would force him to keep his promise. 'And, as for his leaving France, the time of his departure must be kept a secret !'

How could Sir William foresee that in the end Mr. Thomas would renounce such behaviour and marry (in accordance with his father's arrangement) no Nun, but one of the Neville heiresses, the daughter of Lord Latymer !

.      .      .      .

Sir Nicholas Throckmorton was enthralled by the scandal, but his ideas, veering like a weathercock, soon swung in another direction.

In September 1561, he had already warned Her Majesty that a Greek called Maniola de Corfeu 'was appointed by a great personage to take a voyage into England to poison her', and that the Bishop of Aquila 'was privy to the plan'.

And when the Queen was seized with an illness endangering her life, he told the Queen that it was thought not to be smallpox, but the result of poisoning. 'Her friends here [in Paris] fear that it has proceeded of the violence of her enemies. It is believed here for certain that the Grand Prior, disguised, entered her realm, there to practise things that were accomplished with peril to her own person.'

Sir Nicholas could not vouch for the *truth* of this, but 'hoped the rumour might cause Her Majesty to be vigilant of her safety'. For the Princes of the Roman Church, so he thought, were particularly active in their attempts to murder the Queen.

It seems, however, as if the illness were indeed the smallpox, for King Edward's dry-nurse, Sibell Penn, who had been high in the royal favour, had been given, by King Henry, the rectory of Great Missenden, and had been affectionately treated by Queen Mary (to whom she would give presents of handkerchiefs 'edged with passamyne of golde and silke') and by Queen Elizabeth, had died in the rooms allotted to her at Hampton Court, of that illness.

APPENDIX D

# *Don Carlos*

THE Spanish Ambassador de Silva, writing to his King on the 10th of July 1564, told him 'I have been at court at Richmond again. The Queen was in the garden with the ladies when I arrived, and she bade the grand chamberlain bring me to her. She received me with the most pointed kindness. She had been so anxious to see me, she said, that she could not help giving me the trouble of coming.

'She took me aside and led me into a gallery, where she kept me for an hour, talking the whole time of your Majesty, and alluding often to her embarrassments when she first came to the throne.'

After a delightful supper party, during a play which turned on the subject of marriage, the Queen 'recurred', said the Ambassador, 'to the Prince of Spain, and asked about his stature. I replied that His Highness was full grown. She was silent awhile, and then said, "Everyone seems to disdain me. I understand you think of marrying him to the Queen of Scots ?"

' "Do not believe it, Your Majesty," I said. "His Highness has been so ill for years past with quartan ague and other disorders that his marriage with any one has been out of the question. Because he is better now, the world is full of idle stories about him. Subjects are never tired of talking of their princes."

' "That is true," she answered. "It was reported a few days since in London that the King my brother intended to offer him to me." '

This conversation was strange, since the Queen must have known that Don Carlos was, at this time, mad.

On the 11th of May 1562, Sir Thomas Chaloner, the English Ambassador to Spain, had told his Queen, 'On the 19th ultimo, the Prince, by occasion of play, others say in hasty following of a wench' (for, having forsaken his strange affection for his aunt, the Princess Dowager of Portugal, he was now pursuing an unrequited passion for the daughter of the Keeper of the Palace gardens) having found a way to leave the Palace when (at nine o'clock at night) the doors were locked, he had fallen down a dark staircase, his screaming unheard, until, at the bottom, he crashed against a door.

'His hurt', the Ambassador told the Queen, 'is upon the noddle.'

When at last he was found, he was unconscious, was carried to his bed, and doctors were rushed to him.

At first it was thought his injury was slight.   Then erysipelas set in, his head swelled to a gigantic size, and he was delirious and completely blind.   His state grew worse each day.   Fifty consultations with doctors were held, and at fourteen of these the King was present.   Even at the moment of this anguish, the immovable etiquette surrounding the Kings of Spain was maintained.   The King was the King, and untouchable by grief, unapproachable by beings of a lesser order.   Behind his chair, stood the Castilian grandees ;   the Duke of Alva and Don García de Toledo stood on either side of him ;   and the doctors in a half-moon on the other side of the room.   Otherwise, the King's days and nights were spent in prayer.

At the first news of the disaster threatening the kingdom, huge multitudes crowded the churches, processions of flagellants passed in the streets, scourging themselves — the yellow dust flaunting and flaring about them.   Processions walked ceaselessly round and round the Palace, chanting prayers.

But the wrath of Heaven against Spain was not averted.

The yellow body of the Prince, lying slack as a river weed upon his bed, was as fiery as if the flames of the Auto da Fé, at whose judgments, but not at whose executions, he and the Princess of Portugal had been present three years before, at Valladolid, ran in his veins instead of blood ;   as if his body had been formed of the flaming dust, gathered together to shape it, of those burnings outside the walls of the city, in which — their bodies wearing the hideous garb of yellow cloth, their heads crowned with the conical caps of pasteboard, both embroidered with figures of flames and of devils fanning and feeding these — Doctor Agustín Cazalla and his brother Francisco (Catholic priests convicted of hypocrisy), their sisters Constanza and Beatriz, three other women, Catalina

Román, Isabel de Estrada, and Juana Blásquez, with Maestro Alonzo Pérez, Don Cristóbal de Ocampo, Knight of the Order of St. John, Cristóbal de Padilla, a Knight of Zamora, Juan García, a silversmith, Pérez de Herrera, and the Bachelor Herrezuelo, who remained obstinate in their heresies, were consumed.

Only one hope was left. A cold and wintry remedy must quench the fires in the blood of the Prince of Spain.

In the monastery of Jesús María, the bones of the most holy Franciscan, Fray Diego, dead for a hundred years, lay in their iron coffin. The King and the whole Court went in solemn procession to the Church, and the mummy of the holy father, 'still sweet to the nostrils' — so we are assured — was carried back by them to the bedside of the delirious Prince and laid beside him as his bed-fellow.

From that night — in which a vision of the Friar appeared to him — his recovery began. The fever went, his head was reduced to its normal size, his blindness subsided. In less than two months, the Prince was able to walk into the next room, and to embrace his father.

But the King held in his arms a dead man — a body into which some soul risen from Hell had entered to give it a semblance of life.

At first, silence and a strange solemnity, alternating with most peculiar and meaningless questions, seemed the only results of the fall. But according to the English Ambassador's letter to his Queen, King Philip feared the Prince would 'take after the humours of the Emperor's mother', the mad Queen Juana of Castile.

Worse was to come.

Tiepolo, the Venetian Ambassador, long after this time, when the Prince was twenty-two, though acknowledging his extreme arrogance and that he was given to appalling rages, spoke also of his love of truth, his great religious devotion, and his great charity — (for he would ask, 'Who should give, if princes did not ?'). 'He certainly', the Ambassador wrote, 'inspired all who came near him with strong feelings of personal devotion. His letters to his former tutor, now Bishop of Osma, did credit to his heart.'

But his madness increased.

His charity was recorded in the account books published in the *Colección de Documentos inéditos para la Historia de España, tom. XXVII*, by such entries as that of his payment for the maintenance and education of abandoned children, and of his paying the debts of an imprisoned debtor. . . . But there is also the record of 100 reals being given to Damian Martín . . . 'father of the girls beaten by order of His Highness'. Prescott, in his *Philip the Second*, says, 'Perhaps the worst story told of him is that of his having shut himself up in his stables and inflicted serious injuries on more than a score of horses'.

In his wild animal rages, he would attack his servants, and the highest officials of the Court. Throwing himself on his Chamberlain, Don Alonzo de Córdova, he tried to hurl him out of the window. From a corner where he had sat in impenetrable silence, the thin yellow wolf-Prince leapt out and flew at the throat of Cardinal Espinosa, who had, probably at the King's wish, ordered an actor named Cisneros, whom the Prince had wished to perform before him, to leave the Palace. Shrieking with rage, he shook the Cardinal violently by the collar, and, dagger in hand, threatened his life. The Cardinal fell upon his knees, and begged for mercy.

(Cardinal Espinosa became Grand Inquisitor, and was so at the time when the process against the mad Prince was brought.)

Then the day came when the Prince whispered to Don Juan that there was a man whom he wished to kill — a man who had offended him. This was shortly before the Day of the Innocents — the 28th of December, when the Spanish royal family were accustomed to take the Blessed Sacrament in public.

But the Confessor to whom the Prince went the night before the Feast, had heard of that whisper, and refused him absolution.

Don Carlos argued with the priest and was told to seek further advice. But the priests who were called together upheld, in horror, the decision of the first Confessor.

The Prior of Atocha asked him the name of the man whom he wished to kill. He answered in two words : 'My father'.

The priests, aghast, asked if any were to help him commit this murder. Again he replied with the two words, 'My father'.

At two o'clock in the morning, the news reached the King.

On the 15th of January, Philip commanded all the churches and monasteries in Madrid to offer up prayers that he might be guided in a certain action he contemplated. None knew what this would be.

By now the Prince slept behind barred doors and surrounded by weapons. But one night he awoke to find five men standing by his bedside. One was the King, and he was removing the sword which hung at the head of the bed.

When he knew he was to be kept, henceforth, imprisoned in this room, the Prince fell at his father's feet and begged him to kill him — or he would kill himself. His father told him that would be the act of a madman. 'I am not mad', he wept, 'but desperate.'

From that moment, he was as lost to the world as if he were in truth dead. He was not seen, he was not heard, excepting by those who watched him, night and day.

The day after the Prince was imprisoned, the King called the various Councils, and, with tears in his eyes, told them of the steps he had taken.

In his letter to Zusnigo, his Ambassador at the Papal Court, he wrote : 'Although the disobedience which Carlos had shown through life was sufficient to justify any demonstration of severity, yet it was not this, but the stern pressure of necessity that could alone have driven him to deal in this way with his first-born, his only son'. And to his aunt, the Queen of Portugal, sister to the Emperor Charles, he declared that 'the feelings of a father have led me to resort to all other means before proceeding to extremity. But affairs have at length come to such a pass that to fulfil the duty which, as a Christian Prince, I owe both to God and to my realm, I have been compelled to place my son in strict confinement. . . . This determination has not been brought about by any misconduct on the part of my son, or by any want of respect to me ; nor is this treatment of him intended by way of chastisement — for that, however just the grounds of it, would have its time and its limit. . . . The remedy I propose is not one either of time or of experience, but is of the greatest moment . . . to satisfy my obligations to God and my people.'

. . . What remedy ?

Did the King suffer, as he wrote this — the son of the woman who, in giving birth to him, had the light excluded from the room, so that no one should witness her anguish ? He had been a tender father to all his children. But Cabrera wrote of him, 'The dagger followed close upon his smile'.

Now there was the perpetual danger that a plot for the Prince's escape might have been formed outside the Palace, and the King was in constant fear. If any unexpected sound reached him, he would go to the window, and the crowds would see the tepid blue eyes, the limp pale face of their King, usually so inexpressive, looking out at them, distorted now by fear of seeing the face of the madman, the body of the madman, carried and held high by that crowd.

By now the Prince, hidden from the light of day, was almost as emaciated as that strange bedfellow who had been brought to heal him of his illness. The constant fires in his veins and in his brain were so high that, as in that fever from which his madness arose, they might, indeed, have been the fires in which the damned were condemned, by the Inquisition, to their eternal punishment.

His attempts to quench those fires were so desperate that the Papal Nuncio believed that since he was prevented by his attendants from 'laying violent hands upon himself', he had determined to take this way of ending his life. He would pour floods of cold water on the floors of his prison and then, naked excepting for a thin gown of taffeta, would pace backwards and forwards over those icy floors for hours at a time. Several times in each night he would call for a fresh warming-pan filled with ice and snow to be placed in his bed. He would drink gallons of snow water, scarcely waiting to take breath, and, having refused to eat any food for as many as eleven days, he would suddenly (washing them down with three or four gallons of iced water) eat four partridges made into a pasty at a single meal.

Don Carlos had been told by his almoner, Suarez, that some of the deeds he had committed were 'of such a nature that did they concern any other than Your Highness, the Holy Office would be led to enquire whether the author of them were in truth a Christian. . . .'

According to Llorente, the Secretary of the Inquisition, a process that had been brought against the Prince ceased only shortly before his death. He was allowed no defending counsel. The judgment, given on the 9th of July 1568, pronounced him guilty of treason inasmuch as he had plotted the death of the King his father, and had conspired to become sovereign of Flanders.

This judgment was placed before the King by the Counsellor Munatores. The penalty, it said, was death. But the King, by his sovereign authority, might decide that the Heir Apparent was above the law. Or he might decide to mitigate or to dispense with any punishment whatsoever, if this were for the good of his subjects.

To this the King replied that though his feelings moved him to follow the suggestions of his ministers, his conscience would not permit it. He could not think that he would be consulting the good of his people by placing upon the throne a monarch so vicious in his disposition, and so fierce and sanguinary in his temper, as Carlos. However agonising it might be to his feelings as a father, he must allow the law to take its course.

But the King had always been addicted to compromise. He added that it might not be necessary to proceed to such an extremity as a formal execution. The Prince's health was in such a state that surely it was only necessary to relax the precautions in regard to his diet, and his excesses would soon lead to death. This, said the King, was the greatest proof of love that he could give to his son and to the Spanish people. One point, however, was essential ; and that was that he should confess, and make his peace with Heaven.

The Chief Inquisitor, the Cardinal Espinosa (the Prince's old enemy), and Ruy Gómez, in charge of the madman, gained a strange impression from what Prescott justly described as 'this singular ebullition of parental tenderness'. Therefore, this impression was conveyed to the Prince's physician by Gómez, in a manner so veiled, in such mysterious terms, that it could scarcely be guessed that he was hinting at the advisability of a murder being committed.

But Dr. Olivares was a man of the world. It was unnecessary to stress the matter. Say no more! He quite understood. It was only necessary to use a certain *tact*.

According to Antonio Pérez, one of the household of Ruy Gómez, a slow poison was mixed in the Prince's food.[1] In a letter written about a month before the Prince's tactful removal from this life — if, indeed, that removal were not an act of nature — the French Minister, Fourquevaulx, wrote : 'They give him sometimes strong soup and capon broths in which amber and other nourishing things are dissolved, that he may not wholly lose his strength and fall into decrepitude. *These soups are prepared primarily in the chamber of Ruy Gómez* [my italics], through which one passes into that of the Prince.'

The Prince was seized with incessant vomiting, then dysentery. (These may, of course, have been the result of his diet, unaided by any tact on the part of Dr. Olivares.) His death was approaching. Then, said the Papal Nuncio, 'Suddenly, a wonderful change seemed to be wrought by divine grace in the heart of the Prince.

Instead of vain and empty talk, his language became that of a sensible man. He sent for his Confessor, and devoutly confessed.'

Death came to him at four o'clock on the Vigil of Santiago, the 24th of July 1568.

The youth whom the Queen of Scots had hoped to marry, and who had been proposed as husband for the Queen of England, was then twenty-three years and sixteen days old.


NOTE TO APPENDIX D

[1] de Thom, *Histoire universelle*.

# The Mariners

THE Queen of England having shown a strange reluctance to be 'assisted to her permanent repose', her brother-in-law, the King of Spain, was for the moment hampered in his plans for her destruction. But he did not like the English any the better, nor did their feelings for him improve.

Long ago, the sound of the leaves in old Dr. Dee's garden, on that day when young Mr. Hawkins, (who had been with Mr. Drake), visited him, was like the sound of the seas on which that visitor had travelled ; and the June rain fell through the leaves with a patter like that of the gold patacoons pirated from Spanish ships.

The maps were spread on the table, and over these the dark faces, creased into smiles like 'the new maps with the Indies in them', leaned.

In 1562 John Hawkins and Thomas Hampton sailed, with a hundred men, for Sierra Leone, where they encountered serpents with gold bells in their tails that sang sweetly of death, and negroes that when they spoke clucked like a hen. . . . The very soil and sands seemed made of gold. Here the mariners 'collected' — to quote Froude's discreet phrase — three hundred negroes and carried them away to sell them into slavery. The expedition brought back so much spoil that the Queen lent them a fine ship for their next exploit, and Lord Pembroke and others put money into the venture. To Cecil's honour, he refused to do so, 'having no liking for such proceedings'.

The adventurers — these, and Drake and the great Raleigh — knew the experiences of the voyager in Rimbaud's 'Bateau ivre' :

> Et dès lors, je me suis baigné dans le Poème
> De la Mer, infusé d'astres, et lactescent,
> Dévorant les azurs verts, où, flottaison blême
> Et ravie, un noyé pensif parfois descend ;

J'ai heurté, savez-vous, d'incroyables Florides
Mêlant aux fleurs des yeux de panthères à peaux
D'hommes ! Des arcs-en-ciel tendus comme des brides
Sous l'horizon des mers, à de glauques troupeaux.

J'ai vu fermenter les marais énormes, nasses
Où pourrit dans les joncs tout un Léviathan.
Des écroulements d'eaux au milieu des bonaces
Et les lointains vers les gouffres cataractant.

Glaciers, soleils d'argent, flots nacreux, cieux de braises,
Échanges hideux au fond des golfes bruns
Où les serpents géants dévorés de punaises
Choient des arbres tordus, avec de noirs parfums.

They sailed by the Spaniards' discoveries — by 'the Iland of
Madagascar', where, 'in the sea about this iland, great whales are
taken, out of which amber is gathered'.[1]  These monsters were
pleasant — in any case bore pleasantness within them : but there
were others which *might*, so it was thought, have been encountered
which were *not* — 'the Physeter, which in English . . . is called
the Whirlpool' ; . . . 'the ill-omened creature with human face
and a monkish cowl, whose German name is Wassermann ; the
delicate monster whose scaly skin assumed the likeness of a bishop's
garb' (of the Roman persuasion, I imagine), 'the bat-winged demon
worthily named the Satyr of the Sea ; the Grisly Ziphius, the Ros-
marus, an elephant in size, which lumberingly scales the mountains
bordering the sea ; the Scolopendra with face of flame, and eyes
which measure twenty feet across . . .'[2]

It is true that Sir John Hawkins opined that there were both
lions and unicorns in Florida.  Of the unicorns he declared 'they
have many, for that they do affirme it to be a beast with one horne
which commeth to drinke, putteth the same into the river before
he drinketh. . . . It is thought that there are lyons and tigers as
well as unicornes, lyons especially, if it be true that is sayd, of the
enmity between them and the unicornes : for there is no beast
but hath his enemy . . . insomuch as, where he is, the other cannot
be missing.'

But they remained unseen by him and, in the regions they passed,
even the crocodiles seemed pleasant.  'The Spaniards somtymes
met' (wrote the author of the Fourth Book of the Third Decade)
'with crocodyles lying on the sandes, the which, when they fled,

or tooke the water, they lefte a very sweet savour behynde them, sweeter than muske or Castorium. . . . When I was sente Ambassadour for the Catholique King of Castile to the Soltane of Babylone . . . inhabitants tolde me that the fatte or swette of them [female crocodiles] is equal in sweetness with the pleasaunte gums of Arabie. . . .'

Nor were the Crocodiles the only delights to be encountered in Babylon. . . . 'Smaragdes grow in the countrey of Babilon. . . . They grow also in other parts of India. . . . They leave not any greene colour upon the touche.'

Such were the treasures of the earth. . . . In the air flew parrots of whom might be said :

> Thou with thy quills mightst make greene *Emerald* darke.

They sailed by the pleasant 'Iland of Hispaniola . . .' whose form 'resembleth the leafe of a chesnutte tree. . . . There is the golden region . . . stones [of gold] the least whereof was as big as a walnut and the greatest as big as an orange. . . .'

Sailing over the sea whose waves seemed the scents drifting from the groves of spice-trees, they passed the Spaniards' Ilands of Molucca, 'where all things are despicable beside pearls, idleness, and spices'.[3]

The great Drake was to sail in 1579, through the Straits of Magellan, and along the Pacific Coast of America . . . amidst the sound and rumour and light of pearls, plundering the Spaniards.

And, when Spain had taken Portugal, and all the countries of Europe were in fear of her power. . . . Drake seemed to Europe as come to avenge them.

His hatred of the Spaniards had been increased by their cruelty. He had seen the body of a negro who, after being whipped raw, had been set in the sun to be tortured to death by mosquitoes. He had seen an Indian, who had been covered with brimstone, set on fire, then brought back to health that he might be smeared over with honey and chained to a tree 'where mosquitoes flocked about him like moats in the sun and did pitifully sting him — these mosquitoes, being like wasps — than which death were better as he said'.

The man who saw spectacles like this was intent, not only on plunder, but the punishment of such cruelties.

The Queen summoned him to Court, and on New Year's Day

wore a crown of green fires — the emeralds he had brought her. She visited his ship the *Golden Hind*, and knighted him.

In 1587 he was, according to his own phrase, 'singeing the beard of the King of Spain', entering the fortified harbour of Cadiz, and destroying thousands of tons of shipping. He took Cape St. Vincent. He 'rode at anchor in the port of Lisbon',[4] he took a Spanish carrack from the East Indies.

It was only too evident to the Spaniards that he was a devil, as well as 'El Draque' (the Dragon). He was guided by a familiar, the winds obeyed his commands, and he had, in his cabin, a magic mirror which reflected all the movements of the enemy ships, and everything that took place on those ships.[5]

He was never forgotten by the Spaniards. Nor was his friend, Sir Walter Raleigh, the author of the *History of the World* — (with his 'most remarkable aspect, exceeding high forehead', his long face, 'sour eie-lidded, a kind of pigge-eie', and his white satin doublet and ropes of enormous pearls) — the Queen's favourite, the learned and gallant Sir Walter, who, as Aubrey wrote, was 'a great Chymist. . . . He studied most in his Sea-Voyages, where he carried always a Trunke of Bookes along with him, and had nothing to divert him'. Sir Walter had, at one time, been an atheist — indeed, so it was said, he even had a school for atheism, but afterwards turned to God, for he had 'seen the wonders of the deep'.

John Lawson wrote in his *History of Carolina* (London, 1718) : 'I cannot forbear inserting a pleasant history that passes for an un-contested Truth amongst the inhabitants of this Place ; which is that the Ship which brought the first Colonies does often appear amongst them ; under Sail, on a gallant Posture, which they call Sir Walter Raleigh's Ship ; and the truth of this has been affirm'd to me, by memory of the best Credit in the Country'.

.        .        .        .        .

Not content with seizing the jewels and spices from the Spanish ships, Sir John Hawkins formed, at about the time of Ridolfi's activities, a new device for plundering from the King. In 1567, seventy-three of his men had been captured by the Spaniards, and taken to Spain where they were now dying in the prisons of the Archbishop of Seville. All were tortured ; some were burned in the Autos da Fé ; others were dying of starvation.

They were Hawkins' shipmates. He thought of them night and day. It was more for the avenging of his men who had died in prison, and for the rescue of those who still lived, that he formed his plan, than for the sake of plunder.

He made a certain communication to Cecil. Then, paying a visit to the Spanish Ambassador, Don Guerau de Espès, he spoke with such bitterness of his treatment by the Queen and the authorities, their utter lack of gratitude, — asking, at the same time, if nothing could be done to help his men in the Spanish prisons — that Don Guerau felt he had made a new friend. Writing to the Duke of Alva, he told him he believed it might even be worth while to set the prisoners free, in order to earn Sir John's gratitude. With a little care, they might easily make use of him. . . . And how great would be that use !

But nothing was done — at the moment. The sailors remained in prison. So Sir John went a little further.

He now told Don Guerau, in the plainest terms, that he was tired of the Queen's ingratitude and had determined to cease from serving her. If, he said, his shipmates were freed from prison, not only would he enter the service of the King of Spain, but he would bring over with him England's grandest ships, most valiant sailors.

Don Guerau was enchanted. Here, assuredly, was the man Spain had been waiting for. . . . It was true that in the past . . . Still, — let the past bury the past !

Don Guerau was not the only person who was enchanted. Sir John shared his feeling. Now he was determined to approach the King himself. Therefore he sent one of his officers, George Fitzwilliam, to His Majesty to tell him that Sir John and he were amongst the most fervent, if secret, sons of the Holy Church, and that they were aghast at the state of religion in England. They longed only for the moment when the heretic Queen would be overthrown, and the rightful Queen would reign. Therefore he and a large part of the English navy would give their services to the King to forward that end.

The King was more surprised than his Ambassador. He asked the messenger who and what he was, he asked for his credentials, he asked if he had been in communication with the Queen of Scots. To which Fitzwilliam replied that the great name of Sir John Hawkins formed sufficient credentials. The King had received the magnificent offer of the services of Sir John and a large part of the Fleet, and all that he asked was that some wretched prisoners should be released. The sailors would follow where Hawkins led — and all that the King had to do was to pay them their wages, and, also, to give money to equip the vessels, for this Sir John could not afford to do.

The King consulted the Duke de Feria and his English Duchess. They were enthusiastic. They had had most confidential talks with Fitzwilliam, and had suggested to him the course Hawkins should pursue. The King caught fire — if so tepid a person could be said to catch fire — from the Duke and Duchess's excitement and wrote to his Ambassador for further information. He then told Fitzwilliam that if he would return, bearing a letter of introduction from the Queen of Scots, his commander's offer should be considered most favourably, and the King would provide the money for the equipment of the English Fleet.

The indefatigable Fitzwilliam arrived at Sheffield with letters and presents for the Queen of Scots from the Duke and Duchess of Feria. He begged her to intercede that the prisoners should be released — to which she replied that 'she must pity prisoners for she was used as one herself, and that she would do any pleasure she could to an Englishman'. For her heart had once been merciful.

It was obvious that she could speak freely with one trusted by the Duke and Duchess of Feria. . . . She did, and she wrote to the King of Spain on his behalf.

The Ambassador, meanwhile, told the King that Hawkins would be of inestimable value. He had 16 vessels, 1600 men, and 400 guns at his command. The men were burning to serve the King of Spain and the Queen of Scots.

Hawkins reiterated that he asked nothing for himself — excepting absolution for his past sins in the Indies. Beyond this, there was only one condition and that was that the ships should be so restored that they could be of real use to the King. He asked, also, for two months' wages in advance for the 1600 men.

Nothing, he explained, could be more simple than for part of the Fleet to sail up the Humber. For this, only six ships would be needed. The crews would then land, proclaim Mary Queen of England, and the enraptured nation would rise and would overthrow the heretic Queen. The letters from the Queen of Scots had banished all suspicions from the King's mind. Fitzwilliam was introduced to the Spanish Cabinet, and learned from them that the Spaniards were preparing to invade England, and that this was to be done, if possible, in late summer.

The English prisoners were released and sent home — each with ten dollars in his pockets. Hawkins received a full pardon for all his acts against Spain, and the King paid him £40,000, or £50,000, and made him a Grandee of Spain.

The King, pondering over Hawkins' offer when it was first made, may have thought it too good to be true !

It was. Hawkins was in full possession of the King of Spain's plans against England. And the ships that had been so generously fitted out at his expense were used, not in the King's service, but against him.

### NOTES TO APPENDIX E

[1] Eden, *First Four Bookes of America.*
[2] Lowes, *The Road to Xanadu.*
[3] Eden, *op. cit.*
[4] Neale, *op. cit.*
[5] Neale, *op. cit.*

# The Queen's Progresses

IN Warwickshire, 'by the soft wind of whispering silks', in the burning July of 1575, the country ladies rushed backwards and forwards to the chests containing their dresses, choosing the gowns they thought would be most likely to attract Her Majesty's attention . . . farthingales (whose name, says Dr. Linthicum, 'apparently derived from the Spanish "verdigarde" . . . possibly because the garment resembled the bell-shaped growth of twigs on a truncated tree') — gowns made of gros grain (sometimes of hair, sometimes of silk), mackarelle, pomette, perpetuana, satin of Cipres, Spanish satins, calamanco (of which Lyly said in *Mydas* that the weave is as easily deciphered as the characters in a nutmeg) — mockado (mock velvet) plain, striped, and tufted.

Silks and satins falling like waterfalls, dripping like thick cream, drifting like the summer airs.

Colours of 'goose-turd greene' ('merde d'oie') — a yellowish green, of pease porridge, of Popinjay blue, Catherine pear, russet red, 'damned colour' (which may have been either flame colour or black), of 'gingerline' (which, according to Dr. Linthicum, is 'mentioned with nutmegs — a reddish colour containing some violet — it had no connection with ginger, as is commonly thought', of horse-flesh ('the bronze shade peculiar to the hides of bay horses'),[1] 'Murrey' (which the *Oxford English Dictionary* calls 'mulberry colour . . . Vernon, in 1575, says it is synonymous with ferrago, chestnut, a sad blue'), 'stammel', or scarlet, 'lustie gallant' (a light red).

The older ladies would wear gowns of russet, which was, says the same authority, defined by Florio in 1598 as 'violet', and 'judging from Middleton's "Scorch me 'em soundly, burn 'em to French russet" (*A Game of Chess*), the violet-brown of burning paper'. Or they would wear 'maiden-hair browne' ('the colour of light-brown hair').[2]

Some among the younger ladies would wear on the sleeve, 'as a raritie instead of a flower', a wild strawberry plant, 'much like unto the ordinary', but differing 'in that the flower, if it have any, is greene, or rather it beareth a small head of greene leaves, many set thicke together like a double ruffe, in the midst whereof standeth the fruit, which, when it is ripe, sheweth to be . . . somewhat reddish, like unto a small strawberry'.[3]

The Queen arrived at Long Itchington, about seven miles from Kenilworth, on the 9th of July. The heat seemed more fiery than ever, and in the flowers in the gardens passed by the Court, it seemed as if 'the fire meeting the watery substance of these, had burned it up, and thus brought them to a red colour, and, when it had evaporated the substance of the air by its heat, caused the flower to be quite red — a mixture of the elements of fire and air'.

At Long Itchington, the Queen dined under a huge tent, and, at dessert, was brought face to face with two prize exhibits of the district — a fat boy, aged six, nearly five feet in height, the weight of whose stupidity equalled his physical avoirdupois, and a correspondingly monstrous sheep. No remark of hers is recorded.

In the afternoon she hunted, coming gradually to Kenilworth, which she reached at 8 o'clock, being met at the Castle gate by the porter in the guise of Hercules. She, with her train, having passed the gates, came to the lake, where she was greeted by a lady accompanied by two nymphs, who seemed as if they walked upon the water.

A temporary bridge had been built over the main Court, with seven pairs of pillars bearing offerings to the Queen, and guarded by gods and goddesses. Crowning the first pair of pillars were large cages, containing 'live bitterns, curlews, hernshaws, godwits, and such dainty birds, offered her by Sylvanus, god of wood-fowl'. The next pair bore two huge silver bowls, with pears, apples, cherries, filberts, walnuts, 'all fresh on the branches, the gift of Pomona', and on the pair following, 'wheat in ears, oats and barley, waved from the bowls'. After these, two pillars bore a huge silver bowl, filled with purple and white grapes, and, opposite, huge pots of silver filled with claret and white wine — at which the thirsty and tired courtiers, in this night that was almost as fiery as the day, looked longingly.

On the Queen's entry into her bedchamber, a tremendous racket of cannon and the blazing and banging of fireworks began, and continued ceaselessly for two hours.

Next day the Queen and her Court went to church, in the afternoon there was music and dancing, and in the evening the cannon and fireworks began again. The heat was so fiery that often the Queen remained in the shadows of the castle until the evening, when she would hunt the deer. . . .

During her stay she had fresh encounters with the Lady of the Lake, and with a 'wild man' covered with leaves, and bearing the branch of an oak, which, unfortunately, frightened Her Majesty's horse so that it shied.

On the following Sunday, she witnessed, in the afternoon, a rustic wedding. . . . 'Thus', we are told, 'were they [the members of the wedding party] marshall'd. Fyrst, all the lustie ladds and bold bachelors of the parish, suitable every wight with his blue buckeram bride-lace' 4 'upon a braunch of green broom (cause rosemary is skant thear) tyed on his left arme (for on that side lieth the heart) and his alder poll for a spear in his right hand, in marciall order raunged on afore two and two in rank. . . . The bridegroom foremost, in his fartherz [father's] tawny worsted jacket (for his friends were fain that he should be a bridegroom before the Queen), a fayr strawn hat with a capitall croon, steep-wize on his hed : a payr of harvest gloves in his hands, as a sign of good husbandry : a pen and inkhorn at his bak, for he would be known to be bookish. . . . After theiz horsman [sic] a lively morrisdawns, according to the auncient manner, six dauncers, mawd marion and the fool. Then three pretty prizels (maidens) as bright as a breast of bacon, of a thirty-yeere olde apees, that carried three special spise-cakes of a bushel of wheat . . . before the bride Syzely with set cauntenauns, and lips so demurely simpring as if it had been a mare cropping of a thistl. After theez, a lovely loober woorts [a dull heavy lubberly fellow] freckle-faced, red-headed . . . that was to beare the bride-cup, formed of a sweet sucket barrell' ; 5 'all seemly besylvered and parcell gilt [partly gilded], adorned with a beautiful braunch of broom, gayly begilded for rosemary ; from which two brode brydelaces of red and yellow buckeram begilded, and gallantly streaming by such wind as there waz, for he carried it aloft. . . . Then came the worshipfull bride . . . a thirtie-five-year-old, of colour brown-bay. . . .'

One supposes that she was surrounded by 'maidens bearing garlands of wheat finely gilded', for this was the custom.

The Queen left Kenilworth on the 27th of July, having, during her stay, cured several persons of the King's Evil — 'which the Kings and Queens of this realm without other medicine, but only by touching and prayers do cure'.

Long before this time, Her Majesty's visits had begun to be dreaded because of the huge expense and worry connected with them. Lord Keeper Bacon, for instance, 'rejoiced much that Her Majesty intended him so great an honour, but owned himself quite a novice in receiving Royalty. . . .' In 1572, the Earl of Bedford, writing to Lord Treasurer Burleigh, said: 'I am now going to prepare for Her Majesty's coming to Woburne, which shall be done in the best and most hartiest manner that I can. I trust Your Lordship will have a remembrance to provide and help that Her Majesty's tarrying will not be above two nights and a daye : for so long tyme do I prepare.' 6

As for the Queen's train, when she made her extremely frequent visits to Lord Burleigh, his lordship's treatment of the Queen's suite seems not to have been generally acceptable to them.

In 1574, Bowyer, steward to the Archbishop of Canterbury, before the Queen visited His Grace at his summer Palace at Croydon, wrote, driven nearly out of his mind by worry, to the official in charge of the Queen's arrangements, 'For the Queen's waiters [train] I cannot find any convenient rooms to place them in, but I will do the best I can to place them elsewhere ; but if it will please you, sir, that I do remove them, the grooms of the privy chamber, nor Mr. Drury, have no other way to their chambers but to pass through that where my lady Oxford should come. I cannot tell where to place Mr. Hatton ; And for my lady Carewe, there is no place for a chimney for her, but that she must lay abroad with Mrs. A. Parry and the rest of the privy chamber. For Mrs. Skelton, there are no rooms with a chimney ; I shall stay [take] one chamber without for her. Here is as much as I am able to do from this house.

From Croydon.' 7


On the whole, one cannot be surprised that Lord Leycester, writing to the Earl of Sussex in 1574, said, 'We all do what we can to persuade Her Majesty from any progress at all !'

But in the year after this optimistic note was written, the Queen, as we have seen, honoured him with a visit, and Lord North of Kertlinge with a visit, arriving at Lord North's on Monday the 1st of September in time for supper, and remaining until the Wednesday following, 'after dinner'. The cooks, red as midsummer roses, had prepared for the visit : '1,200 manchets, 3,600 cheatbreads, 74 Hoggesheads of beare (beer), 2 tunnes of ale, 1 roundet of sacke containing 20 gallons. 1 hoggesh (hogshead) of vinegar, 11 steers and oxen, 66 muttons, 17 veales, 7 lambs, 34 pigges, 32 geese, 30 dozen and 2 capons, 6 turkies, 32 swannes, 22 dozen and 9 mallards and young ducks, 1 crane, 28 hearnshaws, 22 Bitters (bitterns ?), 12 Shovellers, 24 Chickens, also 19 dozen. 125 Pigeons also 16 dozen, 8 dozen and 10 Pewyts, 68 Godwyts, 17 Gules, 8 dozen and 11 Dottrells, 8 Snypes. 29 Knotts. 28 Plovers. 5 Stynts (?). 18 Redshanks. 2 Yewhelps (?). 22 Partridges. 1 Pheasant. 27 dozen and 1 Quails. 2 Curlewes. 8 dozen Connyes [rabbits, or hares]. 4 Stags made into 48 Pasties. 16 Bucks made into 128 pasties. 8 gammons of Bacon. 24 lbs. of Lard. 11 and also 21 Neats tongs [tongues], feet and Udds [udders]. 430 lbs. Butter. 2 thousand, 5 hundred and 22 eggs. Sturgeons 4 caggs (?). 4 dozen craye fishes. 8 Turbots. A Cartload and 2 horse-loads Oysters. 1 barrel Anchovies. 2 Pykes. 2 Carps. 4 Tenchies. 12 Pearches. 4 hundred Redd Herring. 6 Holland Cheeses. 10 Marchpanes. 6 Gallons Hiporras. etc.'

The fields, the air, the rivers, the sea, must have been completely dispeopled.

But still the Progresses continued. Nothing — not the threats from Spain, the question of the succession, nor the appalling horrors enacted in Ireland — could stay these.

### NOTES TO APPENDIX F

[1] Linthicum, *Costume in the Drama of Shakespeare and his Contemporaries.*
[2] *Op. cit.*
[3] Gerard, *Herbal.*
[4] Laces of this kind were presented to all guests at weddings.
[5] A vessel used for holding sweetmeats, 'suckets' being an ancient word for these.
[6] MS. Lansd. : 14. Act 80.
[7] Sloane MS. 1-4, 160. N. 217. Strickland, I, 434.

# The Bishop of Ely: Leycester in the Marriage Market

WE have seen, in previous chapters, the sufferings endured by the English Bishops as unwilling hosts to the Bishop of Ross. Indeed, the lives of the Bishops in the time of Queen Elizabeth the First were by no means untroubled.

It cannot be said, for instance, that the life of Dr. Cox, Bishop of Ely (once numbered among the tutors of King Edward the Sixth), had been uniformly fortunate.

In the year 1573, he might have been seen dealing, or attempting to deal, with the Family of Love. There were several subdivisions of the Family, all equally troublesome, equally obstinate, and equally at war with all the other subdivisions. Amongst these was the Family of the Mount, and the Family of the Essentialists ; and prominent in one of the Families was 'the faithful servant of Jesus Christ, Mr. John Eaton, that planter in Paul, and father of many children. For . . . he hath begat many in the faith, and the Lord hath blessed his labours.'

In spite of their internecine warfare, there were a few tenets that the various parts of the Family held in common, and refused to be deprived of. It was sinful, they declared, to give any alms to beggars ; 'for that they lived in the consumableness ' (whatever that may mean) and 'that there were no beggars in Israel'. That Adam did not sin at all : it was the woman who sinned, not Adam. That there no man was God's child, but that he could show his pedigree. That the martyre in Queen Mary's days 'ought not to have died : for in dying they destroyed the temples of God'. That a man ought not to 'weary his body by travail and labour' ; for they said that 'the Holy Ghost could not tarry in a body that was weary and vilesome. That Adam was the son of God otherwise than by creation.'

The Bishop could do nothing with them. Their beliefs were in many cases highly convenient to them, and they intended to hold to them. Worn out by his encounters with them, he declared that 'the defenders were wily as serpents'.

The Bishop seems to have had a constitutional incapacity for keeping out of trouble. . . . Knowing that the Queen had a strong dislike of priests marrying, he yet, having married one wife and lost her by death, immediately determined, though stricken in years, to take another.

Cecil was the recipient of his confidences on this subject, made in a long letter dated the 29th of September 1569. He wished, declared the Bishop, 'to spend the remainder of his life without offence to God. The Queen's displeasure was death to him, but the displeasure of the Almighty was more to be dreaded. The Almighty had left him without one special gift, and placed him in the number of those who could not receive the saying of Christ. He was between Scylla and Charybdis ; but it was more dreadful to fall into the hands of the living God. And to avoid this, a second marriage was an absolute necessity.

An awkward situation ! And one that the Queen regarded without sympathy.

Worse was to come. Seven years from this time, he was to leave Ely House and its garden (now called Hatton Garden), wrested from him by the Queen and given to Sir Christopher Hatton (one of the Queen's favourite partners in those endless *fêtes galantes* which she used as a disguise for misery). The payment he received was one red rose each Midsummer Day, £10 a year, a truss of hay, and the right to walk in the garden and to gather a bushel of roses a year. When he resisted, the Queen told the 'proud prelate' that if he did not succumb to her wishes immediately, 'by God she would unfrock him'.

The Bishop shilly-shallied. Whereupon he received a rousing letter from Lord North. 'This last denial', he wrote (20th November 1576), 'being added, my Lord, to her former demands, hath moved Her Highness to so great a misliking as she purposes presently to send for you and hear what account you can render for this strange dealing towards your gracious sovereign. Moreover she determines to redress the infinite injuries which of long time you have offered her subjects. For which purpose, to be plain with Your Lordship, she has given me order to hearken to my neighbours' griefs, and likewise to prefer those complaints before her Majesty's Privy Council, for that you may be called to answer and the parties satisfied. She has given orders for your coming up, which I suppose you have already received, and withal, you shall have a taste to judge how well she liketh your loving usage.

'Now to advise you, my Lord, I wish you from the bottom of my heart to shake off the yoke of your stubbornness against Her Majesty's desires, to lay aside your stiff-necked determination and yield yourself to her known clemency. She is our God on earth. If there be perfection in flesh and blood, undoubtedly it is in Her Majesty ; for she is slow to revenge and ready to forgive. And yet my Lord she is right King Henry her father, for if any strive with her, all the princes in Europe cannot make her yield. You will say to me that you are determined to leave your Bishopric in Her Majestie's hands, to dispose thereof at her good pleasure, and I know that you have so reported among your friends. Your wife has also counselled you to be a Latimer, glorying, as it were, to stand against your normal prince. My lord, let not your wife's shallow experience carry you too far. You see that to Court you must come. Your Prince's good favour and grace will be altered from you ; your friends will be strange. It will be no ease for your age to travel in winter, and I know how well you are horsed and manned for that purpose. It will be no pleasure for you to have Her Majesty and the Council know how wretchedly you live, how extremely covetous, how great a grazier, how marvellous a dairy-man, how rich a farmer, how great an owner. It will not like you that the world know of your decayed houses, of the lead and brick that you sell from them, of the leases that you pull violently from many : of the copyholds you lawlessly enter into, of the free lands which you wrongfully possess ; of the tolls and imposts which you raise, of God's good ministers which you causelessly displace.

'All this I am to prove against you, and shall be most heartily sorry to put it into execution. Wherefore, if you love place, the preservation of your credit, and the continuance of Her Majesty's favour, conform yourself and satisfy her requests, which, if you list to do, no doubt the Queen is so inclined to good as I trust she will not only forget what is past and spare your journey, but also thankfully accept your doing herein.

'Thus all things may be pacified, which I will gladly bring to pass. Her Majesty shall receive pleasure, her servants preferment and some profit, and yourself honour and long comfort. Your loving friend

R. North.'

It is not surprising that the Bishop accepted the advice of his oving friend.

Meanwhile, at the time when the Bishop was engaged in combat with the embattled Family of Love, the future owner of his house was, according to a letter from Gilbert Talbot to his father the Earl of Shrewsbury, lying in his bed and like to die. But he recovered, to live in the Bishop's house.

The courtiers, the flatterers, the magnificent beings with their 'triple quadruple Daedalian ruffles . . . their stiff-necked Rebatoes, that have more arches to row under than can stand under London Bridges' [1] (their ruffs rivalled by those of the ladies, 'speckled and sparkling heer and there with the sunne, the moone, the starres, and manye other antiquities strange to behold'),[2] dragonfly-like, butterfly-like, in their glittering insect quality, danced, hummed, glittered, and buzzed round the Queen.

But there were troubles at Court. These, however, the Lord Treasurer, Sir William Cecil, now Lord Burleigh, was determined not to notice. For you never knew which way the wind would blow.

In a letter to his father, Gilbert Talbot said : 'My Lord Treasurer, ever after the old manner, dealeth with matters of state only, and beareth himself very uprightly. My Lord Leycester is very much with her Majesty, and she shews the same good affection to him that she was wont ; of late he has endeavoured to please her more than heretofore. There are two sisters now in the Court that are very far in love with him, as they have been long ; my lady Sheffield and Frances Howard.' (These were daughters of Lord William Howard whose conduct had aroused so much astonishment in the Duke de Feria, and sisters of the Admiral who was to defeat the Armada.)

'They (of like striving who shall please him better) are at great wars together ; and the Queen thinketh not well of them, and not the better of him. My Lord of Sussex goes with the tide, and helps to back others ; but his own credit is sober considering his estate. . . . My Lord of Oxford is lately grown into great credit ; for the

Queen's Majesty delights more in his personage and his dancing and valiantness than any other.'

(Lord Oxford, described by Gabriel Harvey as having 'A little apeish hat, couched fast to the pate like an oyster', and as being 'In courtly Guiles a singular odd man'.)

The Queen delighted, too, in a present he had given her, 'a pair of gloves ornamented with four tufts of rose-coloured silk, and so deliciously scented that she called it the Earl of Oxford's perfume'.

'I think', said Talbot, 'Sussex doth back him [Oxford] all that he can ; if it were not for his fickle head, he would pass any of them shortly. My lady Burleigh [Lord Oxford's mother-in-law] unwisely hath declared herself jealous, which is come to the Queen's ears, whereat she has been not a little offended with her, but now she is reconciled again. At all these love matters, my Lord Treasurer winketh, and will not meddle any way.'

Lord Burleigh always, as we have seen, had it in mind 'to keep some great man his friend'. And in the Elizabethan age an Earl was regarded as a great man. Therefore, it was not only at love matters that my Lord Treasurer winked.

Before Lord Oxford's marriage to the Lord Treasurer's daughter, there had been the unfortunate episode when Lord Oxford stabbed one of the cooks at Cecil House. But all ended well, and his future father-in-law entered in his diary (July 1567), 'Tho Bryncknell, an under-Cook, was hurt by the Erle of Oxford at Cecill-house, whereof he dyed, and by verdict felo de se, with running upon a poynt of a Fence Sword of the said Erle !'

Nothing could have been more satisfactory. But unfortunately no amount of 'crouching and whining' had the desired effect upon Lord Oxford. He only despised his father-in-law more thoroughly, and, writes Alan Gordon Smith, 'complained to all and sundry of the way in which he was treated, of some unspecified ill-usage, and even had some fantastic delusion that Burleigh had been setting his wife to *spy* upon him !'

.          .          .          .          .

Regarding Talbot's reference to Leycester and the two rival sisters, it was thought by some that Lord Leycester had already by this time contracted that 'strange fondness for marriage' which, according to a contemporary, was to beset him for the rest of his life. And that this strange fondness having come upon him on beholding Lady Sheffield, on one of the Queen's Progresses, he had bribed an Italian physician to poison her husband.

The only two things against this story are that Lord Sheffield did not die until 1568, three years after the time of the Progress in question, and that the gentlewoman who told the story was, at the time of the telling, over a hundred years of age, and apt to wander in her wits.

However, in later years Lady Sheffield declared that she was married in the utmost secrecy to Lord Leycester in May 1573 — (' "for if the Queen should know of it", he said, "I were undone and disgraced and cast out of favour for ever" ') — and that her son Robert, born in August 1574, was therefore legitimate.

After the death of the man whom she did, legally, marry when she realised that Leycester was lost to her, and after the death of Leycester, she brought a suit in the Star Chamber, attempting to prove the marriage to Leycester, in order that her son should be pronounced legitimate. During this, she described the ring set with five pointed diamonds and a table diamond, with which she said he had married her, and quoted from several letters, in one of which she said he did thank God for the birth of their son, who might be the comfort and staff of their old age, signing himself 'Your loving husband'. But she produced neither ring nor letters, and her case was lost.

He tired of her quickly, and the more indifferent he became, the more infatuated and importunate was she. It seems certain that he neither married her nor promised to.

The letters which do remain from him to her show a man who was neither without honour nor without heart. The following, written, one supposes, in answer to some reproach, and part, says Milton Waldman,[3] 'of the collection of papers left by Sir Thomas Egerton, first Baron Ellesmere, who, as Lord Chancellor, tried the case in the Star Chamber, was probably written even before the news of her rivalry with her sister was told to Lord Shrewsbury' : *

'My good friend,

'Hardly [with difficulty] was I brought to write in this sort to you, lest you conceive otherwise thereof than I mean it, but more loath am I to conceal anything from you that both honesty and

---

* The Egerton Papers are now in the Huntington Library in California.

good will doth bind me to impart to you.

'I have, as you well know, long both loved and liked you, and found always that earnest and faithful affection at your hand again that bound me greatly to you.  This good will of mine, whatsoever you have thought, hath not changed from what it was at the beginning towards you.  And I trust, after your widowhood began upon the first occasion of my coming to you, I did plainly and truly open to you in what sort my good will should and might always remain open to you, and showing you such reasons as then I had for the performance of mine intent, as well as ever since.  It seemed that you had fully resolved with yourself to dispose yourself accordingly, without any expectation or hope of further dealing. From which time you have framed yourself in such sort toward me as very much to my contentation.'

The meaning of this involved, but quite honest letter, is that he had told her from the beginning that he could never marry her, and that she had accepted the situation, but that as soon as she had felt she had sufficient hold over him and was in a position to do so, she had gone back on the agreement.

Even a year before the time at which that letter was written, she was trying to force him into 'a further degree than was in our condition', and although 'I did plainly and truly deal with you', a period of 'unkindness' began, and after, 'a great strangeness fell out'.

He had lost such love as he had felt for her.  But she insisted, while making it quite clear to him that she knew this, on holding him to her, by that terrible bond that was once love, and was now only an exhausted and despairing pity made harder by conscience and a sense of duty.  He tried to comfort her — though he was utterly weary of her, of her hold on him, of her undeserved reproaches — by telling her he had not changed towards her (she knew that he had) but that he could never marry her.

'My affection', he wrote, 'was never greater toward you otherwise since my first acquaintance with you than it now is. . . . For albeit I have been and yet am a man frayll, yet am I not void of conscience toward God, nor honest meaning toward my friend ; and having made special choice of you to be one of the dearest to me, so much the more care must I have to discharge the office due unto you.  And in this consideration of the case betwixt you and me, I am to weigh of your mind and my mind, to see as near be that neither of us be deceived.' He must therefore tell her, so that there could be no more misunderstandings, 'that to proceed to some further degree [in other words, to marriage] then is possible for me without mine utter overthrow' could never be thought of.

The impossibility that he could ever marry her was, he told her, tragic. 'It forceth me thus to be the cause almost of the ruin of mine own House; for there is no likelihood that any of our bodies are (like) to have heirs; my brother you see long married and not like to have children, it resteth so now in myself; and yet such occasion is there, as partly I have told you the now, as if I should marry I am sure never to have favour of them that I had yet rather never have wife than lose them, yet is there nothing in the world next that favour that I would not give to be in hope of leaving some children behind me, being now the last of our House.'

He reminded her that her youth must pass; and begged her not, for his sake, to refuse marriage with some good man, 'knowing that for my sake you have and do refuse as good remedies as are presently in our time to be had'. It was not for him, 'considering mine own resolution, to bid you refuse them . . . to carry you away for my pleasure to your great and further grief were too great a shame for me '.

Then, consigning her 'to the Almighty, Who always preserve and keep you as I would myself', he signed himself

'Yours as much as he was,

R. L.'

But she was not deceived.

According to her long subsequent depositions in the Star Chamber, he was already, in 1575, the time of the Queen's visit to Kenilworth, feeling that 'strange fondness for marriage' urging him in another direction, that of Lettice Knollys, Countess of Essex, who was, like Lady Sheffield, to be among the Queen's train on her visit to him. He attempted to have the life of his ex-love taken by poison — succeeding only in depriving her of her hair and nails.

It is true that she would have been an inconvenient guest : but there is no proof whatever, either that he tried to poison her, or that he was, at that time, in love with Lady Essex.

Three years afterwards, when it came to her ears that he had in fact married Lady Essex, Douglas Sheffield made no protest. Instead, she married Sir Edward Stafford, and was taken by him to Paris, where he became Ambassador.

Robert Dudley's letters to Douglas Sheffield were — no matter what the author of *Leycester's Commonwealth* might say — the letters of a gentleman.


## NOTES TO APPENDIX G

1 Dekker.
2 Stubbes : *Anatomie of Abuses.*

# The War in Ireland

THE history of the war in Ireland during the reign of Elizabeth is so long and so complicated, and the behaviour of the English so infamous, that it cannot be gone into in detail in this book.

After an interminable open and guerrilla warfare, during which — to give two instances of the English behaviour — the heads of two young men, Pat Tallon and his brother David, were sent, on the 17th of May 1572, according to the account of the officer in charge, 'like a bag of game to the Lord Keeper' and, within a few days of this, another party of the same family were caught, some killed, and others, to amuse the bored soldiers, 'stripped naked, and put in the bog' [1] — the former Lord Essex, the Lord Deputy,* reported that Ulster was quiet, and prepared to return to Dublin.

But certain of the English army continued their campaign of horror, and turned into Antrim from Tyrone — hunting the Irish as if they were game — this was, indeed, regarded by them as 'sport' ; sweeping into Antrim 'not to conquer but to hunt', said Froude [2] 'to chastise, as it was called, Surley boy and the Scots'.†

There is a small island off the coast of Antrim, not far from the Giant's Causeway. Its name is the Island of Raithlin. Accessible only from one spot, it is dangerous to approach it in rough weather.

Here it was that Surley boy and the other Scots hid their wives and children when Essex came to Antrim.

On the 22nd of July 1575, there was no wind. The sea was like glass.

On passing through Carrickfergus, on his return journey to Dublin, Lord Essex learned that the wives and children of Surley boy and his followers were absent. He therefore ordered John Norreys, the second son of Lord Norreys and the Queen's friend,

---

\* Father of the young man who became the Queen's favourite.

† Surley boy : meaning Sarley or Charley the yellow-haired.

her 'Crow', to take a company of soldiers, cross to the island, rush it, and kill.

There were on the island twenty or more Scots in charge of the women and children, but the gallant Norreys had brought cannon with him. After a rejected offer to surrender, every creature the invaders could find was massacred, with the exception of the chief and his family — reserved, probably, for ransom. But there were others, hidden in the caves on the shore — mothers and their little children. 'These', says Froude, 'were hunted out as if they had been seals or otters, and all destroyed.'

Essex wrote, with pride, that the wives and children of Surley boy and the other chiefs 'were all taken and executed to the extent of six hundred' whilst Surley boy 'stood upon the mainland . . . and saw the taking of the island and was like to have run mad for sorrow, tearing and tormenting himself, and saying that he there lost all that he ever had'.[3]

Essex was delighted with this victory, and the Queen, writing to him on the 12th of August,[4] sent a message to John Norreys, 'the executioner of his well-designed enterprise, that she would not be unmindful of his services'.

.    .    .    .    .

Edmund Spenser, when in Ireland, was the witness of monstrous and varied horrors.

'At the execution of a notable tratour',* he wrote, 'I saw an old woman which was his foster-mother tooke up his head whilst he was quartered and sucked upp all the blood running there and saying that the earthe was not worthie to drincke yt, and therewith also steeped her face and brest and tare her haire, cryinge and shriking out most terrible. . . .' The Irish 'were brought to such wretchedness, as that any stonie hart would have rewed the same. Out of everie Corner of the woodes and glennes, they came crepinge forth upon theire handes, for theire legges could not beare them, they looked anatomies of death, they spake like ghostes cryinge out of theire graves, they did eate of the dead carryons, happye were they could fynde them, yea and one another soone after in so much as the verie Carcases they spared not to scrape out of theire graves, and if they found a plotte of water cresses or shamrockes, ther they flocked as to a feast for the tyme, yet not able

* Murrough O'Brien, executed on the 1st of July 1576.

longe to contynewe therwithall, that in short space there were none almost left, and a most populous and plentifull countrye suddenlie lefte voyde of man or beast, yet sure in all that warr there perished not manye by the sword, but all by the extremitie of famyne. . . .'

'The common sort of the Rebels', wrote Fynes Morrison, another eye-witness, 'was driven to unspeakable extremities (beyond the record of most Histories that ever I did reade in that kind). . . . Captain Trevor and many honest Gentlemen lying in the Newry can witness, that some old women in these parts, used to make a fier in the fields, and divers little children driving out the cattell in the cold mornings, and comming thither to warme them, were by them surprised, killed and eaten, which at last was discovered by a great girle breaking from them by strength of her body, and Captain Trevor sending out to know the truth, they found the childrens' skulls and bones, and apprehended the old women, who were executed. . . .'

'Sir Arthur Chichester, Sir Richard Moryson, and the other Commanders of the Forces sent against Bryan Mac Air . . . in their returne homeward saw a most horrible spectacle of three children, (whereof the eldest was not above ten yeeres old) all eating and gnawing with their teeth the entrails of their dead mother, upon whose flesh they had fed twenty dayes past, and having eaten all from the feete upward to the bare bones, rosting it continually by a slow fire, were now come to the eating of her entrails, in like sort rosted, not yet divided from the body, being as yet raw. . . .'

Oh, look at the little sparrows flying ! Not a sparrow that falleth. . . .

In the churches in England the Bishops thundered. The virtuous preened themselves.


### NOTES TO APPENDIX H

[1] Report of the Officer in Charge, named Agard.

[2] Froude, XI, 184.

[3] Essex to Walsingham, 31st July 1575. Essex to the Queen, 31st July 1575.

[4] Carew Papers.

# INDEX